Boston University
Papers on Africa

PRAEGER SPECIAL STUDIES IN
INTERNATIONAL POLITICS AND PUBLIC AFFAIRS

Boston University Papers on Africa

TRANSITION IN AFRICAN POLITICS

Edited by
Jeffrey Butler
and
A. A. Castagno

Published for the African Studies Center
of Boston University

FREDERICK A. PRAEGER, Publishers
New York · Washington · London

The purpose of the Praeger Special Studies is to make specialized re-search monographs in U.S. and international economics and politics available to the academic, business, and government communities. For further information, write to the Special Projects Division, Frederick A. Praeger, Publishers, 111 Fourth Avenue, New York, N.Y. 10003.

FREDERICK A. PRAEGER, PUBLISHERS
111 Fourth Avenue, New York, N.Y. 10003, U.S.A.
5, Cromwell Place, London S.W. 7, England

Published in the United States of America in 1967
by Frederick A. Praeger, Inc., Publishers

Second printing, 1968

All rights reserved

© 1967 by Frederick A. Praeger, Inc.

Library of Congress Catalog Card Number: 67-16665

Printed in the United States of America

PREFACE

Most of the papers in this volume were given at a faculty Seminar on African Politics at Boston University's African Studies Center (1963-1965). The bête noire of all edited works on the current politics of Africa is the time lapse between presentation of the manuscripts and publication. Were editors to take seriously the common criticisms that "events have outstripped the volume" and that "there is an unevenness in the quality of papers," we would have very few edited volumes indeed. The value of such volumes exists not so much in whether they keep us informed of the most recent events but whether they add to our understanding of political phenomena in Africa.

The Seminar did not aim at developing a central theme. Its purpose was to provide scholars with an opportunity to present original research conclusions to a critical audience. Nonetheless, points of emphasis may be found throughout. Political parties and political theory are the subject of five papers (Behrman, Glickman, Hopkins, Nye, and Rothchild): the geographical stress here is primarily on East Africa, thus reflecting the increased scholarship on the area. Edwards and Rubin deal with a subject infrequently researched by our political scientists, the legal and constitutional development of African states in the context of both modern and traditional sectors. Specific studies of "corruption" and "machine politics" in local government, long a concern of students of American politics, have yet to be given significant attention by Africanists. Jenkins helps to fill this gap with his analysis of Ibadan.

There is a considerable literature on the relationship between religion and politics in the Middle East and Latin America, but very little on Africa. Ferkiss, by treating the subject on a broad basis, introduces some questions worthy of additional research. Finally, our understanding of trade unions and trade unionism is enhanced by the contributions of Friedland, Nelkin, and Zack.

We are grateful to the many who have helped in preparing the papers for publication. Special thanks go to Professor William O. Brown (former Director of the Center), Jacoba van Schaik, and Alyce Havey.

Jeffrey Butler
Al Castagno

October 1966

ACKNOWLEDGMENTS

Dorothy Nelkin appreciates the suggestions and guidance of William H. Friedland during the preparation of her paper.

Research for the paper by William H. Friedland was initially conducted in 1959-1960 under a Foreign Areas Training Fellowship of the Ford Foundation and during the summer of 1963 by travel grants from the New York State School of Industrial and Labor Relations, the Center for International Studies, and the Social Science Research Center, all of Cornell University. The paper has benefited by a critical reading by William Tordoff.

George Jenkins is grateful to many official and private persons in Ibadan who allowed him every freedom of inquiry and expression while he was there in 1962-1963. He trusts that they will not perceive in his analysis any implication that Ibadan is more "corrupt" than other cities, for he suspects the opposite may well be true. Thanks also go to the Rockefeller Foundation and the Program of Comparative Politics and International Relations at Northwestern University, which financed his research, and to the Nigerian Institute of Social and Economic Research of the University of Ibadan where he was Associate Research Fellow. Thanks are also due to colleagues in Milwaukee, members of the Boston University Seminar on African Politics, and Nathan Opoku, for comments on an earlier version of this paper.

Terence Hopkins thanks Immanuel Wallerstein, Perez Kamunawire, Joseph Nye, and Jeffrey Butler for their comments on various versions of the essay, although it is only fair to add that none of them is responsible for the interpretation presented here. A Fulbright research award and a grant from the Joint Committee for African Studies of the Social Science Research Council and the American Council of Learned Societies enabled him to spend 1961-1962 in Uganda. A grant from the Columbia University Council for Research in the Social Sciences permitted the return for the summer of 1963, and one from the Rockefeller Foundation made a three-week visit in late 1965 and early 1966 possible.

Joseph Nye is indebted to Jeffrey Butler, Harvey Glickman, Henry Bienen, and Lucy Behrman for valuable criticisms of his paper. And Lucy Behrman would like to thank Professor A. A. Castagno, Ruth Schachter Morgenthau, and Joseph Nye for their many helpful suggestions and criticisms.

CONTENTS

LIST OF TABLES

I

Religion and Politics in Independent African States: A Prolegomenon

Victor C. Ferkiss
Department of Political Science, Georgetown University

The recent growth of interest in the politics of so-called non-Western areas has given rise to much theoretical controversy.[1] Some scholars hold that the politics of these areas are radically different from those of Europe and areas of European settlement, and postulate the existence of something called the "non-Western political process."[2] Others have insisted that particular areas of the world are not only unique in their politics (as, of course -- strictly speaking -- all areas are) but that this uniqueness makes it necessary for anyone studying them to use a different conceptual framework from that which is applicable to the rest of the world. Africa in particular is claimed to require the use of special conceptual tools and theoretical assumptions by social scientists if they are to understand the nature of the developments taking place there.[3]

To set out to study religion and politics in an African context, even in as tentative a fashion as this paper does, is implicitly to take a position in this controversy. It could be objected against the very notion of such an undertaking that the church-state controversies of Western politics either do not exist in African political life or take on such different meanings that they cannot be discussed in terms of the categories traditionally used in evaluating European church-state relations. It is the contention of this paper that African politics present essentially the same kinds of phenomena for analysis -- including religious-political interactions -- as do Western politics. The actors and ideas involved are different, but the same categories and methods of analysis are applicable. It is contended that this is true whether a political scientist operates as a traditionalist or as a behavioralist.

The conceptual framework of this paper is modest. It is based on the assumption that in Africa as elsewhere there are ideas and ideologies, social institutions, and reference groups which may legitimately be called religious and that these groups become interests which seek power and satisfaction within and through the political process. African religious interests are, of course, somewhat different from those found elsewhere, and they articulate themselves and seek satisfaction within a somewhat different political context. But the task is essentially one of qualifying and specifying the applicability of traditional or universal concepts, not one of developing a new theoretical system to deal with an essentially different political process.

There is a voluminous literature on religion and politics in Europe and areas of European settlement throughout the world (although it is strikingly lacking in methodological or even logical rigor). Special features inherent in the institutional structure of Christianity, and Christianity's linking of moral code to religious cosmology, have given rise to a somewhat broader variety of problems in the relations of Christianity to politics than is presented by religions indigenous to other cultures. Only the faintest beginning has been made in the comparative study of the interrelations of religion and politics outside the modern Western world.[4] Any analysis of the problem of religion and politics in an African context is, therefore, necessarily preliminary -- a prolegomenon or sketchy map of the territory that needs to be covered. Using categories derived from European-type experiences, but presumably of universal relevance, this study attempts to utilize data gathered not specifically for this purpose but in the course of providing general descriptions of African political and social events. It suffers from the fact that field studies of African politics have not noted the presence of religious variables unless they were prominent. The major purpose of this paper is to set forth hypotheses which may suggest lines along which research on religious factors in African politics might profitably proceed, and, hopefully, to stimulate interest in such research.

Categories of Religio-Political Interaction

Three aspects of religion which have political relevance are considered in this study: religion as institution, as idea, and as the basis of interest groups. "Interest group" is here used in the broad sense given it in the neo-Bentleyan definition of David Truman as "any group that, on the basis of one or more shared attitudes, makes certain claims upon other groups in the society for the establishment, maintenance, or enhancement of forms of behavior that are implied in the shared attitudes."[5] Although in reality the phenomena these three categories denominate overlap, they are distinguishable theoretically and offer a useful means for handling the relevant data. Religious ideas shape, support, and guide religious institutions; they constitute a basis of cohesion for interest groups (as well as themselves constituting interests); they determine the goals aimed at by the activity of interest groups. Religious institutions initiate and disseminate ideas, are the subject of ideas, constitute interest groups, and shape interests. Religious interest groups include institutions and also persons shaped by institutions. But, essentially, the idea is the doctrine, the institution is the Church or organized religious body, and the interest group consists of the members of the religious body who accept the religious doctrine or politically relevant portions of it.

Church-State Relations

Religion as a social institution (the primary political manifestation of which is here termed church-state relations) can be usefully divided into two sub-categories:

(1) The formally established church in which state power directly supports organized religious institutions.

(2) Church-state interaction in a pluralistic society in which religious institutions come into direct relation with the state, as they do in the case of educational institutions and various social, intellectual, and economic activities directed or controlled by religious bodies. This second situation is much more common in Africa than the first, as it is in Europe.

The Role of Religious Ideas

In considering the political role of religious ideas, the utility of several sub-categories is indicated by our survey. Religious ideas influence politics in Africa as in the rest of the world in the following ways:

(1) Through the activities of religiously oriented political parties.

(2) Through the direct intervention of religious leadership in politics.

(3) Through the activities of a religiously trained political elite. In the latter connection, it must be kept in mind that in underdeveloped areas, and in Africa especially, limited educational opportunities and the predominant role of mission education have produced a situation in which religiously trained cadres may play a role quite different from that of religiously oriented leaders in countries where religious training and values are more evenly distributed throughout the population.

Ethno-Religious Conflict

The third major category used in this study is that of ethno-religious conflict, or the role of religion in the formation of interest groups which have as their special cohesive factor the tendency of individuals to identify with their co-religionists. Ethno-religious divisions within the population are the basis of groups which have as their binding element a desire to promote certain forms of behavior and to advance the interests of those with whom they feel a mutual solidarity as a result of shared beliefs and values. Such groups constitute

interest groups in the same sense in which, according to such contemporary
American group theorists as Professor Truman, believers in world government
or civil liberties are as much interest groups as are the members of the AFL-CIO,
Chamber of Commerce, or Farm Bureau Federation.

Most systems of classification within the social sciences have in common
the characteristic that they are nominalistic, that they do not refer to physically
separable entities. Their validity is based primarily upon their utility, which
in turn is a function of the degree to which they promote understanding of and insight into social processes, enable observers to classify and manipulate data
more simply, and enhance predictability. The validity of the present system of
categories can, therefore, best be judged by attempting to use it to classify and
analyze empirical data. Because this study is based on data not collected for the
express purpose of testing religio-political variables, the examples cited are
necessarily illustrative rather than exhaustive.

Religion in Africa

The problem of the role of religion in African politics is complicated by
variations in the nature of the religions professed or adhered to in Africa, as
well as by the nature of African politics. The importance of the character of
the religion itself in determining its possibilities as a political force can be seen
by examining the nature of the three major divisions into which African religions
(that is, religions practiced in Africa) are customarily divided: African traditional religion (sometimes loosely and misleadingly called animism), Islam, and
Christianity.

It may be objected that this division is too limited. David Apter, for instance,
has written of the developing areas in general:

> The problem of religious division extends far beyond the competition
> between major religious groupings -- Moslem, Hindu, Christian -- and
> far beyond ordinary variation in values. The classic conflicts in the
> West, between the spiritual and secular spheres of life, is not what is
> at stake here, but rather competing spiritualities: the values of govern-
> ment and leadership, moral properties of state action -- all these are in-
> volved in the religious sphere, no less than what we generally thing of as
> religious matters. It is no accident that the language of nationalism is
> often the language of religious usage, and the "political kingdom" is
> both a claim to secular authority and an ecclesiastical allusion, the one
> reinforcing the other.[6]

But to deal with all the conflicts of value in modern Africa would be an impossible
task, just as it would be elsewhere in the world. In any event, what Professor

Apter here holds to be true of Africa and the developing areas is just as true of
the Western world. Western nations have not only seen the rise to power of such
secular religions as fascism, Naziism and communism, but Western Europe is
the cradle of modern "totalitarian democracy"[7] with its ascription of religious
values to the state; in both Europe and the United States religio-political interaction takes place in a setting where the political community has become a
locus and origin of what might well be called religious values -- including the
political religion of secular humanism. To isolate the more specifically religio-
political conflicts found in Africa is thus fully as legitimate as to do so for Europe
or the United States, and our ability to do this underlines the universality of the
categories of conflict under discussion.

African Traditional Religion

There is a vast anthropological and sociological literature dealing with
African traditional religion as such. Even more vast are the individual studies
of traditional African societies which treat religion as one of the integral elements
of the life of these societies. It is a commonplace of anthropological literature
that in traditional society religion cannot easily be separated out as an element in
the life of the group. Even leaving aside the anthropological functionalism which
postulates covertly religious functions for overtly political and economic activity
and vice versa, it is obvious that, in some sense, the African in traditional
society lived in a sacral rather than a secular world. Virtually everything was
endowed with supernatural or preternatural significance. To talk of the relation of religion and politics within traditional society is to initiate an endless
and semantically bewildering task. In any event, what concerns us here is the
relationship of African traditional religion to the modern state. But the modern
state is one which, almost by definition, comes into existence only if the seamless
fabric of society is somehow rent, and religion separated from other activities;
whether African traditional religion can long survive in a rationalized society
is a moot question.

In a few places particular African traditional cults (that of Ifa in Nigeria
for instance) have taken on some of the appurtenances of Christianity and Islam
-- in much the same way that Buddhism in the United States has acquired churches,
Sunday schools, hymnals, and so on. This seems to be a rare phenomenon,
however. A more prevalent pattern is the absorption of traditional religious
norms and rubrics into a generalized ideology of Negroism or the African Personality. Thus Professor Abrahams of Ghana speaks of African society as naturally
"essentialist" rather than "rationalist" in inspiration, and various proponents of
African cultural revival find in traditional religious folklore a storehouse of
value orientations.[8]

African traditional religion, however, has several characteristics which
make it an unlikely focus for the kind of religio-political conflict in which other

religions are likely to become involved. For one thing, it tends to be highly
decentralized and institutionally fragmented, with little in the way of a professional clergy or hierarchy. Its very permeation of traditional life, combined
with the general overlapping of functions within traditional society, has meant
that it has failed to create such specifically religious social institutions as schools
and hospitals, which for other religions often become a source of religio-political
controversy. Many of the traditional religions have been so localized, so centered
upon particular shrines or within small ethnic groups, that any possibility of
their becoming a source of tension with a national state is remote. Also, the
syncretistic tendency of African religious life tends to blur religious cleavages.
Finally, it can be held that African traditional religion, like many Asian religions
(Shinto for example) is social rather than personal in its moral and ethical im-
port, emphasizing shame rather than guilt or sin; and that therefore it is not as
likely to provide a source of conflict between individual moral beliefs (conscientious scruples) and the demands of the state as are the moral codes of other
religions. What society approves is by definition acceptable. The follower of
an African traditional religion may find himself caught between the norms of two
societies, but he does not have to deal with the internalized and ostensibly universally valid norms of such religious systems as Judaism, Christianity, or
Islam. Traditional society itself is so sacral that a conflict between its demands
and those of a supreme being is impossible.

Islam

Islam presents a different picture. It affords a universal, transcendent
code to which the individual is in theory responsible, regardless of the wishes
of society. But this conflict between individual and society rarely takes place,
for wherever Islam goes it creates an Islamic society. Islam, properly speaking,
is a society, and its rules are largely rules of external behavior which a society
of believers is expected to enforce. Moreover, Islam, although it has religious
orders, workers, and teachers of various kinds, does not have a clergy in the
Christian sense, certainly not a hierarchically organized and governed clergy
of the Christian sort. The relations of religion to politics in most Islamic
communities revolves primarily around the questions of who interprets the laws
of Islam, the degree to which the laws of Islam (as integral to it as its cosmology)
are to be enforced by the state, and the extent to which the political and religious
communities are to be coterminous. But here, as in the case of African traditional religion, the church as an organized group does not ordinarily confront a
separate organized entity called the state.

Christianity

Thus the problem of the relation of religion and politics is posed most
squarely by Christianity, which postulates the legitimacy of a separate organization

or organizations of the citizenry for religious purposes -- organizations which do
not derive their right to exist from the state and which have claims upon the loyalties of individual citizens. At times in Western history the boundaries between
state and church have become blurred and the "two swords" have been wielded
by the same arm, but the theoretical separation of church and state has never
ceased to exist as a basic concept from the time of the introduction of Christianity into the Roman Empire. The Christian concept of religion and the church
-- however its form may differ from one Christian group to another -- is radically
different from that of African traditional religion or of Islam and necessarily
creates special problems for the relations of the Christian churches with the
political community in the newly independent African states.

The Christian church in Africa has problems in relating to the state which
it has not had to face elsewhere in modern times, save in parts of Asia. In
Africa, Christianity is the religion usually of a minority -- often a very small
minority -- of the population. It is usually associated, except in Ethiopia and
Liberia, with colonialism, and thus with the political, economic, and cultural
subjugation of Africa by non-Africans. When someone like President Sekou
Touré of Guinea speaks of the need to "destroy the habits, conceptions, and ways
of conduct" built up during sixty years of French rule, he is obviously setting
forth a program that could result in the destruction of local Christianity.[9] The
problems raised for the Christian churches by such nationalistic impulses are
compounded by the fact that even after independence, few of the governing
personnel of these churches are natives or even citizens of the new African states.

It is against this background of the differing implications for politics of the
differing natures and institutional structures of the three major African religious
groupings that any discussion of religion in African politics must take place.
Our discussion here is confined to the role of religion in the politics of the independent states of contemporary Africa, and therefore does not deal either with
the role of the Christian churches in shaping African nationalism or with the
role of the separatist or syncretistic churches in the early growth of African
nationalism. The use of religious, especially Christian, symbolism by non-
religious African political parties and movements also falls outside the scope
of our discussion.

Church-State Relations

Establishments of Religion

We define religious establishment as a particular religious body or members
which are given special privileges by the state. This may involve state support of
religious activity per se, a special legal status for the moral tenets or sumptuary
legislation of a religious body, or restriction of political office to members of a

particular religious body. The definition of establishment does not extend to
state support for educational or social welfare activities carried on by religious
bodies (which is discussed below under church-state institutional conflicts) nor
to such peripheral activities as financial support of chaplains in public institutions.

In many parts of Africa during the colonial period, particular religious
bodies had special privileges granted by the colonial regime. Although the
Church of England was never strictly speaking established in the African colonies
in modern times, its position in the mother country gave it certain advantages
in the colonies.[10] In areas of indirect rule various kinds of aid were extended
to African traditional religions and, above all, to Islam. The Roman Catholic
church had special privileges in the Belgian Congo (prior to 1946 especially),
most notably in the realm of education. But pre-independence situations did not
constitute formal establishment, and have not persisted past independence. They
therefore fall outside the scope of this study.

Christian Establishment

The one instance of a present-day establishment of a Christian church in
an independent African state is the position of the Coptic (Ethiopian Orthodox)
church in the Ethiopian empire. The very identity of the Ethiopian state
throughout history has been tied up with the adherence of the Amhara to the
church, which was established as the Church of the Empire in the fourth century.
According to Article 126 of the present Ethiopian constitution, the emperor must
be a member of the Coptic church and his name must be mentioned in all religious
services. The emperor controls the bishops, and it was agreed in the thirteenth
century that the church should control one-third of the empire's wealth (though
the true extent of the church's current holdings is difficult to assess). In 1915
an emperor who was converted to Islam was forced from the throne. During
the Italian occupation, Islam was encouraged as a divisive force within the
empire. Over 20 per cent of Ethiopian males are priests according to one estimate
(Ernest Luther in Ethiopia Today, 34), though this seems high even if it applies
only to the Amhara. Other Christian groups are officially tolerated though local
practice varies. Islam is no longer proscribed, and some high military and
administrative posts are held by Moslems. However, the government gives
special support and encouragement to the Coptic church in Moslem areas as a
means of promoting national unification; an index of the government's attitude is
its official estimate of the Coptic percentage of the population at 67 per cent,
while Professor Lipsky puts it at 35 per cent and Professor James Kritseck
estimates that 50 per cent or more of the population is now Moslem.

Protestantism was for a period the official religion of the Merina state in
Madagascar, and, in 1850, of 142 high Merina officials only four were not Protestants. French occupation put an end to this situation. Although, as noted

below, Christian influence remains strong in the Malagasy Republic it,
like the other new states of non-Islamic Africa, is officially secular.

Protestantism has a special social status in Liberia -- being the
dominant religion of the Americo-Liberian ruling elite -- but, as J. G.
Liebenow has noted, power in the state is translated into power in the
church rather than vice-versa. In Rwanda -- just emerging into nation-hood --
the Roman Catholic church still enjoys special influence. But in neither
of these cases is there official establishment of Christianity as the
state religion.

Islamic Establishments

In traditional Islamic thought, the distinction between church and state
is extremely tenuous, since Islam is a community of believers. Modernizing
nationalism, though willing to exploit Islam as a focus of national unity,
seeks to make the state the dominant partner in the community. Even in
the more traditionalistic Islamic states, such as Libya and Morocco,
there is a desire to conform to the modern pattern in which freedom of
religion--part of the nineteenth century liberal credo--is an intrinsic
element. The result is a granting of constitutional preference to Islam
while allowing individual religious freedom (although the Islamic states
differ in the extent to which they seek to make Islamic laws and customs
the law of the land) Tunisia, reflecting the greater cosmopolitanism of
its elite, has gone furthest toward de facto secularization; President
Bourguiba has abolished the practice of polygamy and has made attempts
to alter the traditional observance of Ramadan. In Tunisia, as in some
of the other Islamic states, the leadership is now attempting to use a
re-evaluation of Islamic teaching itself as a lever to promote modernization.

Some Moslem states have found Islam a useful political weapon. The
United Arab Republic has sought to use Islam as a means of undermining
neighboring states and of expanding its influence throughout Africa;
Al-Azhar University has become an important element in Egyptian foreign
policy. President Nyerere of Tanzania is reported to have claimed that
the recent toppling of the Sultan of Zanzibar was touched off by the rebels'
misunderstanding of the purpose of an Egyptian shipment of arms to
Zanzibar -- arms which were in fact destined for a projected Moslem
coup d'état in Tanganyika.[11]

Somalia, where Islam is the state religion, uses it not only as a
means of cementing national unity but also of penetrating its officially
Christian neighbor Ethiopia, with some assistance in the past from
the U. A. R. In the Sudan--faced with an ethnically distinct South
in which paganism and Christianity are dominant--forced Islamization
as a means for Sudanization; a history of conflict with Christian

missionaries in the South has lent religious overtones to a bitter civil war
between distinct ethnic groups. [12]

Elsewhere in dominantly Moslem countries in Africa, Islam enjoys a
special position short of actual establishment. In Northern Nigeria, special
support for the dominant creed is even provided on occasion by police action
designed to secure adherence, in public at least, to the requirements of Islam. [13]
The dominant role of Islam in Northern Nigeria was reinforced by the British
policy-- begun by Lugard -- of strongly discouraging Christian missionaries
from proselytizing in the region during the period of indirect rule. In later
years this policy has been modified, and the regional government has contributed to the expenses of mission schools and hospitals. Allegations have
been made of governmental favor to Islam in Mali,and the teaching of Arabic
in schools in Senegal reinforces Islam there. Government radio broadcasts
in some of the predominantly Moslem states of French-speaking Africa give
Islam additional support by devoting a large part of their broadcasting time
to Moslem religious programs. The influence of the Moslem brotherhoods
over the communications media in Senegal is especially strong. [14]

The alliance between Islam, the state, and nationalist feeling in much of
Africa is well illustrated by the case of Tunisia; there the government and
the Vatican have recently signed an agreement as a result of which most
Christian churches--no longer needed because since independence the overwhelmingly non-indigenous Catholic community has dwindled from 320,000
to 40,000 persons -- will be turned over to the state to become museums and
public buildings. Written authorization will be necessary to say mass except
in Tunis, Bizerte, and Sousse. An Arabic language daily commented on the
agreement by saying that " Tunisia's religion being Islam, it is no longer
possible after independence to preserve those churches which give foreign
visitors the impression that they are in Christian territory. " [15]

African Traditional Religion

In part because of the decentralized nature of African religions, in part
because of the wide variety of sects and beliefs, no attempt has been made to
establish any form of traditional religion in Africa. However, in many areas
cultural nationalism seeks to exalt it -- at least negatively -- over Christianity,
and political leaders pay homage to it by taking part in such local customs as
the pouring of libations, offering of sacrifice, and so forth. Local authorities
may aid local cults in ways which Europeans or Americans would consider
overstepping the bounds of proper church-state relations, but it is noteworthy
that there is no parallel in Africa to such Indian movements as the Rashtiya
Swayamsevak or Jan Sangh (which preach a return to Hinduism as a basis for
political life). Syncretistic churches have played a role in African nationalism,
as have such returns to tradition as those embodied in the activities of the

Kikuyu Central Association, but they have not resulted in the post-independence period in any attempt to identify traditional religion with the state.

Church-State Institutional Conflicts

The second type of religio-political conflict we have termed church-state institutional conflict. By this term we mean any situation in which a religious body comes into conflict with the state, either in a religious context (including actions of its officials taken in their institutional capacities) or as the operator of educational or social welfare activities. The decentralized nature of both African traditional religion and Islam has meant that the primary focus of church-state institutional conflicts in independent African states has been the Christian churches. This situation may also be encouraged by the fact that most of the Christian churches have extra-African affiliates to fall back on for moral, political, or financial support and that many of their ministers know that they have a refuge to flee to if necessary. Such conflict has taken essentially the same form in Africa as it has in the past in Europe, with additional conflicts arising from the fact that the clergy is often largely composed of non-nationals, a phenomenon viewed by Africans as a legacy of colonialism. Even this problem is not unique to Africa, however; similar conflicts have arisen in Asia, including India, and in Latin America (especially with regard to French nationals in the Haitian Catholic clergy and Spanish nationals in the Catholic clergy of Cuba).

Problems of Nationality

Problems of conflict between church and state resulting from the nationality of the clergy and hierarchy, while not unique to Africa, are especially prevalent there, and have occurred primarily in two political contexts: where the church was quasi-established and served virtually as a religious arm of the colonial regime, and in one-party states which emphasize national unity and the need for maximum mobilization of the whole society.

The most obvious example of the first type is the former Belgian Congo, which came to birth in an atmosphere of intense racial animosity and subsequent bloodshed. Behind the facade of Belgian paternalism bitter antagonisms had grown up between the Congolese and the Belgians. The Roman Catholic church had been part of an interlocking directorate of church, corporation, and colonial government which ran the Congo. Over 30 per cent of the Congolese were considered to be Roman Catholics, yet when violence erupted Catholic priests and nuns were its special targets in many areas. It is apparent that despite the influence of the mission schools and the role of individual Catholics and Catholic groups in the nascent independence movement (the inspiration of the Conscience Africaine manifesto is only one example), a deep and bitter anti-clericalism pervaded much of the nationalist movement. The current political situation in the Congo remains too fluid to permit an adequate assessment of the current role of the Christian churches there; but it is apparent that although hundreds of Congolese have entered the Catholic priesthood in recent years, the core of the clergy is Belgian and will remain so for some time, and anti-clericalism is bound up with attitudes held toward the Belgians generally. Thus any stable Congolese state will have to answer two questions about religion and politics:

(1) In principle what shall the role of the churches be in education and social welfare.

(2) In practice, what role can be assigned a clergy composed largely of nationals of the former colonial ruler.

The issue of the nationality of the clergy and hierarchy will undoubtedly be a source of contention in the Congo in the future; its severity will depend on the general political orientation of the Congolese leadership. The same type of problem will almost certainly arise in Rwanda and Burundi (in which the Roman Catholic church had the same relation to the colonial administration as in the Congo) as the political activity of the population increases.

That the general political orientation of the government is important in determining the extent of clashes resulting from the presence of a foreign clergy is suggested by the fact that conflicts involving the nationality of clergy have occurred primarily in those African states which place great emphasis on unity behind or within a single party or political movement and on maximum mobilization of the whole society in support of the objectives of the regime. [16] President Sekou Touré of Guinea has represented the Roman Catholic church as a relic of colonialism, which poses a danger to the state, demanding renewed vigilance against a body "which wants a victory over the Guinean people." [17] Following Catholic protests about the nationalization of Catholic schools in Guinea, Touré expelled the Archibishop of Conakry, a French national. When the archbishop was eventually replaced by a native of Guinea (Touré had said that only an African would be acceptable), the president held a civic reception in his honor at the presidential palace, and relations between the church and state in Guinea now appear -- on the surface at least -- less strained.

The controversy over Anglican Bishop Roseveare in Ghana, although involving more complex issues, also illustrates the precarious position of a non-indigenous clergy. Ghana is a state striving for maximal social mobilization, directed and synthesized by the leader and his party . [18] When Roseveare -- a British subject who had had good relations with the regime in the past --

criticized what he contended were atheistic and pagan aspects of the creed
and ceremonial of the Young Pioneers (including the attribution of divinity to
Nkrumah) he was accused of being a neo-colonialist lackey and expelled on
short notice.[19] His position was publicly supported not only by other church
leaders in Africa and Great Britain but by Governor Sir Francis Ibiam of
Eastern Nigeria and the Eastern Nigerian government organ Nigerian Out-look.
When Roseveare was finally readmitted to Ghana, his expulsion was explained
as the work of left-wing opponents of Nkrumah within the government, and he
was feted by Nkrumah. The Roman Catholic church in Ghana has had similar
difficulties, with the Dutch-born Bishop of Kumasi being accused of having
been a supporter of Nkrumah's domestic opponents, the National Liberation
Movement. This bishop's replacement by a native Ghanaian has apparently
done little to ease relations. Church-state institutional tensions generated
by the activities of the modernizing and mobilizing regime in Ghana persist.
Attacks against Bishop Roseveare have been renewed by the Convention Peoples
Party's newspaper, the Evening News, [20] and accusations of neo-colonialism
continue to be levied against the Christain chruches, accusations to which
their still largely foreign leadership make them exceptionally vulnerable.
In recent years, an especially sore spot has been Ghana's increasingly cordial
relations with the communist nations, especially in so far as this has entailed
the sending of Ghanaian students to communist countries to study.

Intervention of Church Leadership in Politics

Even in nations where the nationality of the clergy is not particularly at
issue, the activities of the churches and their leaders have frequently caused
them to become directly involved in political controversy. In the Sudan, as
indicated above, the Christian missionaries have become embroiled in an
ethno-political conflict which they did not initiate but which directly affects
the future of religion and religious institutions. In Rwanda an ethnic conflict
was apparently sparked by the Roman Catholic church: according to some
observers, the 1959 revolution in which the Batutsi aristocracy was overthrown
was precipitated by a circular letter from the Catholic Archbishop describing
the inequality between the Tutsi aristocracy and the Hutu majority as incompatible with Christian precepts.[21] The Roman Catholic church in Madagascar
urged a "yes" vote in the constitutional referendum of 1958. In Cameroon
criticism by an indigenous Roman Catholic prelate of the treatment of
political prisoners (which culminated in their accidental death by suffocation
while in transit) has created tension between the Catholic church and the
Ahidjo regime, despite the fact that in the area of institutional arrangements,
particularly those concerning education, relations are good.[22]

In Nigeria, native churchmen retain an interest in politics and express it from the pulpit in much the same manner as some clerics in the United States. Anglican Bishop Howells of Lagos--himself a Yoruba -- once criticized Awolowo's leadership in a sermon, only to see members of his congregation walk out in protest. Anglican Bishop Odutola of Ibadan has attempted to act as a peacemaker in internal Action Group struggles, though with limited success. But such intervention by religious leaders in politics does not constitute church-state interaction as normally understood, since the clergy involved were acting primarily as individuals rather than as officials of their churches.

In Liberia, Jehovah's Witnesses -- a group once influential in the creation of syncretistic religio-political movements elsewhere in Africa, especially in the Belgian Congo and Malawi -- has become a party to the same kind of disputes it has engendered in the United States. In Liberia, its members have on occasion refused to salute the Liberian flag. The Liberian government -- which in 1962 instituted Bible and Koran readings in the schools (along with corporal punishment) as a measure designed to increase discipline and curb student strikes -- has now passed legislation requiring daily singing of the national anthem and saluting of the flag, making disrespect for either a criminal offense. But still the incidents continue.

Education and Social Welfare

It is in the field of education that institutional relations between church and state are most likely to be a continuing source of conflict in the near future. Such conflicts have been a feature of political life in continental Europe and Latin America and are not unknown in the United States. In Asia, Ceylon is the most obvious recent example of this kind of conflict. In Africa these conflicts are complicated by the combined effect of two circumstances: first of all, the mission schools were the creation of the colonial era, even when they were not directly sponsored by colonial regimes. Equally important, most African political leaders espouse political philosophies which assign to the state a primary role in all aspects of social life, a role allegedly necessitated by the special problems of nationbuilding. Though these political philosophies are in part the result of European and Anglo-American philosophical influences, they generally postulate control of all educational and cultural formation in the interests of the state to a degree not found in liberal Western societies.

How much clash has occurred and is likely to occur in the future between church and state in the educational field is largely dependent on the nature of the educational systems which the newly independent states have inherited from their former colonial masters. In the Congo, the Belgians had long used mission schools as the primary -- and until 1946 the exclusive -- agent of their educational policy. In British Africa a laissez faire policy turned education over to

the missions by default (save in Moslem areas where such mission activity
was originally not welcome and support was given native authority schools
from an early date). Much later, in yielding to demands for government
support of education, the British channeled a major part of such support through
the existing mission schools. The independent African governments which
succeeded the colonial regimes have for the most part kept up the traditional
practice of supporting education provided by the mission schools, but at the
same time they are establishing their own directly operated schools in the
expectation that as the goal of universal education nears the latter will play
a preponderant role.

Ghana is the scene of an increasingly uneasy co-operation in education
between religious bodies and the government. Ghana has halted the building of new mission schools, although on occasion the government has asked
religious bodies to staff new government-built schools. Dowouna-Hammond,
the education minister, has warned that the "strongest sanctions" will be
invoked against teachers in religious schools "using academic freedom to sow
seeds of indiscipline and disloyalty to the state by using literature of history
as a platform for disseminating subversive ideas." [23]

In Nigeria, which is not yet a one-party state and where the politically
dominant traditionalist forces have not sought maximum social mobilization
under state aegis, the relations between church and state with regard to education have been less uneasy. However, in Eastern Nigeria in 1956-1957 a
bitter political fight was waged over proposals to take over the mission
schools. [24]

In East Africa, mission schools have played an even more important
role than in contemporary West Africa. Tanzania, which has had the long-
est experience of independence of any East African nation, makes extensive
use of mission schools in its educational system (in 1959 the mission schools
enrolled 60 per cent of the school population). [25] But ultra-nationalist and
Moslem elements are strongly hostile to these schools, and President Nyerere
(a Roman Catholic) has made special concessions to Moslem interests, such
as providing for the teaching of the Koran in government schools. By law,
religious teaching must be provided in all schools on a released-time basis.
In Uganda the government has, since August 1963, been engaged in secularizing
the mission schools. Sectarian teaching in mission schools is forbidden by
law. Conflicts between the Roman Catholic church and the education ministry
over school administration have recently led to litigation in the courts.

In French-speaking Africa, the relations of the missions to education
under colonialism varied with time and place, with the particular government
in power in France, and with the regime in control in the colonies. The
result was changing policies and frequent disagreement among the rulers themselves. In some countries, such as Dahomey and the Ivory Coast, mission

schools have played a predominant role in education and still do; in others
their influence has been considerably less. An important stimulus to opposition
to church-operated schools in the former French African states in the past
came from teachers from France working overseas under government auspices;
these teachers have been overwhelmingly anti-clerical and have encouraged
the Africans to laicize education.[26]

In French-speaking Africa, relations between the new states and the
mission schools have, generally speaking, been somewhat better in former
French Equatorial Africa than in former French West Africa, which has centralizing regimes and strong Moslem elements.[27] Only in Guinea, however, has
mission education been abolished outright. In the Ivory Coast, mission schools
have been strongly encouraged by the government and enroll one-third of all
primary school students, despite opposition from younger, ultra-nationalistic
elements within the country. [28] Fear that the disappearance of Houphouet-
Boigny from the political scene will mean a more hostile policy toward religiously controlled institutions has led the Roman Catholic church to suspend
new building. In both the Central African Republic and the Congo Republic
(Brazzaville) there have been bitter legislative disputes over the appropriation
of funds for mission schools. In Cameroon (especially the western region),
there has been close co-operation between government and the missions in
the field of education, and the government is planning to institute religious
instruction in federally operated schools in the western region. Mission
schools also play a major role in the educational policy and planning of
Dahomey, where their long dominance has meant the virtual monopolization
of political leadership by graduates of the Catholic mission schools.[29]
Although the degree of support for mission schools varies widely, some
support is found throughout French-speaking Africa except for Guinea and
Mauritania, where no mission schools were established.

In most of the Moslem nations of North Africa, mission schools have not
been of sufficient importance to be a source of church-state conflict, especially
since they have concentrated on the education of the non-indigenous minority.
In the U. A. R., however, mission schools are forbidden to engage in any
Christian proselytizing and are required to teach Moslems their own religion.
In the Sudan, where mission schools were a focus of resistance to the government's policy of forced Islamization, they have been crippled and virtually
abolished. Mission schools play a very minor role in Ethiopia, but Liberia
and Madagascar continue to rely heavily upon them. [30]

Christian religious groups have played a special role in higher education
in Africa in recent years, a role which in part reflects a conscious attempt
to influence the political and social elites through education even should the

missions lose their predominant role in lower education. Lovanium University in Leopoldville is a Catholic-run institution, as is the new University of Butare in Rwanda. The University of Stanleyville will be Protestant in orientation. Episcopalians, in co-operation with other Protestant groups, operate Cuttington College in Liberia. Despite its secularization, the University of Basutoland, Bechuanaland and Swaziland--founded as the University College of Pius XII -- will continue to maintain a strong Catholic presence; and the Jesuits, who once controlled certain faculties of what is now Haile Selassie I University, are still active there. A residual Protestant tradition is still important at the University College of Sierra Leone, which was once -- as Fourah Bay College -- primarily a divinity school. Individual clergymen serve in various faculty positions at several universities in English-speaking West Africa. Al-Azhar University in Cairo, now operating with a broadened secular curriculum, is a focal point for transmission of Moslem and Egyptian influence throughout much of Africa.

In general the African states have permitted the social welfare activities of the churches to continue unchallenged. Medical personnel are of course in even shorter supply in Africa than teachers, and other social services have been notoriously slow to develop in the new African states, largely for budgetary reasons. In most areas, therefore, religion-sponsored welfare activities encounter little obstruction or even competition from the state.

Religious Ideas as a Source of Conflict

In perhaps no area of possible religio-political conflict is the situation so obscure and complex as in the area of the influence of religious ideas upon political behavior. Such ideas may be transmitted in a variety of ways. At one extreme, a political party may be organized to advance the influence in society of religion-derived values: Moslem and Christian political parties exist in a number of African states. At another extreme, ideas acquired at school or from associates may influence the later political expression of individuals: Patrice Lumumba in an important manifesto quoted the contemporary Thomist philosopher Jacques Maritain on the rights of man.[31] The religious schools, the religious press, speeches and statements by religious leaders, religion-sponsored labor unions, organizations of alumni of religious schools, and political parties based upon religious orientations, all easily overlap in their influence on politics. As Lucian Pye has noted, " In the non-Western political process there is a high degree of substitutability of roles" and "there are relatively few explicitly organized interest groups with functionally specific roles."[32] What applies to non-Western of African society generally applies especially to the role of religion within the society. At the risk of artificiality, however, several broad categories of the influence of religious ideas in the political process may be distinguished.

Religiously Oriented Political Parties and Organizations

Religion-oriented political parties have played an important role in modern politics. Some, like the Catholic parties of pre-Hilter Germany and the contemporary Netherlands, Indonesia, and -- for practical purposes -- Belgium have been openly confessional. During the post-war era there has been a growth of Christian Democratic parties -- largely Catholic in inspiration but confessionally open, such as those in Germany, Italy, France and, more recently, in many Latin American nations. Hindu parties such as Jan Sangh exist in India, and Moslem parties such as the pre-partition Moslem League in India and the now more or less outlawed Masjumi party in Indonesia, are found in a number of countries. Many parties not openly religious in name owe their appeal to their directly religious inspiration or orientation. Examples of the latter are the Peoples Party of Austria and the Democratic Labor Party of Australia. In other nations, even in the United States, various parties have had a special appeal for different religious groups, especially when religion coincided with ethnic elements. In Africa, as elsewhere in the world, it is hard to draw the line between confessional parties and confessionally oriented parties, as Thomas Hodgkin has noted.[33]

Religion-oriented political parties in Africa were strongest prior to independence. Many parties were openly Moslem, in some cases representing the efforts of Moslem minorities to protect their interests against centralizing tendencies or governments dominated by "mission boys." Such parties and political groupings have included the African Moslem National Union in Tanganyika , the Moslem Association Party in Ghana (which demanded state support of Moslem schools) the Gambia Moslem Congress, the Uganda Moslem Union and the African Moslem Political Union in Kenya. The Parti de la Solidarité Sénégalaise represented Moslem traditionalism, as did the Northern People's Congress in Nigeria. In other areas Moslem parties developed which, while not devoting major attention to religious issues, gained much of their support from feelings of Moslem solidarity. The Mouvement Sociale Africaine in Chad, and, originally, the Union Camerounaise were two such parties. In Sudan, prior to the outlawing of parties by the military junta in 1953, the long controversy between the Umma and Ashigga (later National Union Party) largely represented a clash between divergent Moslem sects -- which suggests a possible source of religion-political conflict in other Moslem states should multi-party systems arise.

In the French territories the Roman Catholic Church played an influential role in politics in the pre-independence period; the missions supported groups in Upper Volta (the Union Voltaique) and Cameroon (the Bloc Démocratique Camerounais in its early days) and several movements in Madagascar, notably the Mouvement Sociale Malgache and the Parti Sociale Démocratique de Madagascar. As noted earlier, Catholic interests in the Belgian Congo attempted to influence various segments of the independence movement from the start, operating through a number of the fleeting Congolese groups. In some areas former Catholic priests have been politically active. The roles of Bartolomey Boganda in the Central African Republic and Fulbert Youlou in the Congo Republic (Brazzaville) are a reflection of the prestige of the church, but hardly of its political influence. Abbé Youlou was actually regarded by many of his followers as a successor to the syncretistic prophet Matswa.

In many areas of Africa it appears that religious influence has been exerted primarily in order to prevent specific undesired developments rather than to gain general political power. Thus in the Ivory Coast and Dahomey, the Catholic missions, with some effect, used their considerable prestige against the Rassemblement Démocratique Africaine during the period of its ties with the French Communist party.[34] In Cameroon, prior to the 1955 revolt, they took an especially active and open part in the struggle against the allegedly Communist-dominated Union des Peuples Camerounais of Felix Moumie. Catholics in Basutoland support the Basuto National Party because they fear alleged leftist influence in the Basutoland Congress Party. Catholic mission support for the Liberal Party in Sudan could also be interpreted as a primarily defensive gesture rather than a bid for power.

Uganda presents what is probably the most spectacular example of religious cleavage expressed in religiously oriented parties. In Uganda religious division has been a special feature of the political landscape from the earliest days, especially among the Buganda. Catholic has fought Protestant and both, sometimes in concert, have fought Moslems, even to the point of bloodshed. The Catholic-Protestant rift has played a major role in Buganda politics down to the level of chiefly appointments and patronage. When national politics began to emerge, it was not surprising therefore that the primarily Roman Catholic Uganda Democratic Party (DP) and the Protestant progressive party (the Uganda People's Congress) should also emerge. The abstention from national politics of the Kabaka of Buganda and his followers allowed these groups, especially the Democratic Party, to flourish, and the latter formed the first government. The establishment of the Kabaka Yekka Party in 1962 virtually destroyed the Democratic Party's power, however, as most of Catholic Buganda supported the kabaka. The demise of the DP has been hailed as marking the end of religious divisions in Uganda politics; in fact, even before this event, many Catholics supported the UPC and many non-Catholics the DP.[35]

Malawi was also the scene of religion-oriented party activity during the immediate pre-independence period. Opposition to what some regard as extremism on the part of Hastings Banda led to the formation there of the Christian Democratic Party, dedicated to achieving independence by non-violent means. The Roman Catholic archbishop allegedly intervened on behalf of this party; according to Banda's Malawi News the intervention was one aspect of the plan of the Roman Catholic church for world domination. The Christian Democratic Party had little success, however, and it merged with another small group, the National Liberation Party, to form the Christian Liberation Party. Apparently religious opposition to Banda was far from universal, and in some areas even the Catholic clergy supported him. The Christian Liberation Party's lack of electoral strength has since led to its demise.

Events indicate that religion-oriented parties have little future in independent Africa, as indeed do any but parties of national unity. Thomas Hodgkin holds that religion-oriented parties arise primarily "in response to a definite sense of grievance, and to provide a channel for the realization of certain concrete demands on the part of the community concerned" and that "since they can seldom succeed in mobilizing more than a section of the community which they claim to represent, are almost doomed to be minor parties, extracting what concessions they can from the regime . . . Africans are disinclined to give their allegiance to parties of an exclusively confessional type, whether Moslem or Christian."[36] This judgment appears to be borne out by events, although the emergence of the one-party state which eliminates all rivals (including confessional parties) would seem to be the primary cause of their demise, rather than any African disinclination toward religious bases in politics.

At present only Rwanda (where the Parti Démocratique Chrétien is in opposition), the Malagasy Republic (with its Parti Chrétien, a small opposition group), and Cameroon have active parties of explicitly Christian inspiration, although both Christian and Moslem interests influence many existing political parties. Where religious parties are not submerged into a single broad nationalist one-party coalition or destroyed by mass single-party movements prior to independence, they are ordinarily eliminated soon after independence. A Ghana law of 1957, the Avoidance of Discrimination Act, barred parties based on racial or religious divisions of the population and forced the Moslem Association Party to merge with the United Party; the latter itself disappeared as a legal body following the referendum of January 1964 in which the Ghana electorate approved a constitutional amendment making the country officially a one-party state. One-party rule forces Moslem interests in Tanganyika to work primarily through the dominant Tanganyika African National Union. In Nigeria, although the Northern Peoples' Congress is in effect a Moslem party, it represents the fundamental character of the dominant local society as a whole, rather than a special religious interest; as Carl Rosberg has put it: "Party and society are one, bound together in the theocratic community of Islam."[37] The fate of Moslem political groups in the still fluid Kenya situation will in part depend upon Kenya's relations with

Islamic Somalia. Moslems loyal to the Kenyan state will be under special
pressure to merge forces with Kenya African National Union (KANU), especially
since Kenya African Democratic Union (KADU) has been crowded out of the
picture. In Uganda Prime Minister Obote is pushing toward making Uganda a
formally one-party state (a move opposed by the Democratic Party), citing as
one reason the divisive effects of the religious differences existing in Uganda.[38]
Everywhere in Africa religion-based political parties seem to have little future
and represent but a passing phase in political development.

Transmission of Religious Ideas through the Educated Elite

A more subtle influence of religion on politics in independent African
states has been the disproportionate role which the graduates of Christian mission
schools, and educated Christians generally, have played in the new states; exceptions to this have been the traditionally Islamic states of the Mediterranean
littoral, Somalia, and the special cases of Liberia and Ethiopia. As James
Coleman has noted, "When one examines the religious affiliations of members
of the new political elites . . . the extent of the impact of Christianity is even
more striking" than is its spread among the population at large.[39] Because
in many areas virtually all education was formerly Christian mission education
and because political leadership demands some degree of education, most
students at mission schools found it desirable or expedient to become Christians.
The result in much of Africa is that Christians dominate the political life of
states where the majority of the inhabitants are either Moslems or adherents of
African traditional religions.

According to Victor DuBois, in 1963 nine of the thirteen chiefs of state of
former French African territories were Christians, eight of them Roman
Catholics, including Senghor of predominantly Moslem Senegal. Nyerere of
Tanzania is a Catholic, as are Tsiranana of the Malagasy Republic and Adoula
and Kasavubu of the Congo (Leopoldville). Nkrumah, a product of mission
schools, once was. The late Prime Minister Lumumba and President Olympio of
Togo were Catholics. Banda of Malawi and Tshombe of the Congo are Protestants,
as is Kaunda of Zambia. Just as impressive is the number of Christians holding
cabinet level posts and legislative seats. In 1954, 77 per cent of the elected
legislators in the Ghana legislative assembly were Christians, and Christians
constituted an even higher percentage of the Eastern Nigerian legislators.[40]
Twenty per cent of the National Assembly of Senegal were Christians in 1960.[41]
Moslems, on the other hand, are heads of government only in predominantly
Moslem states, with the exception of Adhijo in Cameroon and the late Balewa in
Nigeria. In both cases political power and prestige have been shared with a
non-Moslem -- vice-president Foncha in Cameroons and President Azikiwe in
Nigeria.

Most of this Christian predominance is simply the result of the nature of the colonial educational systems rather than design, although some missions have encouraged their alumni to go into politics. The alumni associations of mission schools have played a direct political role in providing the nuclei of the cadres both of independence movements and of national political parties. This role was especially noteworthy in the former Belgian Congo.

Transmission of Religious Ideas through the Press and Other Means

In an area of the world where educational progress and the development of modern communications have tended to go hand in hand, religious groups and individuals have had a disproportionate influence on the press. The Catholic weekly Afrique Nouvelle of Dakar is one of French-speaking West Africa's most significant journals; a Catholic weekly L'Effort Camerounais is important in Cameroon; and the former Belgian Congo's most important paper, the daily Courrier d'Afrique of Leopoldville, is controlled by the Catholic labor movement in Belgium.

At one time such religion-oriented organizations in the trade union field as Confédération Africaine des Travailleurs Chrétiens /Croyants / (originally an organization of Christian, later of believing / croyant / workers) played an important role in African politics, and thus still have influence in certain areas. Probably the greatest remaining strength is in the Malagasy Republic where a local successor organization, Confédération Malgache des Travailleurs Chrétiens /Croyants /, enrolls 60 per cent of the organized workers.[42] The thinking of the predominantly Catholic group of economists called Economisme et Humanisme has had much influence in Senegal and Mali; the economic development plans for these states were drawn up by the group's Father Lebret.[43] As the missionary groups widen their interests and broaden their outlooks, their expertise and specialized contacts in many areas may continue to give them special influence over social, political, and economic thought in many African states.

In any discussion of the importance of Christian ideas in the African political process, two important qualifications must be made. One is that as more and more inhabitants of African states are brought into the political picture -- supplementing or even in some cases supplanting the originally more educated leadership -- and as the products of state education become more numerous and more important politically, opposition to the present disproportionate influence of Christian trained leaders will inevitably arise. Suspicion and hostility toward the "mission boys" is already overt in some states, such as Tanzania; but elsewhere, too, by a natural process, ultra-nationalistic impulses will find a ready target in the elite trained under a system associated with colonialism. Similar movements have occurred in Korea, where the American-educated Christians Syngman Rhee and John Chang have been replaced by self-consciously Buddhist military men; the same thing, more spectacularly, has occurred in South Vietnam.

A second and not unrelated consideration is the question of the religious commitment of African leaders themselves. In the case of the adherents of African traditional religions, where external practices are of primary importance, few problems arise. Even among Moslem leaders there is a wide variety in interpretation of the social implications of Islam, especially in Africa where Islam is greatly affected by local traditions. South of the Sahara Moslems have been largely cut off from the contemporary revivals of Islamic social and political thought taking place throughout the Middle East, minimizing the problem of the relations between religious affiliation and its moral and social implications. For African Christians, however, the problem exists in an acute form. The allegiance of many African political leaders to Christianity is nominal; it can sometimes easily be weakened by personal circumstances, as in the case of Nkrumah, or in a somewhat different fashion in the cases of Boganda and Youlou. It can also be destroyed by political pressure if anti-Christian nationalism becomes a potent political force.[44] But even if an open break does not occur, even when the religious commitment of the African leader is deep and sincere, a problem arises. Most African Christians active in politics have at best a rudimentary grasp of the whole tradition of Christian social thought. Many, even among those who received their early training in mission schools, have received their advanced education in institutions influenced by European or American liberalism and socialism. For every African intellectual or political leader with the intellectual sophistication of a Senghor (who has been strongly influenced by the Jesuit paleontologist Teilhard de Chardin as well as by Marx and African tradition),[45] or a Jacques Rabemenanjara,[46] there are a dozen for whom religious commitment and socio-political action are separable worlds. The same, of course, is true of political leaders in Western states, but their commitments tend to be buttressed by the views of their constituents or the traditions of their societies. When this reinforcement is lacking, as in the segregation controversy in the United States, religious commitment may have little effect on social and political attitudes. This reinforcement is largely lacking in Africa; therefore, just how much the religious affiliations of the political elite tell us about the future influence of Christianity as a social and political force in independent Africa remains a moot question.

Ethno-Religious Conflict

A third major category of religio-political interaction in the independent states of Africa is ethno-religious conflict, perhaps the most deep-seated and permanent aspect of the influence of religion in African politics. Religion-oriented political parties may decline, church-state institutional conflicts may be resolved (probably in favor of the state), and establishments of religion may disappear from the scene, but as long as religion is a means of self-identification, even among those who do not know or care much about its formal ideology, spiritual or temporal, it will have a role to play in African politics, as it does in Europe, Asia, and the United States. As long as a religion-derived "we" is opposed to a "they," religion is likely to continue to play a significant political role in Africa, in spite of attempts by African nationalists to minimize it.

The growing importance of Islam in Africa accentuates this situation, since by definition Islam is a religious society. In the Sudan the ethno-religious split is between the Moslem north and the pagan-Christian south. This is true of the Cameroon also. A similar cleavage exists in Chad, where recently several political leaders arrested for subversion after a series of political demonstrations were charged with "stirring up the mainly Moslem north of the country against the predominantly Christian south, and of having maintained relations with certain African Moslem states, notably the Sudan, designed to overthrow the Chad government."[47] Northern Nigeria is differentiated from the rest of the nation by its Moslem religion. In other parts of Africa local Moslem leaders have wielded great political influence. Paradoxically, the Marabouts of Senegal have given their support to the Catholic Senghor. In most of former French West Africa, Christianized coastal areas have been in conflict with the largely Moslem back country. In East Africa Moslems, especially strong in coastal areas, have become increasingly restive under the control of Christianized national leaders, and in Tanzania may actually have been conspiring with Cairo to overthrow the Nyerere government. It is to be expected that as education spreads from the largely Christianized urban areas to the Moslem hinterlands, and as migration of rural people to the cities continues, such tensions will become widespread in other areas as well.[48] So far Moslem-Christian tensions have been minimal in such states as Sierra Leone, the tightly Protestant-controlled Liberia, and the now autonomous Gambia.

Save for a few local areas, such as the Casamance of Senegal, African traditional religions have not been a major source of political division in the period since the heyday of the syncretistic sects; if, however, education and political mobilization spread without proportionate Christianization, Islamization, or self-conscious secularization, this situation could change.

Political controversies within Islam itself have a long history, not only in North Africa but in the Sudan as well; and West Africa has seen jihads throughout the centuries, especially the nineteenth, pitting Moslem against Moslem on religious grounds. Such conflicts seem to have little if any significance for the contemporary independent African states, although it is possible that intra-Moslem sectarian conflicts could in the future become a focus of or vehicle for political dissatisfaction in Moslem areas, especially if other means of expressing such dissatisfaction are blocked. Conflicts between Protestants and Catholics have been important in Buganda in the recent past and in Liberia (where they once played a role in the position of the Kru). Such conflicts existed in the distant past in Madagascar, and they still exist on a local level in Eastern Nigeria.

While conflicts between different religious groups will persist and will continue to have political consequences, such conflicts run counter to the ideologies of African nationalism and the political interests of nation-building leaders. Writing several years ago, Professor Coleman observed that:

> Where religious and tribal cleavages coincide, the religious factor may in time become even more pronounced in provoking political separatist movements. In general, however, the religious pluralism of the new territorial societies has furthered the principle of religious toleration. In most emergent states African leaders seeking election avoid religious issues or sectarian identification, if for no other reason than that most of them confront a religiously heterogeneous electorate.[49]

But the evidence suggests that this negative reason for avoiding religious conflict is less important than the desire to submerge religious as well as other differences in a powerful communal ideology based on nationalism and socialism.

Summary and Conclusions

This brief survey indicates that Africa indeed possesses the same bases for religio-political conflict as are found in other areas of the world. Conflict has existed and does exist, skewed by the special association of Christianity and Christian institutions with colonialism and the special problems inherent in Islam in the identification of church with society.

All the influence of African nationalism can be expected to be thrown against any tendencies for religious cleavages to be reflected in politics. Africans are especially conscious of the need for unity in nationbuilding and are especially willing to see in any kind of sub-national division a device of neo-colonial origin. The All African Peoples Conference of December 1958 passed a resolution condemning religious separatism as a device of imperialism and said governments should "pass laws and through propaganda and education discourage tribal and religious separatism."[50] Religious leadership in the new African states, especially the Christian clergy with its special vulnerability, would be well advised to tread softly as far as politics is concerned in the future. In any event, African religion-based ethical convictions are especially shallow as regards the social order, and the possibility of the development of important political movements such as Islamic or Christian democracy are slight, especially in view of the one-party character of most African states.

At the same time, however, the pressure for unity will in all probability come into severe conflict with demands for pluralism in the religious sector.

The states which have gone farthest in the direction of total social mobilization
have sought to avoid conflict with religious groups when possible. Ghanaian
leaders have insisted that Nkrumahism is "not religion as such" but a "social
philosophy, " and under Nkrumah "religion will continue to play its part in the
life of the people."[51] Ghana has sought to make the churches a junior partner
in nationbuilding, [52] using them in education "provided they operate within the
laws of the state" and are not, as some allegedly have been in the past, used
to spread "subtle propaganda calculated to stem the tide of change."[53] Predominantly Moslem Guinea has managed to destroy effectively the political power of
Islam without offending its devotees. But both Ghana and Guinea have been the
scene of severe church-state clashes, despite Nkrumah's expressed desire
that "the conflict between the church and the State, which plagued several
countries for centuries, would not be permitted to arise in Ghana."[54] In
states in which the government seeks to monopolize the role of agent of social
mobilization such clashes are inevitable.

Africans remain, in spite of a growing affinity for materialistic standards,
people with strong religious traditions. Except for a few African leaders who
adhere to an undiluted Marxism, [55] even African socialists espouse a public
godliness closer to American tradition than to secular European traditions.
"Who is Godless in this country apart from the hypocrite?" the Ghana Convention
People's Party Evening News asked rhetorically in an attack on a sermon of
Bishop Roseveare denouncing materialism.[56] The African states oppose the
temporal power of religious bodies and seek to subordinate Islam and Christianity
to the needs of the state and to use traditional religion for political purposes,
but the impetus to formal secularization is still small by French or even American standards.

Our study leads us to certain variables which will be of especial importance
in understanding and predicting the course of religio-political interaction in
independent Africa. Religious division within the population will offer maximum
potential for political conflict:

(a) If most of the ruling elite are members of a religious group different
from that of the majority of the population. (e.g., Tanzania, Liberia).

(b) If the political power position of two or more groups is relatively
equal. (e.g. Ethiopia, Nigeria).

(c) If the direction of change in the religious composition of the population
is such as to reduce the importance of the politically dominant group.

(d) If differences of religion are highly correlated with other ethnic (tribal,
racial, etc.) or geographical divisions. (e.g., Sudan, Chad).

The more rapid and total the attempts to achieve national unification and social mobilization, the greater is the potential for religio-political conflict (e.g., Ghana, Guinea).

The greater the scope of the educational, social welfare, and other activities of religious bodies, the greater the opportunity for church-state conflict (e.g., Malawi, Congo-Leopoldville).

The higher the proportion of non-citizens in positions of religious authority, the greater the potentiality for religio-political conflict, particularly if the foreigners are nationals of the former colonial power (e.g., Congo-Leopold-ville, Rwanda).

The less stable the political situation, the greater the potentiality for religio-political conflict (e.g., Congo-Leopoldville, Kenya).

Research Needed

It has been the aim of this paper to demonstrate that religious affiliation is an important variable in the African political process. Tentative generalizations have been set forth, based on admittedly inadequate data, attempting to indicate the ways in which religion as idea, institution, and interest plays its part in the political life of independent African states, serving both as a source of cohesion and as a focus of conflict. Before any of these generalizations can be raised from the level of hypotheses to developed theories, however, more research will be necessary.

Most of the additional data required is of a quantitative or quantifiable nature. Studies must provide reliable information on the following:

(1) The religious affiliations of the inhabitants of each independent African state. Such data should, ideally, be collected at regular intervals, permitting estimates of rates of change in proportional distribution of religious affiliation within the population. It should include sub-groups within African traditional religion and sects within Islam as well as the traditional divisions of Christianity.

(2) The correlation of religious affiliation with other politically relevant factors within each nation such as ethnic background, occupation, place of residence, education, and extent and nature of political activity.

(3) The nature and scope of religion-oriented or controlled activity in education, social welfare, and communications media within each nation.

(4) The extent to which religion-derived ideas affect the values and behavior of individuals, especially in regard to political issues.

(5) The social, ethnic, and national backgrounds of the religious leadership in each country.

(6) The religious affiliation of political leadership at all levels.

Items 1, 4, 5 and 6 must be provided on an overall basis in order for the data to be maximally useful. Items 2 and 4 would have to be studied on the basis of samples; this is especially true of item 4 which will require use of intensive questionnaires and interviewing. Each of these five items represents information of a type which has been collected to varying degrees by political scientists and sociologists working in American and European countries. The collection of comparable data for Africa presents few problems in theory. In practice, item 1 would require a collection activity of such scope that it is beyond the resources of any investigation undertaken for the sake of the social sciences, and political scientists will have to depend upon secondary analysis of data collected by governments and religious bodies for their own use. Item 4 presents problems of using standard interviewing techniques in a special cultural setting, but similar problems are constantly presented in working with special subgroups in the United States and elsewhere; imagination and patience should make it possible for standard techniques to yield useful results in Africa as well.

When data is available in all the areas noted above, it will be possible to discuss the interrelationship of religion and politics in Africa with greater authority. Greater knowledge of religio-political interaction in Africa will fill an important gap in our knowledge of Africa, will help us to understand how and to what extent African politics do in fact differ from politics elsewhere, and will contribute significantly to the development of a universal theory of the relationship of religion and politics in the contemporary world, thus extending the study of comparative politics.

All figures on population and religious breakdown are the author's estimates of the situation as of 1964, based on figures from various years, extrapolated to bring them up to date. No other means of producing comparable data is possible.

Table 1. Breakdown of Population by Religion in Predominantly
Moslem States (by percentage)

Country	Religious division			Established religion[a]
	Moslem	Christian	Traditional	
Mauritania	100-	n	n	Islam
Libya	100-	n	n	Islam
Somalia	95-100-	n	n	Islam
Algeria[b]	95-100-	n	n	Islam
Tunisia[b]	95-100-	n	n	Islam
Morocco[b]	95-100-	n	n	Islam
Zanzibar[c]	92-	1	n	n
Senegal	76-	4rc	20	n
Sudan	72-	3rc	25	Islam de facto
Niger	72-	.5rc	27.5	n
Mali	62-	.5rc	37.5	n
Guinea	61-	1rc	38	n
Chad	55-	2	43	n

rc = predominantly Roman Catholic

n = existent but negligible

a. In those states where the Moslem percentage of the population exceeds 90 per cent, Islam has been or is used as a focus of identification by all political parties.
b. The Christian and Jewish minorities here are decreasing rapidly due to migration.
c. Approximately 7 per cent of the population is Hindu.

Table 2. Breakdown of Population by Religion in States
Predominantly Traditional in Religion (by percentage)

Country	Religious Division		
	Moslem	Christian Cath. - Prot.	Traditional
Liberia	15	6 (1-5)	79-
Central African Republic	4.5	21 (12-11)	74.5-
Kenya	10	19 (10- 9)	71-
Togo	5	25 (15-10)	70-
Voltaic Republic	26	4rc	70-
Ghana	10	20 (7-13)	70-
Dahomey	16	16 (10- 6)	68-
Congo (Brazzaville)	n	35 (26- 9)	65-
Ivory Coast	24	12 (9-3)	64-
Sierra Leone	33	5 (4-1)	62-
Rwanda	n	37 plus (37- n)	62-
Uganda	4	38 (30- 8)	58-
Malawi	8	34 (19-15)	58-
Malagasi Republic	5	38 (21-17)	57-
Cameroon Republic	17	28 (20- 8)	55-
Congo (Leopoldville)	2	43 (35- 8)	55-

n = existent but negligible

Table 3. Breakdown of Population by Religion in Predominantly
Christian States (by percentage)

Country	Religious Division		
	Moslem	Christian Cath. - Prot.	Traditional
Burundi [a]	n	64- (63- n)	36
Gabon	n	59- (36-23)	40.5

n = existent but negligible

a. Special influence exerted by the Roman Catholic church.

Table 4. Breakdown of Population by Religion in Mixed States
(by percentage)

Country	Religious Division		
	Moslem	Christian Cath. - Prot.	Traditional
Tanganyika	31	25 (17.5-7.5)	44-
Nigeria [a]	44-	22 (8-14)	34
Northern Region	69-	3	28
Eastern Region	.5	50-	49.5
Western Region	33	37-	30
Ethiopia [b]	40	46-	14

a. Statistics on a four-region basis not available.

b. The Coptic (Ethiopian Orthodox) church is established in Ethiopia.

Table 5. Breakdown of Population by Religion in States with
Special Circumstances (by percentage)

Country	Religious Division		
	Moslem	Christian Cath.-Prot.	Traditional
Non-Sovereign Entities:			
Southern Rhodesia	n	13^a (6-7)	87-
Zambia (North.Rhod.)	n	24 (7-17)	76-
Swaziland	n	39 (32- 7)	61-
The Gambia	76-	5 (3-2)	19
Basutoland	6	76- (40-36)	18
Other:			
United Arab Republic (Egypt only)	91-	8c	1

c = mostly Coptic
n = existent but negligible

a. This figure represents African adherence exclusively.

Footnotes

1.   On this awakening interest see Gabriel Almond and James Coleman (eds.),
     The Politics of Developing Areas (Princeton, 1960); Gabriel Almond,
     "Comparative Political Systems, " Journal of Politics, XVIII:391-409 (1956);
     Roy C. Macridis and Richard Cox, "Research in Comparative Politics, "
     American Political Science Review, XLVII;644-657 (1953): and Harry
     Eckstein, "A Perspective on Comparative Politics, " in Harry Eckstein
     and David E. Apter, Comparative Politics: A Reader (Glencoe, 1963),
     23-26.

2.   See Lucian Pye, "The Non-Western Political Process, " Journal of Politics,
     XX:468-486 (1958).

3.   In essence this is the position of Immanuel Wallerstein, Africa: The
     Politics of Independence (New York, 1961).

4.   Two examples of this new interest in comparative studies in the realm
     of religion and politics are Joseph R. Strayer, "The State and Religion:
     Greece and Rome, the West, Islam, " Comparative Studies in Society and
     History, I:38-43 (1958), and Rushton Coulborn, "The State and Religion:
     Iran, India, and China, " ibid., 44-57. At the time of writing, the author
     did not have available the recently published Relations de l'Eglise et de
     l'Etat dans les Pays d'Afrique Francophone by Alfred de Soras, S. J.
     (Paris, 1964).

5.   David Truman, The Governmental Process (New York, 1951), 33. Interests
     are constituted by shared attitudes.

6.   Eckstein and Apter, Comparative Politics, 651.

7.   See J. L. Talmon, The Rise of Totalitarian Democracy (Boston, 1954).

8.   W. E. Abrahams, The Mind of Africa (Chicago, 1963), 42.

9.   Quoted in David Hapgood, "Guinea's First Five Years, " Current History,
     VL:356 (1963).

10. Notably in Buganda and later elsewhere in Uganda where "Anglicanism was ...
     virtually an established religion." Terence K. Hopkins, "Politics in Uganda:
     the Buganda Question, " in this volume.

11. Russell Howe, dispatch in the Washington Post, Feb. 12, 1964. The Cairo-
     controlled radio, "Voice of Free Africa, " has also called for the establishment
     of an Islamic state in Eritrea.

12. See the discussion in Joseph Oduho and William Deng, The Problem of the Southern Sudan (London, 1963); Helen Kitchen, "Uniform Education: Key to Unity?, " Africa Report, IV:8, 17 (Jan. 1959); and Jacques Baulin, The Arab Role in Africa (London, 1962), 97.

13. See West Africa, Aug. 2, 1961, 947, and March 3, 1962, 243.

14. "Information Media in Mali, " Africa Report, V:8 (Sept. 1960); Baulin, Arab Role, 29.

15. Andrew Berowiec, Washington Post, May 28, 1964.

16. The distinction between the parti unique and the parti unifié is not emphasized in this paper. It should be noted, however, that the parti unique involves a higher degree of ascription of religious values to the state, and that often the elements merged into a single parti unifié represent ethno-religious interests merged in order to prevent an open clash and that the existence of these ethno-religious interests may be major factors leading to the creation of the parti unifié -- the Parti Progressiste Tchadien is a good example of this.

17. West Africa, Jan. 6, 1962, 11.

18. On the concept of social mobilization as used herein see Karl Deutsch, "Social Mobilization and Political Development, " American Political Science Review, LV:493-514 (1961).

19. On the Roseveare case see West Africa, Aug.-Sept. 1962.

20. West Africa, Jan. 16, 1963, 48. It should be noted that the party press in Ghana is usually more nationalistic than the government and is occasionally a source of embarrassment to it.

21. Africa Report, VIII:36 (Nov. 1963); Elspeth Huxley, "The Rise and Fall of the Watutsi, " New York Times Magazine, Feb. 23, 1964, 74.

22. Victor T. Le Vine, "The Cameroun Federal Republic, " in Gwendolen Carter (ed.), Five African States: Responses to Diversity (Ithaca, 1963), 333-334. Ahidjo, a Moslem, was once a member of the Bloc Démocratique Camerounais, a Catholic-supported party. "The Quiet President, " West Africa, May 4, 1963, 485.

23. Dowouna-Hammond, "Young Pioneers in All Ghana Schools, " Africa Report, VII:9 (April 1962).

24.   A one-sided view is found in Joseph B. Whelan, "Our Schools: Victory in Nigeria, " World Mission, VIII: 18-26 (Fall 1957).

25.   Edward Munger, African Field Reports (Cape Town, 1961), 306.

26.   Victor DuBois, "Three Views of Catholicism in Africa: I. Recent Trends in French-Speaking West Africa, " Africa Report, VIII:14 (March 1963).

27.   On Equatorial Africa see Richard Adloff and Virginia Thompson, The Emerging States of French Equatorial Africa (Stanford, 1960), 201-285, 303-304.

28.   Virginia Thompson, "The Ivory Coast, " in Carter, One-Party States, 270.

29.   Virginia Thompson and Richard Adloff, French West Africa (Stanford, 1957), 144; also Thompson, "Dahomey " in Carter, Five African States, 173-174.

30.   They enroll something under 27,000 students as against 207,000 in government schools, 15,000 in other church schools, and 20,000 in private schools. W. H. Lewis, "Ethiopia: the Crisis of Nation Building" (unpubl. seminar paper, Boston University African Studies Center, 1964); Gus Liebenow, "Liberia" in Gwendolen Carter (ed.), African One-Party States (Ithaca, 1962), 342,379.

31.   See "An Appeal to the Belgians, " in Patrice Lumumba, Congo, My Country (London, 1962), 138, 140-141.

32.   Pye, "Non-Western Process, " 469, 480.

33.   Thomas Hodgkin, African Political Parties (London, 1961), 67.

34.   Apithy of Dahomey reportedly quit the RDA under mission pressure. Religion in Dahomey is discussed at length by Thompson and Adloff, French West Africa, 202-205; the authors hold that the correlations of tribal, local, and religious divisions expedited the merger of political parties there.

35.   See letter of A. K. Mayanja, Buganda Education Minister, to Africa Report, VII:13 (May 1962).

36.   Hodgkin, African Political Parties, 67-68.

37.   Carl Rosberg, "Democracy and the New African States, " in Kenneth Kirkwood (ed.), St. Antony's Papers No. 15, African Affairs No. 2 (Carbondale, 1963), 48.

38. New York Times, Jan. 8, 1964.

39. J. Coleman, "The Politics of Sub-Saharan Africa, " in Almond and Coleman, Politics, 278.

40. Ibid.

41. Michael Crowder, Senegal: A Study in French Assimilation (London, 1962), 86.

42. Raymond E. Kent, "Madagascar Emerges From Isolation, " Africa Report, VII:5 (Aug. 1962).

43. Senghor praises their "open socialism" in African Socialism, Mercer Cook (trans.) (New York, 1959), 33. It was the Moslem Mamadou Dia, however, who confided the job in Senegal to Lebret. Crowder, Senegal, 86.

44. Aspects of this problem are discussed in Charles J. Patterson, "Three Views of Catholicism in Africa: Pressures on the Church in Nigeria, " Africa Report, VIII:17-19 (March 1963).

45. See Senghor, African Socialism, 27-28, and S. Kachama-Kroy, S. J., "De Karl Marx à Pierre Teilhard de Chardin dans la Pensée de L. S. Senghor et de Mamadou Dia, " Civilisations, XIII: 98-121 (1963).

46. Jacques Rabemenanjara, Nationalisme et Problèmes Malgaches (Paris, 1958), 153-172.

47. West Africa, Sept. 24, 1963, 1064. Note the loose usage of "predominantly" by the correspondent here, since less than 10 per cent of all Chadiens are Christians. The standard is political influence rather than numbers.

48. A colleague of Nyerere's once pointed out that because of such considerations the leader's goal of universal suffrage could prove his own undoing. Munger, Field Reports, 306.

49. Almond and Coleman, Politics, 279.

50. Colin Legum, Pan-Africanism (London, 1962), 235.

51. Education Minister Dowouna-Hammond, quoted in West Africa, Feb. 25, 1961, 215.

52. In his letter announcing initiation of a National Youth Training scheme, Nkrumah said he hoped all existing organizations, especially the churches, "will play their part in this national crusade for the moral and spiritual advancement of our people." West Africa, May 4, 1963, 215.

53. Dowouna-Hammond, quoted in Ghana Today, VI:7 (Aug. 29, 1962); also West Africa, Feb. 24, 1962, 215.

54. Ghana Today, Aug. 29, 1962, 7.

55. Soviet propaganda in Africa has been actively anti-religious, though making occasional tactical compromises in its attitude toward nationalist movements such as Mau Mau, which utilized elements of African traditional religion. See Alexander Dallin, "The Soviet Union: Political Activity," in Z. Brzezinski (ed.), Africa and the Communist World (Stanford, 1963), 37.

56. West Africa, Jan. 16, 1963, 48.

II

Pan-African Trade-Union Organization

Dorothy Nelkin
New York State School of Industrial and Labor Relations, Cornell University

In May 1963 the Organization of African Unity (OAU) emerged as the political realization of Pan-African ideology and succeeded, at least at the formal level, in dissolving the major conflicting groups on the political scene. Similar triumphs have not yet been registered in the trade-union field; the innumerable attempts that have been undertaken to create a single Pan-African trade-union body remain thwarted. While national and regional interests have severely limited the real political and economic power of the OAU, they have not prevented its existence, which is rooted in an ideological imperative and in the few political issues about which there is common agreement. These same divisive interests, however, have seriously constricted continental trade-union development -- trade unions being pragmatically tied to the real centers of economic and political power. So, in spite of a long-standing belief that the continent's trade-unions could make a dynamic contribution toward supranational organization, the competing continental organizations actually perpetuate divisions that existed earlier at the political level.

The Trade-Union Setting

As a point of departure, several interrelated characteristics of the African trade-union scene at the national level will be delineated; it is these characteristics which have impeded the formation of a viable and unified organization. The first and most fundamental factor is the relationship between national governments and trade unions -- a relationship founded on and justified in terms of the monolithic nature of national goals. A typical view of the role of unions relative to politics has been stated by John Tettegah. Unions must make "political as well as economic or labor decisions . . . The unity of purpose of the nationalist movement predetermines the ultimate attitude of labor to national issues . . . There is then an initial marriage of national interest for social reconstruction."[1] Julius Nyerere has defined trade unions and political parties as "prongs or legs of the same nationalist movement."[2] Tom Mboya sees trade unions as having a dual purpose: to promote the interests of workers and to assist in economic reconstruction. "It may seem a more difficult task to do this than it was to identify the trade unions with the nationalist movement during the colonial period, but there is no essential conflict between unions and government."[3]

   Initially, the dual interpretation of the role of trade unions implied that
trade-union unity could serve as a decisive force in the creation of political
unity. The goal of nationalism was, after all, common to all groupings within
the colony. But once the common revolutionary goal of independence was reached
the relationship between trade unions and governments at the national level has
only served to preclude the formation of a significant and unified union structure
on the continental level. Unions in most African nations are at present inextricably tied to political objectives.[4] Considering the urgency of national
development and the small percentage of the population represented by the
unions, participation in trade-union acitivities is only meaningful when it is
tied to these objectives. Indeed, even where unions search intensively to attain
purely economic objectives, they discover that, in the post-independence
period, economic orientations become political questions. This is one of the
reasons why there is an increasing tendency for unions at the national level to
be dominated by political movements. Because unions are one of the few organized interest groups, they also have a measure of influence of their own on
political parties; this influence, however, cannot always be exercised. It
becomes especially difficult when union pressures are seen as threats to national
political goals. Events such as the dissolution of the Tanganyika Federation of
Labour by Nyerere in February 1964 indicate where power ultimately lies.

List 1

Political and Union Positions of Some African Leaders

Name	Major political position(s)	Major position(s) in trade unions
Cyrille Adoula	Former Prime Minister of Congo	Former leader of Fédératio Générale du Travail du Kongo.
Abdoulaye Ba	Member of National Assembly in Senegal	Co-Secretary-general, Union Nationale des Travailleurs du Sénégal; Vice-president of ATUC.
Alioune Cisse	Senegalese Ambassador to Guinea	Co-Secretary-general of Union Nationale des Travailleurs du Sénégal.
Michael Kamaliza	Minister of Labor in Tanganyika	General Secretary, National Union of Tanganyika Workers; Vice-president, AATUF, 1964.

Name	Major political position(s)	Major position(s) in trade unions
Rashidi Kawawa	Second Vice-president, United Republic of Tanganyika and Zanzibar	Former General Secretary, Tanganyika Federation of Labour
Humphrey Luande	Member of Parliament, Uganda	Organizing Secretary, Uganda Trades Union Congress; President, Uganda Railway African Union; Chairman of AFRO, 1964.
Tom Mboya	Minister for Constituional Affairs. General Secretary of Kenya African National Union (KANU)	Secretary-general of Kenya Federation of Labour. Chairman of AFRO Regional Office. Vice-president of ATUC. Member of first AATUF secretariat.
Ahmed ben Salah	Secretary of State for Planning and Finance, Tunisia	General Secretary of Union Générale Tunisienne du Travail (UGTT) until 1956.
Mahjoub ben Seddick	Active in Istiqlal, Morocco	Secretary-general, Union Marocaine du Travail; President of AATUF.
John Tettegah	Member, Central Committee, Ghana Convention People's Party (CPP)	Secretary-general of Ghana Trades Union Congress until 1964; Secretary-general of AATUF, 1964.
Ahmed Tlili	Policy Committee of Neo-Destour, Tunisia	Secretary-general, UGTT, Tunisia; First President of ATUC.
Sekou Toure	President of Guinea	Founder of the Union Générale des Travailleurs d'Afrique Noire (UGTAN).
William V. S. Tubman	Secretary to the Cabinet in Liberia	President of the Congress of Industrial Organizations. Secretary for Organization of ATUC, 1962.

Further reinforcing the ties to national political interests is the marked shortage of competent and trained leaders resulting in considerable duplication in the leadership of unions and political parties. A fair number of political leaders from many countries had their early training in the unions, and some have been simultaneously active in both national and continental trade unionism.

A second characteristic of African trade unions which has served to obstruct the development of continental organization is the variety in trade-union structures derived from the early days of trade-union organization in the colonial period. In the French territories, unions were organized as branches of the metropolitan unions and from 1944 on, members of the French Confédération Générale de Travailleurs (CGT), the Confédération Française de Travailleurs Chrétiennes, and Force Ouvrière were closely involved in running French African trade unions. In the British territories on the other hand, though British authorities encouraged and facilitated the development of trade unions, African organizations were loosely organized and virtually unconnected with British unions.[5] Such differences have extended into the area of continental organization helping to block agreement as to the type of structure that should characterize African trade unionism.

Unfortunately, conflict over matters of organization is not merely a relic of the past. It strongly reflects the exigencies of the present situation and parallels closely disagreements on the political level about the structure of Pan-Africanism. The Addis Ababa Charter, for example, delicately avoids statements on such controversial questions as regionalism versus continentalism, or whether continentalism precludes the existence of sub-groupings. Because of the fragmentation of the continent, consensus could only be otained by side-stepping those issues which posed threats to the nationalistic focus of the newly independent countries. Until some political and economic power is relinquished by the nations to a Pan-African organization, there is little in the realities of the present-day political and economic environment to motivate continental organization of trade unions.

A third characteristic of African trade unions is the variety of extra-continental influences to which they have been exposed. In the colonial period, international affiliations in the French territories were determined by the affiliations of the parent union. Since the CGT initially was the strongest union in French West Africa, the main link was with the World Federation of Trade Unions (WFTU). In the British colonies, unions affiliated directly to international organizations, in most cases the International Confederation of Free Trade Unions (ICFTU). Since both financial and educational aid have been essential to the survival of many African trade unions, the ties to these external sources are perpetuated in spite of the fact that foreign aid is necessarily given within a political context. Thus, external forces have often served to stimulate union rivalry. At the continental level, the question of international affiliation has

become the predominant source of conflict between the continental groupings.
The conflict arises because of the existence of competing outside labor organizations; it is further complicated by the sensitivity to external pressures that
is characteristic of newly independent nations. That the affiliation issue has
assumed such major proportions reflects a tendency to equate affiliation with
neo-colonialism; at the same time the unions are unable to create financially
autonomous organizations of their own.[6]

Conflicting Trade-Union Groupings Are Formed

A variety of regional confederations preceded the formation of Pan-African
organizations. Some of the earliest of these were established at ICFTU-
sponsored conferences such as the Advisory Committee of French West Africa
formed in 1952. Another early organization, the International Confederation of
Arab Trade Unions (ICATU) was formed with WFTU support in Cairo in 1956
as an expression of Pan-Arab solidarity.[7] 1956 also marked the year of the
formation of the Confédération Africaine des Travailleurs Croyants (CATC), a
group which consisted of former branches of the French CFTU and which became
a Pan-African organization in January 1959.[8]

The first significant Pan-African trade-union organization, the Union
Générale desTravailleurs d'Afrique Noire (UGTAN), was formed at a meeting
in Cotonou, Dahomey, in January 1957 under the leadership of Sekou Touré.
Its nucleus was the group of branches of the French CGT which had broken
their affiliation with the French organization to form the CGTA in 1956.[9] Viewing
trade unionism as the "spearhead" in the struggle for the liberation of Africa,
Touré justified continental organization with arguments similar to those used
in the efforts to create political Pan-African groupings -- arguments based on
the unique situation of Africa as an ex-colonial continent. Trade unions, he
declared, do not function as an agent of class struggle in Africa but as a political
action group, an ally of political parties with similar goals, and as a training
ground for government leaders. In view of the shared revolutionary goal, trade-
union unity was a meaningful and dynamic concept that would be decisive in the
formation of political unity.[10]

That a centralized movement would originate in French West Africa is
understandable. Where trade unions had been branches of metropolitan organizations, officials were accustomed to close guidance from the center; UGTAN
simply provided a substitute for the guidance which had earlier been forthcoming
from French trade-union centers. But, further reflecting the earlier experience
of the West African trade unions as extensions of three ideologically distinct
French parent organizations, UGTAN regarded all international trade-union
bodies as representing ideological and political doctrines inconsistent with
African realities. Though identifying itself with the international proletariat,

it reacted against affiliation or identification with international bodies. UGTAN, however, maintained some contact with WFTU which supported its neutralist policy on the gamble that such a position would, in the long run, serve to further WFTU's ends. UGTAN formally announced its intention of becoming a Pan-African labor movement at its general congress in Conakry in January 1959; but as national interests began to emerge throughout West Africa the organization lost its significance as a continental movement.[11]

The first All African Regional Conference of the ICFTU was held January 14-19, 1957, in Accra. At this conference it was proposed that a regional organization be established to help in the creation of strong national unions with the dual task of achieving economic gains for workers and promoting the political freedom of labor organizations. At this time the ICFTU was more concerned with union issues in particular countries than with continental unity. The question of an African regional organization was discussed again at the Fifth World Congress of the ICFTU in Tunis in July of 1957, but only area activities materialized.[12] It was not until the second African Regional Conference of the ICFTU, in November 1959, that rules were adopted for a regional organization. Even then the organization existed largely on paper.

Meanwhile, pressures for trade-union unity were stimulated by discussions in the political sphere. The All African People's Conference in Accra in December 1958 agreed that an all-African trade-union organization was necessary but did nothing about establishing one. The first step was taken in September 1959 in Casablanca when members of ICATU, UGTAN and several ICFTU affiliates planned a conference to be held in May 1960. Discussing the issue at its regional conference in November 1959, the ICFTU supported in principle the agreement to establish the All African Trade Union Federation (AATUF). However, in the resolutions that issued from the conference, the ICFTU affiliated unions clearly stated the conditions of their support: "We see no conflict in this stand with our continued support and affiliation with the ICFTU. On the contrary, we regard this as an opportunity to project the African personality."[13] At this conference and at the second meeting preliminary to the formation of an AATUF, held in November to coincide with and call attention away from the ICFTU conference, the affiliation question became the basic issue dividing African trade-union leaders. Conflicts within the ICFTU immediately began to erupt. The Ghana Trade Union Congress (GTUC) chose to disaffiliate in December 1959 and, in the same month, a large split in the Trade Union Congress of Nigeria occurred over the affiliation issue. AATUF was similarly beset with internal disagreements and political rivalries; as a result, the congress planned for May 1960 had to be postponed until May 1961.[14] Even then, the actual formation of AATUF was stimulated more by common concern over the Algerian independence struggle (which had been escalating since De Gaulle's unacceptable offer of self-determination in September 1959) and the Congo crisis in the summer of 1960, than by agreement on the key issue of affiliation.

At the third ICFTU Regional Conference in Tunis, November 7-11, 1960, the African Regional Organization (AFRO) finally materialized as an autonomous organization with a secretariat in Lagos, composed of an executive board of six members from three areas, all of whom were Africans. No prominent African unionist could be found to head the secretariat, however, so that the position of general secretary remained unfilled until 1964. McDonald Moses, the ICFTU representative in Nigeria acted as a temporary substitute.

The affiliation issue, plus the rapid achievement of independence in many countries, diverted the attention of ICFTU from local issues to the question of African unity. Reacting against moves by "certain governments to undermine ICFTU efforts to build a strong and effective All-African trade union organization, " AFRO insisted on maintaining "the autonomy of national centers in general and their right to make their own decision on international affiliation in particular."[15] AFRO urged its members to attend the founding congress of AATUF to fight the bloc requiring disaffiliation and, hopefully, to insure the independence of unions from the political controls being proposed in some African states.

Two weeks after the AFRO conference it looked as if AFRO's position on freedom of affiliation had been accepted by the disaffiliators. Tettegah and Mboya signed a declaration warning African countries against being pawns in the struggle between international power blocs. However, though stating that AATUF itself should not be affiliated with international trade-union centers, the declaration "recognized the right of each national center to decide on its inter-national relations."[16] Inevitably, this was a fragile compromise. When the founding conference for AATUF finally convened in Casablanca, May 25-31, 1961, at what was claimed by some to be a "packed" congress, the requirement to disaffiliate within ten months was adopted by acclamation. Tettegah, reversing the position he had taken just six months earlier, threatened those who did not comply: "We shall isolate them, break them, enter their countries and form AATUF unions there. It's as simple as that -- total war."[17]

There is every indication that this was a controlled conference with a selected membership which had at least the informal backing of the WFTU. The vote for disaffiliation, by acclamation, was taken after thirteen members from twelve countries had walked out in protest.[18] AFRO strongly repudiated the meeting as non-representative and regarded the affiliation issue as an extraneous matter interjected in order to create a political weapon for the domination of a power bloc.

Ghana's dominance in AATUF had, in fact, been clear from the beginning. The Ghanaian model of a highly centralized organization was adopted in spite of disagreement on the matter of structure. John Tettegah, who was a member of the Central Committee of the Ghana Convention People's Party as well as the head of the GTUC, became AATUF's secretary general. The secretariat contained eight members, seven of whom had been on the preparatory committee and were all part of the Casablanca Bloc;[19] the eighth was Tom Mboya, the only dissenting voice, whom the Ghana Times called "an imperialist stooge, under the thumb of America."[20]

Mboya's position was strange in view of the fact that he had walked out of the conference with the Kenya delegation and was appointed in absentia. Moreover, his national center, the Kenya Federation of Labor, did not accept membership in AATUF. Mboya was careful to clarify his position as a Pan-Africanist upon his return to Kenya. Trade unions, he declared, cannot be imposed from outside as they must reflect the African environment. However, the right of national autonomy in the making of all decisions must be guaranteed "due to the diverse origins of African trade unions arising from their colonial backgrounds and the diversity of African social, economic and political problems." The AATUF position on the affiliation issue, he indicated, reflected a lack of respect for national autonomy. Though supporting "an AATUF" it must avoid "the emerging political splits at the Pan African level."[21]

With the founding of AATUF, the stage was set for a tactical maneuver, the manifest issue being that of affiliation. Created ostensibly as an act of self-defense against AATUF's "total war," the African Trade Union Confederation (ATUC) met in Dakar, in January 1962, to group all those unions that continued to favor extra-continental contacts or desired the freedom to do so. Although the international union organizations were not invited, since ATUC was to be a neutral organization of African labor only, it is tempting to conclude that it was formed as a convenient and hopefully secure means insuring the continuation of the IFCTU and its AFRO on the continent. Having a neutral organization to defend the right of national centers to affiliate was, after all, more effective than AFRO itself speaking out directly in favor of its own position on the continent. Of ATUC's forty-one members, twenty-one were ICFTU affiliates, twelve IFCTU affiliates, and eight were independents. Of these eight independents, most were insignificant, or were in the process of merging with affiliated groups. The two independents from the Ivory Coast, for example, were implementing an agreement made in June 1961 to merge with an organization affiliated with IFCTU. The UGTS of Senegal was to merge with the IFCTU-affiliated union in April just four months after the formation of ATUC. Though the Gambia Workers Union was officially independent, it was run by Mamadou Jallow, trained at the ICFTU Labour College at Kampala, Uganda; he was later to become the first regional secretary of AFRO. Finally, the Union des Travailleurs de Mauritanie, formed in 1961 by a merger, was reported in the spring of 1962 to have continued its ICFTU affiliation.[22] Whether or not ATUC was conceived as a substitute for AFRO as a Pan-African organization, its formation created a situation in which the Casablanca-Monrovia split between states was paralleled in trade-union organization.[23]

ATUC was given a general council consisting of thirty-five representatives, five from each of seven autonomous regions (see list below). This distribution was an attempt to prevent domination by any one country. The members of AATUF, who were invited to attend the conference but did not come, were included in the seven regions. Ahmed Tlili, secretary-general of the Union Générale Tunisienne du Travail (UGTT) was elected ATUC president and David Soumah from Senegal, president of the Union Pan Africaine des Travailleurs Croyants, became administrative secretary.

List 2

The Regional Structure of ATUC

Region 1:   Algeria, Egypt, Libya, Morocco, Tunisia.

Region 2:   Ethiopia, Kenya, Northern Rhodesia, Sudan, Somalia, Southern Rhodesia, Tanganyika, Uganda, Zanzibar.

Region 3:   Angola, Bechuanaland, Congo (Leopoldville), Mozambique, Ruanda-Urundi.

Region 4:   Cameroon, Central African Republic, Chad, Congo (Brazzaville), Gabon.

Region 5:   Dahomey, Ghana, Ivory Coast, Liberia, Nigeria, Togo, Niger.

Region 6:   The Gambia, Guinea, Mali, Mauritania, Portuguese Guinea, Rio de Oro, Senegal, Sierra Leone, Upper Volta.

Region 7:   Malagasy Republic, Mauritius, Réunion, St. Helena, South Africa, Seychelles.

Source: Afrique Contemporaine, I:4, April-May 1962.

In spite of enthusiastic agreement on the general theme of trade union unity and freedom of affiliation, ATUC was rent by internal disagreements and organizational problems. For one thing, the issue of unification of ATUC affiliates at the national level could not be resolved. The ATUC charter stated that there should be a single trade-union federation within each nation. The

Croyants unions, seeing their identity disappearing in mergers with other
unions, objected. As a result, the issue was left unresolved since no time
limit was placed on meeting the terms of the statute and, pending unification
at the national levels, all unions were eligible for ATUC affiliation. The
Croyants, led by Gilbert Pongault from the French Congo, desired a loose
organization with no ruling secretariat while others, notably Tlili, spoke for
more centralized operation. Representatives from independent and IFCTU
groupings objected to the "framework of genuine Socialism" that was proposed
as the means to rational development of African countries. On a more practical
level, there were disagreements concerning the number of IFCTU and ICFTU
officers to be represented on the general council. This was eventually resolved
in favor of equal representation in spite of the discrepancy in the number of
affiliates.[24]

ATUC's first act was to request that its officers be allowed to present a
policy statement and resolutions for consideration at the Monrovia Conference
of the Chiefs of State; twenty-one countries were represented when the conference convened in Lagos at the end of January 1962. Tlili, Borha, and
Pongault flew to Lagos to submit the request and asked for observer status
so that they could attend the closed sessions. The requests were refused on
the grounds that if it admitted ATUC representatives, the conference would have
to open its doors to representatives from anti-colonialist movements in Angola,
South Africa, and the Rhodesias.

It is likely that the crucial reason for the refusal was the ambivalence
with which the new governments viewed labor unions and their role in political
development. ATUC's goals for national unions -- freedom to strike and bargain collectively and independence from government control -- had been cheered
in the colonial period. After independence, however, new governments inherited
the fear of the colonial regimes that the tactics of protest available to the unions
would undermine national stability. These concerns were probably further
magnified by a latent but ubiquitous sensitivity which emerged when national
governments were confronted with the reality of ATUC's international affiliations.
Tlili's response to the refusal on behalf of ATUC indicates an area of increasing
concern to trade-union leaders, understandably perturbed about the future
status of unionism. "We believe that a free Trade Union movement is absolutely
essential in today's world for the preservation of democracy and industrial
progress . . . Governmental attitude leads to a situation where African workers
are exploited by an independent regime as they had been earlier by the reactionary colonialist regime. We condemn the desire to destroy liberty and we consider
it an avowal of fear and incompetence."[25]

The creation of ATUC crystallized the split on the continental trade-union
scene. After the ATUC conference there was a slackening of developments on
the continental trade-union front until the Addis Ababa Conference of May 1963.
The ATUC Executive Committee did not hold a meeting until December 1962.
However, various changes occurred in the membership of the continental

unions through mergers. The most important of these was the formation of the
Union Nationale des Travailleurs du Sénégal by a merger of the Union Générale
des Travailleurs du Sénégal and the Confédération Nationale des Travailleurs
Croyants du Sénégal. AATUF appeared to be preoccupied with largely propa-
gandistic efforts to unite the labor movement "under the glorious banner of the
AATUF, " and accused other organizations of "confusing the minds of millions
of African workers in their resolute march to unity."[26]

The Divisions Persist

The launching of the Organization of African Unity at the Addis Ababa
Conference in May 1963 was also the occasion of an attempt at accommodation at
the trade-union level, consistent with the OAU resolution to "reinforce the
links between our states by establishing and strengthening common institutions."[27]
At the July meeting of the International Labor Organization, Lawrence Borha
of Nigeria put forward a non-controversial issue, apartheid, as a basis for
unity and suggested a program called Operation South Africa. This was followed
by a proposal by ben Seddick, president of AATUF, that AATUF and ATUC
hold meetings to discuss the question of forming a united organization. ATUC
agreed to attend a preliminary conference of the two secretariats in Dakar in
October.

This meeting was convened as scheduled. The decision was made to
create a single African trade-union center "to tackle the problem of the progress
of the African economy, the welfare of the workers and the strengthening of
democracy."[28] But it was also recommended, in the communiqué which issued
from the joint conference, that the unions free themselves from international
affiliations. "The new movement will maintain friendly relations with all
national and international organizations on the basis of equality and mutual non-
interference in internal affairs."[29] Though Tlili signed this communiqué, he
later maintained that he stood firm on the principle of freedom of action for
individual trade unions -- including the right to affiliate. A fourteen-man
preparatory committee with seven members from each group was created to
meet in January 1964 in Algiers to organize a founding congress for the new
center. Tlili, as chairman of the ATUC group, postponed this meeting at the
last minute until late March.[30]

The AATUF secretariat convened in Algiers in early March, without the
ATUC group, to discuss strategy for the projected meeting. During the discussion, they received another telegram from Tlili asking for further postponement to avoid conflict with the ICFTU Regional Conference in Kenya in April,
in which the ICFTU members of ATUC planned to participate. This was a
somewhat curious excuse since the AFRO conference originally scheduled for
July 1963, had itself been postponed in order not to prejudice the unification
plans. A more likely reason for Tlili's telegram is that groups within ATUC,

confused over Tlili's ambiguous position at the October meeting, feared compromise on the affiliation issue. At any rate, ben Seddick, supported by the Guinea and Ghana delegates, decided to proceed with an AATUF congress which was scheduled for immediately after the AFRO Conference in April.

The mood in Africa Hall in Addis Ababa did little more than inspire a superficial enthusiasm when the fourth AFRO Conference met in April 1964. Attended by thirty-nine delegates from twenty-four countries, the conference not only reiterated the earlier position on issues of affiliation, liberation, and the nation-building role of trade unions, but tried to take substantive steps to strengthen AFRO's organization. The executive board was increased from six to nine elected members. Humphrey M. Luande, a member of the Uganda Parliament, was elected chairman, and, more significantly, the organization acquired its first full-time regional secretary, Mamadou Jallow, leader of the Gambia Workers Union.[31]

The key issue of the AFRO conference, indicated by its slogan, "Free Labour in a Free Africa," was the relationship between governments and trade unions. According to one resolution, AFRO viewed "with great concern . . . the tendency in some countries in Africa to control by legislative or administrative action, trade union organizations." Somewhat inconsistently, however, the conference recommended that unions seek modification of labor laws to "prevent the development of splinter groups which sprout up to harass established organizations."[32] AFRO dedicated itself to the cause of trade-union freedom. The issue of affiliation was brushed aside as the scapegoat for more fundamental ideological issues bearing on trade-union freedom.

> Whereas affiliation to the ICFTU results from a completely free choice and decision of the national trade union organizations concerned . . . whereas freedom of association, including the right to affiliate internationally, is a right laid down by the ILO; the Fourth African Regional Conference of the ICFTU reaffirms the determination of African affliates of the ICFTU to maintain their link with the world family of free workers . . . It needs to be stated clearly and unequivocally that the orientation of each national centre is its own choice. Once the choice is made it is only logical for like-minded national organizations to join themselves together in an international body . . . / because / ICFTU policies and decisions are made without regard to the policies and interests of any particular power bloc, affiliation to it is not contrary to the policy of non-alignment of African States.[33]

Two months later, AATUF held its second congress in Bamako. Although ATUC had warned its affiliates not to participate, possibly recalling the fiasco at the first AATUF Congress, one hundred delegates from thirty-seven unions including twenty-four ICFTU affiliates attended. It is not clear if those from unions affiliated with ICFTU were members of the conference or merely observers, nor how many of them were actually authorized to represent their national trade unions. This confusion, increased by the fact that delegate lists for most conferences had not been circulated, is in part derived from the "free ticket syndrome." Given free transportation and the trappings of prestige, both inexperienced and experienced trade unionists enjoy becoming involved in conference activities whether or not they have national support. Indeed, in the weeks following the publication of the list of countries attending, unions in Chad, Somalia, Uganda, and Upper Volta publicly denied that delegates had been authorized to participate at Bamako. Furthermore, it was in the interest of all the sponsoring organizations to invite as many participants as possible since it is often the number of national groupings represented rather than their size or importance which validates the claim to Pan-Africanism. These features of the Bamako conference have long been common to African trade-union conferences.

The focus at Bamako was on affiliation again. Ben Seddick called on the ICFTU affiliates to cut their ties and invited ATUC to merge with AATUF but only on the terms of the AATUF charter: "It is our task to oppose the maneuvers of our enemies with the real Addis Ababa programme which excludes all imperialist or neocolonialist interference."[34] Possibly as a concession to the need of external financial support, the new charter attempted to draw a distinction between its position on affiliation and isolationism: "Our fight is that of all democratic peoples of the world and as the forces of oppression and exploitation ignore national frontiers so are our objectives the same as those of all workers of the world."[35] The charter adopted at Bamako called for both threatening those countries that were still dominated by colonial powers with strikes and boycotts and for collaborating with "the political apparatus responsible for revolutionary action in the independent countries."[36]

The extent to which the charter was supported by the attending delegates is again difficult to ascertain. It was initialed by representatives from Algeria, Ghana, Mali, Tanganyika, Zanzibar, Guinea, United Arab Republic, Congo (Brazzaville), and Morocco. Although representatives from Togo were not present at the conference, their support was forthcoming; and since the list of officers include W. O. Goodluck from the Nigerian Trades Union Congress his support can be assumed.[37] Although the conference was attended by delegates from unions in the Ivory Coast, Rwanda, Mauritania, Dahomey, Kenya, Uganda, Upper Volta, and Zambia, they did not sign the charter, and there is no indication of the extent of their support.

At the level of continental organizations, therefore, divisions along the Casablanca-Monrovia lines persist in spite of efforts at accommodation. As to the effect of the split on the African trade-union movement, the presence of competing continental organizations has reinforced existing factions within national trade-union centers such as in Nigeria and has added to the ferment among discontented groups. In April 1964 fifteen unions split from the Kenya Federation of Labour to form a rival organization, the Kenya Federation of Progressive Trade Unions, with a plan to "conform to the spirit of Pan-Africanism" by disaffiliating with the ICFTU.[38] A similar movement occurred in Uganda when several members of the Uganda Trades Union Congress (UTUC) launched the Federation of Uganda Trade Unions (FUTU) with the object of transferring both the UTUC and the ICFTU African Labour College to AATUF.[39] In March 1965 several of the founding members of the FUTU, including Felix Bukach and G. Wanyama, switched their support back to the UTUC on the grounds that the FUTU "is directly run by certain embassies in Kampala and financed by overseas countries."[40] Several unions have sought the best of both worlds. When the United Trade Union Congress of Northern Rhodesia split with the ICFTU in early 1963, Tettegah offered automatic AATUF membership. The union accepted but shortly thereafter applied for ICFTU funds.

The Strength of the Continental Trade-Union Organizations

The shifting affiliations and the inevitable inconsistencies that are found in attempts to delineate who belongs to which organization are in part a consequence of the meager information emanating from the conferences. The root cause of the fluctuations and inconsistencies lies, however, in the weaknesses inherent in the organizations themselves. These weaknesses stem from their lack of association with real issues and are perpetuated by the African sensitivity to the possibility of neo-colonialist influence -- a sensitivity which precludes the success of any organization subject to external control. The organizational weaknesses are such that it is possible to contend that the continental trade unions exist only as vague ideological followings rather than as viable organizations.

For what does one expect to find in a functioning organization? The first prerequisite is a working apparatus -- not merely a policy board to expound a philosophical position, but an independent administration capable of carrying out day-to-day activities. Secondly, a publication of some sort is usual from established organizations of this type. Thirdly, in spite of the inevitable need for external financial support, at least some regular support should be required from affiliates if their commitment to an organization is to be considered more than vaguely ideological.

AATUF

In applying the above criteria to AATUF, we first note that there has been

Table 6. Duplication of Officers of National Unions and Continental Organizations

Officers	Ghana (1964) AATUF - 9 officers	Nigeria (1964) AFRO - 8 officers	Senegal (1962) ATUC - 18 officers
Persons known to hold positions in their national unions	M. ben Seddick A. Fahim W. Goodluck M. Kaba M. Kamaliza M. Sissoko J. Tettegah G. Thauley	L. Borha M. Jallow H. Luande S. Nkolokosa M. Ognami J. Rasolondraibe	A. Ba C. Mendy A. Bo-Boliko G. Pongault L. Borha L. Ranaivo R. Delanne S. Shiitah J. Diallo D. Soumah B. Gueye A. Sow R. Jamela A. Tlili A. Kithima C. Tubman T. Mboya A. Wague
Persons known to hold positions in the unions of the host country of the continental trade union organization	J. Tettegah	L. Borha	A. Ba J. Diallo B. Gueye C. Mendy D. Soumah A. Sow A. Wague

no functioning secretariat. AATUF's original charter did not provide for a general secretary although Tettegah assumed the responsibilities of the position which was, finally, established at the Bamako meeting in June 1964. AATUF's officers, all its policy makers, are employed in full-time positions within their own national unions, so that it is doubtful that they have time for the administrative responsibilities of a large and complex organization.[41]

List 3

All African Trade Union Federation (AATUF)

Officers, June 1964

President	Mahjoub ben Seddik (Morocco)
Vice-presidents	Mamady Kaba (Guinea)
	Safi Boudissa (Algeria)
	Mamadou Famady Sissoko (Mali)
	Ahmed Fahim (UAR)
	Michael Kamaliza (Tanganyika)
	Wahab Goodluck (Nigeria)
	Ganga Thauley (Congo-Brazzaville)
Secretary-General	John Tettegah (Ghana)

Source: Africa Report, July 1964, 34; World Trade Movement, July/Aug. 1964, 20.

John Tettegah, whose Ghanaian interests as a member of the Central Committee of the Ghana Convention People's Party (CPP) are obvious, is certainly the guiding and controling force in the organization. Following AATUF's 1964 conference, Tettegah resigned his position as secretary-general of the Ghana Trades Union Congress (GTUC) to devote his full time to AATUF as its first secretary-general. This action invites speculation. The prevailing tendency within Ghana has been one of consolidation of centralized control as efforts have been made to dominate various groups that might threaten the central position of the CPP. In this light Tettegah's shift to AATUF could be interpreted as a "kick upstairs" motivated by two objectives: (1) the elimination of a real or potential threat to Nkrumah's monocratic control of internal Ghanaian politics; and (2) the subdual of the damaging impression that the GTUC was attempting to direct AATUF while at the same time consolidating Ghanaian control. This latter possibility is supported by Tettegah's statement in July 1963 that it was necessary "to stop thinking of himself as a Ghanaian."[42] At that time he had already begun to shift most of his attention to AATUF. The expediency of dis-associating the GTUC and AATUF is further indicated by the fact that the African

Worker was published in Ghana on behalf of AATUF by the GTUC prior to the Bamako conference (when Casablanca was AATUF headquarters). This fact was evidently not intended to be widely realized since no editorial address was printed in the newspaper. Since the Bamako conference, Accra has been designated the permanent headquarters of AATUF; plans to open an office in Lagos, announced in January 1965, have met with objections on the grounds that the presence of AATUF would intensify the ideological conflict already existing between sections of Nigerian society.

As for direct financial support, Ghana undoubtedly pays Tettegah's expenses and the WFTU openly extends a helping hand though the extent of this support is not very clear. Humphrey Luande, president of ATUC, deplored "Ghana based AATUF communist factionalist intrigues . . . Although AATUF loudly preached non-affiliation . . . it maintains close financial ties with the WFTU on whose financial resources and ideological inspirations it pursues a disunited cause to the detriment of the workers of Africa."[43] Such support is, of course, essential as there is no workable system for the payment of dues by affiliates. Information about financial matters is not easily available, and if a system does exist, payment is probably as sporadic and inadequate as it is in the constituent national unions. The fact is that, in spite of the clamor against affiliation, AATUF is no more financially autonomous than any other group.

The financial issue inevitably raises questions of cold war politics. Luande is, in a sense, correct in surmising that "the helping hand" is not entirely free of political strings. One member of the first AATUF secretariat, Lazare Coulibaly, was simultaneously a member of a WFTU trade department; and other indications appeared in the WFTU statements at the founding of AATUF that the WFTU strongly supported its creation as a denunciation of Western imperialist influence. Marcel Bras, secretary of the WFTU, considered the conference "an important event for the WFTU because it will greatly help to strengthen the struggle of the African peoples . . . as laid down by the WFTU Constituent Congress . . . and in itself for being an act of unity, of trade union unification . . . the most powerful weapon of the labor movement, the weapon most feared by our common enemy. For all these reasons, the WFTU, now as in the past, assures you of its full support."[44] At the peak of the disagreement about the affiliation issue, the WFTU was widely propagandizing the proceedings of the Fifth World Trade Union Congress which emphasized its interest in AATUF: "The WFTU will continue . . . to give its full support and practical solidarity."[45]

The African reaction against all outside pressures -- whether from East or West -- the need of external financial support and the willingness of politically opposed international bodies to give that support, continues to deter the creation of a simple and effective continental organization. For while WFTU support is felt by one group to have political strings, ICFTU aid brings neocolonialist accusations from the other.

AFRO

Such accusations have begun to affect AFRO significantly. Though the oldest of the Pan-African groupings, its support appears to be waning rapidly. Hampered by administrative problems similar to AATUF's, it was not able to hire its first full-time regional secretary until the spring of 1964. As the regional arm of the ICFTU, however, it has maintained a central office in Ebute Metta (Lagos), near the office of the Trades Union Congress of Nigeria (TUCN). Indeed, Alhaji Haroun Adebola was simultaneously president of both TUCN and AFRO until the conference of April 1964. When Humphrey Luande of Uganda was elected to the position, another prominent Nigerian trade unionist, Lawrence Borha, became vice-president.[46] The office remains in Nigeria and issues a mimeographed monthly bulletin, African Labour News.

List 4

International Confederation of Free Trade Unions (ICFTU)

African Regional Organization (AFRO)

Officers, 1961

Chairman	H. M. Luande (Uganda)
Vice-Chairman	L. L. Borha (Nigeria)
Vice-Chairman	A. Mwamba (Congo-Leopoldville)
Vice-Chairman	open (North Africa)
Regional Secretary	Mamadou E. Jallow (The Gambia)

Regions	Executive Board Members	Substitutes
Central and Southern Africa	A. Mwamba (Congo-Leopoldville)	B. Lulendo (Angola)
	S. Nkolokosa (Nyasaland)	Luch Mvubelo (South Africa)
East Africa	H. M. Luande (Uganda)	Beyene Solomon (Ethio
	J. Rasolondraibe (Madagascar)	L. Rarete (Mauritius)
West Africa	D. D. Garisi (Sierra Leone)	L. T. Essone N'Dhon (Gabon)

Regions	Executive Board Members	Substitutes
	M. Ognamy (Congo-Brazzaville)	B. Carvalho (Portuguese Guinea)
	L. L. Borha (Nigeria)	A. Gray (Liberia)
North Africa	to be submitted	

Source: ICFTU Bulletin, B9, April/June 1964, 13.

AFRO is obviously a viable institution only because of the financial support of the ICFTU, a remark which could also probably be made of AATUF and WFTU. Though its affiliates supposedly pay dues to the international organization, payments are erratic and there is no indication that national unions contribute directly to the regional organization (see Table 7).

Recent political trends towards non-alignment appear to be further reinforcing the weaknesses of AFRO. Tanganyika disaffiliated from ICFTU and AFRO in February 1964 when the government abolished the Tanganyika Federation of Labour (TFL) and replaced it with the National Union of Tanganyika Workers. More recently, in November 1964, Kenyatta forced the disaffiliation of the Kenya Federation of Labour (KFL) in order to pursue his policy of non-alignment. Prior to the disaffiliation eleven members of parliament in Kenya had condemned the activities of trade unionists, accusing them of acting contrary to the non-alignment policy of the government. They called for a dissolution of the KFL and replacement of the leadership by people loyal to Kenya and Africa alone. Lubembe, KFL general secretary, defended his union as a loyal institution acting in support of the OAU policy to develop a Pan-African Labor movement.[47] Objections from within the KFL to the disaffiliation from the ICFTU were overcome by promises that the government would help to ease the financial problems of the union by legislating a checkoff system of dues payment which would be compulsory for all unions, and by establishing a pattern of required union membership.

The possibility that a similar ultimatum may be issued to the ICFTU operation in Uganda poses serious questions about the future of the ICFTU's largest investment and what is perhaps AFRO's most potent source of stability, the Kampala Labour College. There were indications of troublesome possibilities when Humphrey Luande, president of the Uganda Trades' Union Congress and chairman of AFRO, resigned his membership in the Uganda People's Congress Party to protest against alleged government support of a splinter organization, the Federation of Uganda Trade Unions.[48] The latter organization is an AATUF affiliate and has openly demanded that the labor college be expropriated from the ICFTU. This demand has received some support in East Africa; in January 1965 Morris Mulima, the director of education of the Kenya

Table 7. ICFTU Affiliation Fees and Expenditures (in Belgian Francs)

Funds	1959	1960	1961	1962	1963	1964
Received from African affiliates	144,529	682,496	412,891	681,147	265,869	290,246
Scheduled subsidies for African Regional Organization	1,500,000	2,990,000	2,990,000	Scheduled subsidies for these three years not available		

Source: Report fo the Seventh World Congress, International Confederation of Free Trade Unions (held in Berlin, 1962) (Brussels, 1962), 221, 236; Report of the Eighth World Congress (held in Amsterdam, 1965) (Brussels, 1965), 311.

Federation of Labour, informed the college that no more Kenyan students would be sent until it was removed from ICFTU control.

The request by AFRO's Executive Board at a meeting on November 1-2, 1964, that the college be integrated with AFRO, and that "a supervisory council under the aegis of AFRO"[49] be set up to substitute for direct ICFTU supervision, reflects the feeling that AFRO's perpetuation may be contingent upon its increasing separation from the ICFTU.

ATUC

ATUC is perhaps the vaguest of all the organizations. An examination of the members of the General Council indicates that a number of secretarial offices are held by persons who are important officials in their own trade unions.[50] The treasurer, Delanne, for example, is also general secretary of his union in Niger. This job would seem to leave him little time to run the financial affairs of an organization with forty-one affiliates, claiming a membership of two million. Another striking item in the list of officers and General Council members is that of thirty-five General Council members, eight are from Senegal, where the headquarters are located, in spite of the fact that the charter states that the General Council is to consist of five members from each of seven regions. All eight Senegalese hold significant positions in the Union Nationale desTravailleurs du Sénégal (UNTS). Of greater interest is the fact that six out of the ten secretaries, that is those in charge of organization, economic affairs, etc., are from Senegal. As a practical matter, they are functionally distributed so that they are either in charge of every task or back up the individual who is in charge. One of the delegates to the ATUC Congress, J. Mulenga of the Northern Rhodesia United Trades Union Congress, contended, in fact, that the officers had been nominated and then installed without a popular vote from the delegates.[51]

List 5

African Trade Union Confederation (ATUC)

Officers	January 1962	October 1965
President	Ahmed Tlili (Tunisia)	Lawrence Borha (Nigeria)
Vice Presidents	Abdoulaye Ba (Senegal)	Bechir Bellagha (Tunisia)
	Lawrence Borha (Nigeria)	Alione Cisse (Senegal)
	Tom Mboya (Kenya)	Humphrey Luande (Uganda)
	Ruben Jamela (Southern Rhodesia)	Blaise Robel (Malagasy)

Officers	January 1962	October 1965
	Louis Ranaivo (Malagasy)	P. Randrianoatoro (Malagasy)
	Andre Bo-Boliko (Congo-Leopoldville)	Andre Bo-Boliko (Congo-Leopoldville)
	Gilbert Pongault (Congo-Brazzaville)	Gilbert Pongault (Congo-Brazzaville)
Secretary for Administration	David Soumah (Senegal)	David Soumah (Senegal)
Assistant Secretary for Administration	Bassirou Gueye (Senegal)	Fall-Malick (Mauritania)
Secretary for Organization	Chad Tubman, Jr. (Liberia)	James Bass (Liberia)
Assistant Secretary for Organization	Amadou Wague (Senegal)	Lamine Diallo (Senegal)
Secretary for Economic Affairs	Jean Diallo (Senegal)	Jean Diallo (Senegal)
Assistant Secretary for Economic Affairs	Saalim Shiitah (Libya)	Saalim Shiitah (Libya)
Secretary for the Press	Alphonse Kithima (Congo-Leopoldville)	Alphonse Kithima (Congo-Leopoldville)
Assistant Secretary for the Press	Alassame Sow (Senegal)	Alassame Sow (Senegal)
Treasurer	Rene Delanne (Niger)	Bassirou Gueye (Senegal)
Assistant Treasurer	Charles Mendy (Senegal)	Charles Mendy (Senegal)

Source: U.S. Department of Labor, Directory of Labor Organizations: Africa
(Washington, 1962).   ATUC, Trade Union Africa, Dakar, January 1966.

Several conclusions are indicated. First, that ATUC is inevitably at the mercy of the UNTS which must of necessity handle all administrative responsibilities since the other members are employed full-time in their own national unions

Second, that Tlili, the president and major spokesman of ATUC, being as a rule in Tunisia, probably has little contact with the administrative structure. Third, that it is impossible to assess the present position of ATUC as there have been no public expressions of affiliation by national union groupings, and the original membership has been drastically altered by the many national mergers and changing affiliations. In the Congo (Brazzaville), for example, the headquarters of the Union Pan-Africaine des Travailleurs Croyants was closed in March 1965 and its secretary-general, Gilbert Pongault, who was also a vice-president of ATUC, was exiled. Whether ATUC can be regarded as a viable, autonomous organization will have to await the holding of its second congress. Initially scheduled for February 1965, this congress has been twice postponed. A tentative date, at the time of this writing, had been set for November 1965.

Conclusion

Aware of the conflict between the continental union groupings, the OAU, in November 1964, proposed to set up a secretariat on trade-union policy in order to create a new, non-aligned trade-union body or somehow to resolve the differences that have created the present situation. This move by the OAU was welcomed, a fact which is in marked contrast to the reaction just nine months earlier when AFRO sent a memorandum to the February meeting of the Council of Ministers of the OAU strongly requesting that no action be taken on trade union unity: "Action by the OAU . . . would probably prejudice the chance of achieving unity . . . By patient negotiation and compromise the trade unions are gradually finding solutions to their problems of unity."[52]

Whether the OAU intervention was intended as a move to resolve the antagonisms, or whether in fact it was a move on the part of political leaders to control trade unions on the continental scene, is unknown. However, by November 1964, it was clear that "patient negotiation and compromise" were not leading to satisfactory solutions. Ideological agreement on the value of unity and autonomy has shown no signs of resolving the divergent political orientations of the continental trade-union groupings. On the contrary, align-ments with continental trade unions are determined largely by national political relationships and, therefore, show an increasing instability as unions are co-ordinated with, and dominated by, political parties.

At present, economic and political power is organized on a national basis. The need to stabilize the new governments and the compelling tasks of nationbuilding serve to anchor trade unions and their leadership to national rather than to continental level organizations. While economic and political power remain within the national structure, there will be little serious imperative for the formation of a single continental trade-union organization. Pressures, even assistance without strings, if that were possible, from international organizations would only tend to deter such efforts. Indeed, it might well be asked what major contribution a continental trade-union organization can make, especially under conditions in which the acceptance of assistance leads to such acute disunity. For the fundamental condition persists: African trade unions are themselves weak and many of their activities could not have existed without external support. AATUF unions can afford to advocate disaffiliation on ideological grounds, since this has been the tactic of the WFTU, its major source of support; but for many other organizations the question of international affiliation is one of survival and not merely an ideological stand.

Whether the OAU can succeed in either imposing a new organization on the unions or in bringing together the existing groups depends on its success in stabilizing its own economic and political power. For it is far from clear at this time exactly what power the OAU itself possesses, and its influence in trade-union affairs is unlikely to exceed its influence on general political questions.

Addendum

Since this chapter was written, the second conference of ATUC was held in Lagos, October 1965. At this conference the organization reinforced its position relative to the affiliation issue although the particular circumstances of several of its members had necessarily changed since 1962 as is evident by the increasing ICFTU disaffiliations. Due to amalgamations or government takeovers, some of the founding organizations had ceased to exist. These were unions from Kenya, Southern Rhodesia, Mauritania, Congo-Brazzaville, Cameroo and Tanganyika. Nevertheless, structural changes within ATUC were minimal. Ten out of the eighteen original officers were retained and, in most cases, replacements represented the same countries as their predecessors (see List 5). Thus Senegalese officers still dominate the roster. The pragmatic orientation established at the founding congress was also perpetuated.

Perhaps the event with potentially the most significance to the pan-African labor movement has been the coup in Ghana. Reports of mutual discussions between an ATUC delegation and the Ghana Trades Union Congress have appeared, but at the same time, Tettegah, released from detention after denouncing Nkrumah, led a Ghana delegation to a conference of the AATUF secretariat on April 1, 1966. However, the crucial obstacle remains, for the position of unions vis-à-vis national politics has generally moved in the direction of increased political domination and a reinforcement of national rather than continental interests.

Footnotes

1. John Tettegah, "The African Proletariat," Spearhead, 3:9-11 (Jan. 1962).

2. Julius Nyerere, "The Task Ahead of Our African Trade Unions," Labour, Ghana Trade Union Congress, June 1961, 28.

3. Tom Mboya, Freedom and After (Boston, 1963), 254.

4. There have been many articles on the relationship between unions and politics in Africa. Elliot Berg and Jeffrey Butler, "Trade Unions," in J. Coleman and C. Rosberg, Jr. (eds.), Political Parties and National Integration in Tropical Africa (Berkeley, 1964), 340-381, discuss the political role of trade unions both before and after independence with a view towards clarifying several misconceptions concerning the political aspect of labor organizations and their role in a variety of countries. Bruce Millen, The Political Role of Labor in Developing Countries (Washington, 1963), defines political unionism, using examples from Africa throughout. Katherine Van Eerde, "Problems and Alignments in African Labor," Social Research, 1:73-100 (Spring 1962), discusses the political background of unions in Africa. For a complete bibliography on the literature, see William H. Friedland, Unions, Labor and Industrial Relations in Africa: An Annotated Bibliography (Ithaca, 1965). Index category, "Labor and Politics," 8.

5. The varieties of structure of African unions as influenced by models from European countries are discussed by William H. Friedland, "Institutional Change: A Study of Trade Union Development in Tanganyika" (unpubl. diss., University of California, Berkeley, 1963). Also P. F. Gonidec, "The Development of Trade Unionism in Black Africa," Bulletin of the Inter-African Labour Institute, 2:127-156 (May 1963). Audrey Wipper, "A Comparative Study of Nascent Unionism in French West Africa and the Philippines," Economic Development and Culture Change, 1:20-55 (Oct. 1964), discusses other factors effecting variations among trade unions, particularly the extent of social cleavage within the work force as compared to the cleavage between work force and elite.

6. George Lichtblau, "Communist Labor Tactics in the Colonial and Former Colonial Countries," in Everett M. Kassalow (ed.), National Labor Movements in the Post-War World (Evanston, 1963), 51-101, discusses the role of the WFTU in Africa. Colin Legum, in "Pan-Africanism, the Communists and the West," African Affairs, 252:186-196 (July 1964), outlines a realistic framework in which to estimate the potential influence of external pressures.

Elliot Berg, "The External Impact on Trade Unions in Developing Countries: the Record in Africa, " Proceedings of the Sixteenth Annual Meeting of the Industrial Relations Research Association, Boston, Dec. 27-28, 1963, IRRA (Publication No. 32), 89-101, examines many of the dilemmas that external influences have brought to African unions.

7.   ICATU consisted of Egypt, Jordan, Lebanon, Libya and Syria.

8.   It included members from Algeria, Belgian Congo, Cameroon, French West Africa, Madagascar, Réunion, and Tunisia.

9.   UGTAN included unions from Cameroon, Chad, Dahomey, Gabon, Guinea, Ivory Coast, Mauritania, Niger, Senegal, Togo, and Upper Volta.

10.   Sekou Touré, General Congress of the UGTAN (Paris, 1959).

11.   Margaret Roberts, "Africa's Divided Workers, " in Colin Legum, Pan-Africanism (New York, 1962), 82.

12.   The most important of these was the East, Central, and Southern Area Committee formed in July 1958 and headed by Tom Mboya. It included Kenya, Madagascar, Mauritania, Northern Rhodesia, Nyasaland, Somalia, Southern Rhodesia, Sudan, Tanganyika, and Uganda.

13.   Quoted in John Riddell, Free Trade Unions in the Fight for African Freedom (Brussels, 1961), 34.

14.   It was not until 1961 that ICATU deleted the "I" (International) from its name in response to the goal of non-affiliation.

15.   Riddell, Free Trade Unions, 36.

16.   Roberts, "Africa's Divided Workers, " 84-85.

17.   West Africa, June 10, 1961.

18.   These twelve countries were Cameroon, Congo (Leopoldville), Kenya, Madagascar, Mauritius, Nigeria, Nyasaland, Somalia, Southern Rhodesia, Tanganyika, Tunisia, and Uganda.

19.   The original nucleus of AATUF was the six Casablanca countries: Algeria, Ghana, Guinea, Mali, Morocco, and the United Arab Republic.

20.   Mboya, Freedom and After, 226.

21. Quoted in AFL/CIO, International Free Trade Union News (July 1961).

22. This material, tracing the position of the independents, has been extracted from relevant sections of the United States Department of Labor, Bureau of Labor Statistics, Directory of Labor Organizations -- Africa (Washington, May 1962).

23. All the countries belonging to ATUC were either members of the Monrovia Bloc or of PAFMECSA.

24. Discussions of the disagreements at the ATUC conference appear in the Tanganyika Standard (Dar es Salaam), Jan. 12, 16, 1962; in an article by Arnold Beichman in the Christian Science Monitor (Boston), Jan. 13, 1962, and in the AFL/CIO, International Free Trade Union News, Feb. 1962.

25. Christian Science Monitor (Boston), Jan. 26, 1962, 4. See AFL/CIO, International Free Trade Unions News (April 1962), for the full text of Tlili's message to the heads of state.

26. Editorial in the African Worker, Jan./Feb. 1963, 1.

27. "The Charter of the Organization of African Unity, " reprinted in Boutros Boutros Ghali, "The Addis Ababa Charter, " International Conciliation, 546:53 (Jan. 1964).

28. African Labour News, No. 90, Nov. 1963.

29. Tanganyika Standard, Oct. 22, 1963.

30. ATUC delegates were from Senegal, Congo (Brazzaville), and Liberia. AATUF delegates were from Algeria, Ghana, Guinea, Mali, and the United Arab Republic. It was led by Majoub ben Seddick of Morocco.

31. ICFTU, Free Labour World, 167:2 (May 1964). For a biographical sketch of Jallow see West Africa, May 2, 1964.

32. "The Resolutions of the Fourth African Regional Trade Union Conference, " ICFTU Bulletin, April 1964, 8, 13.

33. Ibid., 3, 6.

34. WFTU, World Trade Union Movement, 7/8:17-18 (1964).

35. WFTU, Trade Union Press, July 14, 1964.

36.   Africa Report, IX:34 (July 1964).

37.   West Africa, June 20, 1964, 687.

38.   Christian Science Monitor (Boston), April 21, 1964.

39.   AFL/CIO, International Free Trade Union News, Oct. 1963.

40.   African Labour News, No. 148 (March 1965).

41.   Of the nine officers, it is known that eight hold positions in national
      unions and three are active in national political parties (see Table 1).
      Note how this situation parallels that in both AFRO and ATUC.

42.   West Africa, July 25, 1963, 824.

43.   African Labour News, No. 123, Aug. 1964.

44.   Marcel Bras, "Speech to the First All African Trade Union Conference, "
      World Trade Union Movement, 1:37-49 (Jan. 1962).

45.   I. Zakaria, "Report to the Fifth World Trade Union Congress: For the
      Abolition of Colonialism, " World Trade Union Movement, 1:37-49
      (Jan. 1962).

46.   Of eight officers, it is known that six hold positions in national unions and
      one holds a position in a national political party (see Table 1).

47.   Nairobi Kenya Domestic Service in English, 1015 GMT, Oct. 29, 1964
      (transcribed in Foreign Broadcast Information Service, Daily Report on
      Foreign Radio Broadcasts, Oct. 30, 1964).

48.   African Labour News, No. 132 (Oct. 1964).

49.   Ibid., No. 135 (Nov. 1964).

50.   Of the eighteen officers all hold positions in national unions (seven in
      Senegal); and four of these also hold positions in national political parties
      (see Table 1).

51.   African Diary, II, 5:372 (Jan. 1962).

52.   African Survey, 21:22 (March 1964).

III

Co-operation, Conflict, and Conscription: TANU-TFL Relations, 1955-1964

William H. Friedland
New York State School of Industrial and Labor Relations, Cornell University

In the period following independence, the relations between trade unions and the nationalist political parties in most African countries have been tempestuous. Originally allied with the nationalist parties in varying degrees, unions have discovered that attempts to maintain the pattern of industrial relations instituted during colonial times have led to increased friction and to substantial restrictions.[1] In country after country the government-nationalist party has sought to bring trade-union organizations under control; and the unions have become more obdurate and potentially competitive. Beginning with the passage of the Industrial Relations Act in Ghana in 1958,[2] increasing controls have emphasized the productionist function of unions and restricted their consumptionist activities.[3] Furthermore, governments have sought to undermine the autonomy of the trade unions through pressure.

This paper analyzes a specific case in some detail in order that the process by which a union is taken over and led into new activities by the government-party may be understood. The focus upon a single union constellation, the Tanganyika Federation of Labour (TFL) and its constituent organizations, reveals insights into the general political process in Africa today. In particular, the TFL illustrates the manner in which changed political circumstances have produced a shift in the relationship between the unions and the government-party, from co-operation to conflict, and illuminates both the informal and formal legislative mechanisms used to resolve the conflict.[4]

Originally a German colony, Tanganyika was mandated to Great Britain after World War I. The British had no intention of developing the country and merely held it as a possible pawn to be used in the international power game. Negligible economic growth in the interwar years precluded the development of a permanent labor force;[5] it was not until after World War II that the labor force began to develop in numbers significant enough to lead the British administration to seek social control through the establishment of trade unions.

Trade unionism emerged out of a strike of dockworkers in Dar es Salaam in 1947. The strikers were organized by an underground committee of illiterate dockworkers; they knew nothing about unions and assumed that they would be arrested if identified. After issuing anonymous demands to the employers, which were ignored, a highly effective strike took place. The British administration subsequently worked with the leaders and guided them towards trade unionism. A British unionist imported to work with the Labour Department as a trade-union adviser helped the inexperienced workers form and register the Dar es Salaam Dockworkers Union. This union perished in a violent strike in 1950, but unionism began again in 1952. Growth was slow until 1954 and early 1955, when a number of small, localized unions were formed. This growth was stimulated, at least in part, by the creation of the African nationalist party, the Tanganyika African National Union (TANU), in July 1954.

In 1955 Tom Mboya paid a brief visit to Dar es Salaam to meet the Tanganyikan unionists. Mboya, who had been elected general secretary of the Kenya Federation of Registered Trade Unions in 1953 (re-named the Kenya Federation of Labour in 1955), was regarded as a highly experienced unionist by the Tanganyikans. Mboya suggested that the existing structure of the unions -- localized, craft-based, and without any central organization -- was inadequate. He recommended that the unions amalgamate on national, industrial lines and create a central federation of labor. His ideas won immediate acceptance and the remainder of 1955 and much of 1956 were devoted to amalgamating the many organizations into the Tanganyika Federation of Labour (TFL). In late 1956 the TFL survived its first major crisis, a general strike in Dar es Salaam. Although a number of workers were discharged for their participation in the strike, one result was the establishment of a minimum wage in Dar es Salaam.[6] The unions thereafter won substantial support among the workers in the capital. Unionism continued to spread during 1957, mainly in the towns; and in 1958 the first significant organization of plantation workers, who constitute almost a third of Tanganyika's employed labor force, was undertaken. By 1959 the unions had emerged as powerful entities, concentrated largely in the centers of population. The growth of the trade unions in Tanganyika is indicated by the following:

List 1

Year	Estimated Membership
1952	301
1953	687
1954	291
1955	2,349
1956	12,912
1957	33,986
1958	44,600
1959	78,100

Year	Estimated Membership
1960	91,770
1961	199,915
1962	182,153

Source: Calculated from Tanganyika, Annual Report of the Labour Department, 1952-1962.

Membership figures can only be considered indicative of the real strength of the unions. Because the criteria for judging membership were based on financial commitments which workers made to unions in the form of dues payments, the data do not reveal the even more significant support given unions in adherence to union ideas or willingness to respond to calls for strikes or other economic actions. The figures, nevertheless, show a substantial growth in membership and indicate that unions rapidly became the second most significant African economic-political force in the country.

TFL-TANU Co-operation

Early relations between TFL and TANU cannot be described easily. Always close, co-operative and cordial, they were, nevertheless, rather cautious. In the period between 1954 and 1958, while both party and unions were growing substantially, the groups occupied a tenuous position relative to colonial government. Neither could be certain just how far it could go without incurring intervention or suppression by the government, and accordingly, formal attachments between them were developed carefully. Although there was co-operation between the two organizations, as will be shown below, the character of this cooperation did not require close liaison. Organizational separation was maintained, although Julius Nyerere subsequently contended that a TANU officers was assigned to work with the unions at an early period.[7] Most of the early unionists were TANU members and enthusiasts, however, and several came to union leadership on the recommendation of TANU.

That relations between TANU and the unions were close in spite of organizational separation is indicated in three ways that will be examined in detail. First, TFL provided increasing support to TANU's program, though formal links were not developed until the end of 1958. Secondly, TFL made it clear by the expulsion in 1959 of E. N. N. Kanyama, general secretary of the Tanganyika Railway African Union, that support of anti-TANU forces would not be tolerated. Finally, TANU provided effective support to TFL during several boycotts.

TFL Support of TANU's Program

The earliest recorded discussion of TANU-TFL relations occurred at
the first annual conference of TFL held in October 1956 in Dar es Salaam.
While many political issues were raised which expressed hostility toward the
colonial government, TFL relations with TANU occupied only a small part of
the discussion. Rashidi Kawawa, who had been elected TFL general secretary
in 1955 after having obtained some prominence as an officer of the Tanganyika
African Government Servants Association and as a movie actor, [8] explained
that, while members of the unions were also members of TANU, the two organizations were separate and distinct. Although most delegates agreed that the
unions should avoid politics, there was a strong feeling that the unions should
be directly represented within the legislature. This raised the problem that,
in choosing a representative, the unions might come into conflict with TANU.
The resolution ultimately adopted on the "Relationship Between TFL and
TANU" stated: "No Trade Union which is affiliated to the TFL should affiliate
itself to TANU at the moment." The resolution "Trade Unions and Politics"
provided that "(i) At the moment trade union leaders should not accept positions
of leadership in political organizations; (ii) The Trade Union movement should
be represented in the Legislative Council and the Emergency Committee of the
TFL should study the means of making this possible."[9]

By the second meeting of the TFL General Council in July 1957, the political
activities in the country had increased considerably. TANU's rapid growth had
led to the formation, in early 1956, of a political countermovement, the
settler-dominated and government-sponsored multi-racial United Tanganyika
Party (UTP). These circumstances led the TFL to come out in favor of independenc
thus supporting the essential element of TANU's program. Fear of possible suppression, however, kept the unions from a formal endorsement of support to
TANU. The resolution adopted by the council stated:

> Africans must be left free to govern themselves . . . To be ruled
> is absolutely unjustifiable today. A date for independence of Tanganyika
> must be fixed without delay . . .

> We want all citizens of this country to be given the right to vote so
> that there can be government by the majority . . .

> Workers and unions cannot keep away from government affairs because
> we are citizens like other people. Our unions are not political but we
> must be given the opportunity to express our views and be heard on all
> issues concerning our lives and the progress of the country. Our unions
> must have representatives in the legislature of the country to speak on our
> behalf and defend the rights of workers.[10]

This resolution enraged the government and the settler-dominated UTP since it was seen, correctly, as an indirect endorsement of TANU.[11]

During 1958, many activities indicated that TFL was moving closer to TANU. In June, the TFL agreed to provide financial support to a proposed TANU college. Later in the year, Rashidi Kawawa, TFL general secretary, became a TANU candidate for the legislature. TFL leaders became increasingly prominent within TANU, and, late in the year, as the country moved to the first general elections, TFL encouraged the registration of workers as voters. By the end of the year, TFL was formally represented, at the invitation of TANU, at TANU provincial committee meetings.[12]

Formal affiliation of TFL to TANU at higher levels did not take place until 1961 when TFL was given two seats on the TANU executive. Until then, although several trade unionists were prominent leaders of TANU and many union leaders were active at lower levels of the party, most held offices by virtue of personal abilities rather than because of formal organizational connections. Although the unions were always supporters of TANU, at no time was there direct overlapping of activities or organization. Nor is there any indication that TANU sought, at any time before 1960, to direct or control trade-union actions.

The Kanyama Affair

E. N. N. Kanyama was general secretary of the Tanganyika Railway African Union (TRAU) during the rapid growth of the unions in 1955-1956. He devoted himself to building his own union and to TFL affairs; by 1958, when his difficulties began, Kanyama was one of the more prominent trade unionists in Tanganyika.

Kanyama's endorsement of Dr. Daya, an Asian candidate for the legislative council elections slated for February 1959, started the affair. At the time Kanyama signed the petition for Daya, TANU had not yet named its candidate. When TANU later endorsed another candidate, Kanyama's action was repudiated by the TFL and, subsequently, by the annual conference of his own union. A meeting of the TFL Emergency Committee in January 1959 determined that Kanyama should be refused recognition as secretary of his union. The same committee upheld the original decision in February; Kanyama was present at this meeting and pleaded his case unsuccessfully. He was subsequently expelled from TRAU and a militant young man, Christopher S. Kasanga Tumbo was elected in his place. Although Kanyama subsequently admitted the error of his ways, offered public apologies, and appealed for reinstatement into membership, his appeals were rejected. It was not until October 1960 that the TFL ban against him was lifted; TRAU continued to refuse him permission to rejoin the union.

There are indications that the reaction to Kanyama's act was not solely a
result of his support of Dr. Daya. Kanyama, a relatively conservative unionist
who probably represented the interests of the educated clerical staff more than
those of the illiterate manual and unskilled workers, had already encountered
opposition within TRAU. Furthermore, Kanyama's activity in TFL affairs
appears to have incurred some antagonism there. It is likely that the first
union caucus held in Tanganyika was directed against Kanyama and that Rashidi
Kawawa played a role in organizing the opposition to him within TRAU.[13]

While full details are not available, there can be no doubt that Kanyama's
support of Dr. Daya provided an excuse for an attack upon him. But more than
that, the bitterness of the attack indicates that the union leadership was deeply
sensitive to any action that might be interpreted as hostile to TANU. Although
no formal resolution had been adopted by any TFL body endorsing TANU, by
early 1959 TFL had accepted the idea that it was committed to its support and
that no action by unionists in opposition to TANU could be tolerated.[14]

The Kanyama case is interesting because it was one of the few times the
TFL became intimately involved in the affairs of one of its affiliates. Although
TFL leadership of the affiliates was well-established, throughout the history
of TFL there has been considerable autonomy of the affiliates and the idea of
TFL intervention in internal affairs has usually be rejected.

Joint TFL-TANU Actions

While TANU played no direct role in the general strike which developed
in Dar es Salaam in late 1956 and early 1957, TANU support of a trade-union
boycott of the Dar es Salaam municipal bus system represented its first instance
of public support of the unions. In this strike, the Transport and Allied Workers
Union, unable to stop the movement of busses manned by Asians and European
supervisors, called for a boycott of the busses by Africans, who constituted
almost the entire clientele. TANU effectively supported the strike and helped
the unions to achieve a partial victory.

A similar situation developed during the bitter strike of brewery workers in
April 1958; strikers were removed from their homes and Kawawa was arrested
for threatening non-strikers. Again, because of the racial division of labor,
it was feasible for production and distribution to be maintained during the strike.
The boycott called by the unions was supported publicly by TANU. A subsequent
conference of the TFL formally resolved "that a letter be written to the Honorable
J. K. Nyerere . . . thanking him and TANU for the assistance offered during
the brewery strike and asking that he notify all TANU branches of our gratitude.
This conference also asks that the present relationship between this organization
and TANU be maintained for the benefit of our country."[15]

Another instance of close co-operation occurred in late 1958 when the first major strike of plantation workers was held against the Mazinde estate owned by David Lead. Lead had been one of the major supporters of the UTP, and the strike had strong political implications. When it appeared that Lead was seeking to recruit strikebreakers from the Washambala tribe, a mission consisting of Kawawa and S. S. Chamshama, a local TANU leader with no connection with the unions, was sent to meet the chief to request his co-operation in keeping his people from being scabs.[16]

Co-operation in such instances benefited both organizations. For TFL wide public support for its boycotts and economic actions provided necessary assistance for its activities because European and Asian supervisors were able to sustain production and services during strikes. For TANU any series of actions which would mobilize its followers and permit them to express some legitimate hostility to European domination was useful to the party in developing mass support; and union boycott activities offered the party another access to the grass roots level.

TFL-TANU Conflict

Origins of Conflict: The Problem of Political Access

Although there was some conflict between TANU and the unions during the early period, this was on a small scale and largely rooted in misconceptions on the part of low-ranking officials. The potentially divisive problem of TFL's nomination of a candidate for the Legislative Council had been resolved by the unions' designation of Kawawa to TANU, which then named him as its candidate in 1958.

As the country moved closer to independence, however, the latent strains inherent in the differing functions of trade unions and political parties became increasingly manifest. Conflict first began to emerge in the aftermath of two major strikes conducted by Tanganyika's unions against services of the East Africa High Commission. The first, a strike of post office workers against the East African Postal and Telecommunications Administration, began in December 1959 and lasted fifty-five days. The second, a strike of railway workers against the East African Railways and Harbours Administration, began in February 1960 and lasted 82 days. Because of the racial division of labor in East Africa, it was possible for Europeans and Asians to maintain basic services throughout the strikes. Although the response in both strikes by African workers was overwhelming, the strikes jeopardized the existence of the Tanganyika African Postal Union (TAPU) and the Tanganyika African Railway Union (TRAU) and called for considerable financial sacrifices by their members. The two

main leaders of the unions, Jacob Namfua of TAPU and Christopher Tumbo of
TRAU, reflecting the feelings of members of their unions, became increasingly
hostile to the East Africa High Commission as a result.

While the unions were moving toward strong public antagonism to the
High Commission, a countermovement developed shortly within TANU. In
June 1960 Julius Nyerere proposed the establishment of an East African federation
composed of the four British-controlled territories in East Africa: Tanganyika,
Kenya, Uganda, and Zanzibar. The proposal, made while he was in Addis
Ababa, came as a surprise as no policy on this issue had been announced by
TANU. The creation of an East African federation would mean delaying Tanganyikan independence until all four territories could be brought to independence
simultaneously. In the period following Nyerere's return to Tanganyika, it
became increasingly apparent that TANU was focusing upon the East Africa
High Commission as the central structure upon which a future East African
federation sould be created. TAPU and TRAU moved toward a position favoring
the destruction of the commission so that ministerial responsibility for the
important services administered through the commission would be handled
inside Tanganyika. In this way the unions believed that they could obtain political
access to the management of those services against which economic actions had
been unsuccessful.

The tone of future conflict emerged in speeches made at a series of
trade-union conferences in July and August 1960. At the first of these, the
postal workers conference held between July 3-6, 1960, Jacob Namfua, TAPU
general secretary said:

> Our view is that the High Commission -- a creation of London --
> should be destroyed. We shall be ready to co-operate with other terri-
> tories in East Africa in the economic field, however.
>
> We think that there can be a working committee in which ministers
> having full ministerial responsibilities can meet and settle problems
> instead of through the Central Legislative Assembly ⌐of the High Com-
> mission⌐. It is unacceptable to us that we risk our freedom and pro-
> gress in some other federation of East African territories before breaking
> up the High Commission.[17]

The conference resolved that:

> As Tanganyika achieves responsible government, the High Commission
> should be dissolved immediately. A minister, responsible and answerable
> to the electorate of this country, should be appointed to handle posts and
> railways . . . if these proposals are not accepted, we shall request the
> cooperation of other unions in High Commission agencies to join together
> and strike to show their objections to the High Commission.[18]

An even stronger stand against the High Commission was taken at the opening meeting of the TRAU conference at the end of July at which Tumbo made clear his vehement opposition. Although stating that the union favored an East African federation, Tumbo drew an enthusiastic response from his listeners when he stated: "We are opposed to the present High Commission. We are opposed, opposed, opposed."

Present at both conferences was Oscar Kambona, organizing secretary of TANU. At the time of the TAPU conference, Kambona had not answered Namfua on the High Commission. Now, in response to Tumbo, Kambona said:

If you want to tell the government, you have to tell it to Mr. Nyerere. But tell the government what? That the High Commission is no good? I agree to that . . . no colonial rule is good and TANU does not want the High Commission.

But, let's consider the matter. Why is the High Commission bad? Is it because of the spirit of the people ruling it who have the spirit of ruling other people? It is not that the house is bad; it is the people inside the house that are bad. But if you live in a house and there are vermin in the house, does that mean that you burn it down? The house has to be rid of vermin but that doesn't mean that the house itself is bad. The High Commission is bad because the people that run it think of themselves as small gods; we have to rid ourselves of them.[19]

From this point on it became increasingly clear that, in spite of trade-union opposition, as Tanganyika moved closer to independence, TANU's policy would be to maintain the High Commission services and to use the organization as the basis of an East African federation. It was thus over the question of the High Commission that initial TFL-TANU antagonism developed.

The unions were not, however, in agreement among themselves on the destruction of the High Commission. The Transport and General Workers Union (TGWU) led by Michael Kamaliza, felt its way toward a position which sought to reconcile the conflict. At the opening session of the TGWU conference in August, the featured speaker was Julius Nyerere, who made no mention either of the East African federation or the High Commission. In Michael Kamaliza's speech of welcome that followed there was a brief reference to the High Commission indicating that TGWU was not, at the moment, in favor of the immediate destruction of the High Commission but felt that it could be appropriately reconstructed. If attempts at reconstruction failed, however, the TGWU stated that it would join its sister organizations in demanding the abolishment of the High Commission.[20]

The Kamaliza speech touched off a torrent of public hostility between the unions. Tumbo and Namfua promptly reminded Rashidi Kawawa, then president of the TFL, that the previous TFL conference had adopted a resolution calling for the destruction of the High Commission as soon as possible. Kawawa, on tour up-country, was not immediately available to silence the volume of abuse that appeared in the press between TRAU and TAPU on the one hand and TGWU on the other.[21]

On Kawawa's return, the General Council of the TFL met on August 27-28 for a lengthy and acrimonious session. A compromise resolution was finally adopted specifying five conditions which would have to be met if the TFL was not to demand that the government withdraw from the High Commission These conditions included approval by TFL of a report on salaries and working conditions in the High Commission agencies; full responsibility for services to be vested with heads of these services in Tanganyika; movement of Africans into responsible positions; a full contribution by the commission to the development of Tanganyika; and satisfaction of all Tanganyika's government claims on the commission.[22]

The specification of these conditions subdued the contending wings of the TFL for the moment: the TANU supporters had obtained a position which was not in conflict with that of TANU while the militants had obtained a commitment to opposition to the commission if their conditions were not met. The entire dispute, however, was portentous of the conflict that would develop once TANU gained control of the government.

The Elaboration of Conflict

The August 1960 meeting of the TFL General Council took place just before the establishment on September 1 of the first TANU government in which Rashidi Kawawa was named minister of local government and housing. Kawawa's departure from the TFL was to open a succession crisis; more significant, perhaps, was the loss of Kawawa's skill at keeping the many internal conflicts within the unions from breaking into open warfare.

Prior to the battle over the High Commission and Kawawa's departure, there had been no clear-cut factions within TFL. With Kawawa absent, three groups crystallized. First, there were the unions of workers employed by government agencies. These included TRAU, TAPU, the Tanganyika Union of Public Employees (TUPE), and the Tanganyika African Local Government Workers Unions (TALGWU). As TANU took over governmental responsibilities and became the employer with which these unions had to deal, their hostility to the party and the government sharpened. The second group, consisting of unions that mainly supported TANU policies, included the TGWU and the

Domestic and Hotel Workers Union. These unions dealt with employers in the private sector and, on the whole, with relatively minor employers. TGWU, not dealing with large employers or with the government, was able to win substantial concessions for its members. The Domestic Workers Union, in contrast, was almost completely unsuccessful in its industrial relations activities and, to the extent that it was capable of projecting a future for itself, saw possibilities only through government regulation. In the middle there was a "swing" group consisting mainly of the Plantation Workers Union (PWU), the two unions of dockworkers, and the African Mine Workers Union (AMU). These unions varied their stance depending upon the relevance of any given issue to their own interests. In many cases, these unions took a neutral stance between the pro-TANU and anti-TANU unions; in other cases, individual unions took anti-TANU stands when some action was taken that affected their interests. There were also several issues that united all of the unions against TANU.

Between September 1960 and March 1962 public disputes between the unions focused on the persons of Michael Kamaliza and Christopher Tumbo. While other union officials played prominent roles, these two personalities stood out in sharp contrast. The conflict between them stood out in sharp relief at the special congress of TFL called in October 1960 to elect new officers. Kamaliza, one of the earliest of the unionists and the leader of one of the most successful of the unions, had some advantages in that he was generally believed to be preferred by Kawawa. While Kawawa's break with the unions was complete after he became a minister, he had previously worked very closely with Kamaliza. Tumbo, in contrast, was a brash young man whose lengthy strike against the railways had been considered untimely by most unionists even though his union had emerged somewhat strengthened. Kamaliza was elected president; but because the delegates were concerned about the split, Namfua was elected secretary-treasurer in an attempt to obtain balance between the warring factions.[23]

In the period following the congress, relations between the opposing factions and between the unions and TANU continued to deteriorate as a series of crucial issues developed. Much of the difficulty originated in the expectations of the unions that the movement toward independence would produce substantial benefits for union members. Having made promises to their members about the benefits of uhuru (independence), the unionists now wanted concrete concessions from the government. In particular, the unionists believed (with some justification) that the colonial government had favored employers; now that an African government had taken over they expected support for their demands. They were to be generally disappointed.

Three major issues as well as many subsidiary but important questions prepared the ground for intensive internal conflict as well as for the disputes between the unions and TANU. The first issue crystallized over a strike at the Williamson Diamond Mines at Mwadui; additional issues focused on the question of Africanization and proposals to reorganize and centralize the TFL.

The Mwadui strike, which took place in December 1960, had its origins earlier in the year.[24] Although a fifteen-month contract had been signed in April 1960, setting wages and other conditions of employment, disagreements developed between the mines management and the African Mine Workers Union (AMU). The mine was owned jointly by the Tanganyikan government and the DeBeers Mining Company, although it was managed by the latter. Since wage rates had been set for fifteen months, management at first refused to make any concessions to the AMU. Subsequently, some small concessions were made which the union found unsatisfactory. The AMU continued to broaden the issues separating them from management while, at the same time, attempting to create pressures on management to arbitrate the disputed issues. When strike threats were unsuccessful, the workers struck on December 7.

The direct financial interest of the government made it a party to the dispute. Thus when the strike began, the minister of commerce and industry, Nsilo Swai, decided to intervene on the spot. He invited Jacob Namfua, the new TFL secretary-treasurer, to fly to the mine with him to help resolve the dispute. During this trip it became plain that the minister was taking a hard line in support of the management by refusing to pressure them to arbitrate. The minister also issued warnings to the strikers that they would be discharged unless they returned to work within forty-eight hours.

This repudiation by the government led the unionists into an attack on the government. The Mwadui strike was the first major industrial conflict that had taken place since TANU had assumed government responsibilities and the unionists had expected intervention on their behalf rather than on management's.

After several meetings between Nyerere and the trade-union leaders, Namfua and TFL Vice-president Kazimoto were flown to Mwadui where the strike was settled, mostly on management terms. The antagonism of the unions toward the government now became public, however. Although excepting Nyerere, who was credited with having helped bring the strike to an end, Namfua launched a vigorous attack on "certain government ministers."

I must equally say that some certain Government Ministers are mainly responsible for the serious situation which existed at the mine. The situation could have turned to complete chaos and possibly bloodshed.

Some Government Ministers have completely ignored the Government policy of encouraging trade unions in collective bargaining. In the Williamson dispute, the Government has absolutely ignored the laid-down machinery of negotiations.

I must warn the Government, trade unionism was put on trial at Mwadui. Trade unionism has sustained that trial and trade unionism is here to stay. We do not and we shall not take orders from anybody other than from the members we represent.

Certain Government Ministers are ill-advised by their so-called expatriate civil servants.[25]

The bitterness between TANU and the unions also erupted at a public meeting, held on December 20, 1960, to demand freedom for Jomo Kenyatta. Called in conjunction with a Pan-African Freedom Movement of East, Central and South Africa (PAFMECA) conference being held in Dar es Salaam, the meeting was addressed by prominent TANU officials as well as by Namfua. During a speech by TANU's co-ordinator Mbuta Milando, the unions were attacked for their role in the Mwadui strike. Tumbo promptly walked out of the meeting and the unionists did not hesitate to announce their dissatisfaction with Milando. TFL denials that workers were deserting TANU to join the miniscule opposition African National Congress or that TFL was breaking relations with TANU indicated that serious organizational strains had developed. Feelings between officials of the unions and TANU reached a point where it was considered advisable to appoint a committee consisting of three government ministers and five union officials to consider TANU-TFL relations. It was as a result of these discussions that TFL was given two seats on the TANU National Executive in February 1961.

While the Mwadui events were culminating in a dramatic strike, a more significant and long-ranging issue was beginning to develop, the question of Africanization. The upgrading of Africans into upper echelons in the administrative structure of government had long been a burning issue for the unions. As a result of the colonial racial division of labor, Africans had been restricted almost entirely to the bottom rungs of the administrative structure of the government and the economy generally. The African unions became, therefore, the key agencies through which a drive for upward mobility of African workers would be sought.

For the TANU government, however, accelerated Africanization had potentially serious consequences for the maintenance of regular government services. The government leaders, argued, therefore, that Africanization had to take place at a measured pace. The demand for Africanization, however, had enormous political implications; TANU could hardly afford to oppose it, especially since many TANU back-benchers in the National Assembly and rank and file party members felt as strongly on Africanization as the unionists. TANU's public position emerged as favoring "localization"[26] (employing local persons qualified to do the job) rather than Africanization. This was unsatisfactory to the unionists since it meant that local Europeans and Asians could continue to be hired in upper-level positions. Thus, the distinction between Africanization and localization had significant meaning to the unionists as well as to the TANU government.

The issues began to become clear at a meeting of the Dar es Salaam Dockworkers' Union at the end of September 1960 when the general secretary, Luk Ngahyoma, demanded Africanization of the port, threatening action if the union's demands were not met. This drew a rebuttal from the European minister of health and labour, Derek Bryceson. TANU policy, Bryceson stated, was to localize the civil service as rapidly as possible but no racist policies would be followed. The minister's opposition to Africanization prompted the TFL to clarify its own stance supporting Africanization rather than localization.[27]

Nyerere then responded with a direct statement of government policies on the subject of Africanization at the first meeting of the newly-elected legislative council on October 19, 1960. Since the civil service had to reflect the basic character of the population of a country, its representatives had to be African. It was to be government policy that appointments would be made locally and priority would be given to Africans if they were available for existing vacancies. However, if no qualified Africans or Tanganyikans of any race were available, the government would go outside the country to fill appointments.[28]

While Nyerere's statement represented a concession to the trade unionists, it was, on the whole, considered unsatisfactory. The Dar es Salaam branch of TUPE immediately volunteered to name at least twenty Africans capable of taking over advanced posts within the administration. The union contended that, while certain skills were not locally available, in most government departments, expatriate department heads simply signed papers prepared by their African assistants who were doing the essential work. The problem was resolved temporarily as a result of a meeting between a delegation from TUPE and Nyerere. However, the issue was to be revived time and again as the unions found upward movement impeded by the slow policies of Africanization.

The subject of Africanization came to a climax in the railways administration in February 1962. TRAU, dissatisfied with the speed of Africanization, made a series of strike threats as well as submitting a master plan to Africanize the railways. The master plan, the first major threat presented to the TANU government, implied that the union would undertake Africanization unilaterally and without reference to management, a procedure which would have challenged the ability of the management to control and operate the railway system and, ultimately, the authority of the government. The TRAU threat was resolved by an agreement to appoint a commission to investigate specific possibilities for Africanization and by a pay increase in March 1962.[29]

The idea of the master plan appealed to the sense of the dramatic in the unionists since there soon developed a rash of master plans, the most significant of which was launched by the Plantation Workers Union in 1962. Details of the master plans never emerged publicly -- indeed, one union official was summarily discharged by his union for revealing elements of the plan prematurely, thus leaving the government and the public to speculate on their meaning.[30] It was clear, however, that the plans projected a series of stages in which the union would act unilaterally to take over control of their industries to implement the goal of the plans -- Africanization.

The third major issue that divided the unions from TANU developed largely as an internal fight within the TFL. This battle ensued over proposals to reorganize and centralize the unions. While purely an internal question, the anti-TANU unions saw the centralization trend taking place at the behest of the government. The dispute developed after a visit to Tanganyika of John Tettegah, general secretary of the Ghana Trades Union Congress (GTUC). Tettegah had been involved in a reorganization of the Ghanaian unions that had undermined the autonomy of the GTUC affiliates by bringing them under government control. While the extent of Tettegah's involvement in Tanganyikan events is still unclear, it appears that he suggested structural changes in Tanganyika's unions to the minister of health and labour, Derek Bryceson, and to TFL President Michael Kamaliza. Although it was Kamaliza who publicly announced the subsequent proposals, there are indications that he was covertly supported by both the government and TANU.

The proposals for a reorganization of TFL's structure were essentially based on centralizing the financial organization of all of the unions within TFL. The Federation, hitherto dependent upon the payment of fees by its affiliates and experiencing continual financial crises, would have had effective control over strike funds. This proposal was resisted strenuously by the leadership of the government workers' unions that constituted TFL's militant wing. The dispute became public when Tumbo led a walkout of four unions, railway, government, local government, and postal workers, from a TFL meeting on April 18, 1961.[31] In the months that followed, the daily bickering became increasingly vitriolic and soon involved prominent government and TANU officials. With Victor Mkello, leader of the Plantation Workers Union, the President of TFL, and the key person in the "swing" group absent in Europe, there was no one to mediate between the factions. The public battle escalated as disagreement over procedural questions were added to the substantive arguments.

During the next few months, TFL held a series of meetings to attempt
to reconcile the differences between the quarreling groups, none of which were
successful. Indeed, the acrimony began to occupy an alarming proportion of
space in the daily press. The Swahili newspapers Nguromo and Mwafrika
were filled not only with news articles and press releases but also with an
increasing correspondence indicating public concern with the issue. In June,
a speech by Edward Barongo, deputy general secretary of TANU, to the effect
that TANU recognized only those unions affiliated to TFL, inflamed the dispute
and drew TANU leadership into public support of the Kamaliza group. A
subsequent assassination threat against Barongo brought TANU Secretary-
General Oscar Kambona into the dispute. The split developed further when
Tumbo was attacked by the TANU newsletter, Sauti ya TANU, in the third week
in June, and again on July 9 by Minister of Home Affairs George Kahama for
hypocrisy in opposing trade-union cooperation with the government while using
the assistance of the minister of labor in a railway strike.

The vendetta continued, thus, through three bitter months; in mid-July
Mkello returned from Europe and began to seek a settlement. An attempt to
bring together the presidents of the eleven unions in TFL turned out to be
futile. It was not until August that a formula was found that brought about a
cessation of the public warfare. This involved mediation by Adam Sapi, a
prominent chief of the Hehe tribe, who, being neither a trade unionist nor a
member of TANU, was considered neutral.

The report of the Sapi Commission was given to a special congress of
the TFL convened on September 9. The report fixed responsibility for the
initial outbreak on Kamaliza for announcing changes in the TFL structure
before obtaining proper authorization. Although the report found Kamaliza
guilty of other misbehavior, it was also sharply critical of the Tumbo wing
for its public attacks on the TFL leadership. The report recommended that
TFL continue to co-operate with TANU but recognized that TANU and TFL were
not a single entity. The TFL special congress accepted the report and Kamaliza
won a vote of confidence by a single vote. Probably the most important consequence of the Sapi report was that it ended the public controversy. However,
although independence was scheduled for December 9, 1961, relations between
the unions and TANU did not improve. Instead, a new series of issues tended
to unite the unionists in opposition to the TANU government.

During the public conflict which ended with the Sapi settlement, an important
government commission had been gathering evidence concerning Tanganyika's
government employees. The Adu Commission (called after its Nigerian chairman, Amishadai L. Adu), issued a report which proposed the establishment of
a minimum wage for government employees of 126 s. ($18) a month. This
recommendation of the report was greeted with substantial hostility by the
unions.[32]

Throughout this period, the Local Government Workers Union had been involved in a series of disputes with the Dar es Salaam Municipal Council whose mayor, Sheikh Amri Abedi, was a major TANU leader. Abedi accused the union of attempting to drain the council's funds through excessive wage demands while the union accused the mayor of draining funds to maintain the mayoral automobile. A strike of municipal council employees was averted only through the intervention of the minister of labor.[33]

Two other incidents early in November did nothing to ease the strain between the unions and government. A meeting scheduled by the Mwanza branch of TRAU was canceled by police because of the presence in Mwanza of Julius Nyerere. The following day, it was announced that a proposed TRAU Youth Club had been refused registration by the government on the grounds that the organization might constitute a threat to the peace.[34]

The tone of TANU's attack upon the unions sharpened; TFL was seen to represent the special interests of a minority of the population seeking to extract maximum concessions for its members at the cost of economic development of the nation. Although much of this strain did not appear publicly, the period just prior to and after independence was one of increasing tension between the unions and TANU. Just after independence, the relations between the unions and the political party became the focus of an issue of Spearhead, a magazine published in Dar es Salaam which sought to become a theoretical organ for the local intelligentsia. The crucial points were set forth in two articles. John Tettegah of Ghana took a pro-government line in calling for an "African Labour Personality."[35] Referring to the traditional approach of unions "for the protection of wages and salaries alone" as "hackneyed," Tettegah stated that unions must be politically involved. Calling "almost all Governments in newly African /̄sic!̄/ states . . . Governments of Workers," Tettegah asked for closer co-operation between unions and governments.

The second article was by John Magongo, general secretary of the public employees union, TUPE, and one of Tumbo's main supporters. In an article titled "Co-operation Not Domination," Magongo agreed that unions had to exercise restraint in making demands. This had to be voluntary, however, and Magongo warned: "There is a tendency on the part of political leaders to exercise authority over trade unions and make them part and parcel of Government. Self restraint is demanded with threats forgetting that such things have to be carried out by co-operation . . . Sometimes such actions are taken by political leaders because of their ignorance of the principles of free labour movement. But in most cases integration of trade unions and political parties is carried out under the banner of Pan-Africanism and nationalism and on the pretext that trade unions have to be moulded on local conditions."[36]

Magongo's article was a public announcement of the antagonism of the unionists to being "captured" by TANU and the government.

Although relations publicly improved between Kamaliza and Tumbo after the Sapi intervention, the basic strain remained. Added to their trade-union differences was the fact that Tumbo had emerged as one of the most persistent gadflies in the National Assembly, attacking and being attacked by the government.[37] Within TFL, antagonism to the government had reached a stage that threatened Kamaliza's position increasingly. Near the end of 1961 the TFL Emergency Committee adopted a resolution calling on all unionists who were members of the National Assembly and of local councils to resign and for workers to withdraw from TANU. Only the barest hints of this drastic resolution appeared publicly. Opposed by Kamaliza, the resolution was later endorsed by a General Council meeting of TFL. Kamaliza argued that the resolution could not be implemented until it had been adopted by a full conference of TFL. This argument was successful and the resolution was given no publicity; it was ultimately overturned at the special TFL congress in March 1962. Under these circumstances it became evident to the TANU government that some solution to the trade-union problem was necessary and that the removal of the two key protagonists might provide an answer.

One important factor contributing to the exit of Kamaliza and Tumbo from the unions lay in the somewhat unsatisfactory situation existing in the ministry for health and labor. The minister, from September 1960, had been Derek Bryceson, the only European in the cabinet. As pressure built up over Africanization, it became increasingly difficult for a European to occupy a ministry that was so directly involved with this issue. An opportunity came to relieve him when Nyerere resigned as prime minister in January 1962 and a general ministerial shakeup took place. The ministry was assigned to Nsilo Swai, whose role in the Mwadui strike made him unpalatable to the unionists. Thus the government still needed a minister for labor who could represent its view but who would not have any special onus resting on him. This requirement and the need to settle the strains within TFL were resolved by the appointment of Kamaliza to the ministry. Tumbo's removal was obtained by his designation as High Commissioner to the United Kingdom.

The removal of the key leaders of the feuding wings of the TFL resolved neither the internal conflict within the unions nor the strain between the unions and TANU. At a special congress of the TFL held on March 15-16, 1962, the election of the new officers indicated a conscious search by delegates to obtain a balance internally. The new president was Victor Mkello of the Plantation Workers Union, but as a result of structural changes, the post lost its administrative significance. Mkello's selection indicated an attempt by the unionists to find a neutral person who had been largely uninvolved in the major diputes.

The key administrative post, that of general secretary, went ot John Magongo, a Tumbo supporter, at the time the general secretary of TUPE; Alfred Tandau, a Kamaliza protegé from the Transport and General Workers Union was designated assistant general secretary. In choosing vice-presidents, the delegates also sought a balance. The first vice-president was N. Kazimoto who had been in Europe with Mkello, and had been uninvolved in most of the disputes. Hassan Khupe of the Mine Workers, a Tumbo follower, was elected second vice-president.[38] For the moment the TFL presented a face of harmony, but the illusion was shortly to be shattered.

Restrictions Against the Unions

The period following the March congress was marked by the intensification of hostilities as general industrial action continued, demands for Africanization became more strident and more master plans were announced. This was to lead in June to the introduction of three crucial pieces of legislation that seriously undermined the position of the unions; and it was to be followed by a series of actions that eroded the autonomy of the TFL and the strength of the unions. From this time until the de facto suppression of the unions in January 1964, there was almost continual conflict.

While the main force of government action was directed toward weakening the unions, this does not mean that the economic position of the workers was being undermined. Indeed, various bills were adopted in the National Assembly which alleviated some bad conditions in industry.[39] Although this legislation was conceived of as beneficial to the workers, some of it led to additional industrial unrest which will be discussed below.

To a considerable degree, the introduction of legislation protective of workers reflected the concerns of Michael Kamaliza as minister of labor. Kamaliza believed that Tanganyika was moving toward a socialist society in which government and unions were engaged in the same work.[40] The introduction of protective legislation occurred when the unions were not doing their jobs. On occasions the government had contemplated the introduction of legislation, but when the unions had undertaken to act on their own, no legislation was introduced. Thus, in the work of the government and the unions Kamaliza saw no conflict of interest. The same situation was true with respect to the development of the country: this was a job in which government and unions had to contribute, it was not just a job for the government alone. Kamaliza still felt himself to be a representative of the workers. These beliefs led Kamaliza into proposing in mid-1963 that the ministry of labor and the trade unions integrate, the unions becoming part of the ministry.

Table 8. Strikes in Tanganyika 1954-1962

Year	Employed African labor force*	No. of strikes	No. of workers involved	Total no. of man-days lost	Ratio, man-days lost to labor force
1954	409,094	43	4,621	7,842	.019
1955	383,100	42	8,877	12,562	.033
1956	394,209	54	17,695	58,066	.147
1957	390,470	114	39,786	165,328	.423
1958	390,547	153	67,430	296,746	.760
1959	393,268	205	82,878	402,693	1.02
1960	357,475	203	89,495	1,494,773	4.2
1961	412,092	101	20,159	113,254	.275
1962	368,816	152	48,434	417,474	1.13

Source: Tanganyika, Annual Report of the Labour Department, 1954-1962.

* Not including domestic servants.

It was under the aegis of Kamaliza, therefore, that the government introduced three crucial bills into the National Assembly. The alarming
strike rates, summarized in Table 8, indicate one major reason for TANU's
concern. Another reason was that one of the most persistent organizations
pressuring the government for Africanization was the Tanganyika Union
of Public Employees. Since the employer that it dealt with was the
Tanganyika government itself, the continual pressure was probably felt
to be unbearable. That TUPE leaders did not hesitate to publicize the issue,
added another element of strain.

Accordingly, in the June 1962 session of the National Assembly,
three crucial bills were introduced.[41] The first bill, a new trade union
ordinance, created a designated federation to which all unions had to be
affiliated if they were to be legally registered and, therefore, able to
operate as legal entities. The ordinance also provided, in a section later
modified, that the minister of labor would have authority to intervene in
internal union financial matters to ensure financial responsibility.

The second bill, the trade disputes settlement bill, was aimed at
substantially reducing the right to strike by instituting a complex procedure
leading to conciliation and arbitration before strikes were legally possible.
Although it was possible for unions to continue to strike under this bill,
the ability of unions to bring out their members on short notice was eliminated.

The third bill, the civil service (negotiating machinery) bill, removed
those civil servants earning over Ł 702 per year from eligibility to membership in a union and provided, instead, representation within a staff advisory
system.

The response of the TFL to the bills was immediate and hostile.
The legislation was seen as undercutting the position of the unions, their
freedom and their autonomy. The legal right of the government to designate
a federation implied that the government could at any time "license" a
competing organization and make the TFL illegal. The power of the
ministry of labor to control aspects of the unions' accounting smacked too
much of Kamaliza's past proposal to centralize union finances within the
TFL that had stimulated the internal crisis between April and September
of 1962. Similarly, while most union leaders believed that the unions should
be affiliated with the TFL, the proposed legal obligation that they be
affiliated or lose their registration meant that TFL could enforce structural
changes over the opposition of its affiliates. The unionists opposed the
trade dispute settlement bill because it severely impeded their right to
strike. The bill removing higher income civil servants from membership

evoked an extremely hostile response from TUPE. To a large extent, the better-paid civil servants provided much of the effective leadership of the union. The separation of this category from membership meant that the union would have to depend upon less talented individuals for leadership.

Crucial to the effectiveness of the unions' response was the position of Victor Mkello, a nominated member of the National Assembly and president of the TFL. Initially opposing the legislation, Mkello found himself in a position where it was evident that he would be alone in the National Assembly in voting against the government. Substantial pressure was brought to bear on Mkello, and he ultimately voted for the three bills after some amendments were made to soften the degree of financial control to be held by the minister of labor.

Mkello's surrender in the National Assembly did not mean that the unions accepted the legislation in good grace. In July, the general secretary of the Dar es Salaam Dockworkers, Luke Ngahyoma, bitterly criticized Nyerere for misleading the population. Oscar Kambona and other members of TANU attacked Ngahyoma's statement and were in turn subjected to attack. The trade unionists resorted to the ultimate in political vitriol when they referred to those supporting the legislation as "stooges" or "Tshombes."[42] Later in July, in a speech announcing the initiation of a TFL economic program to begin its own farms, schools and hospitals, Magongo criticized government ministers and officials for the ostentatious style of their lives. This drew a response by the publicity secretary of TANU to the effect that TANU ministers were the lowest paid in Africa. Nor were matters aided by the announcement by TUPE early in August that the "greatest master plan ever launched" to Africanize the civil service was to be undertaken.

While these events took place, a decision was being undertaken by the TANU government to change the character of local administration, removing the chiefs from their positions of official power. Magongo picked on this issue to launch a further attack on the government. Although there had been general unity within the unions, especially as a result of the passage of three new laws, Magongo's statement on the chiefs precipita- ted a new conflict within the TFL. Heriel Naftal, general secretary of the Transport and General Workers Union, publicly deplored Magongo's posi- tion. This led to a meeting of the TFL Emergency Committee which sought to extricate Magongo from a position which even most of his sympathizers regarded as untenable.[43]

The dispute between TANU and the government was cast in a new light by the return of Tumbo to Tanganyika in August 1962.[44] Although he was silent for several days, it became clear that Tumbo, opposed

to the government's attitude towards unions, was looking for a political
modus operandi. On August 27, TRAU voted to offer him his former post
as general secretary, but Tumbo had decided to become involved directly in politics.[45]
At first offered the leadership of the minute African National Congress (ANC),
Tumbo decided instead to resuscitate an even more miniscule political
organization which had split off from ANC, the People's Democratic Party (PDP).

Tumbo's decision to revive the PDP was announced at a TRAU meeting
on September 8. Ostensibly called to welcome Tumbo back to Tanganyika,
the meeting was addressed by Tumbo, Katungutu, Tumbo's successor in
TRAU, Magongo, and Mkello. Of the four speakers, all but Mkello lashed
out at the government for recent policies, particularly the passage of the
three bills. Tumbo characterized the laws as a "stab in the back" of the
workers. Mkello was far more moderate: "Let there be millions of
political parties. It is the policy of the party that will make it have our
support. We in the TFL are not fools to be lured to supporting any party
foolishly." Declaring that TFL supported TANU Mkellow added: "The
policy of the federation is to support any party which works in the interest
of the workers. At the moment such a party is TANU... Anybody wanting
us to support his party, let him start it and make it more beneficial for
the workers than the party we presently support--TANU".[46]

After the meeting, Tumbo began the organizational activities necessary to
get the PDP underway, and became increasingly removed from the union scene.
Meanwhile, the unions found themselves involved in the Makota affair that
undermined the position of John Magongo as TFL general secretary and brought
about his removal.

Davison Makota was a Tanganyikan who had returned after a long
stay abroad with grandiose plans for establishing substantial programs
of economic development. Few details are available on his background
or the manner in which he conducted a confidence game with a variety of
groups following his return to Tanganyika in the middle of 1962. He established his
bona fides with the trade unions at a time when they were searching for means
to undertake programs for economic development in order to legitimatize
themselves in terms of government goals. Makota apparently won the
confidence of the TFL Emergency Committee and, early in September,
approached Magongo for an advance of £ 200 to initiate an economic program
for the TFL. Magongo states that although he was unable to convene a
formal session of the TFL executive, contact with individual members
established that the advance was approved. On this basis, Magongo issued
the sum to Makota. Immediately afterward, while Magongo and Mkello
were attending a conference in Nairobi, Makota was exposed as a confidence
man. After returning to Tanganyika and visiting the Criminal Investigation
Division of the police, Mkello, on September 15, informed Magongo that he
was suspended from office and that he should remove himself forthwith

from TFL headquarters.

This expulsion of Magongo from the TFL was clearly unconstitu-
tional. A meeting of the TFL Emergency Committee was called to validate
the president's action on September 28. On the 27th, however, Magongo
was arrested and imprisoned for several days before being charged before
a magistrate for stealing from the federation. The TFL Emergency
Committee meeting thus took place while Magongo was unable to defend
himself. The meeting ratified the Magongo expulsion although the militant
wing, represented by Vice-president Khupe and TRAU General Secretary
Katungutu, publicly denounced Mkello and the expulsion. Once again,
the newspapers carried details of a public conflict between the various
leaders of the TFL.[47] In November a special congress of the TFL was
convened to discuss the issue but in the meantime the Emergency Committee
had suspended both TRAU and the African Mine Workers Union for refusing
to accept the decision to expel Magongo. By the time the TFL congress
took place, the president of the Mine Workers Union had intervened and
Khupe had resigned from the union to remove himself as a bone of
contention. The only issue remaining, therefore, was whether or not the
suspension of TRAU should be sustained; the suspension was supported by
the delegates. In January another special TFL conference upheld the
expulsion of TRAU from the TFL. By this time, however, according to
the new legislation, the expulsion of a union meant automatic deregistration by the minister of labor. On February 5, 1963, the minister of labor,
Michael Kamaliza, rejected the expulsion of TRAU from the TFL on the
grounds that the vote had been without a secret ballot. There are indications that the minister's decision was not based purely on this legalism;
to allow the expulsion and deregistration of TRAU might have precipitated
a direct conflict between TRAU and the government. Here the matter
rested, with TFL refusing to permit TRAU into its councils and the government refusing to recognize the expulsion.

The principal result of the Makota affair was to remove Magongo from
the trade-union scene. There is compelling evidence, albeit indirect,
that in suspending Magongo, Mkello was responding to serious pressures
brought by the government. Parenthetically, it might be noted that the legal
case against Magongo evaporated, and he subsequently found employment
in a non-union capacity.

The next set of problems focused on the Plantation Workers Union
following the adoption of legislation in November 1962, ending the kipande
system.[48] The kipande or "ticket" is a system of payment whereby plantation workers worked on a daily basis as they chose as long as they completed
thirty days work within forty-two calendar days. Although this requirement was honored more in the breach than in reality, the kipande system

was favored by many plantation workers since it provided them a great deal of leeway to decide the circumstances under which they would work. The elimination of the system through legislation was strongly favored by most trade unionists with the understanding that a monthly system of payment would be substituted. The adoption of the legislation, however, created three issues over its implementation. First, there was the principle involved in the conversion of the kipande to a monthly wage, which led to a serious disagreement between the Plantation Workers Union and the Tanganyika Sisal Growers Association. Secondly, there was no agreement as to whether or not there was to be an increase in the amount of work performed. Finally, the legislation applied only to adult men. Women and children were excepted but instead of retaining the kipande, they were paid on a daily basis. It is difficult to convey to those unfamiliar with the Tanganyikan industrial scene the strong feelings that exist among Tanganyika workers about daily payment. Placing the women on this intensely-hated payment system undoubtedly served to encourage wives to support their men in the strikes that followed.

A series of wildcat strikes began in late December just prior to the implementation of the new legislation on January 13, 1963. The extent to which the leaders of the Plantation Workers Union were responsible is not clear. The union leadership vigorously denied any connection with the strikes, which reached serious proportions by the beginning of the year. The government, feeling that no other solution was possible, decided upon drastic action, and under orders signed by President Julius Nyerere, and Sheha Amiri, PWU General Secretary and Victor Mkello, its organizing secretary, were detained and rusticated in the Sumbawanga in the far west of Tanganyika.

The rustication of the two unionists was a staggering blow to the trade unions. Although they subsequently showed a considerable degree of unanimity in protesting the detentions, they were unable to mobilize themselves to take any militant action. The various delegations that met with President Nyerere made clear their friendly intent while seeking the release of the unionists. Considering the long and vitriolic history of both TFL internal relations and relations between the unions and TANU, the lack of any demonstration indicates that the unions felt that any hostile actions would produce similar Draconian measures against themselves. It will be recalled that the militants in the TFL leadership, Magongo and Khupe, had been removed, that TRAU was not active in the TFL councils, and that Mkello himself could not be reached. In these circumstances, leadership devolved largely upon Alfred Tandau who, although a competent technician, was personally indebted to the minister of Labor for his rapid rise and never reflected leadership abilities equivalent to other union leaders. Thus, the TFL and its affiliates suffered from a debility from which they were never to recover.

When Mkello and Amiri were released on March 8, 1963, statements were issued promising co-operation with the government. From this point on, while disagreements and resistance to the government continued, the unionists operated in an atmosphere of weakness and fear.[49] Following the release of the two leaders, the TFL leadership sought to reorient the unions in a manner that would make them more palatable to the government. From March into the middle of 1963, most unionists stressed the need to formulate concrete economic programs, emphasizing trade-union responsibility for the economic development of the country.[50]

A secondary manifestation of attempted ingratiation with TANU became apparent in the activities of the acting deputy general secretary of the TFL, Joseph Rwegasira. Although Mkello had now returned from exile, his post-rustication silence was complete. Since TFL General Secretary Tandau was unable to exercise leadership, the task fell by default to Rwegasira. Many of Rwegasira's activities were, almost certainly, covertly encouraged by the upper echelons of TANU. This is indicated by his efforts to move TFL away from its affiliation with the International Confederation of Free Trade Unions (ICFTU), which historically had opposed government domination of trade unions.

The government, through much of 1963, was searching for a more effective way to end the continuous battle with the unions. The legislation which had been adopted in June 1962 had failed to end either the strikes or the continuous generation of opposition within trade-union ranks. During July and August 1963, discussions were undertaken with the TFL leadership on proposals Kamaliza had formulated; these proposals sought to integrate the trade unions directly into the ministry of labor. The discussions, continuing until October, brought substantial pressure to bear on the unionists to agree to Kamaliza's proposals.

In spite of their weakness, the bulk of the unions affiliated to the TFL found integration with the ministry unacceptable, recognizing that it would convert them into representatives of the minister and destroy their autonomous base. A decision was finally rendered by the TFL on October 27, 1963, rejecting the Kamaliza proposals. Two TFL affiliates, however, the Transport and General Workers Union and the Domestic and Hotel Workers Union, denounced the TFL, arguing that the integration proposals would benefit Tanganyika's workers. Once again, the lack of union unity was manifested publicly.[51]

Things remained relatively quiet, however, until early in January 1964, when President Nyerere announced a new principle in the selection of candidates for the civil service. The principle, one of nondiscrimination, undercut the trade unionists' position on rapid Africanization; the announcement brought an immediate reaction from the TFL, which sent a six-man delegation to Nyerere to protest the new policy. By the end of

January, however, the focus of events shifted, as Tanganyika's political leaders sought to come to grips with the army mutiny.

Conscription: The Capture of the Unions

On January 20, 1964, the mutiny of a small number of soldiers brought about the virtual collapse of the central government. Once control was re-established with the help of British troops, the government moved not only against the mutineers but also against an estimated 200 trade-union leaders, whom they arrested and detained.[52]This was a mortal blow to the unions. Within the next few days, a number of leading unionists who had been in the pro-TANU wing of TFL were released, but no public indication has ever been given as to the number of unionists still in detention. There are many indications, however, that the bulk of the leadership of all of the unions has remained under arrest.[53]No public statement has ever been made about the role of the unionists in the mutiny, although rumors have circulated that the mutineers found a sympathetic audience among some union leaders. Since no accusations have ever been made and no unionists have ever been tried, it is not possible to speculate on the extent of contact between the mutineers and the unionists or the degree if any of the union implication in the mutiny.

With the bulk of the leaders in jail, the situation was ripe for the government to effect a permanent settlement of the trade-union problem. Thus it was that when a new Trade Union Ordinance was adopted in February there was no opposition within the National Assembly. The legislation revolutionized trade-union organization in Tanganyika by abolishing the Tanganyike Federation of Labor and its affiliated unions. In its place was created, by law, a national workers' organization, the National Union of Tanganyika Workers (NUTA). NUTA consists of a single structure to which workers are individually affiliated and to which they pay dues. It has nine industrial sections, none of which are autonomous. To ensure that control from above is complete, the legislation provides that the general secretary and the deputy general secretary of NUTA are to be appointed by the President of the Republic. The general secretary, in turn, appoints all subsidiary officials of the new organization. The legislation also requires the new union to be affiliated to TANU. In his speech of intro-duction to the debate, Kamaliza said: "This merely recognizes an existing situation since the TFL already has representation in the TANU executive and is accepted as having been affiliated to TANU since 1958."[54]Several days after the adoption of the legislation, Michael Kamaliza, still retaining his post as minister of labor, was designated general secretary of NUTA. Alfred Tandau was appointed deputy general secretary. During the next few days Kamaliza appointed nine assistant general secretaries and a number of other officers.

Some indication of the drastic change that took place can be seen by
an examination of the officers of the new organization. Of the three top
offices, national chairman, general secretary, and deputy general
secretary, all are held by former officers of the Transport and General
Workers Union. Other TGWU officers (known to the writer) holding office
in NUTA include Assistant General Secretary for Agriculture Heriel Naftal
(formerly general secretary of TGWU), two of three directors of organization,
M. M. Songambele (who is also a director of the Workers' Investment
Corporation and fulltime regional commissioner of the government in Dar
es Salaam, and former president of TGWU), Michael Juma (formerly vice-
president, TGWU), and the education secretary, Carl Kapungu (formerly
a regional secretary of TGWU and education secretary of TFL). Of the
nine assistant general secretaries, only one, Sheha Amiri, had a personal
history of opposition to the government. The remaining officers are either
long-standing supporters of the TANU wing within the unions or are unknown
to this writer.

Since the adoption of the new law, trade unionism has effectively
disappeared from public view as the bulk of its work became enmeshed
in private proceedings. Strikes declined immediately and an economic
program was gotten underway. NUTA did not affiliate itself to ICFTU
and Michael Kamaliza became a prominent participant in the June 1964
Congress of the All-African Trade Union Federation (AATUF) in Bamako.[55]
By the end of the year, NUTA announced a five-year agreement with the
Sisal Growers Association which coincided with the five-year development
plan of the country.[56] In April 1965, President Nyerere reported to NUTA's
first conference that the organization had been successful in raising average
male earnings 44 per cent over 1962, while man-days lost in strikes had
declined from 417, 500 to 6, 000.[57]

The elimination of TFL and the creation of NUTA marked the end of
autonomous trade unionism in Tanganyika. During its short history,
autonomous trade-unionism had shown surprising potentiality in political-
economic strength. Although initially cautious in their relations with
TANU, the unions made an important contribution by mobilizing urban
workers within organizations that operated as autonomous confederates of
the political movement.

Conclusion

During the pre-independence period, there existed a solid basis for
union-party co-operation. Not only were most employers foreigners but
the colonial government was, itself, the largest single employer of labor.

Thus, any action directed against an employer was simultaneously directed against the "colonial oppressor." In these circumstances, co-operation between unions and party as distinct organizations was complementary and almost inevitable.

As independence drew near, the unions drew closer to TANU organizationally by having formal representation in the TANU executive and at the annual conference. The unions, however, already had a firm structural basis. The union leaders had tasted power during the years in which organizational autonomy was enforced by the British; the thought of losing this autonomy was unwelcome to most of them. The response to questions, during field interviews in August 1963, about proposals to integrate the unions into the ministry of labor was universally hostile. Even relatively unsophisticated branch-level leaders recognized that, with integration, they would become "servants of the minister" rather than "servants of the members."

Besides the desire to maintain structural autonomy, the unions' conflict with TANU arose as a consequence of the changing character of TANU's responsibilities. When TANU represented the political opposition to the colonial government, trade-union action against the government coincided with its own ends. Once TANU became the government, a reverse reaction was inevitable. Responsible now for maintaining a government which continued to be the largest single employer, any demand by the unions for wage increases meant that income had to be found through tax mechanisms. In addition, the TANU government was responsible for the maintenance of government services and rejected the speedy Africanization demanded by the unions, for fear that these services would be damaged.

The TANU government was not responsible only for itself as the largest single employer but had full responsibility for general development of the economy. To the extent that the unions constituted the best-organized pressure group, strategically located to extract a maximum of concessions from the economy as a whole, their position posed a threat to plans for general economic development. If the unions were able to extract continually concessions for their members, who constituted about 5 per cent of the total population, it was felt that there would be less funds available either for new investment or for distribution to the rest of the population. For this reason, the pressure of the union members created a situation which was intrinsically untenable in view of the broad objectives of the TANU government.

But perhaps the most salient reason to control the unions lay in the strategic location which they occupied.[58] The unions' main strength lay in the urban centers, in precisely those areas where government, administration, and commerce are located and where TANU itself was relatively strong.

Unlike the co-operatives whose membership is largely dispersed on the land, the unions occupied an enviable position; efficient communications channels and the heightened expectation of workers could be utilized to mobilize them for economic actions. And, since these economic actions always had political implications, the unions were seen as a source of political competition of great potentiality.

It is not surprising then that after several years of abortive attempts to control the unions informally and through the passage of limiting legislation, the government utilized the advantage of the presence of British troops after the mutiny to remove from circulation most union leaders. The legislation which created NUTA was a logical outcome of the need to conscript competing centers of power into the structure of government.

It is this particular factor that stands out as characteristic of the operation of politics in the independent African states. In almost all countries, the unions occupy a position in which they constitute, after the political party, the next most important political force. Since the function of the unions is often incompatible with the ends of the party government, conflict between these two units seems inevitable.

For the party government, concerned with the maintenance of social order and control, with economic development, and with the preservation of the material perquisites which the party leaders have obtained, the existence of competing power centers may become intolerable. The Tanganyika case illustrates the process as it occurred in a single country; in point of fact and with some variation, the same process is taking place throughout Africa. This does not mean that every country will utilize the same Draconian measures employed in Tanganyika. But every political party and government will have to confront an important competing power source which must be somehow reconciled to the primary goals of national development.

Footnotes

1. For an analysis of the variation in alliances between political parties and unions and some of the consequences thereof, see Eliot J. Berg and Jeffrey Butler, "Trade Unions, " in James S. Coleman and Carl G. Rosberg, Jr. (eds.), Political Parties and National Integration in Tropical Africa (Berkeley and Los Angeles, 1964), 340-381.

2. For a discussion of the Industrial Relations Act see Lester Tracht-man, "The Labor Movement of Ghana: A Study in Political Unionism, " Economic Development and Cultural Change, X:183-200 (Jan. 1962).

3. For discussion of the distinction between "consumptionist" and "productionist" activities see Isaac Deutscher, "Russia, " in Walter Galenson (ed.), Comparative Labor Movements (Englewood Cliffs, N. J., 1952), 505.

4. The extent of political control over trade unions varies from country to country. In Ghana, Tanganyika, Zambia, and the Congo (Brazza-ville), there have been, in effect, complete or almost-complete takeovers. Kenya and Uganda have increasingly limited the activities of unions without direct takeovers. In Nigeria, the unions have remained relatively untouched by government. Regular information on this subject can be found in African Labour News, a weekly bulletin published in Lagos by the African Regional Organization of the International Confederation of Free Trade Unions. For a general discussion of the changes in laws affecting labor in the post-independence period in French-speaking countries, see the review of the book by J. Deprez, in the Inter-African Labour Institute Bulletin, 2:95-98 (May 1962).

5. General political background material on Tanganyika will be found in Margaret L. Bates, "Tanganyika, " in Gwendolen M. Carter (ed.), African One-Party States (Ithaca, 1962), 395-483. For background material on labor and the labor market in Tanganyika see J. P. Moffett (ed.), Tanganyika: A Review of its Resources and Their Development (Dar es Salaam, 1955), 267-239; also Annual Report of the Labour Department, prepared by the Ministry of Labour and published by the government printer.

6. A pamphlet was published by TFL explaining the minimum wage and claiming credit for it. See Rashidi Kawawa, Maelezo Juu ya Vipimo vya Mishahara (Dar es Salaam, 1957).

7. Julius Nyerere, "The Task Ahead for our African Trade Unions, " Labour (Ghana Trades Union Congress), June 1961. Roger D. Scott, "Labour Legislation and the Federation Issue," East Africa Journal, Nov. 1964, 23-24, makes somewhat similar assertions, contending that the Tanganyika unions expanded because of their close links to TANU: "The party gave financial aid to assist the setting up of the union centre and the first president of TFL was a prominent party member. The two organizations shared the same office facilities, arranged joint action on issues of common concern and conducted joint recruiting campaigns." Except for joint action in organizing boycotts, none of this is correct. I found no evidence of financial assistance to the unions by TANU (although there was ample evidence of such assistance from other sources). Nor was there any evidence of joint office facilities or recruiting campaigns. The first president of TFL was Arthur Ohanga, a Kenyan who later returned to Kenya; if Ohanga was a member of TANU, he never was prominent enough to obtain any public notice. Rashidi Kawawa, TFL general secretary, obtained prominence in TANU but this was mostly because of his TFL connections. According to personal interviews with me, Kawawa could not join TANU even though sympathizing with the organization because of government regulations forbidding membership in parties to government employees. He did not join TANU until he assumed fulltime responsibilities with the TFL.

8. For a short biography of Kawawa see William H. Friedland, "Tanganyika's Rashidi Kawawa, " Africa Report, 2:7-8 (1962).

9. Minutes, TFL Annual Conference, Oct. 5-7, 1956. Most minutes were written in Swahili and, unless otherwise noted, the originals available to me were in Swahili. Rough translations were made by Mathew Kashindye who worked with me as a research assistant and translator in 1960. The text of the resolutions cited here were part of an English translation made by the TFL itself.

Constitutionally, the annual conference of TFL was its highest legislative body. The General Council of the organization met approximately every six months and was the policy-determining body between annual conferences. Regular decisions were made, usually at weekly meetings, by the TFL Emergency Committee. The Emergency Committee, sometimes referred to as the Executive Committee, was composed of representatives of unions with headquarters in Dar es Salaam.

10. Minutes, TFL General Council, July 4-6, 1957.

11. See, for example, the criticism by a representative of the Govern-

ment Public Relations Department and the editorial in the <u>Tanganyika Standard</u>, Aug. 12, 1957. Neither the adoption of the resolutions by TFL in 1956 and 1957 nor the attacks upon it should be interpreted to mean that TFL devoted itself, in any substantial degree, to political activities or was preoccupied with political questions. Actually, the time spent in discussion of political matters at the 1956 and 1957 TFL conferences and general councils represents a very small part of the proceedings.

12. Minutes, TFL Emergency Committee, Nov. 20, 1958.

13. Personal interviews.

14. A search of available documents has not brought to light any formal resolution by TFL explicitly endorsing TANU. In 1959, when field work was initiated, it was commonly accepted by unionists in discussions that TFL would continue to support TANU until independence had been achieved. In 1960, delegates to the TFL annual conference voted to send two representatives to TANU.

15. Minutes, TFL Annual Conference, Nov. 23-26, 1958.

16. Minutes, TFL Emergency Committee, Feb. 6, 1959.

17. "Address by the General Secretary", TAPU Conference, July 3-6, 1960. From an original Swahili version in possession of the writer. The speech was made at a public meeting which customarily opens all annual conferences of Tanganyikan unions.

18. TAPU Conference, minutes of simultaneous translation, July 6, 1960. For a general statement of the union in English calling for the destruction of the High Commission, see <u>Tanganyika Standard</u>, July 4, 1960.

19. TRAU Conference, minutes of simultaneous translation, July 30, 1960.

20. <u>Tanganyika Standard</u>, Aug. 9, 1960.

21. <u>Ibid.</u>, Aug. 10-12, 1960.

22. <u>Ibid.</u>, Aug. 29, 1960.

23. The shift in the significant position in TFL took place at the December 1959, annual conference. Prior to this meeting, the chief adminis-

trative position was that of the general secretary. In 1959, this post was
eliminated and the key post became that of president. Kawawa, who had
been general secretary, thereupon became president. Kamaliza who had
been TFL president, was elected a vice-president. In March 1962, a constitutional change returned the situation to the earlier arrangement.

24. For an account of events preliminary to the strike see Tanganyika,
Ministry of Health and Labour, Annual Report of the Labour Division 1960
(Dar es Salaam, 1961), 13-14.

25. Tanganyika Standard, Dec. 20, 1960. Articles, editorials, and
letters on the strike appeared almost daily in the Standard throughout
December and early January.

26. Sunday News (Dar es Salaam), Oct. 9, 1960.

27. Tanganyika Standard, Oct. 2-5, 1960.

28. Ibid., Oct. 21, 1960.

29. ICFTU Area Committee for East, Central and Southern Africa,
Bulletin, Nos. 23, 24, March-April 1962.

30. Tanganyika Standard, Feb. 8-10, 13, 1962.

31. Between mid-April and mid-July 1961 there were almost daily
accounts of the battle in the Tanganyika Standard.

32. Tanganyika Standard, Aug. 1, 3, 1961.

33. Summary of the Vernacular Press, Nov. 2, 9, 1961.

34. Ibid., Nov. 3, 4, 1961.

35. John Tettegah, "The African Proletariat," Spearhead, I, (Jan.
1962), 3.

36. R. J. Magongo, "Co-operation Not Domination," ibid.

37. See, for example, Tanganyika, Parliamentary Debates, National
Assembly, First Session, First Meeting, Dec. 11, 1961-Feb. 17, 1962, cols.
53, 59, 60. See also Summary of the Vernacular Press, Oct. 11, 1961.

38. Sunday News, March 18, 1962.

39. A bill providing for severance pay allowances for workers was adopted in the National Assembly in September 1962; a minimum wage law was passed in October; and the November session amended the Employment Ordinance to provide for a weekly rest day, paid holidays, and the elimination of the kipande (ticket) system. For a general summary of legislation adopted in 1962 see Annual Report of the Labour Division 1962, Tanganyika, Ministry of Labour (Dar es Salaam, 1964), 2.

40. Personal interview, Aug. 10, 1963.

41. For the debate on the bills see Tanganyika, Parliamentary Debates, National Assembly, First Session, Second Meeting, June 5-July 3, 1962. For daily reports, including the vigorous opposition of the unions, see the Tanganyika Standard, June 11-29, 1962.

42. Tanganyika Standard, July 11, 1962.

43. Tanganyika Standard, Aug. 10, 1962.

44. In an interview with this writer in August 1963, Tumbo stated, from his base in exile in Mombasa, that he had resigned as high commissioner because of his disagreement with the new republican constitution that was in the process of being formulated, and particularly with the powers allocated to the president under the new constitution to appoint up to ten members in the National Assembly. The retention of this power, Tumbo implied, constituted a carry-over from colonial times. Tumbo said that he made his objections known to various ministers, and when the published draft contained the objected proposal he felt that he was unable to continue to represent his government in London.

45. When asked in August 1963 why he did not return to TRAU, Tumbo responded that there was little point to re-entering trade-union activity since unions in Tanganyika were no longer economic but political units. Whether an independent trade-union movement could exist in Tanganyika was not an economic issue, he claimed, but one which would be settled only through the political process. He also stated his belief that, had he gone back to TRAU, the union would have been regarded as his base for political opposition, which might have led to its suppression.

46. Sunday News, Sept. 9, 1962.

47. See the Tanganyika Standard, Sept. 29, 1962, and almost daily through March 1963, for articles on the internal dispute, the strikes of plantation workers and the subsequent rustication of Mkello. Much of the material that follows is based upon personal interviews with the leading persons as well.

48. See note 39. For the debate on the legislation see Tanganyika, Parliamentary Debates, National Assembly, First Session, Third Meeting, Sept. 25-27, 1962, cols. 103-108; First Session, Fourth Meeting, Nov. 22-27, 1962, cols. 19-26.

49. For the statements of co-operation see Sunday News, March 17, 24, 1963. The fear of the unionists and their hesitation to take any action that might be interpreted as hostile by the government was clearly evident during every interview I conducted in August 1963, with the unionists.

50. On March 5, 1963, TFL announced the formation of its economic wing to contribute to economic development, a first step of which was to organize a workers' investment corporation. Tanganyika Standard, March 6, 1963.

51. Tanganyika Standard, Oct. 27, 30, 1963.

52. Ibid., Jan. 27, 28, 29, Feb. 1, 1964.

53. Ibid., Feb. 14, 1964. By July 1965, no statement had been made about the unionists who remain in detention; nor is their number known, although the mutineers have long since been tried. On March 16, 1965, replying to a question in the National Assembly, the minister of home affairs stated that 120 people were then in detention, but he did not reveal how many of them were unionists. See Africa Report, 5:40 (May 1965). As late as May 1965 the International Transport Workers Federation, an international trade-union body, was asking President Nyerere to release or try the unionists. See African Labour News, 156:3 (May 13, 1965).

54. Tanganyika Standard, Feb. 22, 1964.

55. Ibid., June 23, 1964; Africa Report, 7:34 (May 1964).

56. Trade Union News From Overseas (Trades Union Congress, London), 112:2 (Dec. 1964).

57. The Economist (London), April 17, 1965, 293.

58. The following points have been developed in somewhat greater detail in William H. Friedland, "The Paradoxes of African Trade Unionism: Organizational Chaos and Political Potential, " Africa Report, X, June 1965.

IV

Trade Unionism Develops in Ethiopia

Arnold M. Zack
Practicing Attorney, Boston

Ethiopia, the oldest of the independent African countries, has recently experienced the birth of the continent's youngest trade-union movement. For 3,000 years Ethiopia has flourished as a predominantly agricultural society with relatively few wage earners, even in more recent times. In maintaining its independence it sacrificed the tutelage over its institutions which elsewhere in Africa was provided by British and French colonists. As a result, Ethiopians have had little preparation for handling the problems of labor relations which accompany urbanization and the early stages of industrialization. Industry, which was stimulated in British and French colonies to a moderate degree, did not gain a foothold in Ethiopia at all until very recently. Similarly, the trade-union movements which gained the support of the colonial powers elsewhere in Africa in the inter-war period did not achieve official recognition in Ethiopia until 1962.

This should not be construed to mean that prior to 1962 there was neither a context in which unions could develop nor worker interest in developing such institutions. The opportunites for organization were limited, however, and the government discouraged any organization which had a democratic flavor or orientation. The government itself assumed the responsibility for regulating working conditions and matters that in other societies had come to be accepted as within the purview of trade unions. Thus the Factories Proclamation of 1944, the first legislation in Ethiopia related to labor matters, empowered the minister of commerce and industry to regulate work hours, safety rules, use of equipment, and related issues; it also created a labor inspectorate to examine plants to ascertain whether they complied with the proclamation. Although there was no authorization in the proclamation for the settlement of industrial disputes by the minister of commerce and industry, that power was later assumed by him as being within the purposes of the proclamation.

The first instance of organized worker unrest in Ethiopia occurred no longer ago than 1947 among Ethiopian workers on the Franco-Ethiopian Railway. Workers exposed to the fact that employees from France and Somaliland were protected in their own countries by labor unions, began to express dissatisfaction with existing wage rates, differentials between Somali and Ethiopian workers, and the discriminatory discharge of certain Ethiopian workers. A strike of the railway's several thousand workers was called, leading to the appointment of a government fact finding committee which, in its conclusions, largely supported management's position. Continued dissatisfaction among the workers led to renewed strikes and government investigations throughout the fifties. On several occasions, the workers sought the intervention of His Imperial Majesty, Haile Sellassie I, in accordance with traditional Ethiopian right of direct petition to the emperor. In response, the emperor created several commissions to investigate the disputes and the possible resolutions.

Until the late fifties labor activity on the railway was the only note-worthy protest of workers in Ethiopia; but it provided workers elsewhere in Ethiopia with an example to follow in expressing their own discontent with management control. Thus, in 1961, a strike occurred at the Wonji Sugar Estates (the largest single employer in Ethiopia); the sugar strike was resolved by the minister of commerce and industry while strikes occurred at approximately the same time at Bole Airport, Indo-Ethiopian Textiles, Damar Shoe Factory, and in other private enterprises in and around Addis Ababa.

Interest in trade unions spread to smaller plants in Ethiopia where aroused workers recognized the importance of spontaneous protest. This indigenous expression of worker dissatisfaction in Ethiopia is quite unique in Africa. This uniqueness has at least three aspects.

First, the Ethiopian movement is a contemporary manifestation of a self-help tradition which the Ethiopians had embraced long before the period of wage employment. For centuries, the edir or self-help associa-tion had provided communal assistance in building homes, financing funerals, and supporting impoverished members of the group. When urbanization and widespread wage employment developed after World War II, these self-help organizations evolved inside the factories. A growing sense of worker strength, exemplified by the experience on the railways and the 1961 strikes, led the edir concept from emphasis upon social unity to emphasis upon economic protection and protection against the improper actions of employ-ers. Thus the edirs transformed themselves into unofficial trade unions in several plants in Ethiopia.

Second, early union development in Ethiopia, in contrast to the situa-tion elsewhere in Africa, has been overwhelmingly indigenous. In British and French colonies the metropole undertook conscious programs of trade-union stimulation. This was particularly true in the British colonies after the announcement in 1930 by Lord Passfield of a British commitment to stimulate African trade unions by providing union advisers. Later, in 1940, colonial recognition of trade unions was made a prerequisite for technical assistance under the Colonial Development and Welfare Act.

The French colonies, too, were encouraged, though less enthusiastically. Limited African participation in French trade unions was authorized in 1937, but despite programs of adviser assistance from metropolitan unions, it was not until 1952 that full freedom for African trade-union activity was authorized in the French colonies.

In contrast, in Ethiopia, workers had no opportunity whatsoever for contact with workers outside their country. Ethiopian delegations to the International Labor Organization included no worker members and, in addition, no Ethiopian workers were allowed to travel abroad for trade-union purposes. Indeed, it was not until 1961 when Tom Mboya, then general secretary of the neighboring Kenya Federation of Labor, came to Ethiopia to plead with the government for recognition of the trade-union movement, that a foreign trade unionist was permitted into Ethiopia to discuss labor affairs.

By this time the trade-union movement in Ethiopia had made strong advances on its own without external stimulation and was beginning to cause concern to the Imperial Ethiopian government which had sought, effectively, to isolate it from the heightening fever of trade-union activity elsewhere in Africa. Finally, in 1962, Ethiopia was opened to foreign trade unionists, particularly those from the International Confederation of Free Trade Unions (ICFTU), and the period of quarantine was over.

A third unique feature of the new trade-union movement has been that it developed apart from the intellectuals of the country. In most countries of Africa severe restrictions upon indigenous political activity until the fifties forced those intent upon obtaining independence to identify with the aspirations of the trade unions as an anti-colonial force. More importantly, it led those politically oriented persons to join and often attain leadership positions in a traditionally economic institution. Their leadership was welcomed by the rank and file for the voice it gave the workers in negotiations, for its administrative skill, and for its dynamism in dealing with the colonial governments.

The age-old independence of Ethiopia precluded such an usurpation of trade-union organizations for political purposes; and Ethiopian intellectuals had ample outlet for creative energy in the building of the nation. Of course, many Ethiopian intellectuals, within the government and out, have been in sympathy with the aspirations of the workers, but their role has been advisory, rather than administrative as elsewhere in Africa, and leadership has remained in the hands of the workers themselves. It is quite feasible that a strong trade union may, in the future, provide a rallying point for those interested in changing the government, but insofar as its development to this point is concerned, the Ethiopian labor movement

has been a truly bootstrap development, and indeed the first grass roots
organization to emerge in contemporary Ethiopia.

This fact has had its negative aspects as well. The union has been
handicapped in its negotiations with foreign employers because of language
barriers and lack of negotiating or administrative experience; and the
development of efficient union leadership has been hampered by isolation.
On the other hand, this isolation has helped to preserve the union as a
strictly workers' organization and has made the government somewhat more
receptive to its demands than would have been the case if potential politicians were as active in this union as they have been in unions elsewhere.

The strictly local character of the unions, organized by individual
plants, was viewed by the movement's leadership as a detrimental factor
in their early efforts to build a strong labor movement. Efforts were
made to bring all the workers together into a single union of Ethiopian
workers, but this proved unsuccessful because of the overriding local
loyalties of the workers themselves, and the fear that a unified body of
all Ethiopian workers would be frowned upon, or worse, destroyed, by
the government.

In 1962, a secret assembly of workers was held to form such a body;
it was resolved to federate all Ethiopian labor associations under a permanent
secretariat and invite all worker organizations that had not attended the
initial meeting to join too. The new group was to be called the Ethiopian
Labor Union. Approaches were made to the government for recognition
but these proved unsuccessful. The government's attitude was that "the
essence of your request is equality of master and servant, " and that this
is "alien to the tradition and culture of our country."[1] Failure of the local
unions to support this new federation led to its early demise.

In June 1962, a renewed effort at unification was undertaken at a meeting attended by union leaders from Addis Ababa and other cities where
local plant unions were developing. The new center set as its main goals
the assistance of members with labor relations problems and a unified
effort to settle labor disputes. This time the attitude of the government
was more favorable, and the minister of commerce and industry, and the
Security Department of the Ministry of Interior granted permission to hold
meetings and continue with the establishment of the organization.

This change in the government's attitude is probably attributable to
the fact that the emperor was preparing to enunciate the Labor Relations
Decree. Disturbed, perhaps, by the growing number of industrial disputes
which were coming to him through popular petition for resolution, aware

of the political dangers that might ensue if a trade-union movement were
to be suppressed when it had support of the majority of the workers, and
anxious to attain the voluntary political support of the majority of the
workers by giving them the right to organize legal unions, he authorized
the preparation of the decree.

Internationally, the decree also had its justifications; Ethiopia was
one of the handful of countries belonging to the ILO who sent neither management nor worker representatives to its annual sessions (despite its membership in that body since 1923). Further, the preparation and announcement
of the Labor Relations Decree in September 1962 came at a time when
Ethiopia was preparing for the Heads of State meeting; the decree ended an
uncomfortable situation in which Ethiopia, seeking leadership in the movement for African unity, was the only independent country without a recognized trade-union movement.

The Labor Relations Decree of September 5, 1962,[2] was the first
legislation in Ethiopia granting the right to form trade unions.[3] It guarantees
workers the right to join or refrain from joining labor unions[4] in language
similar to the provisions of the United States Labor-Management Relations
Act; it includes a set of unfair labor practices prohibited to employers
and to worker organizations. Allegations of unfair labor practices are
brought before the newly created Labor Relations Board within the Department of Labor of the Ministry of National Community Development. The
board has the jurisdiction to hear charges of unfair labor practice initiated
by either side, or may initiate such charges on its own. Decisions of the
board are final and enforceable in the courts. Employers and unions are
required to bargain in good faith once the union is registered with the
ministry.

The second intention of the decree is a concerted effort to have the
parties resolve industrial disputes through voluntary means. The decree
encourages the negotiation of collective bargaining agreements and even
empowers the minister of national community development to draft and
circulate model collective bargaining agreements to management and labor
to guide them in their contract negotiations. To date there have been only
two agreements negotiated and signed: one at the Barhar Dar Textile
Mill and the second at the Wonji Sugar Estates.[5] The Department of Labor
is currently training conciliators from their own staff and anticipates
using non-government personnel acceptable to both sides as conciliators
and perhaps as voluntary arbitrators in the near future.

The third aspect of the decree, is that concerned with the failure of the parties to resolve industrial disputes on their own. Undoubtedly, the Ethiopian government shares with most of Africa a fear of industrial unrest. Such threats to production and achievement of development goals, the government fears, may discourage foreign investment by giving the impression abroad of unstable labor relations. Accordingly, the Ethiopian government has assured itself of some labor peace through certain safe- guards, while at the same time encouraging the parties to resolve their own disputes. The safeguards which the government provides are severe restrictions on the right to strike;[6] in addition, the government itself retains the ultimate power to supercede the parties by setting working conditions in any establishment, with or without a collective bargaining agreement.[7]

Since the promulgation of the decree, there has been a marked increase in labor union activity. Within six months of its proclamation forty-two unions with more than 10,000 dues-paying members had registered with the Labor Relations Board. At present there are over fifty unions with combined memberships in excess of 25,000. This compares quite favora- bly with trade-union membership in other African countries, especially when one considers that there are only 42,000 employees in manufacturing, and, excluding government employees, not more than 125,000 workers in the entire country. The incidence of dues payment is also quite high, compared with other African countries; this fact is readily traceable to the traditions of edir and its voluntary payments for mutual assistance.

The development of a considerable number of plant unions and a few general unions does not tell the full story of trade-union development in Ethiopia. The initial efforts prior to the decree to establish a nationwide federation floundered, and renewed efforts were necessary following the decree. The ICFTU, through the efforts of Howard Robinson, established a training program on the campus of the University College of Addis Ababa, to which were invited the leaders of the several unions. This occurred in April 1963. At the conclusion of the training program, the members present voted to establish a Confederation of Ethiopian Labor Unions as the national center. The new CELU applied for recognition to the Labor Boards and was granted a charter. Then in June 1963, Ethiopia for the first time was represented by a tripartite delegation at the ILO.

The most serious difficulty which the new union movement has under- gone occurred in the summer of 1963. At that time leaders of the forty- two member unions assembled to discuss their problems with management and, more importantly, their dissatisfaction with certain provisions of the Labor Relations Decree and its manner of enforcement by the board. In a letter to the ministry dated July 30, 1963, the leaders asked for reinstatement for all workers who had been dismissed from various plants

because of their union activities (most of these cases were already before
the Labor Relations Board). They asked for a prohibition of further dismissals, as well as stronger protective legislation. The letter contained a
sixty-day ultimatum to the Labor Department for compliance with its
demands. Failure to respond favorably was to result in a general strike
of all workers in Ethiopia. Discussions between the ministry and CELU
officials in August bore little fruit. The minister continued to warn that
such a strike would be illegal, that thirteen of the unions which had signed
the demands were not registered and had no legal standing, that there
could be no dispute between union and government, but only between union
and management, that it was beyond the competence of the CELU to force
the government to enact new legislation, and that a strike would cause
grave damage to hospitalization, transportation, and other essential services
throughout the empire. The case was scheduled for hearing before the
Labor Relations Board, but the union leadership sought to get a determination by the emperor, who referred them to the minister. It was recommended that the president of the CELU resign, and that the union withdraw its
demands. In the light of mounting pressure against their activity, and the
lack of public support for the threatened strike, the union backed down,
the president of CELU resigned, and the situation returned to normal.
A serious scar remained in the form of a suicide by the founder of the
CELU at the conclusion of these events. On the other hand, the threat
of strike acknowledged the power which the unions were obtaining, attracted
additional members, and appears to have inspired greater respect, or at
least greater recognition of CELU's potential power on the part of the
government.

Since the summer of 1963, the Ethiopian labor movement has acquired
additional affiliates and new strength. It has worked well with the government officials and processed approximately seventy cases before the Labor
Relations Board. In nearly half of these cases, the board exercised a
conciliation rather than an arbitration role, furthering the concept of
voluntary dispute settlement to achieve labor-management harmony.

Internationally, CELU acquired affiliation to the International Confederation of Free Trade Unions in the early part of 1964, and served as
host of the Fourth African Regional Conference of the ICFTU in Africa
Hall in April 1964. The holding of this conference in Addis Ababa was
not only significant for the ICFTU (its African operations thus being identified with the Spirit of Addis Ababa and the quest for African unity), but it
was also significant for the Ethiopian labor movement because it indicated
to the rest of Africa and the world that the one-year-old trade-union movement had attained international stature. It was also noteworthy that the
government of Ethiopia was willing and indeed enthusiastic about having
the CELU's international organization use Addis Ababa for its international

meeting. This was a far cry from the period only a few months earlier
when the government discouraged any international contact for fear that it
would turn the heads of the Ethiopian labor leaders and introduce into the
movement influences that might turn it against the government or economy.

The prospects for Ethiopian trade-union development appear favorable.
The union has attracted to it Ethiopians of varying religious, regional, and
language backgrounds, making it the first institution in Ethiopia in which
such integration has been attained (non-Amharas have risen to positions
of national leadership). The tribal differences of the membership, for the
present at least, appear to be submerged in favor of presenting a united
front to management and government.

Much of this integration is attributable to the nature of industrial
operations, particularly in large urban areas around Addis Ababa and in
Dira Dowa; in these areas work forces are composed of elements from
throughout the Empire. Workers who had migrated from Eritrea, which
had some exposure to trade unionism under the British occupation prior
to the dissolution of Eritrean unions in 1958, have often been able to move
into positions of prominence; the current general secretary of CELU,
Ato Beyene Solomon, is such a person.

A very noticeable effort toward Eritrean-Ethiopian integration is
also evident. In November 1964, the government permitted CELU to bring
three Eritrean workers to its training course in Addis Ababa. In September
1965, the government determined to stimulate union organization in Eritrea,
sent several officials to Asmara to prepare for registration of new trade
unions in Eritrea under the 1962 law.

The leadership of CELU continues to be oriented toward "Business
trade-unionism" rather than to any ideological conflict. This perspective
was recently confirmed on the return of Ato Beyene from the 1964 ILO
conference. During his absence in Europe the CELU official left in charge,
a graduate of the Israeli Afro-Asian Labor Institute, sought to rally support
for Ato Beyene's ouster. His efforts proved unsuccessful, and the General
Assembly of the union reiterated its support of the present leadership.
What is most striking about this internal crisis is not that the present
leadership continued with membership support, but that both the attempted
unseating of Ato Beyene and his later endorsement were carried out in
orderly and democratic fashion, within the terms and procedures of the
CELU constitution. This lends even greater strength to the union as one
of the few, if not the only, democratically functioning institutions in Ethiopia --
one that is able to function effectively as an integrated organization despite
the diversity of members' backgrounds and the traditional animosities
among the various ethnic elements in the empire.

Unfortunately, in spite of external appearances, the union does suffer from lack of trained leaders and financial weakness. Only a handful of trade unionists have had either any administrative experience or any trade-union training. This is being remedied by the training opportunities available at the ICFTU Kampala African Labor College and at the Histadrut Institute in Israel. The reluctance of the local unions to contribute their just share to the financial support of CELU appears to have been overcome during the recent internal difficulties when, for the first time, being fully paid up in their obligations to CELU enabled the locals to participate in the crucial decisions of the General Assembly.

The government continues to be sympathetic toward the movement and is free to encourage it because of its lack of direct involvement (civil servants being ineligible for membership). In addition, the government sees CELU as a device for improving the conditions of workers in industries that, in large measure, are under foreign control. Furthermore, built into the trade-union movement itself, through the tradition of edir is a sense of worker involvement in the organization and a tendency toward self-help in the social sphere which will, in the long run, give the Ethiopian trade-union movement a strong base for involvement in economic activities, unlike trade unions elsewhere in Africa where initial orientations have been solely or primarily political.

How long it will be before the trade-union movement becomes involved in politics, if it does, remains to be seen. There is none of the pressure to oust a foreign government which has been responsibile for much of the political activity of trade unions elsewhere in Africa, and there is no direct conflict with the government as employer. Nonetheless, the Ethiopian labor movement must be recognized as the first mass base organization in Ethiopia not controlled by nobility or royalty; as such it will undoubtedly attract intellectuals as a rallying point for social reform. If the government continues in its own program of social reform (of which the Labor Relations Decree is one of the most outstanding examples) at a fast enough rate to avoid dissatisfaction among the intellectuals and the workers, the development of the labor movement will probably continue along social and economic lines. If not, it will turn, most likely to political activities, feeling that avenue to be essential to its success. Continued stability and social progress in Ethiopia as a whole appear to be the crucial factors.

Footnotes

1. Letter on file at Confederation of Ethiopian Labor Unions from Ministry of Commerce and Industry, 1962.

2. Negarit Gazetta, No. 18, Sept. 5, 1962, Decree No. 49, 136.

3. A law permitting the registration of labor unions in Eritrea was promulgated by the British in 1958. Under this law (the Employment Act of 1958, Eritrean Gazetta (1958), 44), the chief executive of Eritrea was empowered to recognize and dissolve unions according to the legitimacy of their purpose. The unification of Ethiopia and Eritrea in November 1962 continued in effect all earlier Eritrean legislation unless specifically repealed. Thus legally, the Eritrean Employment Act continued to exist. In mid-1965 the Ministry of National Community Development declared that the Labor Relations Act of 1962 was to be enforced in Eritrea, thus leading to legal registration of local unions outlawed since 1958.

4. Union membership is open to any worker in a plant employing fifty or more employees provided they are not civil servants, management personnel, or domestic servants. Those working in establishments with less than fifty employees may join general craft unions.

5. The minister is also empowered on his own, and through the Labor Relations Board, to provide conciliation services to the parties faced with a deadlock in their negotiations. A conciliation provision is mandatory for all collective bargaining agreements. The model agreement provides for conciliation in the event of deadlock in renegotiating new agreements and a grievance procedure terminating in voluntary arbitration.

6. The decree specifically prohibits strikes which are accompanied by violence, which are non-labor originated, or which are called for political purposes. It prohibits strikes which by their vital public nature are likely to cause serious public injury or interference with transportation, electricity, water, telephone, or telegraph services. It further requires a sixty-day cooling off period prior to a strike, during which time the Labor Relations Board may hear and decide the particular dispute. If a decision is rendered within that period, then the union is prohibited from striking because the strike would be in violation of the determination of the Labor Relations Board. In effect, the only occasion on which strikes are permitted in Ethiopia is when the Labor Relations Board fails to hand down a decision on a dispute within the specified sixty-day cooling off period.

7. Conditions established must not fall below the legal guarantees of minimum working conditions contained in the Civil Code of 1960. So

far, this power has not been exercised by the minister, and it appears
that the mere presence of this provision in the decree has served the
purpose of stimulating the parties to their own settlements or using successful conciliation rather than face the consequences of having working conditions
imposed by the government.

V

Chieftaincy and the Adaptation of Customary Law in Ghana

Leslie Rubin
Program of African Studies, Howard University

To a greater or lesser extent, traditional African political concepts and institutions are to be found within the modern structure of the new independent states. The chief continues to command loyalty, enjoy status, and exercise authority; customary law remains, for many people, the unquestioned determinant of proper conduct in important aspects of their daily lives. In many states the role of chieftaincy and the scope of customary law in their present form are the result not only of gradual modification in response to social change under colonial rule, but also of steps taken since independence to adapt traditional political ideas to the requirements of a modern state.

Ghana has enacted legislation empowering the chiefs and the govern- ment to co-operate in furthering such adaptation, and intends to introduce far-reaching reforms in certain branches of customary family law. The purpose of this paper is to present a detailed analysis of these measures in Ghana and to offer some general observations on the future of chieftaincy and customary law in the independent states of Africa.

Continuance of the Colonial Pattern

With independence, the new states of Africa inherited systems of government. The transfer of power from the colonial regimes to the inde- pendent states took place within a framework of constitutional and administra- tive continuity. This is true of the former French territories as well as the former British territories, although the process by which power was transferred was different in each case. The twelve territories which comprised French Equatorial Africa and French West Africa moved from colonial status to full independence in the short period of fifteen years-- from 1946 to 1960 -- in distinct stages which were associated with far-reaching constitutional changes in France.[1]

The process in the former British territories was gradual and extend- ed over many decades. The Legislative Council proved an effective instru- ment for bringing about increased participation by Africans in the government of a territory, leading, through the stages of representative and responsible government, to complete independence.[2] But in the French and British territories alike, independence produced no significant changes in the machinery of government. The legislative, executive, and judicial organs and processes, as they had been developed under colonial rule, continued; the colonial administrative pattern was taken over.

Embodied in the system of government bequeathed to the independent states were laws and administrative procedures -- the results of the attempts of colonial powers to deal with the political concepts and institutions of the traditional African societies under their rule.

The most important of these institutions are chieftaincy and customary law. Differences in the policies of the metropolitan powers resulted in different approaches to the pragmatic problems of relating the traditional role of the chief and the operation of customary law to social and economic development and the maintenance of order in the colonial territories. British policy, imbued with a sense of obligation to guide dependent peoples to self-government, incorporated chieftaincy into the administration and included customary law within the legal system.[3] But even the French policy of assimilation, notwithstanding its emphasis on the unity of the colony and metropolitan France, was unable to avoid the administrative use of chieftaincy and the recognition of customary law to some extent.[4]

The Chief under Colonial Rule

The traditional status, authority, and power of the chief were considerably diminished by colonial rule. In those African societies which had highly developed political structures, e.g., the Zulu of South Africa, the Ashanti of Ghana, and the Yoruba of Nigeria, in pre-colonial times the chief was the center of an efficient system for maintaining social order. He was usually vested with supreme legislative, executive, judicial, and religious power. His power and authority were extensive but not absolute; they were subject to clearly recognized limitations. In his actions and decisions he was, as a rule, required to express the wishes of his people, ascertained by constant consultations with elders and periodic consultation with larger groups. In the exercise of his functions he had to conform to the traditional law and customs of his people. The sanction for failure to observe these limitations was removal from office, or the defection of discontented members of the tribe to the support of a rival chief. But as long as he satisfied the traditional requirements of his office, he enjoyed great prestige accompanied by heavy responsibility. He was regarded as the Father of the People, the only person endowed with great power in an essentially egalitarian society.[5]

Colonial rule meant that the chief -- no matter how enlightened the colonial policy -- became part of an administration imposed upon him and his people. The continued exercise of his office depended upon his recognition by the colonial administration; it was the colonial administration,

not the traditions of his people, that determined the nature, extent, and
scope of his powers. He was frequently required to carry out duties not
in keeping with the traditional dignity of his office, duties often resented
by his people, e.g., the collection of unpopular taxes, the imposition of
new controls of traditional occupations such as cattle-grazing and land
cultivation. Above all, he was at all times subject in some measure
to the supervision or control of a colonial official.

The conscientious chief had a difficult task reconciling the dual
functions of being the mouthpiece of his people and part of an alien administration. For many of his people the fact that he was able to intercede on
their behalf with a district officer could not compensate for the fact that
he received a salary from the colonial government; these people soon
ceased to look up to him as Father of the People; they distrusted him as
a paid government servant.

The indirect effects of colonial rule therefore tended to weaken
the traditional allegiance of the people to their chiefs. Three other important by-products of colonial rule were economic development, education,
and Christianity. The growth of towns, improved communications, and
the attraction of paid urban employment took young men away from the
tribe for longer or shorter periods--sometimes permanently. The missionary
offered the Christian faith as a substitute for devotion to the ancestral
beliefs symbolized by the chief; they weaned the tribesman from adherence
to traditional practices, like the bride-price and the levirate, which were
enjoined by the chief. Education planted the seeds of individualism and
fostered a spirit of inquiry which caused the chief to be seen as an obstacle
to the quest for independence and advancement. Before long, these influences
combined to produce a class of young men, dedicated to the cause of national
freedom, who saw the chief as an oppressor to be overthrown.

In many African societies chieftaincy was unknown, political authority
being exercised through the interaction of discrete units based on lineage,
kinship, and age groups. In applying the system of indirect rule to these
societies, colonial governments often converted a lineage head into a chief;
he was then vested with extensive power and authority for which there
was no sanction in the traditions of the communities concerned. These
"civil service chiefs," as one would expect, failed to command the allegiance which sustained the traditional chief during the pre-independence
period.[6]

But the hold of chieftaincy on the African people was by no means
destroyed. Reporting in 1949 on the Gold Coast, the Coussey Committee
wrote that "the whole institution of chieftaincy is so closely bound up with
the life of our communities that its disappearance would spell disaster."[7]
More recently Dr. K. A. Busia has written:

In Africa, group and tribal ties are still strong ...
Constitutional problems that have appeared in different
African countries (in Ghana, Nigeria, the Belgian
Congo, Uganda, and Northern Cameroons, among others)
have consistently shown that indigenous, or tribal,
groups wish to maintain their political identity... Among
the tribal groups that have demanded constitutional
arrangements in recognition of their group solidarity
are the Ashanti of Ghana, the Yoruba and Ibo of Nigeria,
and the Baganda of Uganda. Far from being reactionary
groups they are among the most progressive in Africa,
and their respective accomplishments give evidence of
civic maturity as developed as can be found in any
African community. This compels scrutiny of
assumptions that tribalism is reactionary and necessarily
incompatible with nationhood.[8]

Chieftaincy in Nigeria, Sierra Leone, and Ghana

A comparison of the constitutional status of chiefs in Nigeria, Sierra
Leone, and Ghana presents two approaches to the role of the chief in modern
Africa. On the one hand it is recognized that they are entitled, by virtue
of their office, to exercise political power; on the other, while they may
participate as individuals in political processes, their function as chiefs
is regarded as limited to advisory powers in the spheres of customary law
and chieftaincy. The first approach is to be found in Nigeria and Sierra
Leone, the second in Ghana.

The Federation of Nigeria, which is a republic within the commonwealth, consists of four regions and a Federal Territory with a bicameral
legislature for the Federal Territory and each of the regions. One house
in each region is a house of chiefs, comprising a prescribed number of
chiefs, and the general rule is that a bill may not become law unless it
has been passed by both houses.[9] The Federal Parliament consists of a
senate and a house of representatives. Of the total of fifty-six federal
senators, four are nominated, forty-eight represent the regions--twelve for
each region--and four represent the Federal Territory. Of the four senators
representing the Federal Territory, one is the Oba of Lagos, another is
"a Chief selected in such manner as may be prescribed by Parliament
by the White-cap Chiefs and War Chiefs of Lagos from among their own
number." In addition to this direct representation in the federal legislature,
the chiefs of the country as a whole have a say in the choice of the twelve
senators representing the regions since these are selected at a joint sitting
of both houses of each region. The chiefs thus share the legislative power
of the state, with the elected representatives of the people, at both the

federal and regional levels. At the regional level they participate in the exercise of executive power, too; at least two members of the cabinet in each region must be drawn from the house of chiefs. In the case of one of the regions -- Northern Nigeria -- the constitution provides, in addition to a house of chiefs with legislative functions, for a council of chiefs with advisory functions. The governor of Northern Nigeria is required to act in accordance with the advice of this council in exercising powers conferred upon him relating to the appointment or deposition of a chief and allied matters.[10]

In Sierra Leone, the legislature is unicameral. The House of Representatives consists of not less than sixty members, including one member for each of the twelve districts established under the Protectorate Ordinance (this member must be a Paramount Chief). The legislative power thus conferred upon the Paramount Chiefs is reinforced by provisions in the constitution which prevent a law from taking effect when it seeks to abolish "the office of Paramount Chief as existing by customary law, " unless it has been passed by a two-thirds majority of all members of the house, in two successive sessions, there having been a dissolution of Parliament between the two session.[11]

Ghana has a house of chiefs for each of its eight regions, but these bodies are without legislative power and exercise functions related to customary law and chieftaincy, as prescribed by law. Before describing these functions in detail, it is interesting to consider the attempts of the British, in the early stages of progress towards independence, to grant a measure of legislative power to the chiefs.

Among the recommendations of the Coussey Committee in 1949 was the proposal that a bicameral legislature be established to include a senate, consisting of members elected regionally in a manner to be decided by the existing territorial councils.[12] The members of these councils were all the local Paramount Chiefs. Because the proposal was carried by a narrow majority (20 to 19) the committee put forward the alternative of a single chamber with one-third of the seats filled by persons chosen in the same way as the senators would have been chosen. A new constitution was adopted which provided for a legislative assembly of eighty-four members, of whom seventy-five were Africans. Seventy of the African members were to be elected, partly by chiefs, partly by electoral colleges; the remaining five, by direct election.[13] It was under this constitution that Kwame Nkrumah, head of the victorious Convention People's Party, was elected to Parliament in 1951. The six years which followed before independence was achieved saw a losing struggle by various groups seeking to preserve the political power of the chiefs against the growing strength and influence of Nkrumah and his party.[14]

Ghana became independent in 1957 under a constitution which reflected this struggle. It provided for a National Assembly consisting of members elected by adult suffrage, but offered scope for limited and indirect operation of traditional forces in the country by requiring the establishment of regional assemblies with powers in local government, education, and medical and health services. The constitution guaranteed the office of chief "as existing by customary law and usage." All amendments to the constitution required a two-thirds majority. Amendments relating to chieftaincy required, in addition, the approval of two-thirds of the regional assemblies. But these safeguards were shortlived. Regional assemblies were established in September 1958, but following the overwhelming success of the government in the ensuing elections, the constitutional limitations on amendment of the constitution were repealed in December of the same year. In March 1959, a law was passed providing for the dissolution of all the regional assemblies.[15]

The autochthonous constitution enacted when Ghana became a republic in 1960, while preserving the pattern of excluding the chiefs from any say, direct or indirect, in the government of the country, recognized the institution of chieftaincy as an integral part of Ghananian society. The White Paper issued prior to the constitutional referendum includes the following statement: "The draft Constitution is designed to preserve and guarantee Chieftaincy. In order to emphasise the importance which is attached to this institution the draft Constitution specifically provides for the continuance of Houses of Chiefs."[16] One of the fundamental principles to which the president is required to declare his adherence upon assuming office is that chieftaincy in Ghana should be guaranteed and preserved; another is that no person should suffer discrimination on grounds of sex, race, tribe, religion, or political belief.[17]

The constitution provides that there shall be a house of chiefs for each region of Ghana, the house to have such functions "relating to customary law and other matters," as may be provided by law.[18] In 1961 these functions were determined by the Chieftaincy Act, a law which consolidated existing enactments relating to chieftaincy.[19]

A chief has no actual legal authority. The exercise of his powers and functions depends upon recognition by the government. The act defines a chief as a person who is installed as a chief in accordance with customary law, and is, in addition, recognized by the appropriate minister. Once granted, recognition may be withdrawn by the minister at any time he considers withdrawal to be in the public interest. The authority of a chief who has received recognition is protected by a provision which makes it an offense, punishable by the courts, for any person to refuse to recognize him, or to do anything intended to undermine his power and authority.[20]

Chiefs are vested with powers and functions in matters affecting chieftaincy. They exercise these powers and functions as members of traditional councils and houses of chiefs empowered to deal with questions relating to the election of a chief, the de-stoolment or abdication of a chief, the constitutional relations between chiefs under customary law, and allied matters. In addition, a house of chiefs must consider any matter referred to it by the National Assembly. An appeal from the decision of a traditional council on a matter affecting chieftaincy goes to a judicial commissioner. A traditional council has no jurisdiction in a dispute to which the Asantahene or a Paramount Chief is a party; such disputes are dealt with by a judicial commissioner. An official list is maintained which contains the names of all chiefs recognized by the minister, and a schedule to the act sets out the members of the house of chiefs for each region.[21]

Traditional Councils and houses of chiefs are vested with important functions in relation to customary law. These are discussed below.

Customary Law in Africa

The new African nations have been called upon to deal with the problems of legal dualism. The laws of colonial territories immediately prior to independence were comprised of general law, which was enforced by the courts throughout the territory, and customary law, which was recognized as applicable, in certain circumstances, to members of local communities. In the British territories the general law consisted of English common law, the rules of equity, a number of English statutes, and the enactments of the colonial government. Customary law did not, however, constitute a defined body of law integrated with the law of the land. It was recognized in specified categories of suits in the local courts. But in the other courts, it applied, not as a matter of course, but only when proven by evidence in the same way as a question of fact, and only if it was "not repugnant to natural justice, equity and good conscience,"[22] and not in conflict with legislation in force in the territory.

The task which faces the independent African state is to create an integrated national legal system out of this varied material. Apart from the need for integration of the component parts of the general law -- a question which falls outside the scope of this paper -- a number of problems relating to the future of customary law arise. The first, and perhaps basic problem, is to ascertain what customary law is. All measures designed to bring about the integration of customary law within the legal system of a modern state depend for their efficacy on having adequate means for determining what the customary law is. Customary law is inherently both uncertain and fluid. A rule of customary law is often formulated in general terms as a basis for negotiation and compromise; a more precise rule has sometimes

been modified, in the course of time, under the influence of social or
economic change. Furthermore, most of the research relied upon has
been conducted, not by lawyers but by anthropologists, and the absence
of a system of judicial precedent in African courts has militated against
the precise formulation of principles of customary law.

The second problem is that when we speak of the customary law of
an African state, we are in fact referring to the several different systems
which often exist within a single state, e.g., in Ghana, the Ga and the
Fanti. Is it necessary or desirable to unify such different systems? If
so, how is the unification to be achieved? The third question is whether
customary laws can be adapted to modern conditions and requirements
so as to make them universally acceptable and enforceable within the state;
e.g., is it possible to formulate one law of marriage which will be observed
by all the people in a state, irrespective of their tribal or ethnic status?[23]

Customary Law in Ghana

Ghana's leaders have applied themselves constructively to the development of a legal system which, while satisfying the requirements of advancement in a modern state, aims also to provide adequate scope for the use
of traditional institutions and the expression of traditional ideas. Since
Ghana became a republic several important changes have taken place in
the field of customary law.

In terms of the constitution, customary law has ceased to be an
appendage of the general law and is now one of the component parts of
the law of the land. Under the heading "Laws of Ghana" the constitution
provides that except as may be otherwise provided by an enactment made
after the coming into operation of the constitution, the laws of Ghana comprise
the following: (a) The constitution; (b) enactments made by or under the
authority of the Parliament established by the constitution; (c) enactments
other than the constitution made by or under the authority of the Constituent
Assembly; (d) enactments in force immediately before the coming into
operation of the constitution; (e) the common law; and (f) customary law.[24]
It is no longer necessary, in law, for a litigant to establish that rules of
customary law exist in each case before the court will be competent to
apply customary law. "Any question as to the existence or content of a rule
of customary law, is a question of law for the Court, and not a question
of fact."[25]

The court, in every case in which it tries to rely on customary law,
must determine whether customary rules applicable to the community in
question exist and what the relevant rules are. If the court has no doubt
as to either the existence or content of a rule of customary law, it is
entitled to decide the question without further inquiry. If the court entertains
a doubt, it may decide the question after considering submissions by the

parties and consulting cases decided in the courts of any country, cited
in textbooks, or other sources, as appropriate. If, having taken these
steps, the court continues to entertain a doubt, it is required to adjourn
the proceedings and cause an inquiry to be held. The inquiry must be part
of the proceedings, but the manner in which it is to be held is left to the
discretion of the court. The purpose of the inquiry is to enable opinions
on the matter about which doubt remains to be placed before the court.
The court then decides the question according to the result of the inquiry.[26]

The law of Ghana includes the new concept of "assimilated customary
law," According to a statutory definition, the customary law of Ghana
"consists of rules of law which by custom are applicable to particular
communities in Ghana."[27] If any rule which applies to a particular community
is deemed suitable for general application, it may be assimilated as part
of the common law, thus becoming part of the law of the land. Ghana is
the only African state which has made provision for the assimilation of
customary law by means of executive action taken on the advice of the
chiefs.

One of the traditional functions of the house of chiefs, referred to
above, is to advise the government on the assimilation of rules of customary
law. The minister responsible for local government is empowered to
convene a joint committee of all houses of chiefs to consider whether a
rule of customary law should be assimilated. He may do so, either on his
own initiative, or in response to representations from a house of chiefs.
The joint committee is then required to consider evidence and representations submitted and to carry out such investigations as it considers necessary.
If, having taken these steps, the joint committee decides that the rule
should be assimilated, it then drafts a declaration describing the rule,
with such modifications as it may consider desirable, and submits the
declaration to the minister.

If the minister, after consulting the chief justice, is satisfied that
effect should be given to the declaration either as submitted or with such
modifications as he may consider necessary, he makes a legislative instrument embodying the declaration, with or without modifications as the case
may be, and declares the rule as described to be assimilated. The rule
then becomes part of the common law of Ghana, and may be referred to
as a "common law rule of customary origin." The minister is also empowered
to make provisions in the law which are necessary to cases pending at the
time the instrument is being made, or for any other purpose.

The machinery which has been described may also be set in motion
by a traditional council. A council is empowered to consider the customary
law in force in its area. If, having done so, it considers that the law
should be assimilated, it is required to make representations to the house
of chiefs having jurisdiction over its area, which will, in turn, make the

necessary representations to the minister.[28]

In addition, if, having considered the customary law in force in its area, a traditional council comes to the conclusion that the law on any subject is uncertain, it may make appropriate representations to the house of chiefs having jurisdiction over its area, in order to have the uncertainty removed.

A declaration stating the customary law on any subject may be drafted by a house of chiefs. This may be done on its own initiative following representations from a traditional council or at the request of the minister. When a request is made by the minister, the house of chiefs must comply. The declaration is submitted to the minister, and if he is satisfied that it is, either as submitted or with such modifications as he considers necessary, a correct statement of the customary law on the subject in question, he makes a legislative instrument embodying the declaration, with or without modifications, as the case may be. The instrument provides that the law as stated shall have effect within the area in question. Where the question raised is common to more than one house of chiefs a joint committee of the houses affected takes the necessary steps.[29]

Similar provisions empower the minister to give effect to alterations in a rule of customary law which are considered desirable by a house of chiefs.[30]

The changes in the approach to customary law described above (the first two innovations, the remainder improvements) have been in force too short a time to permit a satisfactory assessment of their significance. They do, however, represent a serious attempt by Ghana to face the challenge presented by widespread adherence to traditional law and traditional institutions within a society committed to modernization. The fact that customary law is now part of the law of the land, with its corollary that courts must apply normal judicial processes in disputes relating to a customary law, should have the effect, in time, of making the content of customary law increasingly certain and contributing to its fruitful adaptation to modern conditions. One may also expect from the courts a deeper insight into, and a more realistic interpretation of customary law now that the judiciary, composed exclusively of Ghanaians, has the benefit of special knowledge and experience.[31]

The provisions relating to assimilation, declaration, and alterations of customary law, enable the executive to co-operate with the judiciary in the process of adapting customary law. At the same time, the procedure ensures that the chiefs will play an essential part in that process. For, while it is true that the decision in all three cases rests with the minister, it would seem unlikely that the views of the house of chiefs -- let alone those

of a joint committee -- would be completely ignored by the government.
The provision for modifications by the minister and the fact that the initiative may be taken either by him or by the chiefs suggest that the increased
use of these powers by both could lead to a fruitful reconciliation of political
and traditional attitudes towards the development of customary law.

Marriage, Divorce and Inheritance in Ghana

"The Government has had under consideration some time the question
of marriage and divorce, and the related problem of inheritance. These
questions touch the very roots of Ghanaian society, and it is Government's
intention that they should be freely and dispassionately discussed, and the
principles that would emerge would be taken to form the basis of legislation."
In this introductory paragraph of a White Paper, issued in 1961, Ghana
announced its intention to tackle a complex problem common to all the new
countries of Africa, namely the incompatibility of the changed status of
women in response to modern influences and the customary law to which
they are subject.[32] This is part of a wider problem -- the failure of the present
law to satisfy the needs of modern African society. Education has lessened
adherence to tribal practice: men and women in the process of urbanization have broken with the extended family, and the traditional authority
of parents has weakened; women, in employment, earning and saving
money, have developed an independence and an individualism alien to
tribal ideas. But the special hardships to which the disabilities of women
give rise (with their corresponding harmful effects on children), together
with the growing tendency among African women to assert their equality
with men in the new states, have combined to underline the importance of
creating a blend of traditional practice and modern ideas in the law relating
to marriage, divorce, and inheritance.[33]

The White Paper goes on to declare that its purpose was to provoke
discussion (to call for "as many people as possible" to send their views
to the government), to describe the problems arising from the present
state of the law, and to outline the legislation contemplated by the government as a means of solving them. After the lapse of a year the marriage,
divorce, and inheritance bill was published, but not passed. In January
1963, a new bill was published which superseded the previous bill. An
accompanying memorandum referred to the "wonderful response of public
opinion on the proposal set out in the White Paper" and stated that the new
measure embodied the principles which emerged from the recommendations received from the public and from a parliamentary committee appointed
to examine the bill. The bill sought to deal with problems arising from
the existing state of the law by creating a single legal framework within
which traditional concepts and procedures were combined with western
principles.

The present law of Ghana recognizes two parallel systems of marriage--according to the Marriage Ordinance[34]and according to customary law.
A person married under the ordinance may not, while that marriage continues
to exist, contract another marriage whether under the ordinance or according to customary law. A person married according to customary law,
however, may enter into other marriages according to customary law,
without dissolving the first marriage. The new bill would substitute for
the existing legal provisions a uniform law of marriage applicable to all
citizens, providing that no person may register more than one marriage.
A man is not prevented by law from having a number of wives, but only
the wife whose marriage has been duly registered is entitled to inherit
property if he dies without leaving a will. Thus the proposed new law,
while it does not prohibit polygyny, exposes it to pressures from women
who are unwilling to accept the subservient status imposed upon them by
traditional African society.

The proposed divorce law is another interesting example of the
capacity of traditional concepts to correspond to modern social requirements. Under customary law, divorce, like marriage, is a matter which
concerns the two families as much as it concerns the spouses. The procedure
takes the form of discussions, designed initially to effect a reconciliation,
between the heads of the two families, the spouses, and other persons
invited to participate because of their relationship, status or experience.
If it is clear from the attitude of the spouses that reconciliation is impossible, a decision is made as to whether the marriage should be dissolved.
In the event of divorce, agreement is also reached on such consequential
questions as the restoration of property which has changed hands, the
maintenance of the wife, and the custody and maintenance of the children
of the marriage.

The first step in divorce proceedings under the proposed new law
is a petition by the spouse to a judge of the High Court. On receipt of the
petition, the judge would appoint a divorce committee, of which he is the
chairman, to arbitrate and attempt reconciliation. No standing committee
is contemplated. In each case, four local inhabitants would be chosen as
persons "whose wisdom and experience are respected in the locality and
who would be expected to bring to marriage problems, sympathy and
understanding." The proceedings would take place in chambers, not in
open court, and no lawyers would be admitted except with permission of
the judge; the committee would have power to call and examine witnesses.
When an arbitration or reconciliation failed, the committee could grant
a divorce, which would be announced in open court by the judge.

These provisions reflect a constructive approach to marriage as a
social institution, and their relevance extends beyond Ghana or Africa.
The insistence on attempted reconciliation as an essential prerequisite to
divorce is in keeping with concern throughout the western world, as is

evident in the use of marriage counsellors. The requirement that the hearing take place in the privacy of a judge's chambers, as more appropriate
to the circumstances that the stress of a formal hearing in open court,
is likely to commend itself to a growing number of people in countries like
Britain and the United States. The provision for a committee of local
inhabitants to assist the judge would be, no doubt, less acceptable to the
individualistic communities of western society than it is to African communities with their strong traditions of communal association. But there is
reason to believe that the idea of a divorce judge being assisted by a committee,
for example, of professional social workers and psychologists, would
be widely regarded in western countries as an improvement over present
procedures.

The question of inheritance in Ghana is complicated by the existence
of two systems of inheritance under customary law in addition to the statute
law. Under the patrilineal system, children succeed to their father's estate;
under the matrilineal system, they do not. The proposed law, which
would apply to all inhabitants of Ghana, removes this distinction. It applies
only to property which the deceased could have given away in his lifetime
or disposed of by will; it provides that two-thirds of the deceased's property
go to the children and a life interest of one sixth each to the surviving
spouse and the surviving parents. If the surviving spouse is the wife she
is entitled to inherit only if her marriage was registered, but all children,
whether by a registered marriage or not, are entitled to inherit.

But the government is not yet satisfied that these proposals enjoy
sufficient public approval and support to justify their being put before
Parliament. On July2, 1963, the minister of justice, announcing the postponement of the first reading of the marriage, divorce, and inheritance
bill, informed the National Assembly that a memorandum received from the
John Sarbah Society of the Faculty of Law of the University of Ghana, was
being studied by the Law Reform Committee as a matter of urgency. He
added that it was desirable that consideration of the bill be postponed "so
that the House can have the full benefit of the views of all sections of the
community."[35]

In principle, judicial interpretation is preferable to legislation as a
means of adapting customary law to modern conditions. When legislation
is used to modify customary law in a changing society, there is always the
risk that undesirable inflexibility will result.[36] On the other hand, the task
of doing justice in a variety of cases, when entrusted to well trained and
experienced judges, approaching an indigenous system with sympathetic
understanding, can lead to the eventual formulation of a coherent body of
consistent law corresponding to social needs and capable of further development. But judicial interpretation alone may well prove too slow a process
for Ghana and other new African states. The decision in Ghana to distribute

responsibility for the adaptation of customary law between legislature, executive, judiciary, and the traditional authorities suggests both a realistic recognition of the urgent need for adaptation and an awareness of the dangers inherent in premature modification of traditional laws and practices. A future policy of sustained use of the new procedures for declaration, assimilation, and alteration of customary law, combined with the normal process of judicial interpretation could be fruitful in ensuring continuous adaptation of customary law in response to social and economic progress.

Conclusions

At their present stage of development, the new African states cannot avoid confrontation with the demands of traditional concepts and institutions. The available evidence indicates (with Guinea as the sole exception) that the theoretical rejection of chieftaincy as a feudal institution incompatible with the needs of a modern state has not wiped out the influence of the chief. For the present at least, social stability would seem to demand the recognition of a continuing role for the chief in societies otherwise determined to keep up with the pace of the nuclear age. The nature of that role would seem to be determined by the balance of modern and traditional political forces in the individual countries, resulting from their national histories and the influence of their leaders. It may be that patterns which will persist in the future have already been laid. It is as difficult to see Nigeria, in the foreseeable future, changing to a legislative system which will exclude the chiefs as it is to see Ghana adopt one which will include them. On the other hand, while it may be valid to assume the continuance in Africa of the two categories which emerge from this paper--the chief with political power and the chief with advisory functions relating to traditional matters-- a dogmatic assessment of future trends would be rash. New patterns will probably emerge. In Uganda, when the approach to full independence seemed to have run into an impasse because of the conflict between the traditional power of the Kabaka of Buganda and the ruling party, the conflict was resolved by finding a constitutional formula which accommodated republican practice to monarchical sentiment. The new constitution, although it provides for a president, declares Uganda to be an "independent sovereign state" (not a republic) within the British Commonwealth. And after Lukiko (the Parliament of Buganda) had met in secret session and declared that the kabaka was the only possible candidate for the presidency, he was duly elected, by a substantial majority, as the first president of Uganda.

The future of customary law lies not only in the adaptive processes within individual states, but in the movement towards unity in African law as a whole. As Dr. Allott has written:

In the development of more advanced legal systems
that will conform to the needs of industrialized, socialized,
educated societies in modern Africa, evolution of African
customary law occupies a central place. It will not remain
tolerable much longer that a purely customary unwritten
system of law is administered within the framework of an
introduced written law of an advanced type ... African
law has a certain unity, deriving principally from its
being customary and unwritten character. There are
also certain distinctive complexes or patterns of
features, attitudes and procedures in the legal field,
falling into a restricted number of types, which recur in
African legal systems ... There are many coincidences
of legal rule in different systems; but the wider unity is
more a question of spirit, approach, and the legal complex
than of detailed resemblances.[37]

In the field of customary law a fairly clear pattern is emerging:
the disappearance of differences between systems within a state leading
to a single national customary law; the adaptation of that national customary
law to modern conditions; and the gradual evolution of an adapted customary
law applicable in many spheres through the new Africa.

Footnotes

1. D. G. Lavroff and G. Peiser, Les Constitutions Africaines (Paris, 1961), 7-12.

2. Martin Wight, The Gold Coast Legislative Council (London, 1946); David Kimble, The Political History of Ghana, 1850-1928 (Oxford, 1963).

3. For an early example of the British attitude toward customary law see the Bond of 1844, a treaty signed by the British governor of the Gold Coast settlements and several Fanti chiefs, which provided for the trial of "murders and robberies and other crimes and offences ... before the Queen's judicial officers and the chiefs of the District, moulding the customs of the country to the general principles of British law." (Ibid., 194.)

While British colonial policy was influenced by economic considerations, there is evidence of an embryonic doctrine of trusteeship in the early stages of colonial rule. In 1865 the House of Commons set up a select committee to consider the report of Colonel Ord who had been sent to the settlements in British West Africa (Gold Coast, Lagos, Gambia, and Sierra Leone) to investigate inter alia how far the four settlements could be run more economically by a single administration. The committee's report, which recommended the central administration of the settlements from Sierra Leone, included the following resolution: "That ... the object of our policy should be to encourage in the natives the exercise of those qualities which may make it possible for us more and more to transfer to them the administration of all the Governments with a view to our ultimate withdrawal from all." J. J. Crooks, Records of the Gold Coast Settlements, 1750-1874 (London, 1923), 366-368.

4. Philip Neres, French-Speaking West Africa (London, 1962), 27-28. Guinea is an exception. There, chieftaincy was suppressed by decrees of Sekou Touré's government issued in 1957 and 1958. Writing in 1962, however, L. G. Cowan expressed the view that "it cannot yet be assumed that tribe is a factor to be disregarded entirely, particularly in the balance of political forces at the national level." Gwendolen M. Carter (ed.), African One-Party States (New York, 1962), 198.

5. M. Fortes and E. Evans-Pritchard, African Political Systems (London, 1940), xi-xxiii, 1-23, 25-55; David E. Apter, Ghana in Transition (New York, 1963), 80-118.

6. Audrey I. Richards, East African Chiefs (London, 1960), 158; Lloyd Fallers, Bantu Bureaucracy (Cambridge, 1955), 246-247; H. A. Fosbrooke, "The Application of Indirect Rule to Chiefless Societies," in Raymond Apthorpe (ed.), From Tribal Rule to Modern Government (Lusaka, 1959), 17-36.

7. Report to H. E. The Governor by the Committee on Constitutional Reform, 1949 (London, 1949), Colonial No. 248, 9.

8. K. A. Busia, The Challenge of Africa (New York, 1962), 71-72. Although Dr. Busia's book reflects a personal attitude towards nationalist development in the new Africa, colored by his political experience in Ghana, his assessment of the influence of tribal ties is, in my view, by and large a valid assessment.

9. The powers of the house of chiefs, except in the Northern Region, are subject to limitations similar to those which apply to the House of Lords in England. Their effect is to permit a bill to become law when it has been passed by the House of Assembly, notwithstanding an adverse vote by the House of Chiefs, after the lapse of a prescribed period and subject to compliance with prescribed requirements. In the case of a money bill (i.e. a bill dealing only with such matters as the imposition of taxation, the appropriation of public funds, and the raising of loans), where the bill, having been passed by the House of Assembly, is sent to the house of chiefs at least one month before the end of the session, and the house of chiefs fails to pass the bill within one month of its receipt, it may be presented to the governor for his assent. In the case of any other bill, it may be presented for gubernatorial assent if it has been passed by the House of Assembly, and rejected by the House of Chiefs, in two successive sessions of the legislature (Constitution of Western Nigeria, s. 27 read with s. 29; Constitution of Eastern Nigeria, s. 27 read with s. 29; Constitution of Mid-Western Nigeria, s. 23 with s. 25) . In the Northern Region, where any bill is passed by the House of Assembly and rejected by the House of Chiefs, the conflict is resolved by a joint sitting of representatives of both Houses (Constitution of Northern Nigeria, s. 28).

10. Constitution of the Federal Republic of Nigeria, Act No. 20 of 1963; Constitution of Northern Nigeria, Act No. 33 of 1963; Constitution of Western Nigeria, Act No. 26 of 1963; Constitution of Eastern Nigeria, Act No. 8 of 1963; Constitution of Mid-Western Nigeria, Act No. 3 of 1964.

11. The Sierra Leone (Constitution) Order-in-Council, 1961. Statutory Instrument No. 741, 1961.

12. Richards, East African Chiefs; Fallers, Bureaucracy; Fosbrooke, "Indirect Rule".

13. Gold Coast (Constitution) Order-in-Council, 1950. The new constitution came into force on Jan. 1, 1951.

14. These groups had merged in 1954 to form the National Liberation Movement which called, inter alia, for a bicameral legislature consisting of a legislative assembly and a house of chiefs. D. Austin, Politics in Ghana 1946-1960 (London, 1964), 259-265; St. Clair Drake, "Traditional Authority and Social Action in former British West Africa," Human Organization, XIX:156-158 (1960); D. Apter, "The Role of Traditionalism in the Political Modernisation of Ghana and Uganda," World Politics, XII:45-68 (1960).

15. Rubin and Murray, The Constitution and Government of Ghana (London, 1961), 308; T. O. Elias, Ghana and Sierra Leone (London, 1962), 82-85.

16. "Government Proposals for a Republican Constitution," White Paper, No. 1/1960 (Accra, 1960).

17. The Constitution of the Republic of Ghana, Art. 13. The constitution was enacted by the Constituent Assembly on June 29, 1960, and came into operation on July 1, 1960. The provisions of the constitution were supplemented by eleven laws passed by the Constituent Assembly on the same date which came into operation simultaneously with the constitution. Among these were the Interpretation Act (1960, C. A. 4) which deals with the interpretation of the constitution and other enactments, and the Courts Act (1960 C. A. 9) which deals with the jurisdiction, composition, and procedure of the courts.

18. Arts. 29 and 50. These provisions are not entrenched, i.e., they may be altered or repealed by Parliament in the exercise of its ordinary powers. Many other provisions in the constitution, e.g., those dealing with the courts and the National Assembly, may be altered or repealed by Parliament only after a referendum.

19. The Chieftaincy Act, 1961, Art. 81, which repealed the Houses of Chiefs Act, 1958 (No. 20) and many other laws regulating the powers and functions of chiefs.

20. The chief's power and authority in the republic conform closely to the pattern established by colonial rule. Under the Native Authority (Colony) Ordinance, No. 21 of 1944, the governor was empowered to appoint a chief as the native authority for a specified area in the colony, and to revoke the appointment. Once appointed, a native authority exercised his powers "if and so long as he is recognized by the Governor." A provision penalizing acts which undermined the authority of a chief was contained in the Native Administration Ordinance, No. 23 of 1927.

21. The Chieftaincy Act recognizes the special status of the asantahene. He is defined as "the occupant of the Golden Stool of Ashanti, " and is ipso facto head of the Ashanti Region House of Chiefs, whereas in the case of the other houses, the act provides that the head shall be elected from among the members. A Paramount Chief exercises jurisdiction in a traditional area, formerly known as a state, with divisional and other chiefs subordinate to the Asantahene. In the other regions a paramount chief is a chief who is not subordinate to any other chief. The authority of the asantahene, like that of all other chiefs, depends upon ministerial recognition which may be withdrawn at any time.

Provision is made for as many judicial commissioners as may be necessary to exercise the original and appellate jurisdiction mentioned. A judicial commissioner is appointed by the chief justice after consultation with the president and need not, like a judge or magistrate, be a qualified legal practitioner. Act 81, s.34 read with Judicial Service Regulations, 1963, L.I. 319, ss. 3, 5, 6 and the Judicial Service Act 1960, C. A. 10, s. 8.

22. The repugnancy rule, embodied in section 19 of the Supreme Court Ordinance of the Gold Coast, 1876, followed a similar provision in an Indian law (section 5 of the Punjab Laws Act, Act IV of 1872). Provision for the application of the rule was also included in the colonial laws of Sierra Leone, Nigeria, Northern Rhodesia, and the Gambia. A. N. Allott (ed.), Judicial and Legal Systems in Africa (London, 1962), 15, 48, 52, 57, 61, 65, 152.

23. For a discussion of these and related questions, see "Colloquium on African Law, London, " Journal of African Law, 2:72; W. B. Harvey, "The Evolution of Ghana Law since Independence, " Law and Contemporary Problems (Duke University), XXVII:587-594; A. N. Allott (ed.), The Future of Law in Africa (London, 1960).

24. Constitution of Ghana, Art. 40.

25. The Courts Act, 1960, C.A. 9, s. 67 (1). See note 14.

26. The Courts Act, 1960, C.A. 9, s. 67.

27. The Interpretation Act, 1960, C.A. 4, s. 18 (1). See note 14.

28. The Chieftaincy Act, 1961, Act 81, ss. 58, 62, 63, 64. I have been unable to find a legislative instrument creating a common law rule of customary origin.

29. The Chieftaincy Act, 1961, Act 81, ss. 58, 59, 61.

30. Ibid., ss.58, 60, 61. The provisions relating to declarations and alterations of customary law replace unsatisfactory provisions dealing with these questions in the Houses of Chiefs Act (No. 20) of 1958, since repealed.

31. For examples of past judicial errors in applying customary law see Matson, "Internal Conflict of Laws in the Gold Coast," Modern Law Review, XVI:469 (1953).

British judges, usually without personal knowledge of the law in question, were frequently at the mercy of expert witnesses, called to establish the law, who were ignorant, biased, or corrupt. When they were not, their evidence was often unreliable because of "a tendency to idealize the law, to present what it ought to be instead of what it is; and a failure to appreciate that the ancient traditional law has been modified by subsequent practice, by native court decisions, or by the influence of English ideas." A. N. Allott, Essays in African Law (London, 1960), 78.

32. White Paper No. 3/61

33. J. S. Read, "Women's Status and Law Reform," in J. N. D. Anderson (ed.), Changing Law in Developing Countries (New York, 1963), 210-239.

34. Laws of the Gold Coast (1951), Cap. 127, 1884.

35. Ghana Parliamentary Debates, XXXII, No. 8, Col. 269.

36. An example is the Natal Code of Native Law in South Africa (Law 19 of 1891), see Stafford and Franklin, Principles of Native Law and the Natal Code (Pietermaritzburg, 1950).

37. Allott, Essays, 65.

VI

Political and Constitutional Change in the Bechuanaland Protectorate

Robert H. Edwards
Program Officer, Ford Foundation

A national election was held in Bechuanaland on March 1, 1965, which
provided that vast protectorate of the United Kingdom with an African government. In the great heat which settles over the country in the late summer,
more than 140,000 people, 74 per cent of registered voters went to polling
places throughout the traditional tribal areas, Crown Lands, and European
farming blocks which had been divided into thirty-one national constituencies.
They determined by a ratio of four-to-one that Seretse Khama and his
Democratic Party should assume responsibility for the domestic affairs
of Bechuanaland, sparsely settled, poor in natural resources, and almost
enveloped by Rhodesia, South Africa, and its own Kalahari Desert.

The final count found the red disc voting symbols of the Democratic
Party to be over 80 per cent of the total votes cast, enough to win 28 of
the 31 elected seats in the new Legislative Assembly. Motsamai Mpho,
the radical Independence Party leader, had lost in his own Ngamiland
region of Okavango, and only Philip Matante, president of the People's
Party, survived in Francistown to lead the three-man opposition.

Seretse's triumph occurred only eight years after his return from
a six-year exile in England imposed by his tribe and the British government.
Such is the speed of events in Africa, however, that there was nothing
ironic in the formal array of colonial officers drawn up at the airfield of
the new capital, Gaberones, to welcome the new prime minister when he
answered the formal call of Her Majesty's Commissioner to form a government. As a member of the old Executive Council he had worked closely
for more than four years with the officials who would become his permanent
secretaries and with the resident commissioner. Her Majesty's Commissioner, Sir Peter Fawcus had gained the confidence and co-operation of
Seretse and his lieutenant Quett Masire, as well as that of the Europeans
and traditional chiefs, during the five years in which he guided Bechuanaland
from a classic colonial government with native advisory and European
councils, to a Legislative Council with a large official minority, and through
the discussions which led to the new constitution.

These ties of friendship and respect will give indispensable continuity
to the new government. Seretse promptly named Quett Masire his deputy
prime minister and chose his ministers, including one European, who
would deal with domestic affairs: ministers of agriculture, labor and
social services, local government, works and communications, mines,

commerce and industry. (Finance remains an expatriate post with an
African parliamentary secretary.) But matters of national defense, foreign
affairs, and internal security remain the responsibility of Britain, and thus
of Her Majesty's Commissioner, although he is to keep the prime minister
closely informed on these subjects, and may delegate responsibility to him
on a day-to-day basis. For reasons of economics and geography, Bechuanaland is overshadowed by its vital relations with South Africa, and management of these ties in turn will dictate the nature of Bechuanaland's relationship with the rest of Africa. Co-operation between the new African government and the British government, therefore, on such matters as South
African refugees, economic and monetary arrangements, and transport
and communication relationships with South Africa, will determine how
meaningful Bechuanaland's self-government can be and whether Bechuanaland
can proceed to independence, now being discussed for 1966.

This paper recounts the constitutional changes which have come
about in Bechuanaland over the past five years, and the political activities,
previously non-existent, which resulted from them in a traditional and
conservative society.

The High Commission Territory of Bechuanaland

The country, an expanse of Kalahari Desert and semi-arid veld,
is much like the Bechuanaland which Livingstone entered from Kuruman
in 1841, and where he spent ten years before continuing on his way to central
Africa. It lies far off the main tracks and water courses of Africa and today
contains some 520,000 Batswana, [1] a homogeneous people of similar language
and culture divided into eight sub-tribes. [2] They have been joined over the
past century by approximately 3,000 Europeans, 700 "Coloureds" of mixed
blood, and a handful of Asians. [3] Small bands of Bushmen, the shy, tiny
original inhabitants, live and hunt unobserved in the central Kalahari.

The Batswana live today much as they have always lived, in small
circular brown huts neatly assembled into wards which form the units of
the large, straggling villages--growing like the rings of a tree out from the
central kgotla, the court of the headman or chief. Nearly all major villages
lie near the railway line on the eastern fringe of the Kalahari. There the
more regular rains allow farmers to raise precarious crops of sorghum
and beans. But the Batswana are basically a ranching people: 1.3 million
cattle graze the immense pastures that extend far into the desert.
Raising cattle wholly or partially employs 98 per cent of the population. [4]

The land is harsh and aloof; it breeds stoicism rather than innovation.
When the summer rains do not come, and often they do not, the perilousness
of existence is suddenly exposed, and the sun parches eastern areas as

well as western desert. But when the rains fall, relieving the searing heat and wind of October, water fills the pans--the shallow natural depressions on which the animals depend--and lies in sheets over the territory. Then, in the more fertile eastern regions, ploughing begins with oxen which have not yet regained condition after the annual five-month winter drought.[5]

It was in the scattered railway towns and these eastern farming areas that discontented men made the first ragged attacks upon the lethargy of the territory. In the towns the vague mutterings brought from South Africa and Southern Rhodesia fed upon poverty and unemployment and broke into fitful, ill-articulated annoyance with traders, government, and employers. (The progressive farmers questioned the existing order less openly--their new agricultural methods collided inevitably with arbitrary chieftainship and tribal custom.) Among these rural Batswana, where ancient attitudes toward cattle as social and economic capital are still being eroded, tribesmen have finally begun to treat their beasts as income, as a means to alternative forms of wealth. As these producers bypassed the traditional markets of traders and speculators to sell directly to the abattoir at Lobatsi, cattle sales rose sharply, and the horizons of these rural people have widened.[6] Ranchers increasingly travel with their animals to market, learn the reasons for prices of cattle and for their shipment in rigid quotas to South Africa, and so learn the dependence of their country upon that republic. But modernization is a slow process and droughts and great distances quench the enthusiasm of those who seek economic and political reform.

In 1961, when independence movements were washing over Africa, scarcely a ripple seemed to touch Bechuanaland. That year, however, a constitution was introduced to a largely uncomprehending and uninterested people in a territory where local government remained synonymous with the eight Batswana chiefs and the trusteeship of isolated district commissioners, and where the civil service was entirely European in the upper ranks.

Until the early 1950's it had been assumed as contemplated by the South Africa Act of 1909, that the High Commission territories of Bechuanaland, Basutoland, and Swaziland would be absorbed into the Union of South Africa. For fifty years the Colonial Office was freed from the necessity of producing a High Commission policy. But, with the calcifying of Afrikaner Nationalist racial policy, it was accepted that no such cession would be acceptable to the Batswana, the new African states, or the British electorate. Throughout the late 1950's it began to be assumed, by officials and the few educated Africans, that there was probably a time limit on the pleasantly undefined status of the three territories, shielded by the protection of the Crown, but residing under the more practical shelter of an advantageous customs agreement with the Union, now the Republic of South Africa. In the late 1950's, events on the rest of the continent indicated that self-government, however implausible, was imminent. A degree of economic independence

would have to be encouraged, a local civil service trained, and the administrative capital would have to move from Mafeking into Bechuanaland.

In December of 1960, then, an order-in-council promulgated a cautious
constitution which determined that Bechuanaland should cease to be governed
entirely by an expatriate government. The advisory councils -- purely consult-
ant bodies -- should give way to a territory-wide, semi-popularly-elected
legislature endowed, despite broad powers reserved to the Crown, with
substantial law-making authority.[7] This Legislative Council, complemented
by an Executive Council serving as an advisory cabinet to the resident
commissioner, came into existence in 1961 and was to last for five years.
But its life was cut short. With the Legislative Council just emerging
from less than three formative years, the colonial administration in late
1963 stimulated a new set of constitutional discussions which determined
that Bechuanaland should make a further leap -- with national elections based
upon a common electoral roll -- into internal self-government.[8] The 1965
elections were the result. But with independence already being discussed
for 1966, it is uncertain how long this system will be allowed to test the
slender political base of the country.

Organized political activities date only from 1961, stimulated by the
imperial initiative of 1960.[9] They were the natural, hasty responses of
the more progressive members of the African society to the British decision
to throw part of the burden of legislative authority upon the community -- a
community whose traditional hierarchy of chiefs formed the sole indigenous
framework for political power. Despite a half-hearted attempt by a few
Europeans to form a right-wing alliance with the chiefs, it was the African
commoners of the Bechuanaland People's Party and of the Bechuanaland
Democratic Party who, in the three years of their existence, undertook to
awaken the country politically.[10]

In a territory with an almost total pre-colonial indifference to the
rest of Africa, the awakening was fitful. Bechuanaland's tranquillity has
been unruffled during its seventy-five years of British administration,
thanks to its lack of urbanization and the unique insulation provided by the
calm of South Africa. Too poor to lure many white settlers and cut off
by its desert and lack of seacoast from modern black Africa, Bechuanaland
did not experience the severe economic or racial injustices or conquest
and the dispossession of land which have spurred political development
elsewhere in Africa.[11]

The new political activity, accordingly, produced little discontinuity
with the past; in the absence of exploitable injury, a special interest party
could find only isolated pockets of support. The task of the few weary
politicians of both the People's Party and the Democratic Party, crossing

the desert in their trucks, speaking in the village councils, has been to
explain the unfamiliar concepts of nationhood, independence, and the
"heresy" of a new political power separate from the local chief and molaodi
(lawgiver)-- the district commissioner.

Chiefs and Protection: The Shade of Lugard

From the middle to the end of the nineteenth century the border of
Bechuanaland, on the periphery of the British Empire, was the scene of
spasmodic skirmishing between African tribesmen, Afrikaner farmers,
missionaries, and the British government.[12]Some of the great chiefs of
Bechuanaland, and by their fiat, many of their tribesmen, were converted
relatively quickly and willingly to Christianity and saw the missionaries
as natural allies. A substantial degree of mutual confidence sprang up
between chiefs and missionaries of which the British administration in
Cape Town was unaware; at the same time a related distrust of the
Afrikaner frontiersman was produced. With the mineral discoveries of
the seventies and eighties, the zone of concentrated white settlement moved
nearer Bechuanaland, and the western border of the Transvaal "became a
sort of Tom Tiddler's ground filled with warring Kaffirs and the scum of
Europe -- discharged and deserting soldiers, Dutch burghers from the
Transvaal, the Cape Colony, and Free State whom neither the British nor
South African Republics could control."[13]

Imperial intervention, particularly after the acquisition of South-West
Africa by Germany in 1884 was not long delayed. In 1885, Bechuanaland
was declared to be in a British sphere of influence and in 1895, the Colonial
Office partitioned it, delimiting large reserves to the chiefs and placing
them under imperial control (where they had asked to be) rather than under
the rule of Cecil Rhodes' British South Africa Company. In the best imperial
style the three chiefs (Sechele, Khama, Bathoen), who insisted on going
to England to plead for British intervention, were received by the Queen at
Windsor, with a promise of protection and presents of Bibles and breast-
plated, plumed Horse Guard uniforms. Bechuanaland's first constitution
was duly promulgated by orders-in-council on May 9, 1891, making a
resident commissioner the chief administrative officer, under the High
Commissioner for Basutoland, Bechuanaland, and Swaziland.

Parsimony and indirect rule have characterized the administration
of Bechuanaland. Traditionally and necessarily obsessed with the balance
sheet aspects of the empire, the Colonial Office had little faith that the
country could be made to pay for itself. The imposition of a hut tax was
felt to be a slender hope upon which to base solvency, and although this
cynicism long ago proved to be justified, it was only in 1956 that the United

Kingdom's treasury began to make annual grants-in-aid.[14]District Administration posts had been established before 1895 in each of the tribal areas,
and the central headquarters was in Mafeking -- then in British Bechuanaland
(The cession of the latter colony to the Cape Colony in 1895 left the capital
outside Bechuanaland.) Under pressure of budget, British administration,
personified in the district commissioner, was no more than the thinnest
lamination laid upon the local government of the chiefs.

The district commissioner's most important function was to support
the chief, whose law, in all instances that it did not conflict with common
law, continued to apply. The practice of leaving the tribes alone -- regarding
administration as a passive function of preventing bloodshed, exploitation by
traders, and the grosser forms of local injustice -- was the rule until about
1950. Until then, the district commissioner made only occasional trips
into the remoter areas. All formal directives to the people were channeled
through the chief, and only with his co-operation could the colonial government
express its wishes to the people. Democratization of tribal councils -- the
gradual broadening of local power to a tribal executive group beyond the
person of the chief -- was attempted for the first time in 1961. The result
of indirect rule through the chiefs was predictable: dawning criticism of
chiefly inadequacies became implicit criticism of the colonial administration,
the underpinning of the chief's position.

A strong system of hereditary chiefs and sub-chiefs still exists, an
ancient and autocratic form of local government which has been called the
single greatest impediment to political and social modernization in Bechuanaland. It is fairly clear that such an imperfect system has been able to retain
its effectiveness and substantial popular support only because there have
been so few foreign or local impulses to generate alternatives. The outside
world -- industrialization or modernized plantation agriculture, the need for
a mobile working population and flexible social hierachy, the examples of
a sophisticated and more egalitarian European civilization -- has impinged so
little on the lives of the people that traditional rule has remained meaningful.
Contact with the outside world for most of Bechuanaland, even today, is
provided by the 20,000 miners who leave on nine-month contracts each year
to work in the Johannesburg mines.

A trip with one of the phuti, the royal family of the great ranching
Ngwato tribe, as they tour their cattle posts with a retinue of trucks and
wagons, underlines the problems which face the establishment of democratic
institutions in Bechuanaland, while exposing the great strength of the traditional
order. The personal retainers who set up the chairs, light the fires, prepare
the evening meal, and then retire among the shadows to wait for a word
from Morena, remain in feudal relationship to their master. He feeds
and clothes them, allocates their cattle posts and agricultural lands, and

supplies them with cattle to increase their herds. They, in turn, serve
him unquestioningly with a personal devotion whose strength derives from
a tangle of hereditary loyalities, awe of rank, pride of association, and
economic dependence. Here is the benevolently despotic ward boss of
American cities, the prototype of the African politician who will, most
likely, succeed the chief; he carries for his constituents' physical well–
being in exchange for their broad and unquestioning mandate.

The system is rigid and status-ridden.[15]The chiefs and their subordinate
headmen jealously preserve the traditional patterns of life for their tribesmen, especially the custom of gathering the people into villages, upon which
depends the administrative effectiveness of the tribal regime. A local
tribesman (or an outsider from another tribe, for all Batswana speak the
same language and have the same basic custom) may go to a chief or a
district headman and ask for a place to build his house. A plot in the
village will be assigned to him without question. He may ask for a cattle
post near water and for a plot to plough; these too, will be granted to him
in the tribal cattle area and the tribal lands area. But he must obey the
chief who, as trustee, representative of the collectivity of the tribe, has
issued him a share of the communally held land. This means that the land-
holder must, in most tribal areas, keep his main domicile exclusively
in the village. He may not plough until he is told, reap until the chief has
so commanded, and then he must return to the village. He may live at his
agricultural plot only during the stated crop season (although most chiefs
now permit conservation measures such as winter ploughing), and he must
certainly not plough at his cattle post or graze other than his ploughing
oxen near the tribal lands area. Only his young sons live at the cattle post,
as herd boys, until they are eleven or twelve and go off to school.

Not until recently have these logical customs, arising from the needs
of a cummunal society living a hard life in an arid land, begun to chafe.
In the sandy kgotla under a green acacia in the middle of the village, the
chief, with his council of elders, still sits and hears appeals and disputes
and gives judgment in accord with tribal law. If the point of customary law
is obscure, assessors are called to give their impressions of the unrecorded
law from equally unrecorded precedents. The district commissioner must
then uphold the chief's order if it is supported by verified custom (tribal
law is not codified, rendering its repeal all but impossible), however
contrary to the laws of economics, agronomy, and common sense the order
may appear.

The chief holds the great sanction of land dispossession for failure
to obey his edicts. Allocation of land gives the tribesmen what could
roughly be described as an inheritable possessory right; many tracts have
been in the same families for years, passing from fathers to sons in accordance

with tribal law, for land once assigned cannot be taken away arbitrarily
without remedy. But appeals to the district commissioner's court take time
and land taken unjustifiably is still taken, often at an awkward season. Of
course, no tenant has the right to alienate the land; its use is strictly
controlled, and money cannot be raised on its security.

The economic leverage of the chief, built on his traditional power,
is the root of his authority today. But the breakdown of this power is implicit
in the 1965 constitution, which isolates chieftaincy from the legislature.
Although a few courageous individuals fight a land case in kgotla from time to
time, these efforts are not really relevant, for they necessarily confront
tribal authority on its own ground. In the future events will merely flow
silently around the chief, subjecting him to forces which he cannot control.
An African national government concerned with centralized power and a
modernized economy will surely pre-empt his right to determine allocation,
use, and alienation of land -- especially in the granting of mineral concessions.

In the meantime, political success will remain with the party which
can best comprehend and exploit the traditional attitudes of its electorate.
Throughout the 1964-1965 political campaign, for example, both major
political parties felt constrained to state that tribalism and chieftainship
must sustain the society until the new political order has time to transfer
a little of the flesh of custom to its constitutional bones. The recent national
election will not prevent the chiefs from remaining important figures in
Bechuanaland's local government for some time to come.

Legislative Council: Responsibility Without Power

There was no alternative, when the Constitutional Committee (composed
of four officials plus the four European and four African members of the
Joint Advisory Council) met, in April and October 1959, to basing the popular,
electoral aspects of Bechuanaland's first constitution on the existing framework
of the tribe. Neither tribal, nor white settler, nor colonial administrative
opinion could have performed the psychological leap to a common electoral
roll; and, more practically, neither the public awareness nor the political
organization existed which would permit local elections to take the form
of general public polling. The committee therefore recommended the establishment of a multi-tribal electoral college -- a new African Council -- to select
African members of the Legislative Council, as this indirect system, "is readily
understood by and acceptable to the vast majority of the African inhabitants
of the Territory, whereas elections to the Legislative Council by any sort
of secret ballot system would be alien to them ... The Tribal Council
system combines the best of the traditional kgotla system with more
democratic processes, and is being developed among the tribes of the
Territory as rapidly as the inherent conservatism of the majority of their

members will permit".[16]

In early 1961, accordingly, in every tribal area each village kgotla chose its representative to the central tribal council of the chief, who also nominated several personal representatives. These eight tribal councils and a handful of electors from non-tribal Kalahari and northern regions then chose, in proportion to the population of their areas, the thirty-two African councillors who, sitting with the eight chiefs as the electoral college of African Council, were to elect the ten African members to the Legislative Council. (Under the presidency of the resident commissioner and with seven official government members who did not participate in electoral proceedings, the African Council was also to advise the resident commissioner on a range of matters affecting Africans only.)

Few of the electors in the tribal councils appreciated that by voting in open kgotla for African Council members, they were not only choosing some of the men who would be participating in lawmaking for the country, but were also performing a ceremonial which cut at the roots of chieftain-ship. The chiefs sensed the threat, however, and made known their views on who should go to the African Council.

Occasional skirmishes occurred between a nervous chief and his tribal council over the worth of a man respected by the tribe -- usually a regional headman of impeccable credentials but considered by the chief to be a radical and a threat to his own authority. In these cases the tribal council invariably triumphed and the man was sent to the African Council, deepening the anxiety of the chief; but this involved no great break with tribal tradition which has often found the chief bowing to the will of his council.

This African Council in turn chose its representatives to the Legisla-tive Council of Bechuanaland. Although neither chiefs nor Europeans had shown enthusiasm for the idea, the Constitutional Committee, stimulated by its government members, had decided that it would be a backward step for the constitution to provide for a Legislative Council with a majority of colonial officials. Its report stated: "It is the firm opinion of the Committee that the proposed Legislative Council should have the same balance of composition as between elected members and official members of the present Joint Advisory Council; that is, that the Council should have an unofficial majority and should be what is usually termed a 'representative council.'"[17]

Thus, the Legislative Council was comprised of thirty-five members: ten government officials from the colonial administration (three ex officio: the chief secretary, the attorney general, and the finance secretary; and

seven nominated members); ten African members chosen by the African
Council electoral college; ten European members elected by the European
community in ten constituencies; one Asian; and four (paired African and
European) nominated members. The resident commissioner presided.
(He was replaced on the council in 1963 by a speaker when he became Her
Majesty's Commissioner with powers approximating those of a governor.)
An Executive Council, meeting every week, served as an advisory cabinet
to the resident commissioner, who presided over its five official (colonial)
and four unofficial (two African, Seretse and Chief Bathoen, and two European)
members.

Of the ten members dispatched by African Council to the opening
session of the Legislative Council, four were traditional leaders whose
victory was the predictable result of their patriarchal function. Of these,
two (Kgosi Bathoen and Kgosi Mokgosi) were the strongest chiefs in Bechuanaland; the remaining six, plus the two nominated African members, who
joined the miscellaneous European assortment of traders and farmers in
the council, were younger men -- progressive farmers and ranchers, school
teachers, and former government servants. Naturally drawn together
by interest and age, frequently by education at a common South African
institution (Fort Hare, Tiger Kloof, Lovedale), the latter represented a
sort of undefined bloc. They were an amiable crowd, characterized more
by good fellowship, however, than by parliamentary contentiousness or
sense of purpose.

The Legislative Council opened formally in June 1961, with a speech
from High Commissioner Sir John Maud on the significance of the new constitution. But the tone for the next two years of legislative activity was established by the parading of the leopard-skin-cloaked police band beneath the Union
Jack and by the presentation of Orders of the British Empire to a sprinkling
of the African and European members. It soon appeared that the Legislative
Council would be only another advisory council. In subsequent sessions
the African members courteously, at times eloquently but invariably uncriti-
cally, supported the government's position on transfer of the capital from
Mafeking to Gaberones and on an assortment of other appropriations, fencing,
arms control, and tax bills.

Familiar with Advisory Council formalism and indifferent to the
potential of their new position, the African Legislative Council members
remained passive and uncontentious. The first eight Hansards, covering
two years of debate in the Legislative Council, exhibit full co-operation
with the government by the African members, who seemed to accept their
position on the council as essentially an extension of customary leadership
in their tribal communities.[18]

On the other hand their constitutional circumstances were not designed to inspire flights of inventiveness. Initiative, the constructive leading of a legislative program, was not possible, for the African members were on a track which parallels, but never intersects with, the lines of governmental control. This situation was, perhaps unavoidably, characteristic of pre-independent Africa. Political activity, either subversive and illegal or encouraged by the colonial administration (as in Bechuanaland), is, until the achievement of self-government, sealed off from the channels of power. Either the politician has no chance at all of constitutional legislative expression (e.g. in a pre-legislative assembly situation) or he comes into an elective assembly, in effect as a member of the opposition. In the latter role he is condemned to frustration, for he is popularly elected and responsible to the council or group of people who elect him; yet he remains distant from the sources of substantive policy. All initiative remains with the executive, the colonial civil servants who hold in their departments the files, the confidential memoranda, the quantitative data which are the prerequisites of constructive action. The department heads, the official members of legislatures alone make the decisions, give legislative drafting instructions, and plan policy -- not through ill will or resentment, but rather from the natural short-circuiting of an apparatus which has, in fact, little functional utility in what is still a colonial administration.

The elected African members may then gradually recognize their alternatives. Either they approve what is usually an unexceptionable government program (perhaps with interested and face-saving commentaries) or, having cemented their party organization in the country, they pool their collective strength into a veto in the name of African solidarity (which will frustrate the program entirely, ultimately precipitating a constitutional crisis). But whichever alternative is taken, it is impossible for them to influence significantly the nature of the program.

In Bechuanaland, the Legislative Council remained a rather ponderous body of undefined attitudes for two years. Although an official minority, the government rarely found it difficult to win a vote.[19] Four times a year members trooped faithfully from all corners of the territory to the neat white High Court building among the hills of Lobatsi, a town on non-tribal land. They rarely remained in session for more than a week, cursorily debating bills that they had not fully studied and approving the legislative program with a minimum of criticism.[20] There was little awareness in the territory, inspite of earnest attempts by the government to publicize proceedings, of what was going on or its significance.[21]

It is not surprising then that Bechuanaland, the country, not the Legislative Council, became the forum for political action. While the Africans in the Legislative Council came slowly to grips with their

predicament, the more conventional African nationalist forces were beginning
to harangue the people. The short political history of the territory is
largely an account of how, during 1962-1963, the African members of the
Legislative Council, who personified the educated elite of the territory,
formally united into a political association in reaction not against the
government, or the Europeans -- in fact, not at all as the response of an
opposition to the minority position inflicted upon it by the Constitution -- but
in response to the harassment of a political party which had sprung up
outside the prepared arena. They suddenly found themselves labeled
dupes and servants of colonialism by a zealous band of non-tribal politicians
who called themselves the Bechuanaland People's Party. Suspecting that
tribal status might be weaker than political organization in a national
election and that the publicity afforded by the Legislative Council was
not an unencumbered blessing, the eight non-chief members turned to
politics, and, under Seretse Khama, the most royal and respected African
in the Legislative Council, they launched a party of their own.

Political Change

When the African members of Legislative Council organized their
Bechuanaland Democratic Party to counter the flamboyant attacks of the
People's Party, they brought about a polarity which reflected faithfully
a split in the attitudes of the rural agricultural people of the tribes and the
detribalized laborers of the towns.

The railway determined the political boundaries. It spans Bechuanaland
from north to south, a distance of about 400 miles, from Ramathlabama, a
few miles north of Mafeking, to Plumtree in Southern Rhodesia. The railway
passes through a number of chief towns: Lobatsi, Gaberones, Mahalapye,
Palapye, and Francistown. But the main tribal towns all lie a few miles
off the line: Kanye, the capital of Chief Bathoen's Bangwaketse; Molepolole,
of the Bakwena, the senior tribe of Bechuanaland; Modhudi, of the Bakgatla who
originated in the Transvaal; Serowe, the seat of Khama and of the great
ranching Bamangwato; and, far off on the edge of Okavango Swamps toward
South-West Africa and Angola, Maun, the capital of the Batawana.

In the villages away from the railway, life still follows an orderly
tribal pattern, the residents moving in a body out to the land in the rainy
season and drifting back after the harvest. In these settlements there
is no electricity, no beer hall (if the chief still proclaims a "dry" area),
and no commercial center other than the few dingy Indian and European
trading stores. Public transport is infrequent and erratic. A man passes
his life peacefully attending the kgotla of his chief, traveling out to his
cattle post, journeying only occasionally into a larger town.

In the urban locations of the railway towns which, in Lobatsi and Francistown, are unregimented versions of the South African stads, the tribal grip is relaxed. There also is the poverty and disillusionment which are still unknown in the subsistence environment of the tribal villages. The detribalized towns are neither many nor particularly populous, for there is insufficient employment. But they do contain a poor shifting African citizenry which, especially in Francistown near the northern border, is a rather debased group of temporarily employed, often idle, squatter-tenants.

Francistown lies in the Tati Concession, a block of territory running along the Rhodesian frontier which was originally held by the British South Africa Company. It is now owned by a company of South African specula-tors who sell plots of land to European and occasionally to African farmers and run the town. They own the beer halls, grant concessions for the hotels and trading stores, control gasoline prices, owned until recently the water and electricity supplies, employ their own police, and collect rentals of one sort or another from the several hundred Europeans and about 25,000 Africans who live in the concession. It was here, predictably, after the promulgation of the first constitution and the election of the tribally approved African members, that the People's Party found its base.

The People's Party

The Bechuanaland People's Party (BPP) was born simultaneously with the publication of the draft of the new constitution in 1960. It promptly proclaimed the goal of immediate independence, issued lapel buttons, and produced a flag and some songs. The novelty of these devices and the impressive arrival of a gift of Land Rovers from Ghana quickly drew support from the railway towns in which it established "Freedom Squares" for holding political rallies. The immediate strength of the BPP was due to the skillful use its three leaders made of their well-developed techniques of rhetoric and of the financial aid (to pay for transport, local organizers, and colorful trappings) which they were able to command from sources in the rest of Africa. From West Africa the party also assembled an independ-ence vocabulary." This it faithfully utilized in its party manifestoes, in its demands for "independence now, " Africanization of the civil service, and a complete return to African (i.e., communal) land tenure (an indirect means of nationalizing the holdings of farmers in the European blocks).

The educated, well-traveled president of the BPP was Kgalemang Motsete (M. A., London University), a Bamangwato tribesman and not a man of property. Because of his lack of wealth and an awkward reputation for failure in practical matters, Motsete tended to be scorned by his cattle-owning tribe who, led traditionally by the wealthiest and most distinguished royal house, the highly capable Khamas, regard wealth and birth as the prerequisites of respect. His support came instead from the detribalized towns.

Philip Matante, the vice-president of the party, had much of the self-confidence necessary to breathe fire into a militant proletarian party. His career was erratic: he had been a member of a tsetse control unit; a store keeper; at one point he served as minister of a church, where he developed an outstanding gift for public oratory. At the Freedom Square meetings Matante was highly effective, using organized cheers and antiphonal, chorused questions and responses which lulled audiences into acquiescence rather than eliciting the intellectual, humorous analyses typical of tribal kgotlas .

The third leader was Motsamai Mpho, not a Motswana, but a Moei from the edges of the Okavango Swamps in the northwestern territory. His membership in the banned African National Congress (ANC) in South Africa had forced him to leave that country for Bechuanaland; he nonetheless retained his South African contacts and a strong interest in South African political refugees. His associates were inclined to be in the far left wing of the ANC, but, as with many of the "Communists" in Southern Africa, it was, and still is, difficult to label him. Mpho's chief value to the party was as a contact with left wing elements which gave him access to their techniques of organization and the funds they provided militants in southern Africa. It was his sophisticated political sense, developed from contact with South African nationalists, which stimulated a series of boycotts of local traders' stores. [22]

These devices enjoyed a degree of success, insofar as they managed to worry the government and some traders. The BPP's ability to mobilize the population into specific action appeared to stem from the conventional expediency of wrapping up a more general political attitude--anti-European, anti-chief--in an ardent local issue. With the dismissal of an African employee, or an altercation between an African and a European, the BPP often arrived to provide moral support. This infusion of team spirit--cheerleading at political meetings, solidarity gestures via boycotts, and zealous use of African nationalist vocabulary against Europeans--appealed to the discouraged and idle in the railway towns and, interestingly, to government clerks who despaired of Africanization.

A number of supporters of the BPP were those who hoped to gain by the extravagant demands of the party, especially for land nationalization. For the unemployed of the towns, even in underemployed Bechunaland, are often there because they were idle farmers or trouble-making tribal members. But this element of BPP support was overemphasized by the government, which feared the party's left wing connections; several

regional organizers were intelligent men, earnestly irritated by the government's dilatoriness in moving Batswana into the upper ranks of the civil
service, integrating schools, and improving working conditions at the
abattoir in Lobatsi and in the territory's two small mines.

By the end of its first year, the enthusiastic meetings held by the
BPP suggested that it dominated the towns. Its leaders proclaimed a membership of some 20,000 (some 4,000 of whom, reportedly, paid dues). But
the surge atrophied; when the BPP went into the country villages with jeeps
and loudspeakers, it alienated local leaders (the Bamangwato tribe banned
BPP meetings, yielding only to government pressure to remove the
the ban) and alarmed tribal members.

The party's failure in tribal areas was predictable. The BPP used
techniques which are effective in urban communities where there is an
explosive mass of discontent. In these situations the local organizers
were successful in gaining members. Attacking the domination of chiefs
and Europeans is useless, however, when there is no feeling of domination;
and it is positively distasteful when an institution is cherished, as is
chieftainship among a large portion of the electorate who dwell away from
the railway. The result was a party which, below the competent district
organizers and their urban followers, had a fluctuating and irresolute
membership.

The party's most obvious flaw was its lack of a figurehead who could
command broad-based emotional support. None of the BPP executive were
able, despite various attempts at apotheosis, to generate awe or strong
personal affection. Among the Batswana, the great majority of whom are
uneducated and are confused about election issues, the average voter,
predictably, turns to a traditionally sanctioned leader to whom he feels
a personal loyalty -- just as he did in the 1961 elections to the African Council.
Even so, it would be a mistake to conclude that the rural voter would cast
a blind, slavish ballot for his headman. Education is widely respected in
Bechuanaland, by the young almost to the point of fanaticism, and the
poor education of the chiefs causes increasing criticism. But a politician
who, himself devoid of tribal status, attacks a headman or chief, is taking
a grave risk. The BPP in fact made this mistake and had to retreat from
support of a liquidation of tribal government policy to a house of chiefs
policy, urging the retention of status but the relinquishment of active
authority.

These inner weaknesses of the party pale in dramatic interest,
however, beside the spectacular internal feuds which shook the party,
resulting toward the end of 1962 in an open rupture. To some extent the
break appears to have been the result of a clash of personal views between
the patriotic but more moderate wing represented by Motsete and Matante,

and the activist, international left wing represented by Mpho. The nature
of the factions supplied the antagonists with the labels of anti- and pro-
Communism. A number of colorful skirmishes occurred: duels were
held with loudspeakers, leaders were kidnapped, and thrown over the
border and in law suits, both sides appealed, ironically, to British justice
for custody of the Ghanaian Land Rovers. Mpho, the party's pan-African
contact man, reportedly issued instructions to his financial sources in
Ghana and Tanganyika that no more funds should be issued until party
leadership was settled; he set himself up as the only legitimate officer of
the party. Journeys and appeals to aiding countries were made by both
wings of the party, but the Ghanaians and the Dar-es-Salaam-based agencies
showed little inclination to take sides and were said to have suspended support
to all factions of the BPP.

For a time the Motsete-Matante wing (which won the Land Rovers)
retained a certain vigor, while Mpho and his supporters consoled themselves
by starting an unsuccessful set of boycotts against local traders and engaging
in the South African refugee trade. Both factions were represented at the
constitutional discussions in late 1963, billed as the "Mpho BPP" and the
"Motsete-Matante BPP." The performances of both wings at these discussions
left their public statures badly diminished and resulted in less activity until
early 1964, when a further upheaval resulted in yet another split, this time
between Motsete and Matante.

By April 1964, it appeared that the more conservative, Bechuanaland-
oriented Motsete, the BPP founder, had fallen into a limbo between his
left wing factions and the Democratic Party. Matante, following a trip to
Moscow and north and West Africa, held forth in his narrow base, Francistown, and, mysteriously opulent, renewed operations, using three new
vehicles. Mpho, reportedly supported by Peking, launched a far left-wing
Bechuanaland Independence Party. Despite the confusion, by 1964 it was
clear that some political entity--whether splinter parties, possibly reflecting Moscow-Peking competition, or a single radical internationalist party--
would represent the left-of-center, strongly ideological, outspokenly anti-white
point of view. The argument that anything done by a colonial power is
tainted by its undemocratic, European quality, and therefore is voidable,
was still finding adherents in the towns of Bechuanaland as it has among
city dwelling laborers in other parts of Africa. As long as exponents of
the dogma remained content to use constitutional means to gain support,
however, the BPP never appeared to have a chance with the electorate of
the tribal regions.

But the BPP was responsible for awakening even the backward areas
of the territory to nationalism. Even the Democratic Party acknowledges
that the tumultuous behavior of the leaders and the outside support the
BPP attracted, coupled with the 1961 constituion, encouraged the

institutionalization of politics in Bechuanaland.

Seretse and the Democratic Party

In the African Council, the conflicting attitudes of eight hereditary and thirty-two popularly elected members perpetuated the atmosphere of the old African Advisory Council. On the part of the chiefs, there continued a vague retrenching and a sensitivity on tribal matters (especially on "forced labor," the custom of having certain age groups provide free services to the tribe, and on matimela cattle, the placing of all stray, unclaimed cattle in the kraal of the chief--ostensibly for charitable purposes).[23] On the part of the more liberal African commoners, there appeared an increasing concern with Bechuanaland's awkward dependency on South Africa, and less concern with tribes and tribal governments. Partly, the division was one of age, for the chiefs and their advisers were older men; partly, it was one of intellectual ability and training, for the young men had greater learning and the confidence of fresh ideas.

These attitudes, which were reflected less sharply in Legislative Council debates and spurred on by the Freedom Square activities of the BPP, resulted in the union which became the Bechuanaland Democratic Party (BDP). Eight of the fourteen original BDP organizers were members of the Legislative Council-all younger men of professional or traditional status in their respective tribes men of professional or traditional status in their respective tribes (several were school teachers). This very homogeneity for a time made it difficult to say whether the Democratic Party was a political party or only a loose band of congenial associates-- whether it was a club or a purposeful union whose members were willing to desert their professions and farms to become politicians.

The reluctance of the BDP founders to engage in politics, and their related irritation with the upstart People's Party, appears in the history of the party as described in the party newspaper by the BDP secretary, Quett Masire:

In November, 1961, at Mr. Seretse Khama's invitation a number of us met at Lobatsi. The subject was "the Political Future of Bechuanaland." It was a pleasant surprise to find that we were all aware of the need for a responsible National Political Party. We agreed with one accord upon the formation of such a party. We thought, and time has proved us right, that it would be better to form a new party than try to reform the two parties then in existence, which in our opinion were irresponsible.

One of these parties [the Federal Party] was too indolent.
It had been in existence for years but had never held meetings outside the Ngwato Tribal Territory. Even in the
Ngwato Tribal Territory it had held very few meetings, if
any at all. Worse still though, it started as a middle of
the road, if not a moderate left wing party, it had suddenly
become an extreme right wing party. This change of
policy coincided with its leader becoming a sub-chief.

The other party [the People's Party] had been in
existence for nearly a year when ours was formed. From
the very beginning it had made some grossly irresponsible
statements and was threatening to take some irresponsible
actions such as uncalled-for boycotts and strikes merely
to test its strength and demonstrate the power it had.
It was growing popular on the strength of its irresponsible
statements. We realised that it would be difficult to
reform this party from within as: (a) we were not prepared
to devote our time and energy to fight for leadership; and
(b) it was obvious that due to conflicting policies of its
leaders the party would break into three parts. Time
will prove us right; so far it has split in twain.

In contrast to these attitudes, we felt that a political
party for Bechuanaland should not be the outcome of a
mere academic exercise nor should it be a poor imitation
of a certain party elsewhere: But that Bechuanaland with
her problems peculiar to herself needed a Bechuanaland
Party, formed for the sole purpose of taking care of
Bechuanaland's problems, and we decided to form such
a party.

The tribal administrations were less interested in political nuances.

It was agreed that the first meeting should be held on the
27th of January, 1962, at Modhudi [capital of the Bkgatla
Tribe]. Mr. Maribe [Treasurer and himself a Mokgatla]
was asked to ask the Chief there for permission and the
Secretary was accordingly instructed also to write and ask
the Chief for permission. On the 27th people who were
invited to attend turned up from all over Bechuanaland.
Maribe and Masire carried out the instructions but on
the day of the meeting the Chief turned us away and told
us that he had not been properly informed of the meeting.
Thereupon we applied by phone to the District Commis-

sioner, Gabarones [a non-tribal town]... who kindly granted
us permission. We moved by lorry and car-loads to Gaberones
and met under a big "MORULA" tree between the camp and
the station north of the road.[24]

Speeches by Seretse Khama and Quett Masire opened the meeting, the
party constitution was adopted, party elections held, and the new members
quietly returned to their villages.

Seretse Khama, the chairman, had received far more votes than any
other member dispatched by the African Council to the Legislative Council;
since 1961 he had worked closely with the colonial administration as one
of the two African members of the Executive Council. He is the grandson
of Khama III and heir to the chieftainship of the Bamangwato, the largest
and richest of the Batswana tribes. He was educated in South Africa and
then at Oxford. While in England Seretse married an Englishwoman and
spent a six-year exile in London until the Bamangwato tribe, the Bechuanaland
government, and the Colonial Office (which had feared the reaction of the
South African government to the interracial marriage) were pacified by
the passage of time. Upon agreeing to reject all claim to the chieftainship,
Seretse returned in 1956 to Serowe, the tribal capital, whence, ironically,
he was quickly summoned by the Bechuanaland government to participate
in territorial affairs.[25]

Seretse's dignified conduct during this period won him admiration
and sympathy, strengthened by a common resentment against the government's action extending far beyond his own tribe. Upon this general
popularity and the strong personal devotion of the Bamangwato (who,
oblivious to his legal repudiation of the chieftainship, continue to regard
him as kgosi, chief), the Democratic Party first based itself. Yet Seretse's
very dominance -- his natural leadership qualities, his education and the
sophistication which commanded the regard of Europeans and government
officials as well as tribesmen -- raised the question of whether the party
might not be still-born. For Seretse personified the dilemma of the BDP;
liberal by inclination but conservative by status, it was difficult for BDP's
members to be ardently partisan. Already dispatched to Legislative Council
by wide tribal acclaim, already respected and relatively wealthy, Seretse
and his associates appeared to possess everything that a politicain or a
private citizen could desire. Strong party discipline, frequent meetings,
ostentatious displays of personal beliefs, appeals for public loyalty are
all alien to the aristocratic tribal tradition.

In its early days, the party leadership seemed inspired by little more
than vague sentiments in favor of some future, undefined form of self-
government and the conviction that it was their duty and due to be re-elected

to the next Legislative Council. The prevailing attitude at meetings in
tribal areas was characterized by an elderly resident of a remote village
in the Kalahari. He had watched the arrival one day of the bright green
Chevrolet trucks, emblazoned "Bechuanaland Democratic Party, " and had
heard the reasoned educational talk conventionally given by the party leaders
in village kgotlas. He listened courteously to the questions which followed
Seretse's speech, and then raised his hand to ask: "Is this Seretse, the
son of Khama?" He was assured that this was so. "Why then do you bother
us, " he continued uncertainly, "Is this not our Moses?"

On the railway line the response was less matter-of-fact. BPP
hecklers asked embarrassing questions. What about chieftainship; where
exactly did the BDP stand on that issue, they asked (knowing the difficulty
Seretse was experiencing in restraining his royal tribal uncles from
claiming positions on the party executive and destroying forever its liberal
label)? Did Seretse want to be restored to the chieftainship? What was the
BDP position on independence? On Europeans? Could Seretse still be a
Motswana despite his marriage, his education, and his European associations?
Finally, as the party presently held a number of Legislative Council seats,
why did it not act immediately instead of waiting until the next election?

At these meetings the party leaders delivered their moderate statements of principle, either uninterested in local issues or not deigning to
exploit them. They remained statesmanlike rather than political, lecturing
listeners on the meaning and responsibility of self-government and nationhood
before making general proposals of education for all, overseas scholarships
for those with proven ability, equal opportunity with Europeans in government
service, and one-man-one-vote at the next election to return an African
majority to Legislative Council. But BDP members of the Legislative Council
refused to exploit in the assembly itself the propaganda potential of their
position. Seretse's motion[26]to appoint the Select Committee on Racial
Discrimination to investigate and remove all discriminatory provisions
from the laws of Bechuanaland was eloquent, but apparently, too detached
and moderate to attract attention, and the BDP gained little political advantage
from the establishment of the committee and its ensuing report.[27]

Once again, however, the colonial government broke the calm. In
mid-1963, the British Colonial Secretary issued a public directive in London
that the resident commissioner should begin to consider the next constitutional step for Bechuanaland. From the time of this announcement the
solidarity and self-consciousness of the BDP began to grow. The party
secretary, Quett Masire, following brief visits to London and several
African countries in May 1963, began to warn the party executive that much
of the next election would be fought in the forthcoming discussions. These
conversations between the political parties, representatives of the chiefs,
the European community, and government officials would determine the

nature of the constitution, the electoral roll or rolls, the weight to be accorded rural and urban areas in the districting of electoral seats, and the allocation of seats to the chiefs and to Europeans, if such there would be. More importantly, they would define the content of the self-government likely to be given Bechuanaland. Masire pointed out that failure to establish a majority position by the first election would mean risking permanent loss of the support of independent Africa, which was already tending to gravitate toward radical freedom fighters with continental associations rather than toward the Bechuanaland-oriented BDP.

As part of his program to arouse the country, and despite the indifference of his own party executive, Masire founded the party newspaper, Therisanyo Consulation. He also organized a highly successful meeting of the executive in Francistown. Accompanied by a roasting oxen and speeches by Seretse, it drew district organizers even from the desert villages and aroused enough local interest to eclipse a BPP meeting in its own stronghold.

Masire had been the real moving spirit of the party from its birth, although he entered politics unwillingly, acquiescing to Seretse's request for his assistance. Until he was 14, he had spent most of the year at his father's cattle post far off in the bush. At that time he started school and in eight years attained university standard, before the death of his parents denied him college and forced him to assume the duties of head of the family. He became a schoolmaster at Kanye and one of the most modern, large scale farmers in Bechuanaland. Masire's ability was quickly acknowledged even by his tradition-bound tribe, and, although unfavored by his autocratic chief, Bathoen of the Bangwaketse, he was elected by a strong majority to African Council, then Legislative Council. In the Legislative Council his acute analyses and humorous barbs at chieftainship, respectably clothed a basic support for what he felt was necessary government legislation.[28]His outspokenness there, while making him the intellectual leader of the younger African members, also brought him into contact with the government-favored, sophisticated Seretse Khama.

Upon the foundation of the Democratic Party, Masire became the confidant and alter ego of Sertse, whose failing health and tempermental uncompetitiveness make him a sporadic politician. Moving from village to village, Masire prepared meetings, exhorted members, and explained the periodic failure of his leader to materialize; in time, it became clear that Seretse was leaving a great deal of practical formulation of policy and party organization to his secretary, while Seretse himself performed necessary ceremonial functions in meetings and in neighboring African states. For example, Masire strongly favored making the party multi-racial; the BDP's handful of influential European members, including a member of the Executive Council (now a minister) and a trader who is the party treasurer and who successfully stood for election in March 1965, reflects his stated wish to set an example for the Republic of South Africa.

The activist wing of the Democratic Party, however, personified by Moutlakgola Nwako, worried about the restraint imposed upon party mobility by Seretse's health. Nwako (treasurer of the isolated Moeng secondary school) provided the party with its appendage on the left; he attacked chieftain-ship and was inclined to dismiss the traditional support which the party sedulously cultivated. But he conceded that without Seretse's tribal prestige and fame, the BDP would not easily have gained dominance in Bechuanaland.

In March 1964, Seretse fell seriously ill, and came so close to death that the question of Masire's succession to the party leadership was seriously raised for the first time. His recovery shelved the problem, but Seretse for a time had to become a figurehead, able to engage only in limited campaigning. The stage-managing of his role as party oracle by the reading of his speeches and the tape recording of messages became a fundamental BDP weapon.

Seretse's activity in the 1963 constitutional discussions and his handful of notable addresses left his Democratic Party a valuable legacy in international African politics as well as at home. In September 1963, Prime Minister Verwoerd of South Africa had pointed out to the High Commission Territories (including Bechuanaland) the benefits of association with his republic. Speaking at a time when a number of political refugees were seeking asylum in Bechuanaland, Verwoerd referred to "the delicate question of the future relationship between the Republic and the High Commission Territories". South Africa wanted "good, prosperous and trustworthy neighbors". Therefore, he suggested, "if South Africa were to be, or to become, the guardian, the protector or the helper of these adjacent Territories, instead of the United Kingdom, we could lead them far better and much more quickly to independence and economic prosperity than Great Britain can do, " within the framework of their "natural native democracy. "[29]

Seretse led the African attack on a motion which was introduced in Legislative Council to consider the South African proposal, and caused its peremptory withdrawal. He was equally adamant when South African farmers of the Tati and Tuli blocks advocated cession of their areas to South Africa. "We shall not allow the fragmentation of Bechuanaland, " he stated. "We shall not allow any part of it to be excluded from the whole and thus create a Congo situation. Those who are apprehensive of the future solely on the grounds that Bechuanaland will have an African Government soon, can be assured that the Bechuanaland Democratic Party welcomes anybody who wishes to make this country his home and is prepared to work for its social, economic and political advancement ... Those who feel that they are too dedicated to racial prejudice to want to live here know where to go; but they will not be allowed to take with them any part of Bechuanaland. "[30]

1963 Constitutional Discussions

Joint constitutional consultations between the Queen's commissioner and the principal political parties -- the BDP and both wings of the BPP -- and representatives of the chiefs and Europeans were held during the latter part of 1963. A nationalistic fillip was given the final October and November discussions by the background of Verwoerd's overtures and intense South African irritation over Bechuanaland's accommodation of political refugees. At the November Legislative Council, the Queen's commissioner, Sir Peter Fawcus "reaffirmed that the protectorate would continue to give shelter to refugees arriving from South Africa. He counselled the Legislative Council that the territory must pursue a policy of 'caution but not timidity' toward those 'neighboring countries who are so much stronger than ourselves but with whom we must trade to live.'"[31] Officials privately stated that this would mean attempting to expedite refugees' departures to prevent a buildup of dissidents within the borders of Bechuanaland.

Agreement on the new constitution was obtained swiftly and harmoniously. Sir Peter Fawcus had accumulated a powerful store of personal good will in all communities through the sympathetic but impartial strength of his administration. The trust reposed in him by both Africans and Europeans enabled him to keep the discussions secret. This remarkable self-restraint, faithfully observed by all parties, to eschew the press and public propaganda, prevented escalation of demands and averted the need for the usual pre-independence London conference.

Two predictably voluble factions -- the BPP and the chiefs -- were silenced unexpectedly. The People's Party representatives had arrived with prepared addresses and bands of followers to greet a planned protest walkout. It was later reported that the BPP leaders were staggered by the immediate agreement by all parties, including Europeans and the colonial government, to universal adult suffrage. Having based their bargaining campaign on a "one-man-one-vote" slogan, they never fully recovered from the sudden deprivation of their issue and were content to plead the secrecy of the proceedings to keep their embarrassment to themselves. Following agreement on the constitution they were able to share the triumph publicly by stating (correctly) that their political activities had dictated this concession on the franchise.

The chiefs, on the other hand, were reconciled to the provision that they should not stand for elected office by the establishment of a house of chiefs, a body which would consider for thirty days any bill dealing with tribal office and tribal law and administration, and which would be empowered to submit resolutions to the designated minister on these subjects. After the discussions, the chiefs gradually awakened to the insubstantiality of

their "House of Lords" powers and for a time agitated for renegotiation.
Basic changes, however, were doomed from the start, for all parties,
including the colonial government, feared active political participation
on the part of the chiefs. Their victory would place a dead hand on national
government, but their defeat would cancel much of their tribal authority,
upon which local government would still largely depend.

    With general agreement between the colonial administration and the
Democratic Party (who dominated the discussions for the Africans), the
draft constitution which emerged from the discussions left only a national
election in the way of Bechuanaland's internal self-government on a Westminster
model. A thirty-five or thirty-six seat–Legislative Assembly would have
four of its number specially elected by the assembly itself (i.e., the majority
party), it being intended that some of these seats should be filled by competent
Europeans. The thirty-two (reduced to thirty-one by the Delimitation
Commission) elected members were to be chosen by a common electoral
roll from thirty-two single-member constituencies. A prime minister selected
by the Queen's commissioner would be "the Member of the Legislative
Assembly who appeared to him most likely to command the support of the
majority of the Members of that Assembly." With the advice of the prime
minister, the commissioner would then choose a cabinet (upon which he
would also sit) to replace the Executive Council. This cabinet would include
a deputy prime minister, up to five other ministers drawn from the legislature, and an ex officio minister of finance.

    The final delineation of the duties and powers of the executive -- the manner
in which authority is divided between the appointed British Queen's Commissioner and the elected prime minister -- reflects, in effect, the realistic consent
of Seretse and Masire that foreign affairs is the area in which Bechuanaland
lies most sharply exposed in southern Africa. For, reserved to Her Majesty's
Commissioner are "(a) external affairs and defence (to the extent that
such matters may be dealt with by the Government of Bechuanaland);
(b) internal security (including the organization, use and operational control
of the Police); (c) the making of appointments ... to offices in the Public
Service."

    "External affairs" is of course nearly a misnomer. Bechuanaland
depends upon a foreign country, South Africa, for its survival. Over
90 per cent of Bechuanaland's produce is either marketed via the heavily
subsidized South African marketing boards or passes through a South
African port; Bechuanaland receives valuable income pursuant to the 1910
Customs Agreement (some 1/4 of 1 per cent of South Africa's custom and
excise revenue); and it relies on South African communications, transport,
markets for its labor, and its access by air and sea to the outside world.
Virtually every important Bechuanaland decision thus must be a foreign
policy decision. In recognition of this fact, the draft constitution stated

that "Her Majesty's Commissioner should be required to keep the cabinet fully informed on matters of external affairs and defence and to obtain the advice of the Cabinet in the exercise of his special responsibilities in this respect."

There are, therefore, several individuals concerned with Bechuanaland's external affairs: the prime minister, the Queen's Commissioner, the Colonial Secretary, and the British ambassador to South Africa who, until 1964, was also the High Commissioner for Basutoland, Bechuanaland, and Swaziland. It is predictable that, ill-defined as the subject is, the substance of Bechuana-land's self-government will depend to a considerable extent upon the strength of personality of these figures.

A perennial question which this group will have to accommodate is the destiny of refugees who leave South Africa to seek education, military training, or adventure via the Bechuanaland escape route. Intensely security-conscious, South Africa has protested the unco-operativeness of Bechuana-land's authorities, and there have been incidents (the mysterious burning of an East African Airways DC-3 in Francistown, the "kidnapping" of a South-West African refugee, Abrahams, inside Bechuanaland, and his subsequent release) which periodically disrupt the flow of refugee traffic.

The problem of relations with South Africa continues to hang over the heads of the new African government in 1965 just as it did over the colonial administration. A black government cannot ingratiate itself too obviously with South Africa, whose apartheid policies are eliciting boycotts, UN resolutions, and aid for "freedom fighters"; yet, a responsible Bechuanaland government, acutely aware of the example of the Congo, would recognize its common interest with South Africa in maintaining an internally stable Bechuanaland. In the six months following the constitu-tional discussions there was general acceptance that Seretse's Democratic Party would form the first government. Many Africans and Europeans questioned, however, whether a BDP government would be faced by an opposition, already assisted by rabidly anti-South African states, which concerned itself with Batswana affairs and operated within the constitutional framework. African civil servants stated their fear of a "Zanzibar take-over." It was clear that the 1965 constitution would take effect in an environ-ment of precarious stability and that Bechuanaland would have to remain in important ways -- perhaps even in independence -- a "protectorate" of the United Kingdom.

The Elections and After

The great international South African problem remained a minor issue, however, in what became an unequal campaign between the comparatively

anonymous followers of Matante, Mpho, and a fading Motset, and the
noted and respected personalities who led the Democratic Party. The final
three months leading up to the elections may be passed over quickly.
BDP efficiency increased greatly, and meetings were held regularly in
even the smallest villages. Printed matter was widely distributed, and
Therisanyo blossomed into an acid political commentator on the Peoples
Party and a guide for voters (it published an elaborate issue in January
with pictures and a complete list of the BDP candidates, who contested
every constituency, and an exhortation to voters to "please sleep in the
place you will be voting in the following day (March 1)."

An account of voting day comes from a young officer of the Colonial
Service, a presiding officer at the polls of one of the village constituencies.

> I left home ... at 5 am and drove along a road that
> was a river of people walking excitedly to their polling
> stations. In the half-light at sunrise it was a wonderful
> sight. Then at the Sebele Primary School at Molepolole
> the day began. There were thousands of people sitting
> on the hilltop on which the school perches when I opened
> up the polling station at 6:30 am. They poured in all
> morning to ballot, quiet orderly patient queues of
> people standing in the boiling sun ... But by 9:00 am
> it was obviously Domkrag -- all the way -- you could tell
> from the discarded discs.[32] What so impressed one
> was the determination of the people to vote and to vote
> for the BDP. There were old women who had walked
> 45 miles from their family lands; literally scores of
> blind people; cripples who had climbed the rocky hill
> on their hands; and above all women. The secrecy
> of balloting, about which so much fuss was made, was
> totally disregarded. Many voters collected their
> three discs, threw the yellow and green over their
> shoulders and with 'Domkrag' on their lips popped
> the red into the ballot envelop. By 2:00 pm I
> estimated that 75 percent of the 2500 voters
> registered at my polling station had voted. When we
> closed at 7 pm well over 80 per cent had cast their
> ballots. Some stations recorded polls in the high
> 90's ... No single BDP candidate even lost his
> deposit.

The details of Seretse's victory (he won his seat by 5,909 to 92)
have been described. Of the chief BPP leaders, Matante alone gained an assembly seat (by 4,415 to 1,299 in Francistown); Motsete polled only 377 of
the 5,801 votes cast in his Lobatsi constituency. Mpho, whose Independence
Party failed to win a seat (and 19 or 25 of whose candidates forfeited their
deposits with less than 10 per cent of the votes cast) lost a close race in

his own tribal stronghold by 1,929 to 1,666.[33]

Such a mandate brings responsibility not only to Bechuanaland but to the leaders of Black Africa who, despite general sympathy with her plight, have at times indicated their desire for a Bechuanaland base against South Africa. The South African issue, however, for all its portentousness in world councils and the Organization of African Unity, stirs none of the emotion in the <u>kgotlas</u> of the territory that is aroused by the price of cattle, the allocation and tenure of land, and education of the youth. The Democratic Party long lamented that the resolutions of the United Nations politically oriented against South Africa, are little concerned with the troubles of the three territories:[34] "What help is UNO and her member states offering us -- resolutions or economic aid."[35]

The internal problems are staggering enough: there are only three secondary schools in all Bechuanaland, and in higher education only the recently secularized Roma College for Bechuanaland, Basutoland, and Swaziland (in Basutoland). Only a handful of students attend universities abroad, and outside of the Education Ministry there is the barest handful of senior African civil servants. A minimum of funds are available for economic development, and they come mostly from the United Kingdom. These facts will surely produce explicit demands upon politicians.

And just as the personalities and tribal acceptability of the Democratic Party gained them their seats in the new Legislative Assembly, so these personalities will be held accountable for procuring the benefits of education and economic assistance for their constituents. Inevitably, they will have to face the classic African political dilemma: the few able politicians who have become ministers will find it necessary both to run their departments and sustain their party -- the foundation of their position in the country.

But the shock of self-government -- ministers responsible to a popularly elected Legislative Assembly only five years after the unheeding Batswana received their first cautious national constitution -- must be great. It may be sufficiently dislocating to cause the politicians to adopt the one-party system, the political device which other African countries have employed to compensate for the institutional weakness of a constitution based upon the traditions of a distant and dissimilar nation. Seretse's overwhelming victory already puts Bechuanaland far along that road.

The period of adjustment may, in any event, recall to mind the fact that twentieth-century Westminster democracy was not born in its present form, but evolved from authoritarian origins in the confused days of the Cromwellian dictatorship. But as Seretse and Masire gently explained the coming change to dubious tribesmen in the village <u>kgotlas</u>: the guinea fowl sees the hawk, and the sun, and the jackal and would like to remain in the nest. But a time comes when that is no longer possible and it must enter the veld by itself.

Footnotes

Bechuanaland became the independent republic of Botswana on September 30, 1966. On October 4, 1966, Basutoland became the independent republic of Lesotho.

1. "Batswana" rather than "Bechuana" is the preferred usage; the single tribesman is a "Motswana." 1964 Census and Delimitation Commission.

2. Bakgatla, Bakwena, Bamalete, Bamangwato, Bangwaketse, Barolong, Batawana, Batlokwa.

3. Basutoland, Bechuanaland Protectorate & Swaziland. Report of an Economic Survey Mission (London, 1960), 169. Based on last complete census, 1954.

4. Bechuanaland Development Plan, 1963-1968 (1963), 15.

5. Annual rainfall averages twenty-one inches in the east and eighteen inches in the desert; an average of less than one inch falls throughout the five-month May-October period. Economic Survey Mission Report, 195.

6. Cattle exports rose from 70,000 carcasses in 1954 to 130,000 in 1963; over 90 per cent of these are African produced beasts. When in 1959 overseas markets became available, sales mounted quickly, suggesting perhaps that inadequate markets, rather than traditional attitudes of producers, had hindered sales. Africans supplying direct (not via traders) to the abattoir at Lobatsi rose from 12 in 1954 to 1,500 in 1963. Bechuanaland Development Plan, 15. The abattoir was opened by the U.K. Colonial Development Corporation.

7. The Batswana regard for the courteous, leisurely proceedings of their traditional village and area kgotlas, may explain why the history of the protectorate abounds with councils. Prior to 1920 all Bechuanaland legislation was proclaimed by the High Commissioner of Basutoland, Bechuanaland, and Swaziland, and was prepared in consultation with the chiefs, elders, experts, and any others deemed appropriate as advisers. That year two councils, nominated by the colonial administration, were formed to assist in the process of consultation: the African Advisory Council and the European Advisory Council, each advising the resident commissioner of Bechuanaland on matters concerning its community. Their vague, and, for the African Council, largely symbolic, functions were focused somewhat when, after World War II, the Joint Advisory Council was established, consisting of four government officials, the four members of the European Advisory Council, and four African members chosen by the African Advisory Council from its number. Although the European and

African councils continued to function, the Joint Council was the principal body representing the people of the territory from 1950 until the introduction of the 1961 constitution.

When the formation of the Joint Advisory Council was debated in the African Advisory Council, some speakers stated their preference for a legislative council, but it was not until April 1958, that any formal motion on the subject was introduced, and that was in the Joint Advisory Council, which passed the following resolution: "That in the opinion of this Council the time has come when a Legislative Council should be formed and empowered to assist in the Government of the Territory." More bluntly, the African Advisory Council resolved a month later, "that the time is long overdue for the development of a Legislative Council for the Bechuanaland Protectorate." See The Constitution of the Bechuanaland Protectorate (1961), an account prepared by the Information Branch of the Bechuanaland Protectorate Government, 1962, 8.

8. See Bechuanaland Protectorate Constitutional Discussion, 1963, published by command of His Excellency Her Majesty's Commissioner for the Bechuanaland Protectorate, November 1963.

9. An African association called the Federal Party had existed in name for several years prior to 1961, but faded when its leader, Letile Raditlade, became headman at Mahalapye.

10. In late 1962 and early 1963 a few whites in Lobatsi tried to draw a handful of chiefs and headmen into their new Liberal Party; the party seems to exist today in name only.

11. European farming areas, 2 to 3 per cent of the total area, are blocks of farms along the periphery of the territory: the Tati Concession and Tuli Block along the eastern border (nineteenth-century concessions granted by the chiefs to the British South Africa Company); the Molopo farming area along the Cape Province border (non-tribal Crown lands sold to settlers in the past six years to supplement territorial revenue and provide funds for agricultural loans); and the Ghanzi Farms (a vague area near South-Western Africa in the middle of the Kalahari Desert procured by Rhodes for a mixed group of European settlers as a buffer between German West Africa and the British South Africa Company interests in Rhodesia).

12. The writer is indebted to Anthony Sillery, The Bechuanaland Protectorate (Oxford, 1952), for historical material on chieftancy in Bechuanaland. See also M. Hodson and W. Ballinger, Bechuanaland Protectorate (Johannesburg, 1931).

13. Quoted in Sillery, Bechuanaland, 46.

14. An annual "native" tax of 25s. paid by each male African was increased to 40s. in 1958 It is supplemented by a graded tax, payable by each individual owning more than ten head of stock. The tax is administered by the treasuries of the eight tribes. Economic Survey Mission Report, 44. This system, which distinguishes between African and non-African, will presumably be altered in self-government.

Aid for capital development began in 1945 under the Colonial Development and Welfare Act; but until 1956, budgetary expenditures and revenues were, with the exception of certain inter-colonial loans, roughly equal, thanks to minimal expenditures and to South African customs and excise returns to Bechuanaland. Since 1956-1957, a deficit has occurred annually, the budget being balanced by grants-in-aid from the British treasury. Economic Survey Mission Report, 41-43.

15. The following paragraphs are the product of two years' personal conversations and observations. Isaac Schapera's Handbook of Tswana Law and Custom (Oxford, 1933) is the basic professional text on the subject.

16. Paragraph 29 of the Report of the Constitutional Committee, quoted in The Constitution of the Bechuanaland Protectorate, 14.

17. Paragraph 10 of the Report quoted in ibid., 11

18. Official Reports of Debates of the Legislative Council, nos. 1-8, 1961-1962.

19. In mid-1963, dissatisfaction with the prices and marketing practices of the Lobatsi abattoir caused the African members to table a motion censuring the government's conduct of the meat industry. Its carriage produced the government's first defeat on an issue. Official Reports of Debates of the Legislative Council.

20. The eight meetings of the first two sessions of the Legislative Council averaged three to four days. (See Reports of Debates, 1-8)

21. A supply of the pamphlet Legco Day by Day is circulated to all district commissioners while the council is in session.

22. Organized picketing and boycotts were first used successfully after an African employee was discharged by a trader in Lobatsi in 1962.

23. For a description of "regimental labor" and Matimela customs, see Schapera, Handbook, 110 ff. and 220 ff.

24. Therisanyo/Consultation, Oct. 1963, 6 ff.

25. These sensational events are related in a biography of Seretse's uncle, who was the regent of the Bamangwato during Seretse's minority. Mary Benson, Tschekedi Khama (London, 1960), 173-272.

26. Reports of Debates, 6:118, July 26, 1962.

27. "Legislative Council Report of the Select Committee on Racial Discrimination (Mafeking, 1963).

28. See, for example, Masire's speeches in debates on localization of the Public Service, Reports of Debates, 4:33; on the Export Duty Bill, ibid., 3:131; on the Cooperative Societies Bill, ibid., 7:54.

29. Fact Paper 107, published in conjunction with South African Digest by the Department of Information, Pretoria (September 1963), 12-14.

30. Therisango/Consultation, Oct. 1963, 7.

31. Africa Report, Nov. 1963, 23.

32. The BDP symbol and Motto Domkrag means -- with deliberate irony, in Afrikaans -- wagon jack; the BDP proposed to lift up the country.

33. Bechuanaland Democratic Party Newsletter, I, no. 4, March 3, 1965.

34. On November 4, 1964, the United Nations Committee of Twenty-four did request "the Secretary-General to intensify, in cooperation with the specialized agencies, programmes of economic, technical and financial assistance to these Territories." He was, however, also asked "to undertake a study as to the ways and means of ensuring the economic independence of these Territories vis-à-vis the Republic."

35. Therisanyo/Consultation, Dec. 1963, 4. Among other resolves the U.N. General Assembly warned "the Government of the Republic of South Africa that any attempt to annex or encroach upon the territorial integrity of these three Territories shall be considered an act of aggression."

VII

An Informal Political Economy

George Jenkins
Department of Political Science, University of Wisconsin, Milwaukee

This paper presents some evidence and some speculation about
what I have termed the informal political economy of the city of Ibadan,
Nigeria, and its consequences for that city's political and economic
stability and change.[1] This somewhat cumbersome term refers to economic
activities which are related to formal governmental institutions but not
closely controlled by them. It excludes from consideration, on the one
hand, the formal budget of the Ibadan Council (and its effects on the economy
in terms of labor force, building contracts, and provisions of services),
and, on the other, the economy which functions unregarded by and without
regard to city government (the world of market-women, the cocoa farmers,
and the factories). The informal political economy occupies an area between
the budget and the market economy, but its existence is a direct result
of city government and its functions. It may support or detract from
government efforts, but it operates in areas in which the Council itself
takes no action.

The economic activities of this sector have varied from time to time,
including slavery, pawning, food raiding, and the devastation of property
as a form of punishment for treason or damage caused by unattended fires
(in a city of thatched roofs). Today tax evasion, elections costs, contract
kickbacks, chieftaincy expenses, nepotism, bribery, job-fixing, and the
activities of various economic pressure groups contribute to this economy.
Some of these activities are lawful, but they are not legal functions of the
Council. Others are illegal; some, which are illegal today, were once
publicly acceptable and even today carry little opprobrium.[2]

The concern of this paper is not to determine what is moral or immoral
in these activities but to describe these phenomena and to suggest how
they contribute to or detract from the development of political and economic
stability in the Ibadan social system. Do such activities create stability
in the system, perhaps at the expense of innovation or the accumulation
of capital? Do different kinds of activities attract different types of political
actors? What are the consequences for the political system? Does the
informal political economy create impressions of the real or potential
role of the formal government different from and perhaps conflicting with
those which the government seeks to create of itself? How does this affect
the stability of the system and its ability to grow and change? This paper
attempts to suggest a few answers to these questions and to supply the
historical information to put them in perspective.

Nineteenth-Century Ibadan

Ibadan today is the largest of the Yoruba cities with a population
approaching one million. Until about 1829 it was only a small village.
In the early part of the nineteenth century, the Moslem armies of Uthman
dan Fodio pressed southward from the northern savannah in what is now
the Northern Region of Nigeria into Northern Yoruba territory. Refugees
from this region and military free-booters from other areas flocked to
Ibadan, located inside the rain forest, as a place of refuge and as a base
of operations against the Fulani. In 1852, the first Christian missionary
to Ibadan estimated the upstart city's population at 60,000.[3] Most of the
populace then must have been non-Ibadan born.

In its history and other characteristics Ibadan differs from traditional
Yoruba cities. Divine rulership, such as Oyo and Ife possessed, was
purposely rejected. In the resulting secular state, the Islamic teachers
who arrived in the 1830's, and the Christians who arrived in the 1850's,
seem to have enjoyed a political status similar to that of the Yoruba religious
functionaries. Both groups acted as advisers to the chiefs and remained
outside the formal structures of government.

Ibadan also rejected the idea of hereditary rule and established a
co-optive form of democracy based on the elevation of leaders through the
kinship system and military accomplishment. A young man with wit and
daring might become the leader of a band of fighting men gathered around
his kinship group. Victory in war meant the taking of slaves as soldiers,
farm laborers or wives, and free men were attracted to his following.[4]
A successor to the founder of a lineage was selected from his sons according
to age and ability to manage its corporate affairs-- mainly military, land,
and judicial matters. A certain lineages distinguished themselves and as
the followings attached to them grew, their heads, or mogajis, received
preferential consideration in the distribution of chieftaincy titles. By 1893,
about a hundred of the lineages were known as "ruling Chieftaincy Houses."[5]
Mogajis with military skill, wealth, and political acumen were co-opted
into "lines" of civil, military, young men's, and cavalry chiefs. Since
any lineage member might become its mogaji, and since any mogaji might
be promoted from the bottom to the top of his chieftaincy line, in theory
at least, any free man in Ibadan might advance to the most senior titles,
which in the process passed from one lineage to another over the course
of the years. Thus, no chief or lineage could hope to retain an important
office for great length of time to the disadvantage of other chiefs or lineages.
The system was well designed to prevent transfer of advantage from generation and the accumulation of political power within any one lineage group.

The senior chiefs from each line constituted the central council,
which declared and directed war, acted as the supreme appellate court,
and distributed chieftaincy titles. Its senior office holder was the bale,
whose civil title meant simply "father of the town."[6] He was a retired
war-chief who guaranteed civil order while the balogun, ("lord of war, "
or general) led the army in the field.

War, agriculture, and crafts were the most important means of
production, probably in that order. As Olubadan Akinyele has written:
"The leading enterprise of the age was warfare; very few people were farmers,
and the few were despised. Traders were few."[7] Reverend Johnson wrote
of the period around 1850 that an important aspect of war was slave-raiding,
which became "a trade to many who would get rich speedily."[8] War and
agriculture were closely linked as the food surplus necessary for the
army in the field was produced by slaves taken in war.[9] The head woman
chief at one time, Iyalode Efunsetan, reportedly held 2,000 slaves on her
farms alone, in addition to the "warboys" who captured slaves.

Slaves also constituted large sections of the army; Are Latosisa
lost 500 slaves in a single afternoon's battle in 1878.[10] Plundering for
foodstuffs in the farms of the enemy was a normal part of Yoruba warfare,
and some people believe that it contributed to a neglect of farming in the
nineteenth century and a distaste for it even today. The point must also
be made, however, that war was costly. Guns and ammunition from coastal
dealers had to be imported over hazardous routes into the interior. Newbury
states that most of the 23,000 worth of arms and powder imported into
Lagos between July 1862 and the end of 1864 eventually reached Ibadan.[11]
In 1884, Reverend J. B. Wood of the Church Missionary Society reported
that Ibadan's finances were exhausted by the war, her houses were in ruins,
and the people were angry with the head chief (Are Latosisa) for his
administration of the war.[12] Such a state could hardly have developed had
simple raiding been the most important aspect of Yoruba warfare. On the
contrary, the armies were frequently in the field for years at a time,
organized in a military structure of considerable complexity.

Craft guilds rather than the lineages organized the production of
soap, leather goods, cloth, iron wares, and pottery. When such items
were moved outside Ibadan, they were subject to customs exactions at the
city gates. Certain chiefs were placed at these entry points and given the
right of customs collection in return for guarding them against attack.
These customs were probably payable in kind as well as in cowries, the
shell currency in use at the time, and the amounts exacted flowed into the
purses of the collector rather than into a civic treasury.

A certain portion of the slaves captured in war, a token of the annual
harvest, and part of the customs were paid as tribute to the senior chiefs.

This tribute was paid to them, however, in their individual capacities and
not to a central Council treasury, so that civic wealth   did not accumulate
in a central place for any period longer than the life of the bale (and his
private and public purses were indistinguishable). The costs of his administration were met through the efforts of his own following, the tribute paid
to him, and exactions from those for whom services were rendered. One
of the consequences of this fiscal arrangement was that the Council did not
provide for or maintain any municipal building, market, or prison prior
to 1893 except the Ogboni Lodge at Oja'ba, a rarely used meeting place.

Wealth flowed through the formal political economy in several channels.
Special gifts and fees were required from those seeking a promotion in
rank. The first was a small "title fee, " fixed according to the importance
of the title being sought, which registered the candidate's acceptance of
the Council's nomination for consideration. The second set of charges
varied according to the rank sought, the number of persons contesting it,
the favor in which the candidate was held, and his ability to pay. A candidate
for a senior title might well have had to pay in cattle, cowries, cloth, gin,
and slaves.[13] Those seeking lesser titles might make a less substantial
contribution. The gifts indicated the candidate's willingness to use his
private resources for public purposes and levelled out any great advantage
of wealth the candidate might have. As long as the appointment was in
question, candidates continued to "feed" or "entertain" the senior chiefs
who had the power of co-optation to higher ranks. Of course, candidates
with the military power to become wealthy and the willingness to be generous
were clearly at an advantage; the size of their gifts could compensate for
the lack of other desirable characteristics such as age, seniority, status,
and loyalty.

A "thank-you" gift was also paid by the candidate upon his confirmation
to the title, followed by a relatively smaller investiture fee, a fee for the
symbolic leaves used in the installation ceremony, and a gift to the messengers of the other chiefs who accompanied him to his home after the ceremony.
A final and substantial sum was taken to the senior chiefs whose positions
forbade their presence at his house, where a public celebration was held to
mark the new honor. This celebration, depending upon the rank, status,
wealth, and generosity of the new chief, might cost as much as the fees
necessary to acquire the title. Thus, a promotion could put a considerable
strain on the family purse until the perquisites of the higher office compensated for the investment.

Prior to the imposition of peace by the British in 1893, chieftaincy
titles were of two different sorts. Eleven of them were functional positions, and some with more than one holder at a time. Holders of these
positions may have held only one title in a lifetime, reflecting a particular
military skill, such as the captain of the Rifles. These titles were not

ranked in any order of precedence. Mogajis could be appointed to one of
these positions, or they might be appointed to one of the twelve hierarchical
positions in one of the four lines; these hierarchical titles were senior to
the functional positions, the most senior of them entitling the holders to
membership in the Council. Functional chiefs could also be promoted into
the ranks of the hierarchical chiefs. The hierarchical titles had only one
holder each, and senior chiefs may have held an average of five titles during
a lifetime.[14] Perhaps two promotions in each of the hierarchical sections
of the four lines of male chiefs occurred annually. Even if this figure
were doubled, however, it would suggest that only a fraction of the wealth
in the economy was channeled into promotions and title-seeking. This
interpretation would be in keeping with the accounts that Johnson and Olubadan
Akinyele have given of the importance of military prowess as a criterion
for selection rather than the ability to purchase a title.

The transaction between the candidate and the senior chiefs was but
one channel through which promotions money flowed; followers and family
members of a candidate were expected to contribute toward his fees and
expenses, for the benefits which accrued to him as a result of a higher
position came to them as well. A chief who shared in a candidate's fees
divided his share among his own supporters. It is important to note, therefore, that this aspect of the economy was essentially distributive and re-
allocative, rather than accumulative.

The court system was as decentralized as the military and agricultural systems and it, too, was based on lineage. The lineage court had
initial jurisdiction over marriage, land, petty quarrels, and all matters
affecting lineage members, followers, or slaves. Some of the larger
compound courts may have had jurisdiction over as many as several
thousand people. Such units were large enough to be liable to considerable
internal conflict, and a considerable part of the city's litigation occurred
at the lineage court level. Disputes which the lineage courts failed to settle,
disputes involving members of more than one compound, petty theft, and
disturbances of the peace were dealt with at the court of the quarter chief
or at a chief's court chosen by the litigants. The courts of the balogun
and of the bale served as appellate courts and heard disputes between chiefs
of the respective lines. The town Council had original jurisdiction in cases
with political implications and those involving the death penalty, such as
major theft or murder.[15]

Payment for court cases and litigation had several of the characteristics
of promotion fees. Both parties to a dispute made an initial payment which
recognized the judicial authority of the chief or the court. The second,
"favor-me" gift was clearly meant to influence the decision by means of
criteria extraneous to the merits of the case and was a bribe. Finally,

the successful party usually sent a gift of thanks for the favorable decision. Most litigation took place in the lineage courts where costs were low and the revenues derived from them were distributed throughout the city. In these courts, equity and social cohesion were undoubtedly more important criteria for judicial decision-making than strict observance of legal niceties, but their accessibility to the litigants and the appellate process provided checks against unfair judgments.

Severe punishments also had an economic aspect. Traditionally, Ibadan had no prison where a debt to society could be paid in terms of time. "Fine, ruinous fine" was the punishment for adultery.[16] A person guilty of starting a fire in a city of thatched roofs could be sold into slavery along with members of his immediate family. Chiefs who had earned the disfavor of their peers and who refused suicide or banishment were in danger of having their houses destroyed. Inhabitants of their compound were often sold into slavery, and the chief's tools and articles of clothing were divided among the plunderers before the house was fired.[17]

In the above paragraphs, I have attempted to describe the traditional political economy as it was before the arrival of the British. Ibadan grew from a village in 1830 to a city of 150,000 by 1890, a growth which represents a considerable feat of economic and political organization. Had Ibadan been only an agricultural city, it would be fair to say that it had essentially a subsistence economy, one based on generous natural conditions but, never- theless, oriented primarily toward local consumption of locally produced goods, mostly at the lineage level. The importance of war, however, and the related activities of plundering, slave-raiding, and tribute-gathering from subjugated areas, meant that the Ibadan economy was engrossed in a much larger system which it exploited and from which it accumulated wealth. Even so, the political system, with its marked decentralization based on the lineages, and the methods of distributing goods meant that economic power could not accumulate in a few hands, nor be passed through the generations.

The question may be raised whether the distinction between formal and informal political and economic behavior suggested earlier can be made in nineteenth century Ibadan, where the distinction between public and private spheres was, at best, a vague one. In large part, the answer is no. Tribute exactions, chieftaincy fees, and the lineage-based army fused private wealth and influence into the polity in a manner made unnecessary and undesirable by modern bureaucratic standards. On the other hand, there were clear proprieties which were not to be violated. When wealthy but untrustworthy men were given military responsibility, when favor-me tribes were necessary to achieve justice or used to circumvent it, it was

clear that the normative standards to which all would publicly subscribe,
were being flouted. It must also be remembered, however, that nineteenth
century Ibadan itself was the product of a breakdown in Yoruba order,
and that its entire political and economic growth, by means of intra-Yoruba
warfare and slavery, was contrary to eighteenth century Yoruba conditions
and norms.

Pax Britannica

In pursuit of several economic, fiscal, and moral policies, the
British governor of the colony of Lagos finally accomplished the pacification
of the Yoruba interior in 1893 through a series of treaties, agreements,
and military expeditions. An agreement with Ibadan allowed him to place
a Resident and a troop of Hausa constabulary in the city to enforce the
peace in Yorubaland. The Ibadan military chiefs presumed that the British
would eventually depart, and peace was welcomed as a respite. But the
British remained, peace endured, and a number of other unexpected consequences quickly followed. The simple necessities of life could no longer
be procured by raiding farms or trade caravans. As Governor Carter put
it in early 1894, he had no desire to "interfere with reasonable modes of
obtaining the necessary revenue" which the chiefs needed to support themselves, but "highway robbery" would not be condoned. Such "irregular
methods of Government" must be halted. The chiefs should endeavor
"to fall in with the new order of things" and to put their government on a
"civilized and enlightened footing."[18]

Slave taking was promptly terminated. Since slaves were no longer
needed in the Ibadan army, however, the smaller supply was matched by
a decrease in demand. The number of slaves available for agricultural
labor also diminished rapidly, a development which was compensated for
by the fact that it was no longer necessary to produce a surplus for the
army. Presumably, many slaves left Ibadan to return to their homes;
but beyond the prohibition of further slave taking, the British did little to
change relations between masters and slaves. Slaves were allowed to
purchase their freedom (for £3, 15s.) and charges of brutality were investigated, although slave holding was not outlawed until 1916.[19] Since both the
necessity and the profit of the system were destroyed by peace in 1893,
the number of slaves remaining in 1916 was probably small, and there is
no indication in Ibadan records that any of them complained of their position.

A judicial agreement in 1904 prohibited the entire set of compound
and quarter courts and replaced them with two public courts. The British
hoped thereby to eliminate the "bribery and corruption" which they thought
must perforce exist in secret (private) courts, and to create a public

revenue from court fines and fees. The records suggest that the British
did not understand the principles of family and local jurisdiction or the
appellate process which connected the compound and quarter courts to the
Council of Chiefs. Nor did they ever acknowledge that authority and
legitimacy, rather than corruption and oppression, might have bound the
people to these courts. But in spite of their prohibition, the chiefs openly
admitted in 1909 that the secret courts still existed and that fines and fees
were collected for cases heard in them.[20] The volume of litigation in the
new public courts probably did not exceed that of the secret courts until
about 1930, and, as we shall note later, the public courts were also open
to various private influences. While the senior chiefs spent much of the
day in the public courts, their slaves and servants continued to supervise
the traditional system.[21] This provided income for the chiefs, who were
unable to meet their expenses from their share of regularized court fees.
If the bulk of litigation in pre-British Ibadan was indeed at the family court
level, and if it was relatively inexpensive, the sume of £1,500 which
the British Resident estimated could be collected for fines and fees in a
single quarter of 1903, suggests that the high cost of litigation in the public
courts may have contributed to the continued use of the family courts,
which became indeed increasingly secret.[22] Thus the Council (which was
forced to approve British dictates) itself created an informal system around
the formal institutions.

Captain Elgee, Resident from 1903 to 1913, attempted to prevent
this lapse into informality by restructuring the entire formal political
economic system. The Council treasury was to centralize the collection
of all revenue. Court fines and fees, fees from liquor licenses and rubber
tree tapping permits, and a new system of customs control would provide
the Council's income. Control over this latter perquisite of the traditional
system passed to the Council in 1903. For the final quarter of that year,
Elgee estimated that £1,500 in revenue would accrue to the treasury.[23]
Perhaps both this estimate and that for court revenues were inflated as much
as 100 per cent by Elgee's enthusiasm, for the 1904-1905 estimated expenditure was only half of what this rate of revenue would have provided. Nor
should these figures be thought to represent a sum equal to revenues enjoyed
by the chiefs before 1893, for at least a portion of the court revenue was
derived from cases involving traders and firms which arrived in Ibadan
after the pax britannica, and much of the customs revenue must have been
exacted from goods (such as gin) which began to move freely only when the
roads were kept permanently open.

From these funds, according to Captain Elgee's plan, new projects
were to be financed and supervised by the Council. The chiefs were to
receive salaries to decrease their dependence on other sources of income,
while their involvement with new projects would educate them toward

what Elgee called a "higher standard of municipal life." These projects
never gave the chiefs much political satisfaction, however, for they were all
administrative failures. A pottery school collapsed because the proper
type of clay had not been provided. The Bale's School appeared to the
chiefs to be an attempt to make Christians and monogamists of their sons,
and they refused to send them. Neither the Agricultural Society nor the
plantation of the British Cotton Growing Association effected any significant
changes in agriculture, nor did the attempt to create a planned housing area
at Dugbe opposite the railway station prove a success.

Elgee's response to threatening failure was to hold the chiefs responsible
in their individual capacities rather than to deal with the Council as a whole.
When free labor failed to appear for road construction, when difficulty
developed over the provision of a house for the potter, when sales of
alcoholic beverages dropped by several hundred per cent within a few
months, the chiefs were threatened with a loss of the salaries which were
supposed to relieve them of the necessity for accepting bribes and which
were meager enough to begin with.

From the outset of the program in 1903, a mere ₤ 100 a month was
allotted to be divided among at least twelve and perhaps twenty chiefs.
This was hardly sufficient to arouse enthusiasm about the new system, and
it elevated the chiefs only slightly above the eighteen customs clerks who
drew ₤ 70 per month among them. Three clerks received ₤ 20 all together
and an indeterminate number of police officers received ₤ 30. Thus, by
1903, the chiefs were receiving less than half of the Council's total monthly
salary expenditure of ₤220. Estimated expenditures for 1904-1905 were
₤ 5,697, so that the chiefs, even with additional sitting fees for days spent
in court, probably received only about 25 per cent of the total formal
budget.[24]

Inducements in addition to salaries, as well as the deductions from
them, further mitigated the principle of a salaried chieftaincy. The chiefs
were rewarded with a part of the revenue from the sale of timber from a
Council forest preserve, and the British easily adopted the tradition of
gift-giving in their relations with the chiefs. In 1908 alone, the bale received
from Elgee "a very grand and unusual seat, " as well as a "a silver wrist
watch which I trust you will appreciate" and "my own Gun & a very good one."[25]
Sums of money were also openly given and acknowledged, for in this transi-
tional period, definitions of personal proprieties and institutional scope
and the separation of personal and civic economies so common to British
administration and so alien to Ibadan, could not be effectively introduced
by fiat.

Yet for all the concern over salaries, court fees, and annual estimates of expenditures, the chiefs had lost all control over the formal budget of the Council, which in their eyes must have consisted of inadequate salaries or outlays for projects which were unwanted or unsuccessful, or both. The rapidly expanding European-oriented economy was soon to rob them completely of their role as economic leaders of society. The Spirit Merchants, dealers in alcoholic beverages, were a recognizable group in 1899. Even before the arrival of the railroad from Lagos in 1901, European trading firms had established their depots in Ibadan. A trade council of Iddo Gate merchants first met in 1906. Two-story houses, sometimes with stained glass windows and imported chandeliers, appeared, marking the successes of the rising merchant class. Interest rates of 5 per cent per month on the original loan were prevalent in the 1920's and returns of Ⱡ 50 on a Ⱡ 20 investment for six months and Ⱡ 150 on Ⱡ 100 for four months are recorded from the trade in palm products and cocoa. Those with money to lend became wealthy. They purchased old Ford and Dodge automobiles so as to supervise the produce trade in the bush "scale markets" where cocoa and palm oil kernels were brought for weighing. The Killa Society was formed for the public celebration and consumption of their wealth. The three wealthiest merchants were Moslem commoners. Salami Agbaje, not a native of Ibadan who employed a European bookkeeper, was eventually appointed to the Legislative Council and made an Ibadan chief. Saka Adebisi, of a non-chieftaincy house, by the sheer weight of purse and personality won friends and a title. Okunola Alesinloye, although the son of a chief, came from a family in which the mogajiship had passed into the hands of a regent. Okunola organized a trading operation that extended from Kano to Lagos and became known as Balogun Yam Flour because of his corner on that staple in Ibadan. He wrested control of the family away from the regent during the period when the chiefs were still required to recruit unpaid labor for road construction, each according to his rank. Many of those who were unable to do so were forced to resign their titles. Others were relieved of their embarrassment when the wealthy Okunola sent contingents of his own men to supplement their labor forces.[26] On the death of the family regent, Okunola had built up sufficient gratitude among the chiefs to be given the title the regent had held instead of the much less distinguished title to which he was entitled by custom.

Lack of education, inadequate capital, and traditional dignity prevented most chiefs from moving with the times. They were usually content to live on the sale of perquisites to those who sought and could afford them and could thus bolster the sagging economic and political powers of chieftaincy. The chiefs still had two major functions at this time, which they retained as late as 1954. These were control over the courts and, after 1918, control over the tax collection system. The purchase of chieftaincy titles thus became the channel of recruitment for the courts and tax collection, and both the efficiency and the legitimacy of these two functions decreased greatly as a result. In the next two sections we shall see how the chiefs were removed from control over these remaining functions.

The Courts

The Judicial Act of 1904 had challenged but not broken the hold of the chiefs over judicial matters. A second attempt to regularize the courts came in 1914 in pursuance of what was called indirect rule. An attempt had been made in 1911, before Lugard became governor-general of Nigeria, to institute a schedule of tribute from the outlying towns and villages. The Resident suggested a rate of Ł 1 per thousand persons to avoid the "hand to mouth procedure of the tribute being collected on various occasions throughout the year;" but the chiefs thought the existing tribute collection was "sanctioned by long usage, was not hard on the people and kept them in better touch with their rulers." Nothing more came of the proposal.[27]

By 1914, everyone was willing to admit that Ibadan's government was in a sadly deterioriated state. Elgee's successors blamed this on two decades of British rule which, they said, had confused the morality of the chiefs. Under Elgee, they said, the chiefs lost their customary sources of income and were forced to find illegal alternatives. It was thought that the provision of adequate salaries would obviate the necessity to take illegal presents and allow a return to pre-British morality, particularly in the courts. To ensure, as Elgee had not, that the salaries would be adequate for the purpose, the bale himself was asked in 1914 to declare the amount he considered "sufficient to make these presents unnecessary." His estimate of Ł 200 per mensem was made his monthly salary, and further Ł 2,760 per annum was approved for the eight other chiefs the government was willing to recognize as members of the new Council. Guaranteed incomes were, therefore, not provided for all receivers of gifts, partly because the government did not wish to recognize the Ibadan system of promotion and authority and perhaps because it believed that the recognized chiefs, as they had promised to do, would put all gifts received thereafter into the Ibadan treasury. Wrapped in a new virtue, these chiefs would then attract litigants away from the currupt and secret courts into the new municipal courts.[28]

If we assume that the bale's Ł 200 per month or Ł 2,400 per year, did fairly represent his income in illegal presents, and if we make the same assumption for the eight chiefs who were to receive Ł 2,760 among them, and if we add to that figure an equivalent amount for the chiefs who remained unrecognized and unsalaried, we arrive at a figure of Ŀ 7,920 per annum as the cost of litigation in the secret courts. Such a figure ignores the amount spent in family courts, which we presume had lower costs, but it does suggest that the sum of money involved in the judicial economy made it worthwhile for the British to formalize these processes. Since administrative manpower to begin the tax system was not available during the war years (Lugard insisted that a tax system must precede salaries), the scheme was not begun until 1918. Unfortunately, the records of this period are singularly uneven, and it is not at all certain who received salaries or in what amounts. Certainly, the traditional system continued to operate through 1918; and there is every indication that even after salaries were introduced, other corrupt sources of income augmented them handsomely.

Suspicions and allegations of corruption were levelled at no less a personage than the Resident himself. Since indirect rule required rulers, and since Ibadan had no king, the alafin of Oyo was made king over Ibadan by Lugard. It was thought in Ibadan that the new Resident, who moved the provincial headquarters from Ibadan to Oyo, was profiting greatly through his association with the alafin.[29] A railway clerk tells of the "sumptious gifts" which the Resident and alafin exchanged. The son of one Ibadan chiefs,who went to Oyo with a gift of Ŀ 160 to persuade the alafin to grant his father a promotion, met his rival there with Ŀ 800. He firmly believed that the receipt of such a sum must have been noticed and hence approved by the Resident. The alafin's intervention in a single land dispute between two Ibadan families in 1927-1928 netted him and members of his family Ŀ47.5.-, two turkeys, a case of gin, and twelve bottles of beer -- in a case which had already cost one of the litigants Ŀ48.10.- in Ibadan! Thus, the practices which the provision of a king for Ibadan was supposed to correct were only transferred to another city while they continued to thrive at home as well.

The Resident was aware of these problems in Ibadan. Speaking in 1920 at a teachers' meeting "in brief but touching" terms, he solicited their aid in eliminating dishonesty, but a few weeks later when a delegation of influentials approached him to discuss bribery and corruption in the Ibadan government, he admitted that it existed but that the time was not appropriate to fight it since it would endanger rights of the Council which he was fighting to maintain. An important member of the small literate element in Ibadan wrote: "Corruption, bribery and political insanity are and will for a long continue to reign supreme in Ibadan. Knowing the truth our Chiefs will never tell it. Justice becomes a sort of auction sale; invariably the highest bidder is always the purchaser."[30] This was less an outcry against isolated injustices than a description of the normal political system in action.

Typically, the system worked as follows. Having pleaded a case in
court, a litigant would be informed that the bale, his chiefs, and the police
would have to be "properly fed" if the hard work of his antagonist was
to be overcome. A loan might have to be raised, usually at interest rates
between 25 and 50 per cent. To avoid the word "interest" a receipt would
be signed for the initial amount with the interest calculated in the total.
By the time this had been accomplished, the chiefs might have raised the
price. For some, the sergeant of police could be helpful; for many years
that official was known to avoid accepting gifts unless he could deliver the
expected results. The difference between the sergeant and the bale then
was that the bale could never be trusted not to require and keep "favor-me"
bribes from both sides. The bale accepted bribes, the sergeant accepted
payment for services performed.

During the 1930's salaries averaging about Ŀ 9, 200 per annum were
paid to the chiefs. An average of Ŀ 12, 000 per annum was paid into the
treasury in fines and fees during this decade, so that formal courts were
sources of revenue for the Council. During the 1930's, people learned that
cases decided in the traditional manner could be appealed to the formal
courts, and that it was safe to have the formal courts handle divorce,
land, and debt suits where receipts, payments, and deeds were involved.
Dissatisfaction grew as people discovered that they had to pay twice for
court services, once to the courts as such, and a second time to the chiefs.
Anger developed against some of the chiefs and charges of corruption were
openly made. The charges, however, were not made against all court
judges, but only against those who did not use their incomes in the appropriate
manner. Those court judges who continued to provide the traditional largesse
of a wealthy chief avoided popular wrath.

Not until 1938, when Chief Isaac B. Akinyele assumed the presidency
of the crucial Lands Court, did a significant change in this pattern occur.
Chief Akinyele, brother of Bishop Alexander Akinyele, and a minister of
the Christ Apostolic Church in his own right, was a man of stern Christian
morality. Following an on-the-spot investigation of a boundary by his
court, one litigant commented: "The Chiefs, unlike their former peers
acted well and bribery did not set in to influence their investigation."
This personal example was not followed in all the other courts until Akinyele
became chief judge of the Ibadan customary courts in 1954. In the reforms
which he instituted that year, with the firm backing of the administrative
officers and the Western Regional government, literate presidents of his
own choice, responsible to his own unimpeachable integrity, replaced the
old chiefs in the courts. One new court president, who customarily presented
turkeys, schnapps, and money to judges and registrars as a litigant, seems
never to have made such demands on persons appearing in his own court.
This tradition has been continued under Akinyele's successor. It is a fact

that the Ibadan court presidents supported the Action Group party with campaign contributions, and since 1954 two court presidents have been dismissed because of overzealous exhibition of their party preferences; but no evidence suggests that pecuniary considerations any longer affect Ibadan's courts.

A circumstance which may have supported the moral convictions and administrative vigor of Chief Akinyele is the fact that few decisions are actually made in the courts today. Serious crimes had been transferred to Western Regional magistrates' courts, so that the so-called customary courts now deal mostly with divorce, a most uncustomary legal proceeding. Most judges make no attempt to establish any facts in divorce cases, which constitute about 80 per cent of the schedule, except the length of co-habitation, since this determines the amount of dowry to be repaid. The judges feel that all effective means of reconciliation have been exhausted before divorce cases reach court, and that they can only ratify the situation as the litigants present it.

Taxation

Taxation and salaries, which Lugard saw as essential elements of indirect rule, were not implemented until 1918, due to administrative problems caused by the war.[31] Although armed soldiers stood by at the meeting at which the tax scheme was announced, no violence occurred. The tax was collected from adult males by compound heads and chiefs since it was thought that only they would know whether individual tax payers were in the town or the farms during the "tax season" (which is also the cocoa harvesting season). The number of men from whom each chief had to collect was originally calculated by a room census of each compound adjusted by a ratio of adult males per room. This figure was then multiplied by seven shillings, which was 2.5 per cent of the annual income of Ł 14 with each adult male was assumed to earn. The tax, then, had nothing to do with private incomes of individually specified persons but was a quota assessed against the tax collector. It was really intended to establish a tax quota for the entire city. Collectors were not restricted to collection solely within their own compounds, and, as under the nineteenth century military system, success depended on one's ability to attract a large following. As each warrior chose his own war leader (babaogun), so now each tax payer was free to choose his collector, who was also known as a babaogun. The longer the collector's list of payers, the greater his prestige. This was reinforced by a rebate of 10 per cent paid on the amount collected.[32] After assessment was made against a chief, he collected tax money wherever he could, turned it in, and received the appropriate number of tax tickets for distribution to his payers. It was to his advantage to attract as many payers to himself as he could. This resulted in the raiding of others' lists.

Thus, the "A" family once paid its tax through the "B" family. When Mogaji "A" was made a chief he also became a tax collector and at one point had over a thousand persons on his tax lists, largely at the expense of Mogaji "B, " whose list had shrunk from over a thousand to about a hundred. The names on the tax lists thus shifted continually, but they were not kept up to date. Those who could not attract enough followers to meet their assessments collected as best they could. Wealthier members of the family might have to pay as much as Ł 5. Some paid nothing. From 1926 to 1937, no additions were made to the tax lists, so that collectors continued to pay for men who had died in the interim, while not paying for young men who had come of taxpaying age.[33] This arrangement worked in favor of the collectors, for the expanding population provided more potential, unregistered taxpayers each year from whom the collector might exact something, than the number of men who had died. This helped him to meet his quota without having to collect from everyone in his compound.

Tax season was dreaded by all. Year after year saw huge sums left outstanding after the end of the season. About 1937, street raiding was initiated to correct this situation. Streets and compounds were cordoned off and all men were required to show a ticket corresponding to their names on the tax list. The purpose was not to arrest and prosecute, since the courts were not equipped to process so many cases, but to frighten some pour encourager les autres.

The man in the street therefore calculated closely his chance of getting caught, and one out of every three or four registered taxpayers, in addition to those who have not been inscribed at all, risked not paying every year. It should not be presumed, however, that evasion was limited to the small taxpayer. In 1939-1940, 170 European administrators, military officers, railway employees, and missionaries left Ibadan for other posts without paying any taxes.[34]

Blame for mass evasion was attached largely to the chiefs, and it was thought that only a territorial collection system, based on residence rather than personality, could produce the revenue the city so desperately needed. In 1952, therefore, tax collection duties were shifted from the chiefs, for whom they had become an embarrassing remnant of power, to ward committees appointed by the Council on the recommendation of the local councillor. Everyone was now to be assessed by a committee of his peers and neighbors and to pay a tax clerk in his own ward. This system proved to be no more effective than the previous one, for although the reduction of the rebate to 5 per cent had taken away much of the profit motive for the collectors, the committees—in fact members of the councillor's political ward organization-- were useful means of persuading the taxpayers

of the virtues of the party through their power to fail to inscribe names in
the tax register. Assessments did not increase nor did evasion decrease.
A survey in 1956 showed that government and university employees were
among the most flagrant defaulters.[35] In fact, the system was so inequitable
in its enforcement that one almost had to cheat in order not to be cheated.

To end the evasion, the embarrassing street raiding, and the influence
of political parties in assessment, a pay-as-you-earn system was begun
in 1959-1960 to tax salaried persons at their place of employment. Collection was supervised by the regional government on behalf of the Council,
but when the government found itself in financial straits in the wake of the
crisis of 1962, it became convenient to keep these taxes for regional rather
than city use. As a result of this "reform," the Council now taxes only
35,000 of the lowest incomes in the city, from which it derives only about
Ł 100,000. There is no sales tax. Efforts to institute a property tax
have been made since 1948 to no avail. The Council estimates that property
other than land could be assessed at Ł 50 million and that 2,315 expensive
brick or block houses, plus the commercial structures, could be made
to bear a proportion of the needed revenue that would reduce by two-thirds
the tax paid by those who dwell in the city's 21,658 mud structures.[36]
A meeting at which this scheme was to be explained to the general public
was canceled a few hours before it was to begin. The chairman of the
Council blamed the leader of the opposition in the Council, who is one of
the largest house owners in the city, for leading a last minute attack on
the plan. City officials, noting the quality of the houses which most of
the councillors enjoy, remarked that the opposition leader probably had a
majority of the Council with him. While one of the most pressing needs
of the city, according to the chiefs, councillors and taxpayers, is to lower
taxes, no political party has yet seen fit to offer its constituents a tax cut.

The problem of taxation in Ibadan illustrates strikingly how governmental attempts to institute a program may first require informal participation (the utilization of the babaogun system) and how eventually an attempt
to eliminate informality may result in the loss of control over a crucial
formal function to the national or regional government.

Chieftaincy Today

In spite of its loss of influence over the military, political, and
fiscal powers of the city government, chieftaincy remains important in
Ibadan, mostly because it continues to function as a significant adjunct
of the lineage structure. For, while the mogajis and the lineages are the
most conservative forces in Ibadan today, they also provide more social

stability and cohesion than groups, parties, or any other form of affiliation.
Among them, only the olubadan and a few of the senior chiefs can initiate
or support policy to any significant degree; but the Council continues to
support the whole chieftaincy structure to stave off the ever-present threat
of the massive veto power of the chiefs and to subsidize, in effect, their
important welfare activities as heads of Ibadan's huge families. In today's
informal political economy, chieftaincy has the closest tie of any economic
activity to the Council and its formal expenses. It is discussed in detail
here because it is representative of the replacement of what was once the
formal system by a new and different political form. This replacement
process threatens one day to exclude the chiefs entirely from the immediate
concerns of the modern Council. As early as 1954, the economics and
politics of chieftaincy had become largely internal matters, encapsulated
within lines of traditions which have little relevance to the real work of
the Council.

As chiefs became less powerful over the years, feuds over loss of
power and agitations against the top leaders, whose longevity was increased
by peace, were stilled by the addition of new titles to the lines, the arrangement of titles in strict but untraditional order of seniority, and automatic
promotion to higher titles upon the death of a senior. Sixty-six chiefs now
receive salaries from the Council. A total of Ł 11,774 was provided in
1962-1963 for the "maintenance of traditional offices."[37] Thirty-four of
the chiefs receive less than Ł 50 per annum, the assumed minimum male
adult annual income. Twenty-four receive between Ł57.19.- and Ł194. Seven
receive between Ł 299 and Ł 886. The olubadan receives Ł3,163. Probably
only these last eight receive enough to pay the expenses connected with
the office itself; the others receive only partial maintenance, as the following figures, based on interviews and private records show.

The announcement of one's mogajiship costs between Ł 2.10.- and Ł 5
if no unusual circumstances exist. The sum of all the fees for the first
of the twenty-three titles in each line is between Ł 40 and Ł 50. Since the
hierarchical ranking of all titles in 1936-1937, promotion from one rank
to the next is automatic except in cases of physical disability or a serious
moral blot. One is therefore promoted toward the top position with considerable certainty as long as the fixed fees are paid.

The fees for the next to last title in the line are about Ł75. Taking
Ł 60 as the average fee, four recent senior chiefs with an average of about
seventeen promotions (they were sometimes able to skip some titles upon
the simultaneous death of two of their seniors) could have each paid about
Ł 1.000 in title fees during their careers. Each of them experienced difficulty
at some point where automatic promotion was modified by discretion. One
of them paid at least Ł 160 and perhaps as much as Ł 370 in an attempt to

clear himself. Another man thinks he may have spent twice that amount.[38]

One is also expected to celebrate his new honor appropriately. The head of a large lineage may have to spend as much as Ł 100 on each occasion regardless of the importance of the title. It is therefore reasonable to believe that our four chiefs spent over Ł 2,000 each in reaching the title of otun (second most senior title in each line). Under the present salary scale, which is rather more generous than that in force during the earlier years of their chieftaincies, these four chiefs probably would not have received a total of Ł 2,000 in salaries until they achieved the fourth most senior title.

Fees and festivals at the time of death are equally important and expensive. It costs as much to die as it does to attain the title one holds at death. While a wealthy merchant-chief might make these payments from his own purse, most chiefs must solicit from family members and impose tribute on tenants; gifts from friends may defray a substantial portion of these costs. In any event, the payment of fees creates a vast network of debts, obligations, and gratitude.

Title taking, unless one has other forms of income, has become a costly and risky investment. The four chiefs mentioned above each held titles about twenty-five years while they worked their way through the ranks. Not until they reached the fifth most senior title did their salaries for a year approximate the costs of attaining it. Of seventy promotions during a recent twenty-month period, only seven were in the rewarding upper ranks. Most chiefs die before they recover their investments.

The method in which title payments are made depends somewhat upon the preference of the olubadan. Under Olubadan Akinyele, all fees were paid to him directly, and it was strictly forbidden to do otherwise. He then gave one third of the total to the balogun's line, one third to his own line, and kept one third for himself. Each chief was then "shared" by the head of his line -- a portion more or less commensurate with the salary attached to his title and indicative of his rank. Thus, out of a set of fees of Ł 50, each line divided about Ł 15 in twenty-two scaled portions. A portion is also given to the women's line and, reportedly, to various mogajis as well. In the twenty-month period mentioned above, seventy promotions produced fees totaling about Ł 1,800. It would appear, therefore, that the olubadan enjoyed an extra income of about Ł 600 during this period. Automatic promotion, however, presents problems to an olubadan concerned with the dignity of his juniors. Having accepted Ł 48 from one friend in fees, he returned Ł 50 to him to help meet celebration expenses, thus sustaining a loss of about Ł 35. On another occasion, death found a prominent chief deeply in debt and his family unable to find the money to pay the fees to announce his demise. Until this was done, the poor man could not be buried. It is said that ₺ 800 was needed to rescue his family from its dilemma.

Such costs are added to already heavy demands against the olubadan's salary. The costs of achieving that most exalted title are extremely high. If two candidates contest for the title, expenses of a thousand pounds may be incurred. An equal sum may be spent on entertaining the entire city, and the death of an important olubadan probably costs several thousand pounds in funeral and entertaining expenses. For a period, the Council provided a subsidy for installation costs of ₺ 400, but several of those who received this sum and died shortly after installation, died hundreds of pounds in debt.

Some families have become acutely aware of the high costs and risks of chieftaincy. Among them conversations are going on about the relevant criteria for mogajiship. While seniority has often been a decisive factor, tradition has also demanded that a mogaji must be able to provide well for the lineage's corporate needs. This very structure means that a man sixty years of age, who would have to wait perhaps twenty years to come into a rewarding title, can no longer do this. Thus, one family which includes several honorable, experienced, and senior men, is presently postponing the selection of a mogaji in order to give several men not yet forty an opportunity to prove themselves.

Politicians

During the 1930's, several new types of politicians emerged which eventually displaced the chiefs from any but nominal places in the city's government. In 1933, two educated councillors were co-opted from the Ibadan Progressive Union, a reform group, to act as liaisons between the illiterate chiefs and the administrative officers, and to perform much of the administrative work of the Council.[39] As the three-year term of each pair of councillors expired, it became the practice for the chiefs to offer them titles so that political groups became a channel for revitalizing both the Council and the chieftaincy system. As the number of groups and councillors increased, however, it became impossible to continue these practices and, in 1952, thirty-four seats were opened on the Council to be filled by elections. Members of the traditional political groups fared well that year, for in most wards the mogajis and lineages simply selected a representative by consensus rather than having a contested election. In the 1954 local elections, however, political parties took over both nomination and election processes. Candidates of the NCNC (National Council of Nigeria and the Cameroons) were selected by

Adegoke Adelabu, the party's local chairman; he won a convincing success over the old political groups which had affiliated with the Action Group party. Adelabu's elected councillors replaced the chiefs as the officials responsible for the Ibadan government.

This 1954 Council, in contrast to its predecessor in 1952, was almost completely illiterate and included only four of the thirty-four members of the 1952 Council. Charges of corruption and maladministration led to its dismissal in 1956 and the appointment of a Council by the regional government to act as an interim body. But in 1958 the NCNC was returned to power in an election which included nine members from the previous Council in its body of forty-six. A similar number survived the 1961 election, including two members who had served three consecutive terms. Thus, from one election to the next, only about 20 per cent of the councillors survive. While the Ibadan councillor is similar in many ways to American "machine" politicians, he operates without the support of an organization capable of returning him predictably to office. The Ibadan councillor must, realistically, reckon on only one term in office.

To be nominated one has first to be a member in good standing of the ward organization of his party. Candidates and members in the NCNC state that good standing has meant, among other things, the payment of a fee of up to Ł15 to the party leadership. It is, as one party leader stated, a method of identifying the leader. In 1954, the demagogic appeal of Adegoke Adelabu was a more effective campaign aid than hard cash, although election politics in Ibadan are known as "stomach politics." NCNC councillors report that election expenditures varying from Ł 35 to Ł 50 were generally sufficient, with the support of Adelabu, to overcome literate Action Group candidates who spent up to Ł150. Action Group candidates confirm these estimates. The value of Adelabu's personal appeal is further indicated by the increased expenses of NCNC candidates in an election held in 1958, after his death. The 1961 elections probably cost the Action Group candidates between Ł100 and Ł300 each.

Election costs are not the only ones the councillor must bear; a councillor is expected to help in all kinds of situations. If it becomes necessary for a citizen to pay taxes in order to avoid prosecution, the councillor may be called upon to help. School fees for the child of a sick man, or bus fare to Lagos may be demanded of him. Most councillors probably spend several pounds a week in this way. One party lieutenant in the 1961 Council reports weekly constituency expenses of Ł 10. Election and constituency expenses for a single three-year-term may range between Ł 125 and Ł 800 or Ł 1,000.

The councillors, according to their own reports, are not wealthy men. Less than 25 per cent of them report an income of over Ł 100 per annum and most state their incomes to be between Ł 50 and Ł 60. While their homes are comfortably appointed with armchairs, curtained windows, radios, and linoleumed floors, ready cash incomes reportedly are not theirs. How then do they meet their heavy political expenses?

Each councillor receives approximately Ł 60 per annum in sitting fees from the Council to recompense him for the loss of income he is presumed to suffer by attendance upon official duties. This figure is equal to what most councillors claim as their annual income. Contributions from ward organizations do not exist, for councillors are expected to distribute largesse rather than to be the objects of it, although friends and supporters may contribute to election costs. A major portion of one councillor's costs were paid by his father, a powerful mogaji in the ward, who wished to have the councillorship secure in the family. Still, a rather sizable figure remains to be earned in political services. Nearly everything the councillor does is subject to detailed review and approval by the Council. Thus, each hawking license, every land rental, each butcher's permit, is reviewed by a Council committee. It is said that fees for such services accrue to councillors at the rate of ten shillings to several pounds per item. It is also alleged that the authority the councillors reserve to themselves to locate sites for refuse bins and the much sought after water taps is a remunerative one. Difficulties in the transfer of land and leases are the specialties of some councillors who can be met daily as they go about their constituents' business at the Council offices. A final source of income is said to lie in the discretion the councillors have in the allocation of contracts. Contract awards are controlled by the Tenders Board, the Works Committee, and the Finance Committee. Depending upon the nature of the service or goods to be supplied, their decisions are reviewed by various officers of the Council and regional ministries. These officials suggest that a 10 per cent kickback to councillors on these committees is usual. Selection for committee posts at the beginning of each year is therefore extremely important for the councillor. Some councillors say that bargaining for committee posts is related to agreements reached among members of the majority party regarding the Council chairmanship, which is also re-allocated annually.

There are other types of politicians in Ibadan today, such as the regional and federal parliamentarians. Their nominations depend on ties to the regional or national party which controls use of the party name and allots the campaign funds which most candidates need. While Nigerian election regulations forbid offering "food, drink or entertainment ... receipt of gifts, loans, or employment for corruptly influencing elections," political parties usually supply each candidate with about Ł 400 which he must spend precisely in these forbidden areas if he is to appear a generous and responsive candidate. It is impossible to calculate how much of the candidate-constituent relationship is a continuation of traditional conceptions of largesse and how much of it is calculating opportunism. One regional NCNC assemblyman suggested that election bribery would cease only when all voters in the Western Region would follow the example of Ibadan, "that is, to take Action Group's money and vote against them."[40] Most people of Ibadan understand little of the work of their federal and regional representatives. Since the city councillors are daily about their political business, on which the parliamentarians spend but a few days a year, the impression is re-inforced within the electorate that the parliamentarian does not return full value for his salary, although he is less dependent upon fees for his services than the councillor.

Conspicuous by their absence in the informal political economy are the senior staff members of the Ibadan Council. They are among the best-trained, best-paid members of the unified Local Government Service of the region, which has the power to send away to new posts staff members who become too deeply engrossed in the informal ways of doing things. This has never been necessary with Ibadan staff members, who see in scrupulous observance of the formal rules a major guarantee of independence vis-à-vis the legislative branch of the Council, for while the staff is often forced to administer Council decisions arrived at by methods which they question, the independence granted them in policy-making matters makes them some of the most powerful figures in the entire political system.

Conclusions

Even if one defines an urban area simply as a large, densely populated area, certain social and political consequences result which distinguish rural from urban communities. Size and density alone call for social rather than individual solutions to problems such as water, fuel, food, transporation, and housing. When the polity is called upon to provide these solutions, an opportunity arises for a series of arrangements between the polity, the economy, and the society, which are also markedly urban. Nineteenth century urban America developed the machine to supervise these arrangements. A brief look at the American machine may help put Ibadan politics in perspective.

American cities were immigrant cities, dominated by ethnic groups of predominantly rural backgrounds, inadequately prepared for urban employment. They arrived in the city during a technological revolution which made possible the construction of a highly sophisticated physical plant.

Water was supplied through pipelines and pumphouses, not wells and water wagons. Transport was provided by electric street cars, not bicycles. This vast labor was not performed by virtuous and efficient local governments, which proved either incapable (or unaware) of the need for change. As Professor Scott Greer has said, "When ... the burdens of government became too much for the legitimate systems of government, ways were found to circumvent the system."[41] The machine was the American way of circumventing formal systems. In order to control local governments which dispensed contracts and franchises for construction and operation of the new physical plants, machine politicians needed the ethnic bloc votes. These were purchased with favors (jobs, gifts, and protection from the law) which the machine controlled through connections or from the "honest" and "dishonest" graft taken from government contracts. The machine dominated the informal polity and linked social needs to inadequate formal institutions. In the process, a vast wealth of public, indivisible goods such as roads, buildings and utilities was created for American cities.

In Ibadan, however, there is no machine.[42] The ethnic minorities are in fact the British, Lebanese, Ijebu, Hausa, and American economic dominants, and none of them have machine constituency interests. Although most Ibadans are still in, or only slowly escaping from a subsistence economy, their relative poverty vis-à-vis the economic dominants does not mean they live in insecurity. The social system is relatively intact and poor do not die of starvation. The absence of an industrial technology means that there is little opportunity for individuals to become rich or for the city to develop a new physical plant. The ethnic elites are not interested in public housing, transportation, or the improvement of water service, nor do these problems attract the attention of local entrepreneurs. For the Council to undertake these tasks would require the taxation of people who have an annual income of little more than ₤ 50; this to purchase equipment priced according to the European industrial economy and increased by the costs of importation.

The Ibadan population, however, generally seeks individual and divisible values, not a new physical plant, the development of which might provide funds to run a political machine. Such large-scale projects as a new abattoir and a new water plant are under consideration, but they are being undertaken by the regional and federal governments and not by local politicians. Neither the problems, the politicians, the technology, nor the levels of political action in Ibadan are conducive to the development of a political machine in the American style.

The informal political economy of Ibadan is a strikingly individualistic sphere, catering to the individual needs of a traditional clientele that does not see itself as oppressed or alienated. In their councillors they find entrepreneurs who can get things done for them. Perhaps the speed and methods by which councillors must recover their investment contributes to the brevity of their tenure.

The councillor-constituent relationship must leave a certain impression of the nature of politics in the voting public's mind. It can be stated with certainty that this impression has little to do with the implementation of town planning, property taxes, or expensive and modern improvements. When most people think of "the Council" they think of the councillors but not the senior staff members who create and effect technical policy. The petty nature of the councillors' concerns alienates most doctors, lawyers, teachers, and engineers from local politics; for they see little satisfaction in handing out market stalls or allocating butchers' licenses. Their talents, therefore, are presently not utilized by the Council.

It might be argued, that the demands placed against the Council by its traditional constituents, cared for in large part by the councillors as entrepreneurs, are all that the Council in its present financial state could hope to meet regardless of who its councillors might be. Reform, in the sense of formalization of the informal political economy, has cost the Council its jurisdiction over courts and taxation and threatens to make contracts a matter for the regional government as well. The Council may become less "corrupt" in the process, but it will also become even less interesting to the alienated professional classes in terms of providing opportunities for substantive decision-making.

Ibadan is part of Nigeria, politically and economically, and it would be misleading to suggest that stability, growth, and development are solely dependent upon local conditions. It may be that Ibadan's informal political economy is producing considerable local political stability by satisfying divisible and individualistic needs, while legitimacy (in terms of loyalty) is lacking at all levels, particularly at the federal and regional levels which are estranged from the masses. So, while the local society grows committed to personal material satisfactions, the system as a whole remains vulnerable to revolutionary criticisms of its legitimacy. The informal system creates stability, but it does so in a manner which creates conditions favorable to instability in other areas. It frightens off the professional classes with their innovations, it invites the distant regional government to intervene to correct what it feels to be intolerable practices, and, in the area of tax evasion, it prevents the accumulation of capital necessary to establish projects which would make the Council a vigorous, modernizing agency to the community.

There are some who would suggest that all informal activities in developing systems such as Ibadan's must be immediately rooted out. Yet there may be some grain of utility in them. Perhaps the councillors might best be left to their present concerns, where they absorb uncertainty in the system and tie the masses to it. Where well-trained and selfless civil servants are available, as they are in Ibadan, it would be more useful to strengthen their policy-making powers than to attack the councillors. For an interim period, the councillors may indeed profit from an increase of local contracts which can be tapped through kickbacks; but other cities have gone through such experiences and survived. Should the Council through its professional staff be able to create modern improvements which would appeal to the loyalties of the masses and spark the civic imaginations of the alienated professional classes into more vigorous political action, the informal economy, rather than the power of the Council, may indeed wither away.

Footnotes

1. The reader will wish to consult Corruption in Developing Countries by Ronald Wraith and Edgar Simpkins (New York, 1963). My interpretations, run closer to those of Nathaniel Leff in his article, "Economic Development Through Bureaucratic Corruption, " in The American Behavioral Scientist, No. 3:8-14 (Nov. 1964). Leff demonstrates that much of the problem of corruption is how one thinks about it. The proper-transfer-of-institutions-and-practices approach of Wraith and Simpkins may be usefully contrasted with the model of the prismatic society presented by Fred W. Riggs, Administration In Developing Countries (Boston, 1964). For a discussion of Ibadan's politics from 1893 to 1963 see also George Jenkins, "Politics in Ibadan" (unpubl. diss., Northwestern University, 1965).

2. It used to be that a district officer could accept a horse as a gift from a chief to whom he might present money and watches in return and be praised for his generosity. The last British administrator employed by the Council scrupulously avoided giving or accepting as much as a chicken and was greatly praised for his honesty.

3. Rev. David Hinderer, "Journal, " Oct. 23, 1852, Church Missionary Society(CMS) file, CA. 2/049 (b).

4. In Samuel Johnson, The History of the Yorubas (CMS: London, 1921, reprinted 1956), 389, the Osi Seriki, third officer of the cavalry, is reported to have had 2, 000 followers in a campaign in 1873.

5. They are listed in Olubadan Akinyele's Iwe Itan Ibadan (privately published in England, 1959), 246-281. Mr. Hinderer in 1852 referred to Ibadan as "a military aristocracy, " although he noted that wealth was also a means of attaining office in Hinderer, "Journal, " Oct. 23, 1852.

6. Contrast this with Oyo, where the oba, or king, held the title of alafin, meaning owner of the palace.

7. Olubadan Akinyele, Outlines of Ibadan History (Lagos: privately published, 1946), 72.

8. Johnson, History, 321.

9. The army attempted to live off the land on short expeditions. When camps were established for long periods, crops were planted and provisions from Ibadan were brought up. It is impossible to estimate the relative importance of the various means of provisioning the army. Hinderer notes

in his "Journal, " Oct. 23, 1952, that some of the Ibadan chiefs had
thousands of slaves on their farms and that farmers and the "working class"
were looked down on by the warriors. A letter from F. L. Akiele to
Archdeacon MacKay suggests that complex trade relations existed which
were capable of functioning even in the troubled period of the Ijaye war.
"I remember that during the Ijaye war which took place in 1860 to 1862
this woman whose name was Ogunsola was a great friend of Mr. and Mrs.
Hinderer who supplied them with all necessaries then. She used to send
her slaves to Lagos ... as she has many, to buy and sell during the war
time. She has no title but she was a rich woman ... It may be that she
assisted John Glover the Governor of Lagos at that time to keep open the
road as the Alafin of Oyo used to send her slaves to Lagos to buy and sell
during the war time. She was a relation of the Alafin of Oyo." F. L.
Akiele to Archdeacon MacKay, July 7, 1926 (courtesy of Canon Olunloyo).

10. Johnson, History, 393, 421.

11. C. W. Newbury, The Western Slave Coast and Its Rulers (Oxford,
1961), 72-73.

12. Reverend J. B. Wood to Reverend R. Lang, Dec. 10, 1884, CMS
Archives G3. A/203, Jan.- June 1885.

13. One supporter's contribution to Are Latosisa's costs of taking
office in 1880 included 800 bags of cowries (valued at £ 800 in the late
1860's), a house, a sword, and gowns. Johnson, History, 375, 390.

14. Estimated from the sketches of chieftaincy houses in, Akinyele,
Iwe Itan Ibadan, 246-281.

15. Akinyele, Outlines, 72-73.

16. See a letter from Council Secretary E. H. Oke to Resident of
Ibadan, n.d., in Annual File, Ibadan Council, Mapo Hall, 1912.

17. The case of Aiyejenku is described by Johnson, History, 407-410.

18. Governor Carter to Bale, March 2, 1884, No. 37/17, in Historical
Papers File, Ibadan Council, Mapo Hall.

19. Several chiefs have pointed out to me persons living in their
compounds who they said were descendants of their former slaves. Private
records show that slaves remained in their masters' service into the
1920's, by which time they were known as "retainers." A slave redemption

registry existed, but could not be traced.

20. Ibadan Council Minutes, May 18, 1909.

21. Thus the district officer complained to the bale in 1914: "I want you to be very careful to stop your slaves or servants trying cases. I know it is the custom of the country, but it is a bad custom." Grier to Bale, April 10, 1914.

22. Ibadan Council Minutes, Oct. 10, 1903.

23. Ibid.

24. Ibid. This disadvantageous position in terms of income, recognized by the British as legitimate, is further illustrated by the fact that the chief customs clerk received a salary of Ł 30 in 1914.

25. Bale to Resident, June 26, 1908; Resident to Bale July 16, 1908, No. 322/1908; Resident to Bale, Oct. 28, 1908, S.N. 715/1908, all in Correspondence Ledger 1907-1908, Ibadan Council, Mapo Hall.

26. Part of the labor force may have consisted of slaves.

27. Ibadan Council Minutes, March 30 and July 22, 1911.

28. Southern Provinces file 14935, Nigerian National Archives, contains records pertinent to the implementation of indirect rule.

29. The following examples and allegations are taken from three different private sources.

30. Diary of Akinpelu Obisesan, Aug. 30, 1927, Aranran, Nigeria.

31. See G. Oke Orewa, Taxation in Western Nigeria (London, 1962), I, for a historical account of taxation in Nigeria from 1917 to 1927.

32. Ibadan Native Authority File "Rebate" (1934), Mapo Hall.

33. Handing Over Note of Feb. 19, 1938, in Oyo Provincial Papers (Oyoprof), National Archives, list I, Vol. II, 931.

34. Oyoprof, list I, 902.

35. Oyoprof, list I, 547/S.8, Vol. I.

36. S. O. Ajibola, Secretary of the Ibadan City Council, "Ibadan City Versus Progress and Improvement, " July 1963 (mimeographed).

37. Approved Ibadan City Council Estimates for 1962-1963.

38. Difficulties, unusual circumstances, and "trouble" are to be avoided in such a system, as a celebrated case in 1945 shows. First, a fee of Ł 5 was paid to the olubadan to announce the death of the previous family head. On the day after the death, eight chiefs who came to console with the family were given a total of Ł 7.10s., and 5 shillings were presented to their messengers. Ł 2.10s. was given to the balogun to gain his approval for the family's nominee for mogaji. The Ł 5 was given to the olubadan and Ł 2.10s. to his son, who acted as his major domo, for the same purpose. Up to this point all seemed to be going well. Then, the olubandan's son reminded his father that the candidate had once opposed him during an agitation. The candidate's backers later complained that this reversal of opinion was prompted by a gift from another branch of the family of Ł 105 paid to the olubadan, his son, and two other chiefs. None of the original candidate's fees were returned, and he took the case to the Western Region courts, where he was defeated. The cost of the litigation is not known, but the defeated candidate was forced to leave the family compound and begin a new house, of which he is now a recognized chief. Provincial Administra- tion Department, Ibadan Division, File 2225, National Archives.

39. See Richard Sklar, Nigerian Political Parties (Princeton, 1963), Ch. VII.

40. The Honorable D. K. Olumofin, Debates of the Western House of Assembly (Western Region of Nigeria), Dec. 13, 1955, 243.

41. Scott Greer, Governing the Metropolis (New York, 1962), 48-49.

42. It is sometimes suggested that Adegoke Adelabu, whose party controlled Ibadan from 1954 to 1958, had a machine. Richard Sklar, although he uses the term, emphasizes Adelabu's charismatic and demagogic talents. See Sklar, Nigerian Parties, Ch. VII. A commission of inquiry which investigated "six instances of corrupt or dishonest acts" by Adelabu and his principal lieutenant while Adelabu was council chairman, revealed Ibadan political life to be an opportunity for the individual politician, but not for organization men. See E. W. J. Nicholson, Report of the Commission of Inquiry into the Administration of the Ibadan District Council (Western Region of Nigeria, 1956).

VIII

Dilemmas of Political Theory in an African Context: The Ideology of
Julius Nyerere

Harvey Glickman
Department of Political Science, Haverford College

The Problem of Ideology in Africa

All revolutions develop ideologies in order to help make choices and
justify them afterward. Africa is no exception even though in the changing
political systems of many older states on other continents during the last
half-century, most non–Marxist politicians have steadily come to believe
that ideological formulations are not relevant to current political problems
and, in fact, undermine practical solutions. But the reverse view prevails
today in the new African states. As recent dissenters -- claimants of power
rather than wielders of it -- Africa's new political executives move more easily
on ideological than on administrative terrain. They have seen the rapid
fruition of their appeals for justice, dignity, and the right of self-government,
and experience which could, quite understandably, suggest to them or their
followers that appeals have merely to be made in order for Africans to
achieve results that have come far more slowly to other colonial peoples.
Some of the most telling maneuvers in the course of the de-colonizing
Africa would seem to have taken place in debate: in the assembly halls
of the United Nations, in the parliamentary chambers of the metropolitan
powers, and in the legislative councils of their colonies. Frequently,
debates on constitutional matters were forced to consider fundamental
questions about the nature of government and who should rule.

The ready availability of anti-imperialist doctrine, the persistence
of the issue of colonialism in southern Africa with its potential for wringing
favors from competing great powers, have all served to delay the complete
conversion of doctrinal formulas into designs for post-colonial nation building.
Colin Leys once noted the constitutional opportunity for President Nyerere
to construct "a national social ethos" for Tanganyika.[1] In varying degrees
each of Africa's new states faces the same responsibility. Although African
governments have achieved sovereign status in international relations,
they have barely established civic authority within their own borders.
Nation building, i.e. the acquisition, particularly by leaders, of the capacity
to govern and the extension of loyalty to the civic entity of the territorial
state, by leader and followers, has hardly begun. The idea of a public
purpose that informs responsibility to government, and the notion of a
relationship between popular participation and the eventual policy of
government, remain, of course, exceedingly vague to the vast majority

of the population. To render meaningful the role of citizen in a new state like the United Republic of Tanzania is to undertake a great architectonic task. Even more urgently than in the period of organizing for nationalist victory, the politics of African nation-building is the politics of vision, i.e., the capacity to foresee problems ahead, and to coin the ideas and symbols which create in people a sense of helping in a common task.

Despite the prominence of ideological discourse and its significance for the style of African leadership, several problems face the analyst. Although there are obvious similarities in the circumstances in which all African nationalist leaders find themselves -- and therefore a certain uniformity of vocabulary -- the new states vary according to social structure, relationship of nationalist parties to that structure, and the controls and supports available to the central government. While there is agreement on the lineaments of African socialism as an overall guide for official policies, there is no single body of orthodoxy from which African leaders draw their ideas. Each of Africa's political theorists, therefore, deserves individual attention.

Africa's political theorists are also her governors, and in the midst of the numerous burdens of office protracted concern for conceptual matters is hardly to be anticipated. Often major ideological statements are circumstantially oriented rather than premeditated; African political theory is still in the era of the pamphlet, not the book. One journalist observed despairingly that a political utterance in Africa "is merely a sympton of the situation in which it is made. A speech here is not conditioned by circumstances; it is created by them. It is therefore often impossible, indeed, to give it any precise verbal meaning."[2] Indeed, most of the evidence we have of ideological preoccupation is in the form of speeches, in which the ideas are accompanied by considerable rhetorical baggage and argumentative flourish. Nevertheless, the business of state-creation is going on, and if we hope to comprehend the preconceptions which condition the choices that leaders are making, we must work with the materials at hand.

A major dilemma confronting those involved in the construction of ideology in Africa concerns the somewhat contradictory nature of the job. If the inhabitants of a territory are to develop citizenship ties to the state, the emergent civic culture must reflect some part of their social experiences, i.e. their traditions. Yet the residues of traditional culture pose serious obstacles to the creation of attitudes conducive to the growth of modern institutions.[3] The problem is acute in Africa where traditional attitudes have only just began to give way to the demands of new loyalties. The situation is, therefore, particularly volatile and potentially divisive. At the same time as an African ideology must face toward tradition it must act as an agency of modernization.

The paradox in this is that political modernization aims toward the construction of a democratic state; yet to encourage democracy, to solicit popular
participation in public affairs, leaders must invoke attitudes still embedded
in traditional loyalties and outlooks. One way to evade the difficulty is
to hold that African traditional society is inherently democratic and that,
therefore, no basic conflict exists. Another escape is to reverse this
stratagem and redefine democracy so that its essentials reflect the realities
of the emerging national political system. Julius Nyerere, the president
of Tanzania and one of a handful of current African leaders who can be
called a political theorist, executes both these maneuvers; their implications
pose a central problem for the character of his country's political system.
At some future date Nyerere may have to abandon some parts of his eclectic
ideology: traditional conceptions of communal co-operation, Christian notions
of brotherhood, Western liberal-democratic conceptions of self-government,
and European socialist ideas of abolishing economic exploitation.[4]

In any society the propagation of ideas goes on at different levels.
It is important, therefore, to distinguish between the forensic ideologies
of political thinkers and the latent ideologies of the common man.[5] In
Africa the gap is perhaps wider than elsewhere and the links between them
are extremely tenuous. Although previous analyses of political ideologies
have indicated the durability of traditionalist ways of thinking and underscored
the mixed character of all political cultures, it would be misleading to focus
on latent ideology in order to comprehend the probable lines along which
a mobilizing regime will move.[6] The growing body of forensic ideology of
African political leaders, especially those of a speculative bent, offers a
more promising quarry for our purpose. Touré, Nkrumah, and Nyerere,
for example, have each developed a line of thought which exposes the
determining features of their social and political condition, describes the
future society to be created, and prescribes the means necessary to achieve
the ends in view. Classic questions of political theory are dealt with,
though sometimes too briefly: who shall rule, how will they be selected,
and by what principles should they govern. As "founding fathers, " they
have dwelt on programs for the defense or reform or abolition of important
social institutions, arguing to persuade or to counter opposition.[7] This
paper deals with the political thought of Julius Nyerere, focusing on his
conceptions of the nature of a reconstituted polity in Tanzania.

Ideology is approached here as a precursor of broad political issues
and as a source of inspiration for the shape and style of political reconstruction. The genealogy of ideas or their uniqueness are not fundamentally at
issue; the measurement of the impact of ideology requires a different form
of analysis and is left to another occasion.[8] The present approach to the
discussion of political ideology requires clarification of the conceptions of

society and government and an assessment of their implications for a
developing political order.

The Problem of Brotherhood

Commenting on his domination of the politics of Tanganyika, an
observer has aptly compared Julius Nyerere to Pandit Nehru.[9] Almost
all the first presidents and prime ministers of Africa's new states so
control the early politics of their countries that each appears of paramount
importance; but only a few have also been celebrated internationally for their
integrity and perspicacity. In this way, Nyerere is close to Nehru, but in
other ways as well. Like Nehru, Nyerere is at home in the environment of
European-style politics, within which he has been adept at using against
his colonial masters their own weapons -- democratic doctrines and parliamentary skills. Both men sprang from families of high status in traditional
society and achieved high position in the class system of the modern sector.
Finally, like Nehru, Nyerere has pushed his political discourses to their
philosophical foundations. Indeed Nyerere's intellectual forays are probably
taken as seriously now as Nehru's were, if we are to judge from the increasing
frequency with which his publications are cited in illustrating Africa's new
departures in politics -- one-party democracy and African socialism.

The feat is all the more impressive, since as late as 1958 Nyerere
did not face the necessity of thinking about an overall policy for the nationalist movement beyond the achievement of independence, gained in December
1961. When, in March 1955, during Nyerere's first appearance before the
Trusteeship Council of the United Nations, he was asked how TANU proposed
to eliminate ignorance and poverty in Tanganyika, Nyerere replied: "I
cannot say that my Union is contemplating anything because it is not like
a party in opposition to the Government, which is itself likely to be the
Government a little later so that it can make up its mind what it would do
if it were in power. We do feel, however, that two things can be done.
The first is that our own people should be able to help our own people; if
we had an African holding a responsible position he might have more influence
on the people ... there is a need for co-operation and people ought to be
told that they must co-operate. If we were in a position to do that, they
would obey."[10] Nyerere's political thinking, like the program of the Tanganyika
African National Union -- the nationalist movement which Nyerere helped found
in 1954 and which he serves as first and only president -- developed in response
to issues which arose in the course of mounting the assault on the British
administration and, later, in acquiring formal authority to govern. From
1955 to 1958 he concentrated on tactics that would result in a "West African
solution" to Tanganyika's constitutional problems in contradistinction to the
policy of the colonial government to give all racial groups parity of representation

Nyerere wanted self-government with Africans in control, and his justifications were in the tradition of European liberal democracy. Responsibility
for government should be in the hands of the people, and representation
should be based on the legal equality of all inhabitants. One man-one vote
and majority rule with equal and uniform rights for all were the familiar
premises on which Nyerere operated. "Government belongs to all the people
as a natural and inalienable possession, it is not the private property of
a minority, however elite or wealthy or educated, and whether uni- or
multi-racial. Government is properly instituted among men not to secure
the material or cultural advantages of a few, but to promote the rights
and welfare of the many. Therefore the many must inevitably be genuinely
consulted, and the just powers of government derived from them. Government
by representatives in whose selection most of the governed have no part
is not rule but repression."[11]

   The policy of the colonial government of Tanganyika in this period
was so blatantly anti-"democratic," depending on parity of representation
for each of the two minority racial groups with the overwhelming African
majority, that it really was not necessary to spend much time arguing at
the level of ideology. "What will satisfy my people is a categorical statement
both by the [Trusteeship] Council and the Administering Authority, that
although Tanganyika is multi-racial in population its future government
shall be primarily African. Once we get that assurance, everything else
becomes a detail."[12] Such an assurance was not forthcoming until TANU
could demonstrate decisive support among the Africans permitted to vote
in the first elections for seats in the Legislative Council in September 1958.
In order to do this, as well as to capture a majority of the fifteen seats
at issue (five for each race, with candidates nominated by each racial
group but elected on a common roll) and to show its willingness to work
with all races, TANU decided to endorse those Asian and European candidates
who were not committed to the United Tanganyika Party -- the party of multi-
racialism and official government policy. All the TANU-supported candidates
of all races won handily in the twelve contested seats, and the margin in
virtually every case was provided by African support for TANU.[13] In one
swoop, Nyerere had demonstrated TANU's overwhelming popularity and its
acceptance of non-racial co-operation.

   Nyerere probably first came to the notice of foreign observers through
his steadfast rejection of racist arguments. His reputation as a moderate
was helped when a small group of members split with the party at the Annual
Conference in January 1958 over the combined issues of co-operation
with other races and participation in the forthcoming elections. On this
subject Nyerere later made a particularly moving appeal as the leader of
the multi-racial Tanganyika Elected Members Organization in the Legislative
Council: "Let not the world point a finger at us and say that we gained our

freedom on a moral argument -- the argument of the brotherhood of man -- and then threw that argument overboard and began to discriminate against our brothers on the grounds of color."[14] He has also staked his position on support for his policy. In October 1961, he faced bitter criticism from a sizeable number of African members of the National Assembly on the question of the eligibility of non-Africans for Tanganyika citizenship. Nyerere rebuked his critics, comparing their ideas to "Hitlers and Verwoerds ... this Government has rejected and rejected completely any ideas that citizenship, with the duties and rights of citizenship of the country, are going to be based on anything except loyalty to this country."[15]

In January 1964, Nyerere applied the same principle when he announced that preference for Africans in the recruitment, training, and promotion of civil servants would cease immediately. This implied an end to the policy of Africanization, which had gone forward rapidly since independence. Skill and experience would determine qualifications for service and "the skin in which this skill is encased is completely irrelevant."[16] It is not clear to what extent this helped spark the army mutiny which occurred a few days later, but to the extent that it did, it was another instance in which Nyerere risked the life of his regime, knowingly or not, on the principle of non-racialism.[17]

At the level of his popular following, there is no doubt that Nyerere's ideal of non-racialism meets with considerable resistance. But this fact should not be explained merely by the assertion that Africans have simple-minded notions of the meaning of independence or unabashed cupidity in the face of the advantages possessed by Asians and Europeans. Long after there was no tactical advantage to limiting membership to Africans, Nyerere could not convince the National Executive of TANU that non-racial doctrine should extend to membership in the party. Not until he was ready to announce a statutory one-party system in 1963 could he get the restrictions repealed. The difficulty goes deeper; it can be traced to the fundamental problem of preaching universal brotherhood when the reconstruction of society depends on the assertion of the uniqueness of African culture. Underlying Nyerere's explanation of democracy and socialism in Africa is the message that Africa is different. And, while Nyerere argues that the civic attitudes of the new society in Africa should reflect the kinship ties and communal loyalties of the extended family, he would also have us believe that these are peculiarly African traits, which non-Africans do not share and indeed avoid. As we shall see, Nyerere has not been able to escape this conceptual difficulty, as well as others which lead to more critical dilemmas, i.e. those with practical implications.

Conceptions of Society and Polity

Nyerere's insistence on Africa's uniqueness pervades his attempt to construct an ideology socially meaningful to his countrymen. The two basic strands represent reinterpretations of socialism and democracy, each involving an endeavor to render a cluster of beliefs and values (that have had long and honorable but previously non-indigenous connotations) into a form with recognizable claims to African origins and appropriate to the solution of local problems. Through this effort Nyerere hopes to establish a national political identity for his people that is neither wholly negative--a rejection of colonialism and capitalism--nor as wholly imitative as a constant emphasis on the artifacts of a modern developed society would be. His task is to infuse dignity and worth in the way Africans are and to demonstrate that what they are doing reflects what they are.

The Solidaristic Society

In what promises to endure as one of the classic opening sentences in the literature of political tracts, Nyerere has observed, "Socialism-- like democracy--is an attitude of mind."[18] This attitude of mind, according to Nyerere, springs from the traditional relations of African society, which are communal (as distinguished from individualist-associative) and egalitarian (as distinguished from elitist). The structure of that society is classless and its characteristic institution is the extended family. For Nyerere any valid African political philosophy must express this underlying reality, which he calls "socialist," but which we label "solidaristic" in order to distinguish it more clearly from more conventional ideas of socialism.

Let us look more closely at Nyerere's picture of Ujamaa ("familyhood"), the expression of Africa's solidaristic society. Its basic egalitarianism is expressed in a rejection of individual acquisitiveness and the desire for domination over other people, which Nyerere believes to be parasitism-- a direct product of the capitalist system. "But the man who uses wealth for the purpose of dominating any of his fellows is a capitalist ... Acquisitiveness for the purpose of gaining power and prestige is unsocialist." The analytical emphasis is on "an attitude of mind." It is not the possession of wealth but the value attached to wealth and the use made of it that matters. Nyerere is raising a moral and psychological standard, not one of objective structure. "A millionaire can equally well be a socialist; he may value his wealth only because it can be used in the service of his fellow men." Similarly, socialists can behave in a capitalistic manner. "But I believe that the Socialist countries themselves, considered as 'individuals' in the larger society of nations, are now committing the same crime as was committed by the capitalists before. I believe that on the international level, they are now beginning to use Wealth for the purpose of acquiring power and prestige."[19]

Africa's traditional society could be called socialist, in Nyerere's view, because it concerned itself with the problem of distribution, making sure "that those who sow reap a fair share of what they sow."[20] But, of course, everybody had to be satisfied that his share was a fair one. Nyerere does not make clear why this should be the case, except to emphasize the rough equality of rewards and relatively even distribution of wealth that prevailed in traditional African society. He goes so far as to suggest that the reason there were no African millionaires is that the social organization did not permit private accumulation. (This is somewhat at odds with the history of several traditional African kingdoms.) In any case, it is right not to permit sizable differences in rewards: "there must be something wrong in a society where one man, however hard working and clever he may be, can acquire as great a 'reward' as a thousand of his fellow can acquire between them."

Justice implies equality, and equality for Nyerere also means sharing in one another's concerns. People did not have to hoard wealth for themselves, the communal ethic secured everyone against the chief hazards of life. "We took care of the community and the community took care of us. We neither needed nor wished to exploit our fellow men ... One of the most socialistic achievements of our society was the sense of security it gave to its members, and the universal hospitality on which they could rely ... For when a society is so organized that it cares about its individuals, then, provided he is willing to work, no individual within that society should worry about what will happen to him tomorrow if he does not hoard wealth today. Society itself should look after him, or his widow, or his orphans. This is exactly what traditional African society succeeded in doing."

One way to restore vestiges of that security is to emphasize types of economic organization which seem to reflect traditional African principles. In Tanganyika this was not difficult since Africans were active in co-operative production and marketing societies under British administration. Co-operatives, by themselves, it should be pointed out, do not guarantee socialism in action, of course, since a desire for individual gain could re-assert itself. Nyerere continues:

> Much as we respect the Rochdale principles of co-
> operation and the fine example provided by foreign co-
> operative movements, co-operation in its real sense as
> we all know, has provided the basis of our African society
> for thousands of years ... the whole Society was one vast
> co-operative.[21]

"Ujima" [co-operation] is indeed the instrument of "Ujamaa" just as the commercial company is the

> instrument of capitalism ... the two main instruments
> of Ujamma [are]--the Government and the Co-operation
> Movement.[22]

Nyerere has observed in private that if he had an entirely free hand, government policy would seek the complete elimination of private profit and would substitute co-operative methods of sharing the rewards of enterprise.[23]

Equality existed also in the relative uniformity of labor--"in traditional African society everybody was a worker"--and in a classless social structure. According to Nyerere, classes have arisen as a result of alien intrusions, "for aristocracy is something foreign to Africa. Even where there is a fairly distinct African aristocracy-by-birth, it can be traced historically to sources outside this continent ... In my own country, the only two tribes which have a distinct aristocracy are the Bahaya in Bukoba, and the Baha in the Buha districts. In both areas the aristocrats are historically 'foreigners' and they belong to the same stock." In pristine African society, he argues, status came only with age and with doing a job well. The divisions in present-day African societies are also due to outside intervention; the distinction between employer and employee and between landlord and tenant, Nyerere claims, were introduced by colonialism and foreign capitalists. In the solidaristic society the African saw "no conflict between his own interests and those of his community."[24]

What made all this possible was the extended family: "the structure of society was, in fact, a direct extension of the family."[25] Nyerere wishes to extend the spirit of the family tie throughout the whole contemporary society. "The foundation and the objective of African Socialism is the extended family. The true African Socialist ... regards all men as his brethren--as members of his ever extending family." Ujamaa--"familyhood"-- is, therefore, the term that Nyerere enlarges to fit the African conception of the good society. It is also an historical conception; i.e. it once existed.

Nyerere believes that the virtues of traditional African society can exempt the continent from the bitterness which accompanied the political and economic development of Europe. The philosophy of socialism that has emerged there, though it shares several characteristics with the African variety, stands quite opposed on the question of conflict and its uses. "As prayer is to Christianity or to Islam, so civil war (which they call 'class war') is to the European version of socialism--a means inseparable from the end." By accepting the fact that socialism develops out of capitalism, the European socialist are actually glorifying social conflict, something which Africans, if they perceive their heritage in the proper light, can avoid completely. "The European socialist cannot think of his socialism without its father--capitalism. Brought up in tribal socialism, I must say I find this contradiction quite intolerable." African socialism can take its own separate

and independent philosophical path, " opposed to capitalism, which seeks
to build a happy society on the basis of the exploitation of man by man ...
opposed to doctrinaire socialism which seeks to build its happy society
on a philosophy of inevitable conflict between man and man."

Nyerere singles out the institution of individual ownership of land
for special condemnation, and it serves as a dramatic illustration of the
social damage wrought by the intrusion of the capitalist principle of personal
acquisition, which leads to the injustice of domination of man by man. The
traditional African conception, according to Nyerere, recognizes communal
ownership but permits personal use. "The foreigner introduced a completely
different concept -- the concept of land as a marketable commodity." But
Nyerere does not argue against individual sale of property, concentrating
instead on the irrationality of variable market values, which are reflected
in rent and in fluctuating sale prices. He is willing to grant that "a member
of society will be entitled to a piece of land on condition that he uses it."
Nyerere concludes that the only way we can make sure that people do
utilize their land (of course, they will also have to utilize it in accordance
with socialist guidance) and concentrate their interest in land in the development of it and not in speculation is to eliminate private proprietal rights.
"Unconditional, or 'freehold', ownership of land (which leads to speculation
and parasitism) must be abolished."

The possibility that the colonial administration might begin the transformation of customary tenure into freehold tenure in 1958 provided an
occasion for Nyerere for extended introspection on the institution of property.[26]
Nyerere dealt in detail with the legal and administrative objections to enlarging
freehold ownership of land in Tanganyika at that time; but first he argued
that individual proprietary rights in land are not only unnatural to Africa,
but also probably wrong in conception.

"What is the basis of the right of owning property?" asks Nyerere.
His answer fits the social teaching of the Roman Catholic Church, in which
Nyerere was reared and of which he remains a member: "A person cannot
be the property of someone else ... his health, intellect and strength cannot
be the property of someone else. Therefore when he uses these things ...
in making anything, the thing belongs to him, it is his own property ... the
efforts of a person himself are the foundation of possession, and that
foundation comes from a natural law that makes a person his own property
... God did not give us any way of obtaining our wants except one, and that
is by Sweat."[27] Certain things exist on earth as a gift of God for everyone's
use, such as air, water, and land. "I can say about a piece of land, 'here
is my place.' But it is evident that what is mine is not the land itself --
which I found where it was and where it will continue to be for generations

until the end of the earth -- but only the ground that I cleared for my own needs. By clearing the place I have made it valuable, in that I have improved it and made it useful for satisfying human needs. If you want that ground you must pay for the value which is a product of my own strength, for that is not a gift from God." What belongs to us, then, is what we make useful. (Nyerere does not expand on the limits involved, but he intimates that we should not try to make "useful" more than we need.) It follows, also, that a piece of land we are working remains ours only as long as we work it: "we ourselves are only tenants and our time will expire and others will come to replace us." Neither can we pass it on to succeeding generations. "The present generation cannot give the next generation things like air, water and land. These things belong to the next generation under the natural law and not by good will or practice or human law." We cannot treat land like a pen or a pencil, because in the nature of things it cannot ever belong to anyone. People may think they can make claims on land which their families have worked and the government may try to sell land to individuals. But "a robbery is a robbery even if it is defended by law."

Not only is it wrong to grant individual proprietary rights in land, it is also dangerous. It permits people to charge rent, capitalizing on artificial values that are created by natural or man-made shortages. It also allows rich foreigners or cunning Africans to buy up the best land in the country. "And these blood-suckers will not even let the poor workers get fair wages for their toil. They will forcibly take everything which the workers harvest and call it taxes for using 'their' land (as if they made or created it) ... One group will harvest without planting, while the other group will plant the seeds without harvesting the crops!" The remedy suggested by Nyerere in 1958 for this "disease" of freehold ownership is to permit leasehold arrangements under specified conditions.

Four years later Nyerere stated: "the TANU Government must go back to the traditional African custom of landholding."[28] Nyerere's desire to abolish freehold has been described as a specific example of ideology which led directly to policy consequences. In 1963, the government dissolved freehold titles and indicated methods for converting to leasehold arrangements. Leasers were obliged to develop their lands in the future in the best interests of the whole nation. In November 1964, the government confiscated thirty-seven leasehold farms (some were absentee-owned and in debt to the government) because, as Nyerere said, "they did not conform with the requirements of land tenure."[29] The significance of the fact that the leaseholders involved in these holdings were all Europeans and Asians was not lost on the African population.

Communal responsibility enforced by ties of kinship is at the heart of Nyerere's vision of the solidaristic society. This vision serves to invigorate Tanganyika in its task of nation-building because it springs from Africa's own pattern of social organization; but it is perhaps even more important that the vision represents a set of attitudes that embody what is natural and right for human beings today. In Nyerere's view, it is necessary to recall these indigenous values because they have been emasculated by capitalist imperialism, which forcibly implanted its own institutions in African society. The sin of capitalism then is that it introduced conflicting interests -- in the form of social stratification reinforced by racial inequality -- into an environment where previously only natural harmony existed. Nonetheless the harmony has been shattered, and the construction of the new order becomes a political problem. It is not easy to restore attitudes of social responsibility after they have been crippled by an alien system that glorified personal gain. The way that has been made available by the advent of self-government and the power of the TANU government to enforce measures which revive the exercise of communal obligations. The difficulty of restoring the solidaristic society necessitates a theory of centralized democracy.

Monopolitical Democracy

"True Democracy depends far more on the attitude of mind which respects and defends the individual than on the forms it takes."[30] In adopting this approach to the nature of good government, Nyerere again seeks to detach African institutions and practices from alien varieties and yet tie the goals of African government to familiar verities. It is not very difficult to indicate the unsuitability of certain European parliamentary forms to Africa, but it requires some redefinition of respect for and defense of the individual for Nyerere to hold that such a notion underlies African political attitudes. Once it is recognized that Nyerere defines individual freedom as equal opportunity for access to deliberation on policy, and not as the preservation of certain inviolable individual rights, then it is clear how his conception of African democracy can also involve individual freedom."A small village in which the villagers are equals who make their own laws and conduct their own affairs by free discussion is the nearest thing to pure democracy."[31]

In any case, Nyerere is not willing to admit that the more familiar Western liberal notion respects and defends the individual: "The West seems to have exaggerated its idea of freedom beyond the point where freedom becomes license; to have accepted a society in which, provided a man does not too obviously steal or murder, he can defend any form of self-indulgence by calling it 'freedom of the individual.'"[32] The African's conception

of individual freedom flows from the ethos of the solidaristic society. This
is not identical with the suppression of the individual in a totalitarian regime:
"the individual in a Communist society is secondary to something called
the state."[33] Rather, it is a direct extension of ujamma, the organic
relationship between individual and community, which makes basic conflicts
of interest between individuals and between individuals and the state, impossible.

In the course of his inquiry Nyerere re-states a classic dilemma.
"Here, then, I think is the problem: where does society or the state draw
the boundary of its rights and obligations; and where does the individual ...
Our problem is just this: how to get the benefits of European society --
benefits that have been brought about by an organization based upon the
individual -- and yet retain Africa's own structure of society in which the
individual is a member of a kind of fellowship."[34] It is a Rouseauan problem,
which, of course, can only spring from the Rousseauan quest for individual
and community good that is simultaneous and equal.[35] Nyerere's interim
solution is to invoke a core of African morality which somehow will cause
us to re-evaluate individuality in a novel manner: "I feel that Africa's own
tradition, her moral strength, her lack of ties with one power bloc or the
other, and that sentiment of oneness which the centuries of suffering have
built among all her peoples can together fit her for the role I have suggested --
the role of champion of personal freedom in the world today."[36]

From a Rousseauan problem Nyerere travels inevitably toward
Rousseauan formulations. Social solidarity and personalization of leadership
are not only conducive to mobilizing popular energies for public welfare,
they also combine with the consensual method of deliberation and decision
making. This achieves a form of government that retrieves Africa's
contribution to the restoration of human dignity by reflecting a "form of
organization of society which solves the fundamental conflict between the
individual and society."[37] In practice this leads to eliminating associations
that cannot be organically related to the community-in-action and to obviating
the need for any organized political opposition. The national political
union, which strives to embrace all political endeavor and to penetrate all
activity, becomes the center of the monopolitical system.[38]

Let us turn first to the merely expediential factors in the development
of monopolitical democracy, the reasons why, according to Nyerere, it is
the nature of the decolonization process that forms single-party systems.
He describes the drive for independence as "a patriotic struggle which leaves
no room for differences, and which unites all elements in the country."
The same applies to the economic and social development of the post-independence government. "This, no less than the struggle against colonialism, calls
for the maximum united effort by the whole country if it is to succeed. There
can be no room for difference or division."[39] Nyerere describes as ridiculous

the idea that "the country should divide itself" at this time.[40] The circumstances can be compared to the wartime parliaments in Western Europe:
"it is an accepted practice that in times of emergency, opposition parties
sink their differences and join together in forming a national government.
This is our time of emergency.[41]

"The problems of government in the new state are also just too
formidable to permit political divisions ... the demands of the common man
in Africa ... the lack of men, the lack of money, above all the lack of
time" plus ethnic and racial disunity; and "as if the natural challenge were
not enough, with the raising of each new flag come the intrigues of the
international diplomacy of rivalry." The crowning embarrassment stems
from the nature of opposition groups withing the new states: "a few irresponsible individuals" who abuse the privileges of democracy "by creating problems
of law and order, " people who display "neither sincerity, conviction nor
any policy save self-aggrandizement. They merely employ the catch phrases
copied from the political language of older, stabler countries in order to
engage the sympathy of the unthinking for their destructive tactics."[42]
Although the nationalists achieved a certain unity in the course of overthrow-
ing colonialism, it remains fragile and uncertain in the new post-colonial
circumstances. The establishment of government for Nyerere in the changed
situation of independence is then partly a Hobbesian problem. Order requires
an imposed unity, the single sovereign who will forcibly bring an end to
endemic divisions.[43]

To the necessity of unity and its institutional expression, the single-
party system, Nyerere adds the naturalness of such an expression in Africa.
Africa's heritage of a classless social structure, according to Nyerere,
reasserts itself in the united national movement and single-party government.
"It soon became clear to us that, however ready we leaders might have been
to accept the theory that an official opposition was essential to democratic
government, our own people thought otherwise; for the idea did not make
sense to them."[44] This extends beyond party competition, embracing the
whole conception of the relationship of ruler to the ruled. In Africa, the
attitudes that attend family obligations also define political ties. To the
question "who rules?" Nyerere answers that the reply intelligible to an
African is a chieftain related to him. The African's "conception of government
was personal, not institutional. When government was mentioned the African
thought of the chief; unlike the Briton, he did not picture a grand building
in which a debate was taking place."[45] In re-constituting the government
on the lines of a presidential system, Nyerere noted that the republican
constitution "adapts our historical experience of government to the new
circumstances."[46]

More significant, however, is the linking of natural attitudes toward
the procedures of deliberation to the contemporary situation. "This 'talking
until you agree' is the essential of the traditional African concept of democracy."[47] Nyerere's point is that to the African the whole purpose of
discussion is to agree. To continue to oppose it after a decision has been
reached is regarded as embarrassing and even mischievous, an attitude
which carries over to the present refusal of the Tanganyikan masses to support
any opposition to TANU and their tendency to equate opposition with sedition.
Nyerere does not mean to deny disagreement among African politicians,
in the traditional context or otherwise. Instead, he confirms that Africans
are more comfortable with methods of reaching political decisions that do
not choose up sides, but rather depend on arriving at the sense of the
meeting. Discussion revolves around a central authoritative presentation
and subsequent argument and decisions are not dependent on the presentation of prefabricated alternative positions emanating from several opposing
viewpoints. Nyerere, the extraordinarily successful campaigner, even
scorned the process of argument by alternative candidates for leadership.
"Campaigning for elections is not a traditional African practice. It is one
we have inherited from the Europeans. It smacks of pride, vanity and
sometimes stubbornness -- a man standing before the public outlining his
good qualities. This is a shameful thing."[48]

It might be remarked in passing that, decision making by consensus --
"talking until they agree"-- seems to characterize formal deliberation in
many African organizations. William Friedland describes discussions in
the local branches of African trade unions in which three principles are
operative: discussion is open; it is lengthy; decisions reflect public opinion.[49]
That the process of deliberation among Africans tends to avoid votes and to
continue long beyond the time that the result is apparent to all participants
has been observed as long as outsiders have written of their experiences
of African "palaver."

Nyerere, however, does not claim that all participants must remain
agreed. In fact he counsels good citizens to persist in their views if they
feel they are right. But they must contribute to discussion within TANU,
for "basically democracy is government by discussion."[50] When advising
his own people, Nyerere need not stress obedience to authority, for he is
genuinely interested in participation (to the extent of sounding like John
Stuart Mill):

> The wishes of the majority are made know through
> discussion. If the minority does not clearly mention
> their wishes, the discussions are useless. Sometimes,
> after discussions are over, the Minority -- even if they
> have agreed to obeying the conclusion of the majority --

can still believe that their own opinions (i.e., the opinions
of the minority) are right or are in the best ones, and
that those of the majority are wrong. Democracy gives
them the right and truth makes it their duty to continue
holding their opinions until most of them feel that their
opinions are right. Without that, progress in opinion
is impossible, for often a good opinion originates from
one person only. At first it may be opposed, sometimes
strongly, by the majority, but afterwards most of them
support it. This is the basis of progress in the opinion
of mankind.[51]

Nyerere's desire to encourage popular participation along with his
belief in the suitability of single-party government provides the background
for an elaborate attempt to provide for more flexibility in the operation
of government and for enhanced opportunity for discussion. To this end
he calls for more than merely one-party system; in effect, he demands a
constitution which implements the monopolitical system.

Nyerere's final justification of the statutory one-party system in
Tanganyika rests on more than its congruity to African cultural attitudes
and its expediency in present circumstances. He broadens his defense into
an attack on the two-party system as it operates elsewhere and on the notion
of opposition as an integral part of democratic government. "Is it seriously
suggested that a Government can be democratic only if it is rejected by
nearly half of the people?"[52] Since party systems always reflect class
systems he writes, a two-party system is justified only if the parties are
divided on some fundamental issue. The origins of "Anglo-Saxon" parties
are cited as evidence. Fundamental differences lead inevitably to civil
war, which becomes one extension of party conflict in the West; or, according
to Nyerere, multi-party politics degenerate into a game. "It is hard to
avoid the conclusion that people who defend the two-party system are
actually advocating 'football politics,' that they consider a spirit of purely
artificial rivalry, like that which exists between a couple of soccer teams,
is appropriate to the relationship between opposing political parties."
According to this view, two-party politics are either impossible -- lead to
civil war if differences are on fundamental issues -- or illegitimate -- lead to
football if they are not fundamental enough. Africa is presently involved
in a business much too serious to afford the luxury of football politics.
Nyerere believes that as the process of finding logical reasons for the
utility of such a system is rather difficult, the defenders of the two-party
system have equated it with democracy merely out of force of habit.
Nyerere remarks that "other people, who also claim to be democrats,
are now beginning to ask: 'How can you have democracy with a two-party
system?' ... I have found myself questioning the democracy of the two-party

party system very seriously indeed."[53]

The spectacle of one party trying always to embarrass the other, despite fundamental agreement on important issues, offers considerable material for humor, and Nyerere utilizes the opportunity to ridicule artific- ial arguments, regular reversals of policy, and emphasis on personalities. But he studiously avoids the one point that usually occurs to "Anglo-Saxon" defenders of their own system; that is that opposition parties can act as an effective check against the abuse of governmental power. By starting from the assumptions that the only legitimate origin of party is class and that the national interest is palpable and can be represented by one group only, Nyerere discovers no raison d'être for more than one party. "Where there is one party and that party is identified with the nation as a whole, the foundations of democracy are firmer than they can ever be where you have two or more parties, each representing only a section of the community!"[54] In any case, in Nyerere's view, the whole problem of balancing or checking power appears unreasonable in Africa's present circumstances. Power needs to be generated, not divided. "Our need is not brakes -- our lack of trained manpower and capital resources and even our climate act too effectivly already."[55]

Finally, he sees opposition parties as unnecessary and unnatural for Tanganyika because their growth would be dangerous to the society TANU wants to create. "In the future it is possible that a second political party will grow in Tanganyika, but in one sense such a growth would represent a failure by TANU. The existence of two or more stable political parties implies a class structure of society, and we aim at avoiding the growth of different social and economic classes in our country. If we do avoid this, then the opposition will take the form of disagreement on how to do things which we agree should be done. It is not essential that this type of disagree- ment be expressed through a two-party system."[56]

The question then becomes what positive advantages accrue from a one-party system for the practice of democracy. Nyerere is careful to distinguish the Tanganyika single-party system from other forms, such as those associated with "our friends, the Communists." Given the opportunity to escape the rigidities of the parliamentary two-party system, the Tanganyika system must be alive to the possibilities of enlarging democratic relation- ships. "In a One Party system, party membership must be open to everybody and freedom of expression allowed to every individual."[57] Nyerere hopes to draw all available talent and skill into enthusiastic implementation of national policy and to expand opportunities for popular participation in political discussion at the same time. Obviously, the anomaly of limited membership in TANU had to end and this has been accomplished. All

citizens, including non-Africans (who were excluded by TANU policy) and
civil servants (who were excluded by law), are now eligible for TANU
membership. Civil servants are all but required to join. Other aims of
a statutory one-party system await constitutional revisions. Nyerere is
on record, however, as expecting that open membership in TANU and the
demise of party discipline -- such discipline makes sense only in the face
of an opposition party -- will encourage free debate in parliament and in TANU
committees in the countryside. In addition, he anticipates that people outside
central TANU headquarters and outside the local TANU hierarchies will take
part in choosing candidates for local and national offices. Until appropriate
constitutional changes are recommended (progress has been slow due to the
intervention of new and broader constitutional problems, such as planning
for an East African Federation and integrating Zanzibar in the new United
Republic of Tanzania), matters like the free choice of candidates in nominations and elections have had to be put off. It is also not clear that the TANU
hierarchy is ready to face a situation in which "any member of the Movement
(which in this context means any patriotic citizen since it is a National
Movement we are talking about) would be free to stand as a candidate if
he so wished. And in each constituency the voters themselves would be able
to make their choice freely from among these candidates."[58] Several local
TANU units have experimented with informal soundings of opinion, similar
to American primary elections, before choosing TANU nominees for seats
on the local council. At present it is doubtful if there is much canvassing
prior to nominations around the country. In any case there are no elections,
since TANU candidates are invariably returned unopposed. Even the local
independent has disappeared, as every seat on every local council filled
in the past year-and-a-half went to the TANU nominee.

An even greater advantage of the one-party system is the elimination
of dual lines of authority. "In our case, for example, the present distinction
between TANU and the TANU Government -- a distinction which, as a matter
of fact, our people do not in the least understand -- would vanish. We should
simply have leaders chosen to do a job." Nyerere adds an astonishing
suggestion (which has never been elaborated or discussed): "And such
leaders could be removed by the people at any time" (my italics).[59] The
possibility of popular recall, if implemented, would contribute to local
responsiveness that harks back to the most radical democratic creeds.
"And anybody who continued to occupy a position of leadership under such
conditions would do so because the people were satisfied with him; not
because he was protected by a law which made it impossible for them to
replace him until the next General Election."[60]

It is difficult again to avoid noting the similarity between Nyerere's
overall conception, manifested in his plan for a one-party democratic system,
and Rousseau's great vision of the continuously self-governing society. Such

a society was possible for Rousseau only when each individual asked himself "the right question"--what is the community's interest?--and when everyone in the community participated in deciding it. Putting aside the problem of the size of the community in which this would be possible, the only relationship that would foster such a system is one that permitted each individual to feel that his interest would find expression in the will of the community-- the organic, "communitarian" society.[61] Nyerere's hope that the processes of politics can be accessible to everyone in the society at all times must be seen against the background of ujamaa, the feeling of familyhood which would prevent such continuous participation from foundering in a welter of conflicting individual interests.

But ordinary people are notoriously short-sighted and self-oriented. How can they be prevented from insisting on immediate local benefits and tribal advantages, instead of resting satisfied with long-term national progress? Nyerere's answer is to develop a system in which all enterprises and associations are related to and identified with government-party policy. Nyerere has not yet elaborated on the neo-corporative trends obvious in the construction of the new relationships among all organized groups and efforts in the society, except for some remarks about trade unions. Briefly, he told the unions that they may not arrive at any aims that cannot be integrated into government policy. "If a government is a socialist government, represent- ing the working people of the country, then it must be acknowledged and treated as such, not only by the capitalists, but by the workers themselves. The workers can be no more independent of it than it can be independent of the workers."[62] Tanzania's trade unions, the last faintly effective opposi- tion group to the government, have been reconstituted into one giant union with the minister of labor as general secretary. A similar pattern is slowly taking shape in the case of the co-operative unions, the employers associa- tions, and so on.

If everybody joins TANU, then TANU branch meetings can serve as local focuses for the discussion of all matters affecting the comprehension of national policy. As civil servants have come into TANU in the past eighteen months, they have not joined branches in their home neighborhoods. Instead they have been forming branches in their offices. Newspapers carry regular announcements by TANU headquarters of new branches springing up in army units, among prison warders, in government offices, and among policemen. The officers of these branches usually duplicate the staff hierarchies involved. It is too early to say whether these branches with occupational orientations will partially replace or merely supplement existing neighborhood branches, but they may be a sign of the eventual emergence of functional orientations within TANU. At present, however, TANU recognizes special activities but no differences of interest. For Nyerere the central role of TANU at present is in facilitating support and understanding of the program of the political leadership. "It is the establishment and maintenance of this channel of communication which is the real problem of democracy in Tanganyika, not the establishment of an artificial opposition."[63]

If the population is united on the central goal of economic betterment and on the means of a single channel of political authority, then the task for TANU is less political than educational--even technical. "It is also necessary to have a strong political organization active in every village, which acts like a two-way all-weather road along which the purposes, plans and problems of the Government can travel to the people at the same time as the ideas, desires and misunderstandings of the people can travel direct to the Government. This is the job of the new TANU."[64] In acting as transmitter and receiver of ideas Nyerere sees TANU branches developing into local welfare and fraternal societies. He counsels TANU to take an interest in sickness, bereavements, harvests, accidental losses, etc., and to treat all people as tribal brothers. "Even if we build enough schools, enough hospitals and enough roads, still we shall not be a union of people if we do not deal with their daily difficulties and complications and enjoyments."[65] Recently "cell leaders" have been appointed in Dar es Salaam in order to increase the influence and control of TANU over the urban population. Leaders, who are responsible for ten houses each, help in regulating internal migration and have been active in clearing the city of idlers.[66]

Dilemmas and Drift

One way to evaluate the emergent ideology of Julius Nyerere is to de-emphasize the logic of his substantive argument and to concentrate on the functions it may serve in light of the goals advanced. Solidarism and monopolitical democracy then can be seen as the basis for the myths which underlie the development of a sense of national identification. What is important, therefore, is not the nature of the myth, but its role as an instrument of unification and modernization. This appears to be the conclusion of Fred Burke in his searching inquiry into popular understanding of ujamaa and its influence on certain policies.[67] He agrees that "so long as the President of Tanganyika is in a position to direct policy, the country's development will be determined in part by that philosophy." If it is true that "there seems to be little evidence that the 'attitude of mind' termed ujamaa can be extended to the point where it could serve as the underlying ethos for a Tanganyikan nation," then it seems worthwhile to reflect on the more likely implications of Nyerere's attempt to construct an ideology.[68]

Clearly, serious difficulties stand in the way of translating solidarism and monopolitical consensus into policy and practice. The virtues of traditional society are bound up with tribal life, which is particularistic

and backward-looking. The African is being asked to abandon tribalism at
the same time as he is supposed to retain an attitude of mind associated
with it. It is hard to see how the very processes of modernization can avoid
instigating even greater disruption of customary, communal interdependence.
New and perhaps equally durable associations may emerge, but they will
probably be linked to a broadening emphasis on intitiative and individual
differentiation as the requirements for the varied skills to run a modern
state are filled from the ranks of the generation currently acquiring technical
training. In this context the interpretation of obligations growing out of the
relationships identified with the extended family can mean little more than
a vague humanistic concern for brotherhood. What we know of the modernization of societies elsewhere indicates that the transformation of rural social
organization assumes a high priority on the agenda of political leaders.
Although it is possible for a set of irrelevant rural virtues to endure during
the process of spurring social reconstruction, it is hard to see how they can
actively inform that process.

The social reorganization accompanying modernization already poses
a threat to the ideal of a classless society. Aside from the fact that the
basis for traditional classlessness -- similarity of economic function -- grows
more attenuated, the makings of a class system are quite obvious, especially
in the towns but in the countryside as well. The direction of social reconstruction remains confined to a small group of public servants who have acquired
the perquisites of the previous governing class of colonial administrators
and their private clients. Despite some attempt to reduce the gross disparities
of income within the African community, the rewards for performing jobs
previously done by non-Africans can be decreased only so much without
creating serious problems of morale and inviting charges of racialism in
reverse.[69] Ironically, Africanization in the public services and in foreign-
owned private corporations, coupled with the popular notion that independence
meant expropriation of the agencies of alien exploitation, has led initially
to a widening of the social gap between African leaders and their followers.
Above all, the enormous differences in privilege and power among Africans
is supported by the requirements of centralized regulation of social and
economic development. As long as African college graduates are scarce --
and relative to the need the prospect is that they shall remain so for quite
some time -- they will retain a high market value. In such a situation equality
can dissolve into no more than a pious hope.

The thrust of Nyerere's notion of democracy is to expand discussion
and participation in matters of public concern. In September 1965 the first
election under the new system took place. Through TANU machinery two
candidates were chosen for each constituency and were warned to keep
their debates and discussions within accepted national policy as defined
generally by TANU. About 76 percent of registrants turned out to cast

ballots, and about 78 percent turned out in the presidential poll, which was
held simultaneously, although Nyerere had no opposition. It is still too
early to assess the effects of the election on matters such a parliamentary
discussion or continuing grass roots participation in politics. At present
it appears that the trend toward restricting public discussion has been
halted. Nevertheless, past practices offer disquieting auguries. Significantly,
Nyerere announced the idea of the statutory one-party system without any
prior public consideration of its implications; that is standard procedure.
The National Executive of TANU had raised the issue in January 1962 at
a stormy grievance session which culminated in Nyerere's dramatic resigna-
tion as prime minister; but the decision was not considered worth discussing
in the TANU branches. No public hint was given that the first important
matter to be taken up under the new presidential constitution was its own
revision. For a reform that was to stimulate free discussion, its introduction did not set an inspiring example. Making TANU the only legitimate
political arena has served to choke off any public discussion that does not
originate from TANU sources; this, in turn, has led to a decline in discussion
itself, the very reverse of what Nyerere's theory intended.

The political climate since the dissolution of opposition parties
reflects the concern for the individual that Nyerere finds so basic, only in
a peculiar way, for a remarkable conformity characterizes political comment
in the country. My point here is not to harp on the failure of the inchoate
political system in Tanzania to develop a concern for civil liberties or public
participation as we know them. Rather, it is to suggest that although there
exist more immediate causes, this drift of affairs is implied in the unresolved
dilemmas in Nyerere's efforts to construct an ideology of nation-building.
The whole emphasis on the natural recognition of communal obligations in
Africa is a denial of the conflict of interests in the "good society." And when
conflicts do arise, they are explained as the legacy of colonial-capitalist
attitudes or the consequence of foreign elements who are intriguing in hopes
of re-establishing some form of domination. The classless community,
i.e., the real African society, is supposed to be re-asserted in the emergent
nation; its instrument is the Africans' own organization, the only agency with
the resources and character to accomplish the task, the national movement,
which has merged with government. For Nyerere, TANU is the builder of
the new nation and the valid expression of the traditional African community.
Leadership in TANU and decision making in the organization are seen to
reflect the traditional mode of deliberation which always mirrored the
agreement of the community.

It is clear that Nyerere desires a continuously self-governing society,
but he also wants to make certain that self-government serves the right
purposes. Like Rousseau, he aspires to a society which solves the fundamental conflict between individual interests and community needs, but he

insists, like Rousseau, that the outcome represent the general will. Despite
the conservatism connoted by the appeal to the traditional community, such
a formulation has served revolutionary purposes. Successful revolutionaries
have understood, however, that as far as their followers were concerned,
they had "to force them to be free." Nyerere's emergent ideology creates
no barriers to that conclusion, especially when we remember that the force
may be most necessary in the years immediately following the transformation
of the leader from a claimant to power to a wielder of power.

Footnotes

1. Colin Leys, "The Constitution of Tanganyika, " Journal of the Parliaments of the Commonwealth, XLIV:142 (April 1963). "Tanganyika" will be used when reference is made to activities before the country was united with Zanzibar in April 1964. The union was re-named Tanzania in October 1964. References to subsequent activities use the new name.

2. "Fighting the Forces of Circumstances, " The Times (London), June 25, 1962. Most speechmaking in Africa is extempore, contrasting strongly with the carefully prepared performances of Western leaders, in or out of office.

3. See Clifford Geertz (ed.), Old Societies and New States, The Quest for Modernity in Asia and Africa (New York, 1963), especially contributions by Geertz and Lloyd Fallers; also Harvey Glickman's "Traditional Pluralism and Democratic Processes in Tanganyika, " delivered at the 1964 Annual Meeting of the American Political Science Association, Chicago, Sept. 1964.

4. For a concise discussion of the origins of the ideas of African nationalism, see Thomas Hodgkin, Nationalism in Colonial Africa (London, 1956), 170-175. For a discussion of the origins of African socialism see William H. Friedland and Carl G. Rosberg, Jr. (eds.), African Socialism (Stanford, 1964).

5. See Robert E. Lane, Political Ideology, Why the American Common Man Believes What He Does (New York, 1962), 15-16.

6. Ibid., 433-434; Gabriel A. Almond, "Introduction: A Functional Approach to Comparative Politics, " in Gabriel A. Almond and James S. Coleman, The Politics of the Developing Areas (Princeton, 1960), 9-11.

7. Lane, Political Ideology; also Colin Leys, "The Need for an Ideology, " Darubini Yenu, Kivukoni College (Dar es Salaam) Yearbook, 1961, 3-7.

8. For an excellent first assessment of the effects of ideology in Tanganyika, see Fred G. Burke, "Tanganyika: The Search for Ujamaa, " in Friedland and Rosberg, African Socialism, 194-219.

9. Martin Lowenkopf, "Outlook for Tanganyika, " Africa Report, VI:3-6 (Dec. 1961).

10. Reprinted in TANU katika UNO (Dar es Salaam, 1955), 44.

11. Julius K. Nyerere, "The Entrenchment of Privilege, " Africa South, II:87 (Jan.-March 1958). Nyerere's eclecticism also takes the form of making use of ideas from varied national sources. Note the strong American inspiration of this statement.

12. TANU katika UNO, 23.

13. For a clear and concise account of nationalist politics see Margaret L. Bates, "Tanganyika, " in Gwendolen M. Carter (ed.), African One-Party States (Itchaca, 1962), 412-431.

14. December 1959, quoted in ibid., 449.

15. Quoted in J. Clagett Taylor, The Political Development of Tanganyika (Stanford, 1963), 201. Nyerere called for a free vote and promised that he and his government would resign if the bill did not receive a majority of the votes of the elected members. He won without even a tally. Later he explained his reasoning to a special meeting of the TANU elders in Dar es Salaam. The speech is reprinted as Uraia -- Maelezo ya Kweli ya Waziri Mkuu (Citizenship -- The True Explanation by the Prime Minister), Dar es Salaam, 1961.

16. Quoted in The New York Times, Feb. 2, 1964.

17. For a preliminary assessment see Harvey Glickman "Some Observations on the Army and Political Unrest in Tanganyika, " (Duquesne University Press, African Reprint Series No. 16:Pittsburgh, 1964).

18. Julius K. Nyerere, 'Ujamaa' The Basis of African Socialism (Dar es Salaam, 1962). My quotations from Ujamaa are from the original unpaged pamphlet. It has since been reprinted in Friedland and Rosberg, African Socialism, 238-247.

19. Julius K. Nyerere, The Second Scramble (Dar es Salaam, 1962), reprinted in part in Paul E. Sigmund, Jr. (ed.), The Ideologies of the Developing Nations (New York, 1963), 205-211; see also Nyerere, Address to the Afro-Asian Solidarity Conference, Moshi, Feb. 4, 1963 (mimeographed).

20. Ujamaa.

21. Speech to the Pan-African Co-operative Conference, Moshi, Nov. 14, 1962 (mimeographed).

22. President's Address to the National Assembly, Dec. 10, 1962 (Dar es Salaam, 1962), 20.

23. Personal interview, Feb. 25, 1963. Burke reports the cancellation in 1962 of a program by the Tanganyika Agricultural Corporation which involved granting 80-acre plots to individual farmers, "for fear that it would be contrary to a classless society, communal agriculture and agricultural cooperatives." Friedland and Rosberg, African Socialism, 215. The elimination of private profit among Africans does not necessarily clash with a policy of permitting private foreign investment. Nyerere anticipates the eventual reduction of dependence on foreign aid and the absorption of many functions performed by foreign enterprises into corporations owned or controlled by the government. When he was minister of commerce, George Kahama stated that "establishment of business in this country by foreign investors will not interfere in any way with our aim to build African Socialism. In actual fact foreign industries will help us to increase our total wealth which in turn will enable us to achieve this aim of African Socialism." National Assembly Debates, n.s., 1st S., 2nd M., June 15, 1962, c. 500.

24. Nyerere, "The African and Democracy, " in James Duffy and Robert A. Manners (eds.), Africa Speaks (Princeton, 1961), 30, 32.

25. Subsequent direct quotations from Ujamaa.

26. Mali ya Taifa, Maoni Juu ya Ardhi (The Nation's Party, Opinions on Land) (Dar es Salaam, 1958?). The precipitant to Nyerere's pamphlet is Government Paper No. 6, 1958, "Review of Land Tenure Policy." The connections between land and politics under colonial administration are explored at length in Margaret L. Bates, "Tanganyika Under British Administration, 1920-1955" (unpubl. diss., Oxford University, 1957).

27. Mali ya Taifa, 9, 12. For suggestions concerning the connections of Nyerere's thought to Catholic social teachings, which in turn are linked through Catholic missionary activity to Senghor and other African leaders in French-speaking areas, see Ruth Schachter Morgenthau, "African Socialism: Declaration of Ideological Independence, " Africa Report, VII:3-6 (May 1963). Subsequent direct quotations from Mali ya Taifa.

28. Ujamaa.

29. Reporter (Nairobi), Nov. 20, 1964; see also The Nationalist (Dar es Salaam), Nov. 21, 1964.

30. Nyerere, "One Party Government, " Spearhead, I:8 (Nov. 1961), reprinted in part in Sigmund, Ideologies, 197-202.

31. Nyerere, "The African and Democracy" in Sigmund, Ideologies, 29. This article is almost identical to "One Party Government" in many places.

32. Nyerere, "Africa's Bid for Democracy, " African and Colonial World, VIII:3 (July 1960). This article repeats most of "Africa's Place in the World, " Symposium on Africa, Wellesley College, 1960, 153-164, which was reprinted in part as "Will Democracy Work in Africa?, " Africa Report, V:3-4 (Feb. 1960).

33. "Africa's Bid, " 3.

34. Ibid.

35. Thomas Hodgkin has suggested a similarity to Rousseau in the formulation of ideas of African nationalism in "A Note on the Language of African Nationalism, " in Kenneth Kirkwood (ed.), African Affairs No. One, St. Antony's Papers No. 10 (London, 1961), 22-40.

36. "Africa's Bid, " 3.

37. Ibid.

38. William H. Friedland suggests the term "focal institutional society." See "Basic Social Trends" in Friedland and Rosberg, African Socialism, 26-30.

39. "One Party Government, " 8.

40. "Will Democracy Work, " 3.

41. "One Party Government, " 8.

42. Ibid., 9.

43. The utility of the Hobbesian formulation is noted in Immanuel Wallerstein, "The Political Ideology of the P.D.G., " Présence Africaine (Eng. Ed.), XII:30-41 (First Quarter 1962).

44. "One Party Government, " 8.

45. "Africa's Bid, " 3.

46. Speech by the president-designate at the inauguration of the
Fountain of the Republic, Dar es Salaam, Dec. 8, 1962 (Tanganyika Information
Service press release).

47. "One Party Government, " 7.

48. Speech to the TANU elders and TANU Youth League, Dar es
Salaam, quoted in Tanganyika Standard, Oct. 4, 1962.

49. William H. Friedland, "Institutional Change: A Study of Trade
Union Development in Tanganyika" (unpubl. diss., University of California,
Berkeley, 1963), 154-167.

50. "One Party Government, " 7.

51. Tujisahihishe (Let us Correct Ourselves) (Dar es Salaam, 1962), 4.

52. "The Challenge of Independence, " East Africa and Rhodesia,
339, Dec. 7, 1962.

53. Democracy and the Party System (Dar es Salaam, 1963). My
quotations are from the unpaged pamphlet which reproduces the mimeographed
English version distributed when the speech was delivered on Jan. 14, 1963.
It was also reprinted in Spearhead, II:1, 12-23 (Jan, 1963) as "One Party
System" and in the Tanganyika Standard, Jan, 16-18, 21, 22, 1963.

54. Ibid.

55. Interview quoted in The Observer, June 3, 1962.

56. "Challenge of Independence, " 339-340.

57. Democracy and the Party System.

58. Ibid.

59. Ibid.

60. Ibid.

61. Nyerere first used the term in his speech at Wellesley, Feb. 16,
1960: "One must not think that the African is therefore a 'natural Communist'
... He is, if I may coin the expression, 'communitary. ' He is not a member

of a 'commune' -- some artificial unit of human beings -- but of a genuine com-munity,or brotherhood." "Africa's Place in the World, " 159.

62. "The Task Ahead of Our African Trade Unions, " Labour (Accra), June 1961, reprinted in part in Sigmund, Ideologies, 202-205. For preceptive comments on the role of trade unions in Africa see Friedland, "Basic Social Trends, " 15-34.

63. "Challenge of Independence, " 340.

64. From Nyerere's press conference upon resigning as prime minister, quoted in the Tanganyika Standard, Jan. 23, 1962.

65. TANU na Raia (TANU and the Citizens) (Dar es Salaam, 1962), 3.

66. See The Nationalist, Nov. 6, 1964; also Reporter, Nov. 20, 1964.

67. See Burke, "Tanganyika, " in Friedland and Rosberg, African Socialism, 194-219.

68. Ibid., 209, 208.

69. Nyerere explains the problems involved in the equalization of incomes in a way that ordinary citizens can understand in TANU na Raia, 6-11.

70. This paper was written before the elections. For early yet remarkably penetrating analyses, see William Tordoff, "The General Election in Tanzania, " Journal of Commonwealth Political Studies, IV:47-64 (March 1966); Belle Harris, "Tanzania Elections 1965, " Mbioni, II, no. 5, Kivukoni College, Dar es Salaam, 1965; also, Ruth Schachter Morgenthau, "African Elections: Tanzania's Contribution, " Africa Report, X: 12-16 (December 1965).

IX

TANU and UPC: The Impact of Independence on Two African Nationalist Parties

Joseph S. Nye, Jr.
Department of Government and Center for International Affairs,
Harvard University

Julius Nyerere founded the Tanganyika National Union (TANU) in 1954. Within two years, TANU claimed 100,000 members; but the massive gains which brought membership to over a million in 1960 were made only after it had made a strong showing in the first elections in 1958.[1] At first glance these gains seem to prove that in African nationalist organizations, as in so many other areas of life, nothing succeeds like success. But, if success is defined as achievement of the major goal -- independence -- TANU was hurt by achieving it. In neighboring Uganda, however, the weaker Uganda People's Congress (UPC) was helped by independence.

Why did independence have a different impact on the two nationalist parties? The answer lies in the differences of their organization and the different party systems in which they participated. African nationalism, we have been rightly told, is not like nineteenth-century European "nation makes state" nationalism. Rather, it is an assertion that a nation made by African leaders to destroy the legitimacy of and ultimately gain control of the colonial state. Only when these ideas are wed to an organization is nationalism successful.[2]

Recent work on African nationalist parties has tended to characterize these organizations as dichotomous types: the mass type versus the elitist, patron, or caucus type.[3] Roughly speaking, TANU is a mass party and the UPC a caucus type, if we use Kilson's distinctions. Mass parties are perpetually active; caucus parties display greatest activity during crises such as elections. Mass parties tend to monopolize the aura of legitimacy and have a charismatic leader, caucus parties less so. Mass parties have large-scale memberships and a large number of branches; caucus parties have fewer members and build their organizations, around notable men in local society.

Yet, it is not useful for analysis to include the UPC, which has approximately 500 branches and membership somewhere in the six figures,[4] with the small cliques of leaders in the capitals of some formerly French states. In other words, the dichotomy is merely the two ends of the same spectrum.

Where the idea once stimulated thought, it now hinders it. It is time for
students of African parties to fill in the distinctions between the two ends
of the spectrum. Before we can generalize, however, we must compare
party organizations in some detail and not remain content with the existing
typology.

The Organization of TANU[5]

TANU has four levels. At the former administrative subchiefdom
level 1, 200 party branches -- the basic organization.[6] Each branch
has a secretary appointed by the Establishments Committee in Dar es Salaam,
after the regional commissioner, who is also the regional party secretary,
has interviewed local applicants. In practice, the regional commissioner
appoints them and reports to TANU headquarters.

The branch secretary does not receive a salary, but received a 10
per cent commission on the funds collected.[7] Membership in TANU costs
two shillings; annual dues are six shillings, and some branches number
more than 5, 000 members. Thus, a secretary could earn up to 300 shillings
if his people worked hard. Working hard may mean keeping up local interest
and morale, or it may mean standing in the market to shove membership
cards into people's hands when it is clear they have money and can make
no excuses. At times it seemed that the local TANU organization is a
regressive form of taxation as much as an opportunity for mass political
participation. Most branch secretaries, however, probably earn less than
the minimum wage for house servants in Dar es Salaam -- about 150 shillings
a month.

The branch elects a chairman at an annual meeting attended by members
from constituent hamlets. The chairman receives a commission (less than
the secretary's), and, although he presides at meetings, he is considered
less important than the secretary. Branch powers are limited: branches
recruit members, but cannot drop them; branches explain policy but cannot
communicate with headquarters except through the district and regional
offices.

The sixty districts are more important. Since 1962, their secretaries
have also filled the former government job of district commissioner under
a new title, area commissioner. A deputy district secretary handles the
daily administration of the party. The deputy is subordinate to the area
commissioner, who is still secretary of TANU and tends to drop in at the
district office once a day. The TANU headquarters in Dar es Salaam
appoints deputy district secretaries, sends them to an area (often not their

home areas), and pays them a regular salary of 250 shillings a month with differentials for length of service.

The district chairman receives a monthly allowance (so styled because he is an elected and not a salaried employee) of 150 shillings. The annual conference of the district numbers about sixty. Membership is not always predictable, but usually the conference is composed of three members (chairman, secretary, elected delegate) from each branch (there are fifteen to twenty branches in a district), the ten members of the district executive committee, the district party officers, the local Member of Parliament (constituencies are usually based on districts), and the one or two members of the district working committee who are not included under another category. Besides the chairman, whose re-election is by no means automatic, the conference elects the executive committee for the next year and a delegate to the TANU Annual Conference.[8]

The regional structure of the party is similar to that of the district, with a deputy regional secretary appointed from Dar es Salaam working under the regional secretary who is also the regional commissioner (incorporating the former government job of provincial commissioner). A regional annual conference of between twenty-five and fifty persons (composed of the chairman, secretary and elected delegates from each district, the executive committee, working committee, other officers and Members of Parliament from the region) elects a regional chairman and a delegate to be, along with the regional commissioner, the region's representatives on the important TANU National Executive.

The fourth, or top level of TANU has two sides: the party headquarters on the administrative side, and three policy bodies on the decision-making side -- the Annual Conference, the National Executive, and the Central Committee The largest of these, the Annual Conference, is composed of a representative of each district plus the members of the National Executive -- about 120 people in all. While it seldom makes major changes in policy, the Annual Conference is not a body that the leaders can ignore.[9] More important in policy making is the National Executive, whose fifty-eight members[10] include the nineteen members of the Central Committee, three representatives (chairman, secretary, and National Executive member) from each region, two trade unionists and four representatives of the parliamentary group (the total body of MPs).[11] The National Executive meets quarterly, debates freely, sometimes for several days, and is more important than the parliamentary group, although half the members of the Executive are also MPs. Comparison of membership lists show that approximately a fifth of Executive members are new each year.

The Central Committee, located in Dar es Salaam, includes the
eleven national party officers and meets almost weekly. Slightly more
than half its members are also MPs, but it is concerned mainly with party
business and is less important in formulating policy than the National
Executive.

On the administrative side, the top level of TANU is the headquarters
in Dar es Salaam. The president of TANU, Nyerere, was elected by the
Annual Conference for five years; the vice-president, Rashidi Kawawa, and
treasurer, Nsilo Swai annually. The secretary-general, Oscar Kambona,
and his deputy, Edward Kisenge, hold office at the pleasure of the National
Executive. The deputy secretary-general, who is responsible for the daily
administration of the party, was changed three times between 1961 and
1963, primarily because of the difficulty of the job.

There was an administrative staff of twenty in the headquarters
building in 1963, plus ten or so messengers and drivers. The staff included
administrative secretaries, financial and publicity secretaries, accountants,
and filing clerks. The deputy secretary general described his job as
"just like running a ministry only with a less well-paid staff and longer
hours."[12]

Although party headquarters also settles minor disputes and issues
directives, the great bulk of administrative work is in communications--
reading reports and sending out information. Communications are channeled
hierarchically through the levels. Branches send reports and minutes of
meetings to districts, which send monthly and annual reports to the regions,
which send them on to headquarters. Four administrative secretaries
read these reports, act on those they can, and send the others to higher
officers. Headquarters is in contact with the regions almost daily by mail
or by telephone, and through them with the districts. Both general circulars
(like Central Committee and National Executive meeting minutes with
explanatory notes) and specific directives are sent out. Usually communications are sent to the regions for duplication and distribution, but sometimes
headquarters sends them directly to the districts. TANU's Swahili language
weekly paper, Uhuru, is mostly handled by commercial news agents, but
also by the branch office in remote areas. The paper claimed a circulation
of 15,000 in 1963 and deals with issues in a radical tone.

TANU's annual budget (which Margaret Bates estimated at
Ł 50,000) is based on district estimates sent to headquarters for approval.[13]
Districts estimate what they can raise by dues and special appeals (for Land
Rovers, etc.), and their estimates are checked. They are not allowed to
spend all they collect, though rich areas are allowed to spend more than

poor areas. Each district has its own account, remits funds to headquarters, and is sent checks or vouchers according to their estimated expenses. They send monthly returns to headquarters.

There are few official disciplinary actions. Most of them in the past have stemmed from members' opposition of official TANU candidates in elections. Abuse of police power and embezzlement are left to the courts to handle. Regional and area commissioners can suspend individuals from membership pending action by the National Executive; it is possible, although rare, to appeal to the Annual Conference. In general, TANU shows an extremely high absorptive capacity where repentent sinners are concerned.

Members of Parliament are supposedly selected by district committees which send a list of three or four names from which the National Executive chooses a candidate. Although several districts have complained, to no avail, that candidates are imposed on them, traditional and local factors are taken into account by the National Executive. Six out of fifty TANU candidates in 1960 were chiefs;[14] about 70 per cent of all MPs in 1963 represented the areas in which they were born.

There are no corporate groups or blocs in TANU, though the constitution provides for labor and co-operative representation.[15] Two National Executive seats were formerly reserved for members chosen by the Tanganyika Federation of Labor (TFL), subject to confirmation by the Annual Conference. In practice, however, labor representatives are often on the executive committees of the regions and districts.

There are also three extra sections of TANU: the women's elders' sections and the TANU Youth League (TYL). The women's and elders' sections have district chairmen, without a vote, but no regional chairmen or secretaries; they have no dues or separate admission. This arrangement gives status to the older men and capitalizes on the enthusiasm of women without letting them become an autonomous organization with their own channels of communication which might compete with the TANU secretaries.

The Youth League (TYL) enrolls youths between the ages of 18 and 35 for a fee of a shilling; TYL claimed 85,000 members in 1962.[16] Established in 1958, its members provided ushers and choruses at meetings before independence. The Youth League has had a fluctuating relationship with the party. Originally the TANU district secretary and the TYL secretary were the same person. Then separate secretaries were tried. After the secretary of the TYL deviated from top party leaders on two important issues in 1960, and local TYL leaders became, in the words of a TANU official, "drunk with power," the president's brother, Joseph Nyerere was made TYL secretary, the TANU district secretaries became responsible for the district TYL, and TYL secretaries were gradually moved to other jobs.

As the above indicates, TANU is an efficiently run and centrally directed party with both an impressive bureaucracy and powerful policy-making bodies. While individuals and local factors are often significant, the party presents a unified front, and no section of the party is able to become a law unto itself. When we turn to Uganda, we discover a very different picture.

The Organization of the UPC

The visitor to TANU headquarters enters a modern three-story building built by the party for its own use. Up the road is an even bigger and better building loaned to the party by the University. In contrast, the UPC inhabits a dozen or so rooms on the third floor of an office building in Kampala. Both headquarters partake of the aura of chaos created by the inevitable hangers-on, but there is a more business-like feeling about TANU headquarters. This difference is true of nearly everything else about the two parties.

UPC officials explain the difference by pointing out that they are a young party which had to fight two elections in the first two years of its existence while TANU was able to settle down immediately to being a party of administration.[17] One of the main reasons that the UPC is a young party is that its predecessor, the Uganda National Congress (UNC), founded in 1952, which may have had up to 50,000 members, was unable to overcome the loyalty of most Baganda (the inhabitants of the central and wealthiest part of Uganda) for their kabaka (king). In addition, the UNC is poorly organized and it has, for a number of reasons, failed to integrate Roman Catholics into the nationalist movement. As a result, Uganda has had a three-party system since independence. Many Roman Catholics support the Democratic Party (DP), which won 46 per cent of the votes outside Buganda in 1962. The UPC also has had to govern in coalition with a Baganda Party, Kabaka Yekka (Kabaka Alone).[19]

The UPC was formed in March 1960, when Milton Obote's wing of the UNC, which had strength in the north and to some extent in the east, merged with the Uganda People's Union (UPU), a party of seven Legislative Council notables whose strength was mainly in the west and Busoga but which, by its own admission, had only 3,000 members.[20] As the history of the UPC was written in its conference program in 1962, the "dynamic wing of the UNC" under the "able leadership of Comrade Obote" initiated talks with

the UPU and "answered the call of the people for freedom."[21] The new party
was committed to uphold the dignity of hereditary rulers, preserve unity,
and create a welfare state. While it had no Baganda on its executive,
during its first year it was heavily laden with fourteen elected officers.[22]

The new party is diverse in nature. In the north, particularly in
Acholi and Lango, the old UNC continues; local officials have said that they
merely told people that the name had changed. With 121 branches in Acholi,
approximately fifty in Lango and continuity going back to 1953,[23] the party
in the north has the membership criterion of a mass party. In other areas,
like Busoga, the party is strong because of its association with traditional
leaders. In still others like Kigezi and West Nile, it is associated with
the Protestant religion. It is a decentralized party, but it is not a pure
elite or cadre party as defined by Kilson. While officials do not know exact
party membership figures -- presumably this is true -- because of the lack of
organization, they claim to have at least one branch per gombolola (subcounty)
outside Buganda or nearly 500 branches.[24] During 1963, the UPC opened
a number of new branches in Buganda as well. Thus the 1961 description
of the UPC as "essentially an amalgamation of district clientages" united
"in their fear or resentment of Buganda" was only partially correct by the
end of 1963.[25]

The individuals involved in the party are particularly important. Four
UPC cabinet members are former Legislative Councillors from as far
back as 1954 (Obwangor, Lwamafa, Babiiha, and Magezi). Four were elected
to the Council as independents in 1958 (Obwangor, Lwamafa, Babiiha, Ngobi)
and three others as members of the UNC (Obote, Magezi, and Kirya).
More recently elected figures, like Felix Onama, also brought their own
support, in this case from Catholic and co-operative movement sources in
West Nile. Nor is the importance and relative independence of individuals
limited to former UPU members. Even in Acholi, an old UNC stronghold,
the local party was able to resist an expulsion from the national center.[26]
And in June 1963, when a popular DP member of the National Assembly
joined the UPC, he was almost immediately elected chairman of the UPC in
his home district, Sebei.[27]

Like TANU's, the UPC constitution was modelled on that of the
Convention People's Party (CPP) in Ghana. Moreover, UPC officials have
visited TANU a number of times and several expressed privately a desire to
make the party more like TANU. The tribes and a shortage of money are
two of the factors that prevent the UPC from developing an effective and
centrally controlled bureaucracy as TANU did after 1958. Another factor
is a difference of opinion about the desirability of developing such a bureaucracy.
Tribe is a much more explicit reference group in Uganda, often being reinforced

by linguistic differences between Bantu, Nilotics, and others. As we noted above, in 1963 70 per cent of Tanganyikan MPs represent their own tribal areas. But in Uganda, more than 90 per cent of the MPs represent their own specific tribe. In the words of one minister, "we are not a mass party because most of our MPs are here for tribal merits."[28] Similarly, nearly all local party officers are members of the major tribe of their area.

Below national headquarters, the most important party level is the region, which is based on the administrative districts set up by the British. With two exceptions, all districts in Uganda have one dominant tribe. For This reason, more radical members of the party, including the secretary general, hope to downgrade the importance of the region and increase the importance of the constituency. As of 1963 this had not happened and the constituency party, a new innovation, which lies below the region and above the branch, is important mainly at election time. Radical members of the party also hope to increase the number of branches, then (1963) at one per gombolola (except in Acholi), in order to develop more mass support. They freely admit that the branches are virtually autonomous. At the Annual Conference, one member said he hoped no more branches unknown to headquarters would be formed -- this situation is reminiscent of TANU in 1958, but not in 1963.

Tribal differences are not the only factors preventing free transfer and control of personnel. There are not sufficient funds to pay for a large bureaucracy; in fact, there are no salaried officers in the party. People in the national office as well as the district offices draw an allowance when funds are available.[29] Each level of the party seems to handle its own funds. Receipt books are issued by headquarters and expenditures above 500s are supposed to be checked at the center; but the UPC constitution allows regional treasurers the right to withdraw funds from the regional bank accounts, and donations made to regions are retained by them.[30] Attempts to change this financial system at the 1962 Annual Conference failed, and regional officers have said that they experience very little central control.

The 1962 conference decided to reduce dues from three shillings to one. Donations, particularly by Asian businessmen, are the major source of funds for the UPC, in contrast to the 6 s. dues of TANU; the donations tend to be associated with campaign funds. As one district secretary put it, the whole party changes when there is an election -- major party figures tour the country or the district concerned, and communications and activity as well as donations increase.

The eight UPC officers were re-elected unanimously at the 1962 Annual Conference. Of these, the secretary-general, John Kakonge, spent

most of his time at the party office until he also became director of economic
planning in Uganda. Kakonge was defeated for re-election at the 1964
Annual Conference by Grace Ibingira, who was also minister of state.
The President, Prime Minister Obote, and the treasurer, Minister of
Justice Cuthbert Obwangor, come to the party office about twice a week.
In mid-1963, there was a headquarters staff of ten: one administrative secretary, one finance secretary, two men for research and information, and one
organization secretary who directs four field organizers, including one
woman's organizer (unlike TANU, this position involves more title than
activity) and one youth organizer. In addition there were several hangers-on
and messengers.[31]

Below the central office are fourteen regional offices (district level),
approximately sixty constituencies (outside Buganda), and about 500 branches
at the gombolola (sub-county) level. Officially, the Annual Conference
of each level elects its officers and Executive Committee, which appoints
its organizing secretary; officers are not appointed from above. Branches
and regions receive some funds from dues, but constituencies rely entirely
on donations, often from Asian merchants. Organizational activity, in the
sense of committees and meetings, hardly exists at all below the district
level. Nonetheless, certain people are known as UPC leaders and their
presence at social functions and market days is a UPC presence. The absence
of organization does not prevent the party from having an image among
the uneducated.[32]

Communications are irregular. Headquarters receive no direct
reports from branches, but claim that regions are supposed to send monthly
reports containing news of branches. Regional officers say that they send
a copy of their minutes, somewhat haphazardly, about four times a year
and visit headquarters in person every few months, except during elections
when communications are more frequent. Headquarters has tried to send
out mimeographed material once a week and its research branch has carried
out a few policy studies; but the party has no official newspaper. The most
important form of communication is through visits of MPs to their home areas.

A major difference between the UPC and TANU is in the appearance
they present to the public. While TANU is not a monolith, it is very difficult
to find members admitting differences or washing dirty linen in public. On
the contrary,the former secretary general of the UPC, Kakonge, freely
admitted to the press before the 1962 conference that there was opposition
to him from "the old guard"; and after his defeat at the 1964 Annual Conference
he and his supporters claimed that the conference had been rigged against
him by Obote.[33]Earlier, Kakonge had fled the country after he was left
out of the government, claiming betrayal and saying that seats had been
used to pay political debts to Asians who helped finance the campaign.[34]

Party discipline is also problematical. The regional party can suspend members, but expulsion has to be by the Disciplinary Control Commission. Five Youth League members were expelled for supporting an unofficial candidate in 1961, but other cases were handled less decisively. The 1962 conference passed a resolution that all candidates who opposed official candidates were to be expelled automatically. But when one party official applied this rule to Otema Allimadi in Acholi, another party official denied it, and Otema remained a member. In another instance, which reflected internal differences in the party, the treasurer and chairman fired three headquarters' officials, all radicals, who made statements at variance with party policy. But three months later the men were officially reinstated in new jobs by the Central Executive, and in fact they had never left the office.[35] More serious was a dispute between young radicals and the minister of internal affairs in November 1963. The former detained the minister briefly and closed party headquarters for a six days as a protest. A subsequent National Council meeting failed to discipline the radicals.[36]

The selection of parliamentary candidates is by the constituency executive, which is elected by the Constituency Annual Meeting (composed of two delegates from each branch) with the approval of the National Council. There have been a few cases in which the national office has intervened but most local choices seem to be respected.

The policy-making, as opposed to the bureaucratic, side of the party is slightly more centralized than TANU. The Annual Conference is a huge affair of nearly 1,000 delegates, two per branch, which goes on for several days. Conferences were held in 1960, 1962, and 1964, but not in 1961 or 1963. The real work of the 1962 conference was done in the four committes -- finance administration, foreign affairs, and economic policy -- which reported to the conference. While there was open disagreement and debate in the conference, on financial reform and foreign policy, it is significant that the debate was primarily between disagreeing leaders rather than between the leadership and the floor delegates. Yet, at the 1962 conference, when the chairman prematurely closed debate on the foreign policy issue and lost the ensuing vote, a compromise resolution had to be worked out by the National Council.[37]

The National Council consists of the Central Executive plus the chairman, treasurer, and secretary of each region -- about sixty people. It is supposed to meet at least twice a year, or when needed-during the six months from November 1962 to May 1963 it met three times. The secretary-general claims that it carries more weight than the Central Executive because the regions are represented. This does seem to be true in crisis situations, such as the April 1963 threat to the government coalition, when the Central Executive feels in need of extra support; but in normal situations the relationship is reversed.[38] In September 1963, when a difficult constitutional

amendment bill was before the Assembly, the Central Executive met one
day, and the National Council the next. On other occasions, the leaders
discuss policy problems only in the parliamentary group.[39]

The Central Executive is composed of the eight elected party officers
and twelve others appointed by them. In 1963, half its members were
ministers, four fifths were MPs. It meets at least once a month in Kampala
to supervise the work of the party. It has the right to expel members.
Unlike the central committee of TANU, which tends to be concerned more
with party affairs, the importance of Parliament in Uganda plus the fact
that some members are not in Parliament makes the Central Executive an
important policy-making body in all but crisis situations. Of course,
within this group as within TANU, there is said to be a small group of
more influential ministers who meet informally.

The ideology of the UPC is somewhat more diffuse than that of TANU,
but the language of the militants of the parties is similar. The 1962 Conference
Program spoke of the "downtrodden masses, " the "fires of revolution, "
and printed a Pan-African manifesto, a poem by Patrice Lumumba, and
pictures of "freedom fighters" Kenyatta, Nyerere, and Nkrumah. Conference
delegates spoke of being "freedom fighters" and "fighting neo-colonialism."
And on May Day 1963, Obote sent fraternal greetings to all workers' movements.[40]

The UPC wants the labor movement to affiliate with the party but
union officials fear that affiliation would jeopardize their independence.
Party officials attribute labor's absence from the party to the influence of
foreign ICFTU (International Confederation of Free Trade Unions) ideas.
In 1961-1962 the UPC even covertly supported a Ghana-financed splinter
union in Uganda, but this venture failed to attract worker support. Humphrey
Luande, MP, president of the Uganda Trade Union Congress (UTUC), was
a member of the UPC Central Executive but frequently differed with party
leaders.

Several executive members have past associations with co-operatives,
but these were personal links. There is a woman's section, but unlike TANU,
it is not active. There is no elders' section. In 1963, a number of central
office workers were trying to build the amorphous Youth League into a
centralized organization to act as a "ginger group" in the party. They held
two Youth League Conferences in 1963, the party held none, and by the end
of the year a number of incidents indicated that the radicals who staffed
the party office had increased their importance by identifying with the youth.
Their organization, however, was still minimal. As the UPC deputy secretary
general described the Youth Wing, it was "a gathering of job-seekers ... not
even on the register as Youth Wingers."[41]

In short, the UPC is a very different organization from TANU. While
the latter is close to the bureaucratized end of the spectrum, the UPC is
closer to the non-bureaucratized end. But with its 500 branches, its comparatively strong organization in the north, and some most important leaders
bent on rapid social change, the UPC is not merely a collection of notables.
The following tables summarize some of the important differences between
the two parties.

Table 9. Decision-Making Structure of TANU and the UPC, 1963

Level of organization	TANU		UPC	
	size of body	frequency of meeting	size of body	frequency of meeting
Central Executive or Committee	19	weekly	20[a]	fortnightly
National Executive or Council	58[b]	3 months	60[a]	2 months
Annual Conference	120	yearly	1000	2 years

[a]The Central Executive and the National Council are the two most
important levels for policy formation in the UPC.
[b]The National Executive is the most important level for policy
formation in TANU.

Table 10. Administrative Structure of TANU and the UPC, 1963

Level of organization	TANU: size of body	UPC: size of body
Regular headquarters staff	30[a]	10[b]
Regional (provincial) branches	10[a]	-
District Branches	60[a]	14[c]
Constituency branches	-	60
Sub-chiefdom or gombolola branches	1200	500

[a] Levels with salaried officer paid by the central party. These levels are the most important from an administrative point of view.

[b] Officials receive an allowance.

[c] Most important level in UPC.

The Impact of Independence

TANU

Since, and even immediately prior to, independence, TANU has been concerned with maintaining its organization in the face of declining participation, potential opposition, and internal staffing problems. As independence approached in December 1961, a TANU MP admitted publicly that the party's momentum was beginning to slacken in his area (Kondoa); only 15,000 of 100,000 eligible voters registered for municipal elections in the capital; and Nyerere had to threaten to resign in order to insure the passage of his radically criticized non-racial citizenship bill.[42] Soon after independence, relations between TANU and the Tanganyika Federation of Labor began to deteriorate; the treasurer of the TFL threatened to start a new party and Joseph Nyerere accused TFL of trying to set a trap for TANU.[43]

In January 1962, Julius Nyerere persuaded the National Executive to let him resign as prime minister so that he could "reorganize the party," to make it a "two-way all weather road" between the government and the people. During the next ten months, he traveled widely in the country. His main function was to instill a new sense of purpose at local levels, both by his mere presence and by promoting self-help projects. However, very little was changed in TANU's machinery or personnel. One major exception that we have already noted was the merging of the post of party secretary at provincial and district levels with the government post of commissioner, economizing on salaries and manpower for TANU. This financial aspect was important, as several local officials confirmed that dues began to fall off after independence.

Late in 1962, Tanganyika became a republic with a strong presidential system-- a change which had been urged by the TANU National executive -- and Nyerere was elected president. The election and celebration of republic status provided a stimulus for local party activity, and party officials say that dues payment and membership improved. In 1963, headquarters officials claimed to have between one and-a-half and two million members. Membership, however, included everyone who had ever bought a TANU card rather than only those who paid dues regularly. In 1960, Lowenkopf estimated dues-paying members at a quarter of the total membership.[44] In 1962, John George has said, the party had 450,000 dues-paying members.[45] Slightly more than a million people voted in the 1962 presidential election, more than in earlier elections under more restrictive franchises, but considerably fewer than the more than million and-a-half members TANU officials claim to have.[46]

In January 1963, Nyerere announced that the TANU Annual Conference had approved a National Executive resolution to make TANU the only legal party -- converting a de facto one-party state into a de jure one. Threatened opposition did not seem a major problem; despite extreme racial stands, the African National Congress had polled only 337 votes in the 1960 elections. ANC's candidate, Zuberi Mtemvu, made a poor showing as Nyerere won 97 per cent of the poll in the presidential election in 1962.[47] Possibly more serious opposition came from the Peoples Democratic Party, whose leadership was assumed by Kasanga Tumbo, onetime dissident leader of Tanganyika's strongest union, after he resigned as High Commissioner in London in the summer of 1962; but Tumbo himself could claim no more than 8,000 members for his party.[48]

In 1962, as relations between TANU and the unions worsened, Tanganyika had passed laws limiting trade-union independence and providing for preventive detention. Not only did TANU and the TFL disagree on several issues, but as one MP from Tabora explained: "The trade unions are the only other body than TANU which have effective access to the masses ... In my own constituency, I find there that almost every time there is an election, either for officials within the party or alternatively to the Local Council ... the trade union officials are in a position to suggest candidates and often to persuade people to adopt these candidates."[49] In the words of another MP, "the quarrel at present between the trade union leaders and the political leaders of Tanganyika is for power and personalities."[50] In January 1963, the government rusticated the secretary-general of TFL, Victor Mkello, for several months; and after the army mutinies in 1964, it arrested some two hundred trade unionists, dissolved the TFL, and replace it with a single government controlled union.[51]

In 1963, TANU leaders had also become concerned about attempts to use religious divisions between Moslems (31 per cent of the population) and Christians (25 per cent of the population) as a basis for opposition. Christians, because of better education, filled more important jobs than Moslems did. Five of seventeen cabinet ministers were Moslems in October 1963, as were four of twenty parliamentary secretaries, nineteen of sixty-two area commissioners and four of fifteen regional commissioners.[52]

The post-independence political situation affected TANU in two ways. It shifted power within the party, and, more important, it shifted power from the party to the government.

Within the party, according to Lowenkopf's description of TANU before independence, the district was the key level of the party while the regions, then provinces, were merely unimportant links in the formal chain of command. This may have been true as long as the party was concerned with organization and recruitment at branch levels. After independence, however, administration and communication became more important, and the region became the important point of control.

An even more important change within the party was the gain in the importance of the policy-making bodies relative to the administrative side of the party. During the struggle for independence, the party's purpose was generally assumed and bureaucratic control by the party administration was most important. Lowenkopf described the TANU of this period as autocratically led.[53] But as Leys points out, after independence a single purpose could no longer be assumed, the bureaucracy was weakened by loss of personnel, and the policy-making bodies, along with regional and area representation, became more important.[54]

Symptomatic of this shift was the increased importance of the National Executive over the Central Committee. After independence, Nyerere came to rely on his cabinet for the small, informed discussion of daily problems which the Central Committee had provided before independence. The Central Committee became concerned almost entirely with party administration, and its previous dominance over the National Executive disappeared; indeed the position was reversed. As one official said, "now the National Executive sometimes gives the Central Committee a persecution complex."

The second change, the shift of power from party to government can be seen in the locus of decision-making, recruitment of administrators, and control of economic development. The cabinet has become the critical point for daily decisions. The higher educational level of its members, weekly meetings, and its position as recipient of information gathered by government machinery, put the cabinet in a better position to make critical decisions than any party organ.

Party and government decision-making bodies are co-ordinated in three ways. First, the most influential people in both organizations are the same, and they tend to meet and discuss certain problems among themselves. In 1963, there were six cabinet ministers among the nineteen members of the Central Committee and ten among the forty-eight members of the National Executive. Second, National Executive resolutions serve as a backdrop for cabinet discussions. In Nyerere's words: "the National Executive is the final authority but conflict with the cabinet is unlikely because we know their views when we discuss things in the cabinet."[55] Third, the National Executive and the Annual Conference often summon ministers to appear before them to explain government policies. Rather than policy-making, this is something like the question period in a British-type parliament.

So, while the party organs are more important in shaping policy than Parliament (which includes many political nonentities), they are less important than the cabinet. One minister has stated that in case of conflict, the cabinet view prevails. Another explained this cabinet dominance by its position in the communications network: "it is hard to debate or decide on what you don't have information about." Large decisions -- changing the constitution, admitting non-Africans to the party, legalizing the single party, and hastening the formation of an East African federation -- are made by the National Executive. But execution of these decisions and important daily decisions -- such as bargaining at the federal negotiations, deciding to include a project in the development plan, signing a large contract with a foreign corporation, recognizing a new government, or rusticating opponents -- is carried out by the cabinet.

The abolition of the distinction between party and government servants appears at first glance to be a sign of the increased importance of the party. On the contrary, it is a sign of weakness in TANU, for educated manpower and skilled administrators are the country's scarcest resource. After independence the party's share of this scarce resource was depleted by rewarding party officials with better paying government jobs or scholarships. This seriously weakened the local party administration. The creation of political regional and area commissioners to replace former provincial and district commissioners was the first attempt to solve the problem. The legalization of the single-party state was a second attempt. By requiring all civil servants to become party members, leaders hoped to break down the distinction between the two institutions; but in the immediate post-independence period different educational backgrounds and self-images made the distinction meaningful and made it possible to speak of the comparative strength of the two institutions.

In practice, however, regional and area commissioners spend more of their time at their government posts than in their party offices and communicate through government channels with the vice-president's office more often than with TANU headquarters. As one regional commissioner described his job, "it's just like the PC [Provincial Commissioner] and the Governor."

The abolition of the distinction between party and government service seems to have enhanced the importance of the civil service as a recruiter of administrators. The first two regional commissioners appointed after the announcement of the intention to make TANU the single legal party, were civil servants rather than party secretaries as in the past.[56] Too much should not be made of the distinction, given roughly the same ideology amongst civil servants and politicians, but nonetheless, the styles of party and government institutions do differ and it is interesting that the change enhances the position of the civil service in recruitment.

Finally, TANU defined its purpose after independence as spearhead-
ing the fight against "poverty, ignorance and disease." But the institution
with the machinery to carry out economic and social development policies
is the government. Before independence, it was TANU that established the
Tanganyika African Parents Association to run TANU schools, established
Kivukoni College for adult education, instigated self-help projects in rural
areas, and promoted mass literacy campaigns.

After independence, faced with a decline in its supply of funds and
administrators, the party tended to let the previously colonial government
machinery take responsibility for nearly all these development institutions.
Perhaps the most illuminating case concerned the fate of the self-help
projects which were a major feature of Tanganyika's social policies in the
first year of independence. The party was supposed to "mobilize the population" to build roads, dams, dispensaries, and community halls. It was soon
discovered, however, that it was not enough for TANU Youth Leaguers to
get everyone to the building site. Someone had to make sure that there
were enough hoes for everyone who arrived; that tin arrived in time to cover
newly constructed mud walls before they were washed away; or that a skilled
mason built a bridge to make a new road usable. The party administration
was less efficient at these tasks than the Community Development Department, and gradually the organization of self-help projects became primarily
a government responsibility.[57]

UPC

TANU's main concern after independence was <u>maintaining</u> its impressive
organization and the national integration it had previously created, in the
face of declining participation, potential opposition, and internal staffing
problems; the UPC, on the other hand, was primarily concerned with
<u>improving</u> its position and achieving the national integration it had failed
to create prior to independence.

At the end of Uganda's first year of independence, Milton Obote stated
that the major accomplishment of the year had been the maintenance of the
unity of the country.[58] Other ministers have said that UPC strategy strove
to limit the federal concessions to Buganda and the other kingdoms it had
had to make before independence while increasing its power as a party.
To accomplish these goals, control of the government machinery is essential,
and the activities of UPC leaders are concentrated on government control.
Party reorganization, which was announced by Obote in August 1962, and
which might have threatened a number of the notables within the party, was
minimal.

But the UPC did gain in strength after independence. Although it had
won by only a small majority among the three-quarters of the country
(outside Buganda) which went to the polls in 1962, and so had to govern by
coalition, Obote managed to create the impression that the UPC would not
relinquish control of the government machinery. At one point, when his
coalition was in danger, he stated publicly that the UPC was the major
nationalist party in the country and would not relinquish power even if the
Kabaka Yekka members left the coalition and joined the DP to form a new
majority in the Parliament.[59] At the local level, the UPC promises that an
area will prosper, or fail to do so, at the hands of the government machinery
to persuade local electors to return UPC majorities to district councils.
In 1963, the DP lost its last base of support in a local council (Ankole).

Similar persuasion is used to entice MPs to cross the floor and join
the UPC. In one case, a DP member's constituents came to the capital
and pleaded with him to join the UPC so that the district would benefit from
government funds. He did. By slightly more than a year after the 1962
election, Obote had managed to achieve a UPC majority in Parliament.[60]

In January 1964, Obote announced plans to make Uganda a single-
party state. No party with fewer than twenty-five seats in Parliament would
be allowed to put up candidates for elections to the council in Obote's home
district, Lango.[61] Apparently, the mutiny of the army which was composed
largely of northerners, upon whom Obote had felt he could rely, disrupted
plans for this more active use of the state machinery to build the UPC.
The surprising show of opposition strength in the municipal elections shortly
after may also have caused second thoughts.[62]

Control of the state machinery has not only helped the UPC to increase
its strength to the detriment of the DP in the areas outside Buganda, it also
has helped the party in Buganda. Although the UPC failed to win a seat in
the 1963 Lukiko -- the Buganda Parliament -- it established several branches in
the kingdom without fear of local police reprisals. Most important, the
existence of the Uganda government as a source of status and power alternative to the kabaka's government, gave enough confidence to seven MPs
among the progressive group in the KY to allow them to break with the
kabaka and join the UPC. But at the same time that he used a stick on Buganda,
Obote also used the carrot; UPC party discipline in Parliament was sufficient
to pass Obote's constitutional amendment making the kabaka the figurehead
president of Uganda.

Not only has the UPC prospered in Parliament and local elections
through control of the government machinery, it has failed also to suffer
any internal decline similar to TANU's drop in dues. The party depends
on donations rather than dues, and its perpetually low funds are not affected
by any decline in mass participation. At the same time, government funds

and scholarships give it a new source of patronage. Nor has the party suffered, as TANU has, a depletion of administrators, partly because it had so
few, and partly because the independent position of the civil service in the
three-party system makes it almost impossible to reward party people with
government jobs. The DP and KY are both quick to protest any open attempts
to use the government to bolster the UPC -- a problem not faced in single
party Tanganyika.

As for decision-making, the cabinet makes the important decisions
in Uganda, or more accurately, a group of the important UPC members
within the cabinet does. While some of the party's headquarters staff
hope to influence government policy by establishing a research staff, it
has had little effect. Because of the party system and the small UPC
majority, Parliament remains an important body -- much more so than its
Tanganyikan counterpart.

In crisis situations, when the cabinet group feels in need of extra
support, they call on the Central Executive and then on the National Council
or the parliamentary group -- sometimes all three at the same time. With a
weak regional and district structure, there is little competition between
bodies incorporating regional delegates and bodies at the center as there
sometimes has been in TANU. The leaders did not even feel compelled to
call an Annual Conference in 1963.

This reliance on central government activity has meant a shift of
power in the party. Almost by default, a group of younger militants have
manned the party offices. Building on unemployed youth and using the
name of the Youth Wing, they made themselves a clique important in
deciding on the expulsion of various Europeans, Africanization of certain
jobs, and some foreign policy stands.[63] Yet on most issues, such as the
East African federation (which they supported), signing contracts, or changing the constitution, they have no influence. By mid-1964, however, the
immediate post-independence period during which the party gained strength
less by organization than by identification with the government seems to
be over, and political leaders have begun to consider improving the party
bureaucracy.

Conclusions

Why did independence have this different impact on TANU and the UPC?
Unfortunately, we cannot answer the question for two reasons. First, two
cases are not sufficient to allow us to control all the variables and thus know
the limits of our generalization. Was the difference in party system or in
the internal bureaucratization of the parties more important? To what

extent must we make allowances for differences in traditional systems and the influences of personalities? To answer these questions we need more cases. This study is a plea that those cases be constructed in detail and that we no longer rely on the elite-mass polarity idea in treating African parties.

The second reason it is impossible to generalize with certainty about the impact of independence on these two East African parties is the short time involved. Even if we accept the descriptions of the different impacts as accurate, we do not know whether what we have observed is the beginning of a continuing trend or one limited to the immediate post-independence period. A good case can be made for viewing it as a post-independence period phenomenon. As we have said Uganda government leaders finally did turn their attention to the internal organization of the UPC in the spring and summer of 1964. Whether this was a result of the disruption of other plans by the January army mutiny and the shock of DP successes in the February municipal elections, or whether it would have occurred in any case is an open question.

In Tanganyika, where a commission was appointed to study the role of the single party after the January mutiny, a good case can be made for viewing the post-independence experience as a unique phase. As Henry Bienen points out, the distinction between party and civil service may be expected to become blurred with time as the norms of the two institutions become increasingly similar and the British model becomes more remote.[64] The important point is that TANU will set the norms which become common. The Tanzanian government has recently hastened the abridgement of distinctions between the institutions by requiring that all civil servants become party members.[65]

With this understanding of the impossibility of making any firm generalizations about the impact of independence on TANU and the UPC until we have more detailed case studies of African parties and until a follow-up study is made in East Africa after more time has elapsed, let us relax our discipline and offer a hypothesis about the difference.

Might not the root of the difference in the two parties' development after independence be traced to the nature of African nationalism? This nationalism made control of the old colonial government machinery the vital factor in the creation of a nation.

During the last days of colonialism in Tanganyika and Uganda two parallel organizations existed -- the government and the nationalist party. Party organization was needed to educate the people to nationalist ideas and to create a widespread sense of the illegitimacy of the colonial government. After the party achieved its goal, independence, the very nature of African nationalism made the government more indispensable than the party. According to this hypothesis, the difference in the impact of independence on the two parties is attributable to the importance of the old colonial government machinery in a condition of scarcity of skilled administrators. In Tanganyika, the government competed with a bureaucratized party for this scarce resource and in doing so weakened the party; in Uganda the government served as a substitute for a non-bureaucratized party and in building up this scarce resource, strengthened the party.

The value of this hypothesis in explaining the differences in the immediate post-independence period cannot be judged until we have more case studies. Whether the condition of the parties after independence was unique or will continue cannot yet be judged. We are, therefore, left with the case with which we started -- that independence affected the major nationalist parties in Tanganyika and Uganda in very different ways -- and with a tentative hypothesis. If we are suprised that this should be so, it may be evidence that our analytical tools are far from being sharp enough.

Footnotes

The author wishes to note that this paper was written in early 1964
and the present tense refers to 1964. Subsequent events, particularly the
Tanzania elections of 1965 have altered the situation. This paper should be
viewed as a snapshot of two different parties two years after independence.

1. See Tanganyika Standard (Dar es Salaam), Dec. 9, 1961; Cranford
Pratt, "Multriacialism and Local Government in Tanganyika, " Race,
II:46 (Nov. 1960).

2. Zuberi Mtemvu, who quit TANU in 1958 and rejoined it in 1963,
tried to gain support by propounding radical and racial ideas, but he failed
to build an organization for his African National Congress. On the other
hand, the colonial government-sponsored United Tanganyika Party failed
through lack of attractive ideas.

3. Thomas Hodgkin, African Political Parties (London, 1961), 68-75;
Ruth Schachter, "Single Party Systems in West Africa, " American Political
Science Review, LV:295 (June, 1961); Martin Kilson, "Authoritarian and
Single-Party Tendencies in African Politics, " World Politics, XV:264-268.
Kilson points out that a caucus-type party may have mass support at the
polls.

4. UPC officials themselves did not know the exact number of party
members as the secretary-general, Grace Ibingira, admitted. Reporter
(Nairobi), July 31, 1964.

5. This section is based on interviews with fourteen officials in the
capital and three areas in the early part of 1963. Some prefer not to be
cited. I have tried to make the descriptions as accurate as possible, but
there may be minor errors in details or numbers. Since this field work
was completed, the number of regions has been increased to seventeen
and Tanganyika and Zanzibar formed a union. This paper deals with the
situation in 1963 before these changes.

6. This approximate figure was given both by Deputy Secretary–
General Edward Kisenge, and Administrative Secretary T. A. K. Msonge.

7. Estimates of paid TANU employees, which range in the thousands,
include people receiving commissions, not just salaries. See Julius Nyerere
quoted in Uganda Argus (Kampala), April 10, 1962; Martin Lowenkopf,
"Outlook for Tanganyika, " Africa Report, Dec. 1961, 4.

8. See for an example, Tanganyika Standard, March 21, 1962.

9. Colin Leys, "Tanganyika: The Realities of Independence, " International Journal, XVII:259 (Summer 1962).

10. The creation of the new regions automatically expanded the National Executive membership. In January 1964, seventy-eight members attended the National Executive meeting. East African Standard (Nairobi), Feb. 1, 1964.

11. List of Attendance at National Executive Meeting, April 23, 1963 (mimeographed at TANU headquarters).

12. Edward Kisenge, interview, March 5, 1963. Kisenge, an experienced administrator, was also a parliamentary secretary in the vice-president's office at the time that he held his party post.

13. Margarat Bates, "Tanganyika" in Gwendulen M. Carter (ed.), African One-Party States (Ithaca, 1962), 456.

14. Tanganyika Standard, June 3, 1960.

15. TANU, Sheria na Madhumuni ya Chama (Dar es Salaam, n.d.). After the army mutiny in January 1964, TANU leaders decided that company leaders would be TANU chairmen and that the army would be represented on the National Executive. Reporter, July 3, 1964.

16. Tanganyika Standard, April 6, 1962.

17. Interview, A. M. Kirunda-Kivejinja, director of research, March 26, 1963. Until 1958, TANU also was little bureaucratized. One factor which made it easier to build a party bureaucracy in Tanganyika than Uganda was the existence of Swahili as a lingua franca, allowing secretaries to be shifted easily. See George Bennett, "An Outline History of TANU," Makerere Journal, No. 7 (1962); and Martin Lowenkopf, "Political parties in Uganda and Tanganyika" (Unpubl. diss., London University, 1962), 149.

18. Neal Ascherson, "The Uganda National Congress" (unpublished paper in the files of the East African Institute of Social Research, Kampala).

19. For details, see D. A. Low, Political Parties in Uganda, 1949-1962 (London, 1962); David Apter, The Political Kingdom in Uganda (Princeton, 1961).

20. George Magezi, Uganda Argus, Aug. 18, 1959.

21. Uganda People's Congress, Second Annual Delegates Conference (Kampala, n.d.). The language used by headquarters officials was far more Marxist and militant than language used in normal political discourse in Uganda.

22. Uganda Argus, March 23, 1960.

23. Interview, Acholi District Secretary, April 2, 1963.

24. Interview, Secretary-General John Kakonge, April 29, 1963.

25. Lowenkopf, "Political Parties," 68.

26. Otema Allimadi was declared expelled but retained control of the local party and was quickly reinstated.

27. Uganda Argus, June 29, 1963.

28. Interview, Attorney General Godfrey Binaisa (UPC chairman in Buganda), April 26, 1963.

29. The secretary-general was paid an irregular stipend of 300 shillings a month -- about the same as a TANU deputy district secretary. See, Second Annual Delegates' Conference.

30. The Constitution of the Uganda People's Congress (Kampala, n.d.).

31. Ibingira remarked in 1964 that it was not even clear who was and was not on the headquarters staff because so many people had the habit of "hanging around the office." He installed four new officials of his own and closed the party offices to all but the officials. Reporter, July 31, 1964.

32. Aidan W. Southall, "Micropolitics in Uganda -- Traditional and Modern Politics," Proceedings of the East African Institute (Kampala, 1963).

33. Uganda Argus, Aug. 1, 1962; Reporter, May 22, 1964.

34. Uganda Argus, May 10, 1962.

35. Ibid., Jan. 17, 1963.

36. Ibid., Nov. 22, 26, 29, 1963.

37. I am indebted to Cherry Gertzel for letting me use her extensive notes on the 1962 conference.

38. Reporter, April 20, 1963.

39. Uganda Argus, Dec. 6, 1963.

40. Ibid., May 2, 1963.

41. Ibid., Nov. 26, 1963. Many "Youth Wingers" were unemployed school drop-outs who turned to politics to release their frustration.

42. Tanganyika Standard, Oct. 5, 7, 19, 1961.

43. Ibid., Jan. 11, 1962.

44. Lowenkopf, "Political Parties, " 165.

45. John George, "How Stable is Tanganyika, " Africa Report, March 1963, 5.

46. Interviews, E. A. Kisenge, T. A. K. Msonge, March 2, 5, 1963.

47. Though as a general rule, election results become suspect as figures approach 100 per cent, there seemed to be no important reasons to question the honesty of the 1962 election.

48. Tanganyika Standard, May 9, 1963. Tumbo was extradited from Kenya and detained in Tanganyika in 1964.

49. Speech by A. M. Short, Tanganyika, Parliamentary Debates (Hansard), June 27, 1962.

50. Speech by E. B. M. Barongo, ibid.

51. Reporter, Feb. 14, 1964.

52. East African Standard, Oct. 18, 1963.

53. Lowenkopf, "Political Parties, " 169.

54. Leys, "Tanganyika, " 259.

55. Interview, Feb. 13, 1963.

56. Tanganyika Standard, March 13, 1963.

57. For details, see J. S. Nye, Jr., "Tanganyika's Self Help." Transition, II:35-39 (Nov. 1963).

58. Quoted in Uganda Argus, Oct. 9, 1963.

59. Uganda Nation, April 12, 1963.

60. Uganda Argus, June 18, 1964.

61. East African Standard, Jan. 5, 1964.

62. Reporter, Feb. 28, 1964.

63. Uganda Argus, Nov. 22, Dec. 9, 1963; Reporter, Nov. 30, 1963.

64. Henry Bienen, "The Party and the No-Party State: Tanganyika and the Soviet Union, " Transition, IV:13 (1964).

65. See statement by Vice-president Kawawa, Reporter, July 31, 1964.

X

Politics in Uganda: The Buganda Question

Terence K. Hopkins
Department of Sociology, Columbia University

In a speech to his constituents early in 1964, Dr. Milton Obote, then prime minister of Uganda and president of its ruling party, the Uganda People's Congress (UPC), intimated that he would shortly lead the country along the well trodden path toward a one-party state. Not long before however, on October 9, 1963, the first anniversary of Uganda's independence from Great Britain, the most powerful of the country's traditional rulers, His Highness Sir Edward Frederick Mutesa II, Kabaka of Buganda, replaced Her Majesty Elizabeth II, Queen of England, etc., as Uganda's head of state and became, in addition, His Excellency the President of Uganda.

Coming as they did within a few short months of one another, these two seemingly contradictory developments, the one towards a Ghana-Guinea kind of political structure, the other towards an Ethiopian-style "Moderniz-ing autocracy" (to use David Apter's phrase), led some observers to infer that Uganda politics were reassuming after a brief spell of predictability the complex patterns they had exhibited in the late 1950's, when they were considered by many to be among the more unstable and baffling on the African continent. On the surface, Uganda's politics have been indeed complex. But they have not been unstable, and they are probably no more baffling than those of any other country, once the underlying tensions they reflect are understood.

Among these tensions one in particular has decisively shaped the country's politics, the tension between the Baganda and the other peoples of Uganda. Politically, this tension takes the form of the Buganda question, the dimens-ions and ramifications of which are many but the core of which can be simply stated: what place should Buganda, its ruler the kabaka, and its people the Baganda occupy in the emerging national society? It has not been an easy question for Ugandans to answer. To many Baganda they are an elite people, endowed with a superior culture, superior economic wealth, and superior political traditions. To those among them who have thought about the matter at all, it was until fairly recently almost inconceivable that they should not provide the leadership for the new state. To many non-Baganda such claims have appeared pretentious, the wealth not wholly deserved, and the traditions a liability. While valuing much that Buganda has attained, particularly the relative well-being of its people and its politi-cal successes during the colonial period, the others have been no more prepared to put up with the Baganda overrule than with British overrule.

The Buganda question and its organizing role in Uganda politics
form the principal subject matter of this essay. It is, for such a young
country, an old problem, for its roots lie in actions taken at the very
beginning of the colonial period. Only in the 1950's, however, when the
nationalist movement was getting underway Ugandans began to concern
themselves with how the new state should be organized, did it come sharply
into focus. But at that point it rapidly developed into the overriding political
problem for the country, and it retained that position throughout both the
period immediately preceding independence and the first four years of nationhood, from 1962 to 1966, the period with which this essay is mainly concerned.[1]

The Historical Background

The Colonial Period

The roots of the Buganda question lie deep in Uganda's history and
social structure. The area encompassed by Uganda contains two major
kinds of tribes. In the southern two-thirds are Bantu-speaking peoples:
the more numerous of these are the Basoga and Bagisu, in the southeast
near Kenya; the Banyankore, Bakiga, Batoro, and Banyoro, in the south-
west and west above Tanzania and Rwanda and adjacent to the Congo; and
the Baganda, in between these two groups in the south central area along
the shores of Lake Victoria. In the northern part, bordering the Congo
on the west and Sudan on the north, are Nilotic-speaking tribes, the largest
of which are the Langi, Acholi, and Lugbara. A third group, the Nilo-
Hamites, who live mostly in the northeast, in the area adjacent to Kenya
and the Sudan, and among whom the Iteso are the most numerous, present
a minor classification problem; for the purposes of this analysis they are
discussed along with the non-Baganda Bantu.[2]

In the earlier phase of the colonial period, the three way relations
among the British, the Baganda, and the non-Baganda were most important.
Later on, the distinction between the northern peoples and the Bantu-speakers
becomes almost as important. Today in consequence, with the demise of
overrule an accomplished fact and the end of British influence virtually so,
Uganda's politics are shaped to a large extent by the varying relations
and alliances among and within three major groupings. Of these, the northerners (the Nilotic and Sudanic peoples) constitute about a quarter of the population, the Baganda form about a sixth, and the other Bantu peoples plus most
of the Nilo-Hamites together make up over half of the population.

When the British appeared on the scene in the last quarter of the
nineteenth century, the Baganda were in an expansionist phase, the area
under their well organized administration having been more than tripled

in the preceding two centuries. The Baganda saw in British power a means
of securing and possibly furthering their gains, and the British in turn saw
in the Baganda armies and administrative system a means of extending their
rule throughout what was shortly to become the Protectorate of Uganda
("Uganda" being a Swahili version of "Buganda"). The two made common
cause.

By the beginning of World War I, when the present boundaries of the
country were fairly well established, most areas were under one or another
form of British rule, thanks largely to their Baganda collaborators, who not
only helped pacify reluctant tribes but also set up and manned the local
administrative systems through which order was maintained, taxes collected,
roads built, and cash crops introduced. So extensive was Baganda participation in the creation of effective overrule that even in the neighboring Kingdom
of Ankole, which was itself already highly centralized, Baganda at one point
occupied well over half of the administrative chieftainships; in the northern
Nilotic areas, where decentralized clan structures were common, their
participation was even more extensive. Their frequently arbitrary and
capricious ways, however, and their rapacious approach to local administration, inadvertantly encouraged by British methods of tax farming, often
provoked the populations under their rule to open revolts in which Baganda
chiefs were killed or driven from the area. In due course, as mission-
educated sons from within a district became available, the Baganda were
withdrawn, and the period of their collaboration with colonialism came
to end. But the experience left in the minds of Baganda and non-Baganda
alike certain attitudes regarding one another, which developments both at
that time and later largely reinforced and which in consequence still permeate
Uganda society today.

These reinforcing developments have been of many kinds, but they all
occurred because British colonial policy strongly favored Buganda and the
Baganda. The capital of the protectorate, Entebbe, and the commercial
center, Kampala, both arose within Buganda's geographical boundaries, with
the result that all major lines of communication and transportation radiate
from Buganda. Missionaries first set about their tasks in Buganda, and
the competition among them, although prevalent throughout Uganda, was for
a long time more pronounced there than elsewhere. The result was that
the system of formal education began earlier and became more extensive
in Buganda than in the rest of the protectorate. Moreover, for a very long
time almost all efforts to develop cash-crop farming were concentrated in
Buganda and in the area east of it (the Eastern Province, adjacent to Kenya),
the colonial government taking the view that the Northern and Western
Provinces should form a labor supplying hinterland, which in fact for many
years they did. Politically, too, the Baganda were at an advantage: because
of their geographical and historical position in the protectorate, they dealt

with the British at much closer quarters, on more familiar terms, and on
a much more regular basis than others did. They therefore developed
considerable proficiency in the fine art of neutralizing and evading protectorate government controls, and Buganda managed to reduce the colonial
administration's influence over its affairs both sooner and to a far greater
extent than the other areas did.

These developments, by furthering the growth of Buganda relative
to, and in part at the expense of, the other parts of the protectorate,
sustained the sense of superiority felt by Baganda and indeed provided that
sense with some factual support. In money terms the difference between
them and others can be easily summarized: in Buganda the cash income
per person has been about twice that in the Eastern Region and about four
times that in the Western and Northern Regions. The differences in other
respects are less easy to summarize but are similar: relative to other
Ugandans, Baganda have been better educated, far more numerous among
professionals and upper civil servants, more active in trade, and more
likely to be found in the country's 200-odd small towns and trading centers,
more of which have been located in Buganda then elsewhere. And when the
pressures for independence began to be exerted, it was largely Baganda
who initiated them.

To many Baganda these differences have justified their claims to
superiority and leadership. To many non-Baganda the differences have
justified instead national policies specifically designed to reduce them.
The Baganda approach to national politics, then, expressed publicly as a
desire to protect the institution of the kabakaship, has rested on two premises:
that they should lead, and that their privileges, being the legitimate fruits
of their superiority, should remain intact. The non-Baganda have rejected
both premises. Historically they have more than once emulated Baganda
in matters of colonial politics, adopted voluntarily or otherwise a number
of Kiganda patterns, and to a large extent framed their personal and communal
aspirations in the light of Baganda attainments. But with respect to the
emerging national society, they have held strongly to the twin view that
there are no compelling reasons why Baganda leadership is either necessary
or desirable and that existing differences in material well-being between
Buganda and the rest of the country should give way to a more equitable
regional distribution of wealth and opportunity.

The Politics of the Nationalist Period

Buganda's initial response to this rejection of its claims to leadership was to emphasize its superiority and on that basis to pursue a policy
of separatism. In the early 1950's when the kabaka of Buganda and his

ministers turned their thoughts to independence, they sought the end of overrule not for Uganda as a whole but just for Buganda, the only part of the protectorate, they argued, that was ready. As an interim arrange- ment they proposed the transfer of Buganda affairs from Her Majesty's Colonial Office to Her Majesty's Foreign Office. It was as if, having played the game of colonialism with extraordinary success, at least in part because they had sat on the dealer's right throughout, the Baganda decided that if they could not themselves become the dealer, which it seemed from the others' attitudes they could not, they had better pick up their winnings and leave before the dealership changed hands. Neither the proposal nor the motives it implied, it seems scarcely necessary to add, were received with great enthusiasm by the other players.

The moves were rebuffed by the British but not before they had further divided Baganda and non-Baganda. Indeed, from the point of view of the nascent nationalist movement, the breach was all but complete, since apparently the only structure keeping the country intact was the colonial government. Thus the healing of this breach and the reincorporation of Buganda into Uganda became the principal object or the critical considera- tion of practically all major political moves in this period. The considera- ble amount of maneuvering that occurred, and that gave Uganda politics baffling appearance, concerned not so much the question of whether Buganda would be reincorporated, although it sometimes seemed to be that, but rather the terms of its reincorporation, the place it and its leaders would occupy in the new society.

The British government's response to Buganda's proposal for a separate and foreseeable independence was to reiterate their intention of keeping the protectorate together and to require the kabaka, Mutesa II, to support that intention. This he was unable to do, and in consequence, in the fall of 1953, he was summarily deported. It is a minor irony of Uganda's brief national history that the deportation of Mutesa, for insisting upon Buganda's separate independence, should have brought about the first healing of the breach which this very insistence had furthered. But it did, for practically all nationalists found themselves united in their opposition to this arbitrary exercise of colonial power. Moreover, since the affair intimately concerned the Baganda and they were therefore far more engaged than anyone else in the negotiations to secure the kabaka's return, it effectively put the Baganda in the forefront of the nascent nationalist movement.

Following the success of these negotiations and the return of Mutesa in 1955, however, the Baganda ceased to play the dominant role in the nationalist movement. This occurred for two reasons. First, they came under attack from non-Baganda. The principal party, the Uganda National Congress (UNC), which several Baganda and a few northerners had founded

in 1952 and control of which formed the base of Baganda nationalist leadership, began to split over issues related to the Buganda question and finally
splintered decisively in 1959. A year earlier, nationalists mainly from
the Western Province and some from the Eastern Province had formed the
Uganda People's Union (UPU), and in 1960 UPU and the wing of UNC led by
Milton Obote (a Langi, or northerner) merged to form the Uganda People's
Congress (UPC). UPC's most striking characteristic at the time was the
virtual absence of Baganda among its members.

Second, with the return of the kabaka in 1955, the common front among
the Baganda politicians split badly as they jockeyed for position in relation
to Mutesa. And here it becomes necessary to introduce another of the
principal axes of Uganda politics: Catholic-Protestant tensions. At the risk
of drastically oversimplifying a very complex subject, the two basic sources
of these tensions may be simply stated: Anglicanism virtually became the
established religion, first in Buganda and subsequently throughout the
protectorate, and appointments to the administrative chieftainships came
to a very large extent to be governed by religious considerations. In consequence, and right from the very beginnings of Uganda, the normal competition
between missionaries became a continuing struggle for power among their
adherents, with Protestants trying to maintain their substantial hold on the
chieftainships and Roman Catholics trying to increase the number they
controlled. In 1956, a group of leading Catholic Baganda, with the active
support of the Catholic bishops, took a new tack in their struggle to alter
their position in Buganda society and formed the Democratic Party (DP).
In short order DP became a national party. The hierarchy of the Catholic
Church, seeing in DP's formation something akin to the Christian Democratic
parties of Europe, used the Church's organization to further its spread,
while leading Catholics outside Buganda, most of whom also felt discriminated
against, saw the new party as a means of securing for themselves a fairer
share of their district's administrative posts and began establishing local
DP branches.

In 1961, direct elections were held throughout the country. Earlier,
Buganda had renewed its claims for development as a separate state, which
the British government had again rejected, and Mutesa and his advisors
decided on the tactic of boycotting the elections. The boycott, it is estimated, was 97 percent effective -- which clearly indicated to all concerned
that the kabaka could exercise considerable power through his administrative
system, and that, in consequence, if Uganda were to secure its independence
it would only be through a coalition between the kabaka and his followers on
the one hand, and leading non-Baganda nationalists, on the other. As it
was, the 3 percent in Buganda who did vote voted overwhelmingly for the
DP candidates, giving the party 20 of the 21 Buganda seats in the national

legislature. These together with the 23 out of 61 seats they won in the rest of the country permitted DP to organize the first democratically elected government in Uganda.

It was to be a short-lived government, however. For soon thereafter a conference held in London decided that new elections would be held in April 1962, and Uganda would become independent six months later, in October. A number of difficult constitutional questions concerning Buganda's place in the new state were at issue in the conference, but what was never seriously at issue, it seems, was whether or not Buganda would take part in the new state. A plan was evolved between UPC leaders and several leading Baganda, including Mutesa, which by granting Buganda a good deal of autonomy, made the necessary political arrangements for Buganda's participation. At the same time, however, the fundamental question of leadership in the new state was left unsettled. Constitutionally, it was agreed that Buganda was to stand in a federal relationship to the national state, which meant, among other things, that its own legislature, the lukiko, was to decide whether Buganda's representatives to the national legislature were to be elected directly, by the Buganda electorate, or elected indirectly, by the lukiko acting as an electoral college. Politically, it appears, the following was agreed upon. One, UPC would not contest the coming election for Buganda's own legislature, but instead a new group would be formed under the aegis of the kabaka. On the strength of the showing in the boycott, this group could count on winning the election in Buganda, after which the newly elected Buganda legislature would opt for indirect elections to the national legislature. Two, the 21 Buganda representatives would then join with the UPC representatives to form a coalition government in which Obote would be the prime minister and the Baganda would hold several ministries. And three, in the following year, Mutesa would become president replacing Queen Elizabeth II as Uganda's head of state.

The plan appears in retrospect to have been well conceived. In the elections for the Buganda legislature, the new group, called Kabaka Yekka (KY), which combined rather disparate elements among Buganda's political factions, soundly defeated DP by winning 65 of the 68 elected seats in the lukiko and then chose Buganda's 21 representatives to the national legislature. Two months later UPC won 37 of the seats outside of Buganda, to DP's 24, and with KY formed a coalition government headed by Obote. Then, eighteen months later, on the first anniversary of Uganda's independence, Mutesa succeeded Queen Elizabeth as Uganda's head of state.

Post-Independence Politics: 1962-1965

The agreement worked out at the 1961 London Conference and subsequently put into effect did no more than it was intended to do, however. In particular, it was not intended to settle the issue of leadership but only to establish
the initial position of the participants and some rules for carrying on the
game. It was not intended to resolve the Buganda question but only to permit
the struggle to be carried on within an independent Uganda. And that struggle
indeed went on, in several forms and in several contexts.

Constitutional Issues

It appeared first and most obviously in disputes between the Buganda
government and the national government over interpretations of their
respective powers. For example, considerable strain occurred in February
1963, over the terms of a bill before the National Assembly which detailed
the powers and responsibilities of each. At about the same time the
Baganda were disconcerted to find the national government's public prosecutor
intervening in a case being heard in a Buganda court, and a few months
later questions arose about the running of police posts with Buganda. (By
early 1966, the jurisdiction and autonomy of Buganda's parallel legal
and judicial system had been so reduced through a series of constitutional
rulings that it could safely operate only in the area of customary law, and
even here it was limited to laws not contrary to or pre-empted by national
government laws.) In the same year, 1963, in conjunction with talks that
were held regarding the establishment of an East African Federation,
which at the time was to include Uganda, Kenya, and Tanganyika, a minister
of the kabaka's government resurrected Buganda's claims to separate state-
hood by demanding that its entrance into any such federation should be as
a federal unit by itself rather than as a part of Uganda.

The two matters that probably proved most divisive of all were
Buganda government finances and what are called the "lost" counties. The
former can be briefly summarized as pertaining to rights to taxes collected
in Buganda and to Buganda's degree of autonomy in determining expenditures.
Even as late as 1965 some issues in regard to taxation remained sufficiently in dispute for the Privy Council to hear an appeal from the Uganda High
Court regarding rights in the graduated income tax collected in Buganda.

The other issue, that of the "lost" counties, cannot be summarized
so briefly. Certain areas that in the nineteenth century were part of the
Kingdom of Bunyoro, to the northwest of Buganda, were ceded by the British
to the Baganda in return for their services in the period of pacification.

The Banyoro, however, never accepted this action and referred to the areas
as their "lost" counties. The dispute between them was serious, violence
was frequent in the area, and the counties were in consequence often declared
"disturbed areas" by the central government, which thereupon imposed
special regulations, curfews, etc. and sent in detachments of the Uganda
police. How to dispose of the issue was one of the most difficult questions
which the negotiators at the pre-independence conferences had to face.
Eventually it was agreed, on the basis of recommendations by a special
commission of inquiry, that in the two counties with particularly large
numbers of Banyoro a referendum would be held among the inhabitants to
decide whether they would remain with Buganda, revert to Bunyoro, or form
a new district directly under the Uganda government's jurisdiction.

Following independence, the kabaka's government opened up large
tracts of uninhabited land in these counties and settled on them several
thousand Baganda, mainly ex-servicemen, a tactic obviously not designed
to ease the situation. Moreover, Mutesa himself several times spent
long periods at his hunting lodge in Ndaiga, an area within the "lost" counties,
thus making plain his personal interest in the scheme. The Uganda government was technically not a party to the dispute, but as it provided another
opening for the Buganda question to appear, it was not surprising that
several non-Baganda ministers openly sided with Bunyoro and that on at
least one occasion the Uganda government, on learning of one of the kabaka's
visits there, promptly declared the counties a "disturbed area", an action
to which Baganda spokesmen just as promptly objected strongly. Tension
continued to build until, in accordance with the pre-independence agreement,
a bill was introduced into the National Assembly in the summer of 1964,
scheduling the referendum for that November. Not only was this date about
as early as the agreement permitted, but also the bill contained a clause
restricting the right to vote to people resident in the counties prior to
independence.

By this time, as is described below, UPC had acquired an absolute
majority in the National Assembly through a series of defections from KY
and DP, and passage of the bill was virtually assured. Its introduction,
and in particular the earliness of the date and the exclusion of the recent
settlers from the voting lists, so upset the Baganda that in August 1964,
the remaining KY members of the National Assembly, including two Baganda
ministers and a parliamentary secretary, crossed the floor and sat with
DP on the opposition benches. In the event, the voters chose to become
again a part of Bunyoro. Many Baganda did not accept this decision, and
the situation was exacerbated by the refusal of Mutesa, in his capacity as
president of Uganda, to sign the bills scheduling the referendum and
implementing its result. (The bills nevertheless became law by virtue of
a special clause, described below, that was introduced into the Constitution
prior to his becoming president). Withing Buganda the government fell,

and a new katikiro (prime minister) had to be elected. (In this election,
it is worth noting, the Baganda chose a moderate, national-level politician,
Mayanja-Nkangi, until then one of the Baganda ministers in Obote's government, to become katikiro, rather than a spokesman of the separatist faction
within Buganda, an action that both reflected and furthered that faction's
declining influence.) Even a year later, 1965, feeling among Baganda
continued to run so high that when six Bunyoro officials and a civilian attempted to enter the kabaka's lodge at Ndaiga, all seven were killed, and the
Bunyoro government considered it necessary to declare officially that the
lodge was its property and to ban the Buganda Ex-Servicemen's Association
from the area.

Political Parties

With the introduction of the bill to hold the referendum, the UPC-KY
alliance gave way, for, as was mentioned, the remaining KY contingent in
parliament thereupon crossed the floor to sit with DP on the opposition
benches. Until then the alliance had formed another context in which the
struggle between Buganda and the rest of the country was carried on, and
in which, again, the drift of developments was against Buganda. So far
as UPC was concerned, KY was merely a temporary organizational device
for securing, indirectly, the support of the Buganda electorate, a view which
a number of Baganda national politicians also held. The reason for its
existence thus came to an end, in this view, with the 1962 electoral victory,
and several voices were raised at the time suggesting KY's dissolution.
The core of KY, however, viewed the party much as they did the Consitut-
ional provisions regarding Buganda's federal status, as one of the major
means available to them for protecting their traditional institutions and
furthering Buganda's interests, and they therefore strongly rejected any
suggestions that the party be disbanded.

Shortly after independence, its dissolution nevertheless began,
for two of the five Baganda ministers in Obote's cabinet, Dr. E. B. S. Lumu,
Minister of Health, and Dr. Joshua Luyambazi-Zake, Minister of Education,
switched from KY to UPC, as did several other Baganda members of the
National Assembly, including three parliamentary secretaries. Mutesa's
election to the presidency of the country in 1963 further undermined the
grounds for KY's continuing in existence. Strong statements calling for
it to be banned were made by, among others, Godfry Binaisa, a Muganda
and Attorney General of Uganda, John Kakonge, a Munyoro (westerner)
and then Secretary General of UPC, and Joseph Kiwanuka, also a Muganda
and founder of the old ANC. Their argument -- that as a tribal party,
KY had no place in Uganda's politics -- found increasing support, among

Baganda as well as others, and further defections to UPC occurred. These along with several converts from DP gave UPC an absolute majority in the National Assembly by the time the "lost" counties bill was to be introduced, and UPC therefore could, and did, dispense with the alliance. Thus, in less than two years, KY had lost not only a substantial portion of its representatives in parliament but, more important, its usefulness to UPC, and when that went, it lost its veto power over national legislation as well. To an increasing number of Baganda it thus seemed to be an obviously failing organization, and pressure from within Buganda for it to disband was joined with the pressure from without for it to be banned. As a result of these pressures, and of certain changes within UPC described below, several more leading members of KY joined UPC in 1965, mainly during the summer months, and so within three years of Independence KY found itself with exactly one third of its original strength in the National Assembly: of the twenty-four members with which it started in 1962 (twenty-one indirectly elected by the lukiko plus three specially elected by the National Assembly), only eight remained.

Earlier, foreseeing the inroads UPC or DP might make among its members in Buganda, KY had moved to organize followings outside Buganda, particularly in the adjacent Bantu-speaking kingdoms to the west (Ankole and Toro) and the district of Busoga to the east, where its main theme, the need to protect traditional and semi-traditional institutions from radical modernists, would presumably have an appeal. It met with little success in this endeavor, certainly less than UPC met with in its efforts to recruit within Buganda, but in any case the tactic became a failure when, in 1965, the local governments of Bugisu, Bukedi, Busoga, and Teso in the east and of Ankole in the west, all banned the party from their districts. By this time KY was under attack from all directions, its original leadership had been decimated, and its remaining leadership was quarreling. It was not even clear that it continued to enjoy the kabaka's support. Hence, when in February 1966, the National Assembly, following up on Obote's promise in December to have KY banned, passed an amendment to an existing law that effectively barred the party from operating, at least under that name, the action served mainly to confirm what was by then a virtual fait accompli.

Even within DP, a leadership struggle occurred in which the principal contestants were a Muganda and a non-Muganda. Here Baganda were, in a sense, more successful, for they did retain control of the party. But they did so at considerable cost. Following KY's decisive victory in Buganda in 1962 and UPC's success elsewhere, lengthy discussions took place within DP concerning the future of the party. Among those who lost their seats in the National Assembly was the first prime minister of Uganda and the president of DP, Benedicto Kiwanuka, a Muganda Catholic. Basil Bataringaya, the Secretary-General of DP and a Munyankole Catholic

(westerner) won his re-election with a large plurality, however, and became
DP's leader in the National Assembly. An extremely energetic man and a
perceptive politician, Bataringaya enjoyed a good reputation among almost
all segments of Uganda's politics, which Kiwanuka, for various reasons,
did not. Bataringaya also saw clearly that if DP was to become stronger
as a national party it would have to cease being the creature of Baganda
Catholics, and at the party conference after the 1962 elections, he opposed
Kiwanuka in the contest for the party presidency. In order to win, he needed
a sizeable fraction of the Buganda delegation's votes, however, and this he
was unable to obtain. Following his defeat, DP steadily lost members to
UPC and when, finally, in December 1964, Bataringaya himself crossed,
along with five of his followers, the DP contingent in the National Assembly
was left with only nine of its original twenty-four members. It was difficult
to avoid the inference that this steady attrition, as well as Bataringaya's
eventual crossing, resulted at least partly from his having been blocked
by the rest of the party leadership, mainly Baganda, from carrying out the
reforms he and a number of others had considered necessary.

What were losses to the other parties were gains to UPC. In 1962
it had less than half of the 91 seats in the National Assembly, 37 directly
elected members and 6 specially elected members. By the end of 1965,
it held 74 of the National Assembly's 92 seats (the extra seat having been
added in 1964, when the Attorney General was made a member ex officio).
The following crossover table summarizes the changes in this period:

April 1962	December 1965				Total
	UPC	DP	KY	Ind.	
UPC	42	--	--	1	43
DP	15	9	--	--	24
KY	16	--	8	--	24
Independent	--	--	--	--	--
Total	73	9	8	1	91
Added in 1964	1	--	--	--	1
Total	74	9	8	1	92

With its ranks thus swelled, particularly by an increasing number of Baganda, UPC changed. From being one of the means used by non-Baganda in their struggle with Baganda, it became, in itself, the principal arena in which various sides of the Buganda question carried on their fight. But this transformation, and the outcome of the conflict within UPC, will be easier to follow after more of the background to the events in 1966 has been presented.

The Bureaucracy

A third arena where the Buganda question expressed itself was composed of the national government's two main organizational arms, the central government civil service and the armed forces (army and police).

As was mentioned, the Uganda civil service, insofar as it contained any Africans at all in its middle and upper reaches during the colonial period, contained mainly Baganda. By the time Africanization of the higher civil service positions began in earnest, however, which was not until independence was in the offing, that is, not until 1960-1961, non-Baganda were available in large enough numbers to challenge the heretofore virtual Baganda monopoly. The non-Baganda, furthermore, had behind them a powerful organization, UPC. Given the prevalence of Baganda in middle-level positions, though, and their seniority, any attempt to make the civil service regionally more representative had to entail promoting some non-Baganda who, in civil service terms, were less deserving than some Baganda. And given the Baganda sense of superiority and their sensitivity to their position in society, it is hardly surprising that in a very short time they came to see the Africanization program as an attack on them and to protest against being "victimized". To some extent, they were probably right: non-Baganda were given preference in several instances. Partly this occurred because UPC wanted to redress the imbalance that grew up during the colonial period, and partly because it needed to have the willing co-operation of the civil service to implement its policies and was not at all sure it could count on Baganda civil servants. As a result, a good many rumors circulated, and when the principal organ of the civil servants, the Public Employees' Union, was unable to obtain enforceable promises from the government, Baganda middle- and upper-level civil servants grew increasingly restive in their positions and increasingly apathetic about their work.

In a new state in a developing country, the loyalty of the civil service and its morale are critical. Both political stability and economic develop-

ment depend to a very large extent on the energies civil servants are
willing to expend in their jobs. Any substantial degree of alienation among
them is, in consequence, a serious matter. It is of course difficult to
tell, but what seems to have prevented demoralization from going further
than it did in the Uganda civil service at this time, and from seriously
impairing the day-to-day operation of the government, was not any reversal
of policy, but, rather, the election of Mutesa to the presidency of the
country. For with that election, the national government no longer seemed
to Baganda to be composed mainly of "the others" -- on the contrary, it
now obviously included in a very key position their leading figure and the
symbol of what some have gone so far as to call the Buganda nation. In
any event, in the period following the kabaka's election, their discontent
appeared to lessen markedly.

The Uganda Rifles (the army) and the Uganda Police stood in marked
contrast to the civil service, for both were predominantly manned not by
Baganda, nor even by non-Baganda Bantu, but by northerners (Langi and
Acholi) and easterners (Itesos) from Nilotic- and Nilo-Hamitic-speaking
tribes. The predominance of these men in these two forces, and the relative
absence of Baganda, occasioned considerable concern among Baganda
politicians. For there was some fear that one or another northern political
leader might in a crisis try using tribal and regional appeals to the army
and police in order to resolve the Buganda question by force. Owing to
this concern, leading circles among the Baganda particularly, but also among
other southerners, continually encouraged young men in their areas to join
the armed forces. If the army and police were more nearly representative
of the national population, they reasoned, the chances would be less that
anyone would attempt to resolve the Buganda question, or any similar
communal tension, through an unconsitutional resort to force. They were
only partly successful in their efforts, however. By design the British
had done most of their recruiting for the army and police in the northern
districts and Teso. Service in these forces had thus become an expected
opportunity among many of the younger men in these areas, and for this
and other reasons those responsible for these organizations were reluctant
to change their recruiting patterns, despite frequent appeals from southerners to carry out more recruitment in the Bantu-speaking areas. In addition, among virtually all Baganda (and to a lesser extent among other southerners as well), service in the army and police was not generally viewed as

a particularly worthy vocation. It is not clear whether this view was a direct evaluation of the burdens of such service or derived from the well known fact that these forces were manned mainly by northerners. But in any case the attitude existed and hindered the recruitment of southerners into the non-commissioned ranks of the army and police.

As it happened, force was used eventually, and it was used against the Baganda. Whether it would have been, had the army been differently constituted, is impossible to tell.

One thing it is possible to say, however, that the role of the army and police in the events of 1966 has irrevocably altered their place in Uganda's politics and society. It will take time for the implications of this change to become clear, but the adjustment is unlikely to be without incident, particularly in the light of the attitudes towards the armed forces that had been prevalent among southerners. For a situation in which an organization is at once powerful and not particularly prestigious is an inherently unstable situation, and civil-military relations are likely to become a major source of politically relevant strains in Uganda in the not too distant future.

Even before the most recent events there were signs of discontent in the armed forces. Throughout the entire post-independence period they have been called upon to perform a number of taxing and rather frustrating police actions. In Rwanda, to the southwest of Uganda, a tribally inspired revolution in which the once dominant but numerically much smaller Batutsi were overthrown by the Bahutu shortly before Uganda's independence, resulted in a large number of refugees settling in Uganda along the border. From there they regularly engaged in hit-and-run attacks, which provoked retaliatory raids from Rwanda, and the Uganda Rifles on several occasions had to patrol the border in a UN-like peace-keeping operation. In the north, the smouldering warfare in the Sudan, between the more or less Christian negroes of the southern part of the country and the ruling Moslem Arabs of the northern part, also continually sent refugees into Uganda, and similar across-the-border raids have from time to time required the army's presence there as well. Internally, too, the army and special police detachments have had to carry out a number of police actions. For example, their presence has been necessary not only in the "lost" counties, owing to the Baganda-Banyoro dispute, but also in a district in the far northeast, Karamoja, where cattle-raiding and related marauding have remained popular pastimes,

particularly raids across the Kenya border, and in the kingdom district
of Toro, in the west, where a portion of the population has been threatening
to secede if they cannot form a separate district. In the last case, the army
as well as the police have been employed under emergency regulations
to maintain some semblance of order in the area, but as the rebellious
tribes live on the slopes of the Ruwenzori Mountains, they can and do fade
with ease into virtually inaccessible areas and if necessary cross into the
Congo and thus out of reach entirely. In all these instances, skirmishes
have occurred, men have been wounded, on occasion killed, yet there has
been no enemy who can be properly defeated. The army's tasks have thus
been trying and frustrating, and although it has not been entirely successful
in carrying them out, it has been fairly clear to everyone that its presence
has been a condition of such order as has obtained in these areas.

Yet, despite the significance of their functions, the army and police
have not been particularly esteemed, as was said, and until a mild mutiny
occurred early in 1964, this attitude received concrete expression in a
system of remuneration that put soldiers and police (but not the officers
of either) among the lowest paid people on the national government's pay-
rolls. Partly in response to this, possibly partly for other reasons, some
Uganda army units, like their counterparts in Tanganyika and Kenya, struck
for higher pay and better conditions, among other things. In Uganda it
was not a serious matter and was quickly settled, but on terms rather
favorable to the soldiers. Whether their success at that time, coupled
with their increased power in Uganda's politics, will feed their ambition
or salve it, remains to be seen. Similarly, only one clash had occurred
between off-duty soldiers and civilians in the first two years of independence.
But then the army was doubled in size in 1964, to about 4,000 men (in response
to the fighting in the then Stanleyville area of the Congo, not too far from
the border with Uganda), new military posts were constructed in the southern, Bantu-speaking part of the country, and existing posts were expanded,
and in 1965 several incidents occurred -- at least partly, it would seem,
because the nearly universal civilian-soldier tension was in these areas
compounded by the specifically Ugandan north-south tribal tension. The
local authorities in the areas involved subsequently tried to have the posts
removed, but their efforts were unsuccessful. In the light of the army's
actions in Buganda in 1966, such incidents may well continue to increase,
thus making even more salient and pressing the question of the army's
place in the society.

Religious Bodies

Yet another sphere where the Buganda question appeared, although not necessarily with specifically political implications, was within the religious groups in Uganda. For example, when the English archbishop of the Anglican Church in Uganda announced that he would retire in 1965, much maneuvering took place and eventually the election was postponed for several months, in order to make it possible for a Muganda prelate to be among the candidates. Considerable indignation was felt by some over what they judged to be the rather unseemly tactics of his supporters, however, and the electoral college, a body of nine bishops, included only two Baganda, the others being from the eastern, northern, and western regions of Uganda and from Rwanda and England. When the college finally did meet, in January 1966, it chose someone else to be the new archbishop, a Munyankole (westerner). Whether or not pro- and anti-Baganda feelings actually played a part in the whole process is difficult to say. Certainly other, more specifically religious issues were involved. The event was talked about in those terms, however, and the newly elected archbishop felt it necessary to use the first occasion on which he spoke to the public to deplore the use of these terms and to express the hope that such feelings were not in fact involved.

A more explicitly political appearance of the Buganda question occurred within the African Muslim community in Uganda. A numerically much smaller group than either the Roman Catholics or the Anglicans, the Muslims have nevertheless been of some importance in Uganda politics because of their overrepresentation among the small traders and taxi-drivers. These positions put them regularly in touch with relatively large numbers of people in the ordinary course of their work, and they consequently played an important role in organizing local UPC and KY branches. If the Roman Catholics have felt somewhat aggrieved about their position in Uganda society, however, the Muslims have felt really discriminated against -- which, in the kind of consciously Christian society that was being developed in Uganda during overrule, they undoubtedly were. Consequently, when it was announced in the fall of 1965 that a new group, the National Association for the Advancement of Muslims (NAAM), was being formed to promote the Muslim cause, considerable interest was aroused.

The interest was provoked as much by NAAM's principal sponsor, however, as by its aims, for its leader was A. A. Nekyon, a Langi

(northerner) and relative of Obote, who was not only in Obote's cabinet
but also one of his closest associates. The traditional head of the Muslim
community in Uganda, Prince Badru Kakungulu, was a Muganda and relative
of Mutesa, while another Muganda, Abu Mayanja, a Cambridge-educated
lawyer, founding member of the old UNC, and leading spokesman for
KY until he joined the exodus to UPC in the summer of 1965, was its most
articulate representative in national politics. Nekyon naturally coupled
the announcement of the new organization with an attack on the community's
existing leadership, and specifically challenged Kakungulu with being,
among other things, too much of a Muganda and too involved in KY. It
was both a well-timed move and an effective appeal, and NAAM quickly
gained support not only where it would be expected to, in the northern districts
and Bunyoro, but also to some extent in the other western districts and
in the east, and not only among the ordinary Muslims but also among
the sheikhs. The Baganda leadership reacted promptly, for they saw in
NAAM a clear threat to their hegemony within the Muslim community and
an instrument of a distinctly political nature, and among other steps,
they resurrected an organization they had started some time back but had
then let disintegrate, the Young Men's Muslim Association (YMMA).
YMMA immediately initiated several projects to counter NAAM's influence,
one of which, the translation of the Koran into Luganda, suggests that
NAAM may even have made some headway among Baganda Muslims.

Something more should be said at this point about another important
source of strain in Uganda, the tension between Roman Catholics and Anglicans.
Uganda, as was said earlier, has been somewhat of a battle ground between
the adherents of the two religions throughout its brief history, and their
competition, which always had a highly political character to it, took an
openly political form outside of Buganda in the 1961 and 1962 elections,
when virtually all Catholics supported DP and all Anglicans, as a result,
supported UPC. Uganda in this period thus exhibited an unusual politics
for an African country, because until then there had been no place on the
continent where political and religious lines of cleavage had paralleled one
another quite so closely. Even before the 1962 elections, however, the
Roman Catholic Church had begun to reconsider its policy, and during
those elections the upper levels of the hierarchy openly deplored the virtual
equivalence of church membership and party preference. Following the
elections the four groups involved, the two churches and the two parties,
called for a lessening of the politically exacerbated religious tensions and
a withdrawal of religious groups as such from participation in politics.
The appeal was fairly successful, and the heightened feelings of the election
years died down following Independence. But the basic tension remains
near the surface and may once again become important in Uganda's politics.

This would seem especially likely to happen under conditions of

political instability and uncertainty, when those who are merely one's
competitors under normal conditions all of a sudden seem to be wearing
masks and engaged in conspiracies. In October 1965, for example, a good
many rumors were circulating about possible communist and counter-
communist coups in conjunction with the Independence celebrations, and
there was in general an air of suspense and impending change. (Nothing
in fact happened at the time, although not all the rumors, apparently, were
unfounded.) In this expectant atmosphere, it is worth recording one of
the rumors which circulated quite widely and was even printed in a local
newspaper as an unconfirmed report to the effect that Uganda's Catholics,
in order to bring about the national government's downfall, were clandestine-
ly organizing a program of passive resistance against the government.

Even under normal conditions, UPC's educational policies may make
the tension once again a salient feature of Uganda's politics. All education
in Uganda was initially in the hands of the two missions, and although the
protectorate government eventually played an increasingly important role
through financial grants-in-aid and curricular reform, practically all
elementary schools and a good many high schools were still under mission
control at the time of Independence. It is largely through the school system,
however, that national sentiments are inculcated, and to national leaders
it seemed obvious that the more Uganda's schools concentrated on turning
out good Catholics and good Anglicans and good Muslims, "good" precisely
because they saw themselves as basically different from those believing
in other religions, the less they would be turning out good Ugandans.
Shortly after the elections the Minister of Education, Dr. Luyimbazi-Zake,
broached publicly the possibility of secularization by pointing out that the
process had in fact been begun a decade earlier, when Sir Andrew Cohen
was governor. The reaction to his idea was strong and negative, as anticipated, but the Anglicans stood to lose much less than the Catholics, since they
in fact gave much less religious instruction in their schools, and as they
came to realize this their opposition to the program weakened. About a
year later, in August 1963, the government considered it possible to begin
a gradual secularization of the schools. Although strong Catholics were
almost all opposed, as were some strong Anglicans, the response was
a good deal more muted than some had thought it would be, and the program
having fared relatively well has been continued. It has not ceased to be
in dispute, however, and in fact the Catholic Church's antagonism has
probably increased, as well it might, since each step forward from the
government's point of view is yet another step backwards from the Church's.
Thus in May 1966 the hierarchy issued possibly its strongest statement so
far in defense of religious instruction in schools and implied that Catholics
might have to resist the government actively should Dr. Zake attempt
to enforce a suggestion he had made a few weeks earlier to the effect that
such instruction be discontinued entirely.

Uganda's Political Elite

One of the most important arenas in which the struggle between
Baganda and non-Baganda occurred was formed by what may be called
the "leading circles" of Uganda politics. This arena is difficult to define,
and its composition has shifted from time to time, in at least one instance
dramatically. But it was, and is, an important feature in a country whose
structures are still very much in the process of formation.

In the immediate post-independence period, three key figures stood
out: from the Northern Region, Dr. Milton Obote, then Prime Minister of
Uganda and President of UPC; from Buganda, Sir Edward Frederick Mutesa II,
Kabaka of Buganda, subsequently President of Uganda, and principal voice
in KY; and from the Eastern Region, Sir William Wilberforce Nadiope,
Minister of Internal Affairs in Obote's government until becoming Vice
President of Uganda in 1963, the semi-traditional ruler (kyabazinga) of Busoga,
and a prominent and powerful member of the UPC executive. No one from
the Western Region quite approached these three in power at the time of
independence, although Grace Ibingira, a Munyankore, Minister of Justice
in Obote's first cabinet, and later Secretary-General of UPC, would in time
come increasingly close. Each of the three had a sizeable, well-organized
local following, considerable impact on national policies, and several
followers who were "his" men well distributed among important decision-
making groups (such as the UPC Executive Committee, the cabinet, the
officer corps of the army, the higher civil service, and so forth).

The principal contender for the presidency of Uganda in 1963 appeared
for a while to be Nadiope, who was influential not only in nationalist circles
but also among the traditional rulers (the abakama) of the kingdoms of
Ankole, Bunyoro, and Toro. His election, however, while it would have
satisfied many nationalist and traditionalist groups, would almost certainly
have deepened the cleavage between Baganda and non-Baganda. The hypersensi-
tive Baganda might well have inferred that national positions were closed
to them unless, like the Baganda ministers in the national government,
they forsook their specifically Buganda allegiances. Moreover, it would
have violated the pre-independence agreement which called for Mutesa's
election to the presidency with Obote's support.

The implementation of that agreement, it now appears in retrospect,
required that certain conditions be met. For the presidency, while mainly
an honorific position, did have certain emergency powers in the event of
a government crisis, and its occupant was ex officio head of the armed
forces. If by supporting Mutesa, Obote were not to increase materially

the power as well as the prestige of his most formidable opponent for national
leadership, it was necessary that UPC be firmly in control of the government,
Obote himself be firmly in control of UPC, and in the event of a serious
policy difference between his and the kabaka's governments, that is, between
Uganda and Buganda, that he be able both to resolve the issue in the national
government's favor by constitutional means and to count on the support of
the army and police should the difference lead to an open dispute and a
Baganda boycott or similar disturbance. As we have seen, most of these
conditions were met or were in the process of being met. UPC was well
on the way to gaining an absolute majority in the National Assembly. Obote,
working closely with Ibingira among others, was consolidating his power
within UPC (mainly at the expense of various local-level leaders but to some
extent at the expense of the party's left-wing at the national level as well).
And, as was explained above, owing to the regional composition of the
armed forces, the national government could count on the army and police
in the event of a serious dispute with Buganda. There remained only the
question of the powers of the presidency.

The Uganda Independence Constitution had given the Queen's representative, the Governor-General, absolute discretion to appoint the Prime Minister
after a general election, provided only that the person appointed appear
likely to command a majority of the members of the National Assembly.
If this power were left unrevised and incorporated into the Office of President,
Mutesa would be in a position to appoint a KY leader as prime minister,
even though the KY members constituted but a small proportion of the National
Assembly. Hence, prior to his election the Constitution was amended to
require the President as head of state to call upon the leader of the party
having the most members in parliament to form a government and to prohibit
him from calling upon anyone from a party with less than twenty members
in the assembly. In addition, the Independence Constitution made no provision
for occasions on which the governor-general's action was required but
on which he in fact did not act as he was advised to do by the cabinet. It
was anticipated, though, that there might well be bills, for example the
"lost" counties bill, which would require the president's signature before
becoming law but which Mutesa might resist signing because in his opinion
they ran counter to Buganda's interests. And so this potential veto power
was removed from the presidency by another constitutional revision, which
stipulated that if the president failed to act in cases where his action was
constitutionally required (e.g., declaration of a state of emergency, making
a bill into law by signing it, and so forth), the prime minister could act
for him, and that action would be construed as the president's.

Despite considerable opposition within UPC to honor the pre-independence agreement, Obote threw all his weight behind Mutesa's election and,
with the help of the principle of unanimity, carried his cabinet with him.
Subsequently, the National Assembly elected Mutesa president. Thus,
with only minor and temporary alterations in the alignment of forces, the
Baganda were at this point incorporated further into the developing state,
rather than pushed further out of it.

At the same time, the action seriously strained the unity of UPC,
and the alignments within the cabinet prefigured to some extent a division
that in time would deepen and eventually split the UPC leadership into
contending camps. Just below Obote, Mutesa, and Nadiope in Uganda's
visible power structure at this time stood several men, each with considerable room for independent action: Joseph Cuthbert Obwangor, an Itesot
(easterner), then Minister of Regional Administration, a man with a strong
local base and substantial support within the armed forces; Ibingira, already
mentioned; Basil Bataringaya, then Leader of the Opposition but subsequently,
after crossing the floor in 1964, Minister of Internal Affairs; Dr. Lumu,
a Muganda, then Minister of Health and a principal organizer of UPC in
Buganda; B. K. Kirya, a Mukedi (easterner), then Minister of Works;
John Kakonge, a Munyoro (westerner), then Secretary-General of UPC and,
in 1966 Minister of Economic Planning and Development; A. A. Nekyon,
a Langi (northerner) and relative of Obote, then Minister of Information;
Godfrey Binaisa, a Muganda but not a supporter of the kabaka, Attorney General;
and George Magezi, a Munyoro (westerner), then Minister of State.
Bataringaya, who as parliamentary leader of DP could scarcely be expected
to support the kabaka's nomination, was in any case not involved in the
cabinet decision. Among the others, Obote could count on Lumu and Ibingira,
because both were working actively to avoid alienating the Baganda establishment without at the same time conceding too much power to them, and on
Kirya because at the time he was personally close to Obote. Obwangor
was known for his independent line of action and apparently did not give
Obote his full support in this case. The rest apparently strongly opposed
the decision and supported Nadiope instead. But Kakonge, because not a
member of the cabinet at the time, and Binaisa, because not a member of
parliament then, were limited in their influence, while Magezi and Nekyon
were similarly limited because their views were discounted -- Magezi's,
because as a Munyoro he could not be expected to support the
kabaka while the "lost" counties issue was still pending, and Nekyon's,
because he was well known for a generally intransigeant stand against
concessions of any kind to Buganda. Despite the opposition, then, Obote
was able to pull the cabinet with him, but there seems little doubt that his
action supporting the Baganda cause occasioned more than a little difficulty
within UPC. (The action also apparently caused him some difficulties

among his constituents, the Langi, a northern Nilotic people with a history of strongly anti-Baganda attitudes; for his speech intimating evolution towards a one-party state, alluded to earlier, appears to have been given in his home area rather than elsewhere in order to counter rumors that he was afraid to be tough with the Baganda.)

It was all a portent of things to come. Initially, however, following the kabaka's election, the main locus of strain was between Mutesa and Obote, for despite the constitutional changes, the presidency did give the kabaka a national aspect he did not previously have and it thus made him more of a contender for national leadership, more of a competitor to Obote, than he had been. Relations between the two, never noticeably warm, steadily worsened throughout 1964, when, besides the conflict over the "lost" counties issue, Mutesa and Obote clashed over who should represent Uganda at the Cairo conference of non-aligned nations and the London conference of Commonwealth countries, the head of state or the head of government. More was at stake here, it seems, than the relative prestige of the two offices, although that too was involved. For in terms of foreign policy -- which in time came to play a considerable part in Uganda's politics -- Mutesa was strongly pro-west, in particular, strongly pro-British. Obote, in contrast, adhered much more closely to a policy of non-alignment, which meant, given the existing relations between Uganda and Britain and, through these, between Uganda and the west generally, a preference for relaxing some of the ties with the west and for developing some ties with the east. Obote in fact attended both conferences, but the effect of Mutesa's claims was to transform what, at the national level, had been a more or less personal competition between the two men into both a constitutional struggle over the powers of their respective offices and a political struggle with marked ideological overtones, concerning the position Uganda should take on international issues and the place Uganda should assume in the international political spectrum.

In time, the relationship deteriorated to the point where, in a succession of actions over the course of the first few months of 1966, Obote announced that he was suspending the sections of the Constitution which define the powers of the president and assuming the powers himself, then later gave Uganda a new constitution with an executive presidency and filled that position himself, and eventually ordered the army to search the kabaka's palace for weapons -- an operation that resulted in a day-long siege and ended with Mutesa fleeing to Burundi and then going into exile in London.

Uganda People's Congress

Prior to this forceful resolution of the tension, however, opposition to Obote's leadership arose and became organized within UPC itself. The growing conflict after 1963 between Obote and Mutesa symbolized the shakiness of the 1961-1962 compromise arrangements. A less symbolic but in some ways more significant tension developed between Obote and Ibingira, the two men initially most responsible for UPC policy. At first, it appears, the Buganda question played but a small part in their disagreement. Subsequently, however, it loomed large, and there is little reason to doubt that when matters came to a head in February 1966, and Obote had Ibingira and four other ministers arrested and detained in remote parts of the country, one of the issues on which the two men held markedly different views was on whether and to what extent to maintain the compromise arrangements intact.

Following the 1962 elections, Obote and Ibingira worked together closely consolidating their power with UPC. To this end, Ibingira challenged the incumbent Secretary-General of the party, John Kakonge, in the election for that post at the annual delegates' conference in 1964, and in a bitterly fought contest managed to win. Obote supported Ibingira at this time, as did Nadiope and Obwangor. Mainly at issue, it seems, was control of the party organization. But Kakonge was, and is, an articulate spokesman for the left in Uganda, and he was strongly supported by Godfrey Binaisa, the Attorney General, also of the left, and not unnaturally many participants and observers defined the outcome semi-ideologically, as a victory of "moderates" over "radicals" or "militants".

These terms gained currency over the succeeding two years as the groups associated with the labels became increasingly well-defined. For in this period both the alignments on various issues and the kinds of issues on which people aligned themselves took on definite patterns. During 1964, Tshombe's mercenaries were operating in the northeastern part of the Congo, in the then Stanleyville-area, against the Gbenye-led national liberation forces, and the question arose as to how much assistance Uganda should render the Stanleyville government. Obote, it appears, wanted Uganda to commit itself to give as much support as it could reasonably afford, while Ibingira, for a variety of reasons, favored less involvement. Among those in the cabinet who it seems supported Obote's position were Adoko Nekyon, mentioned earlier; Felix Onama, a northerner from Madi and Minister of Defense; Alex Ojera, also a northerner, from Acholi, and then Minister of Community Development and Labor; and Sam Odaka, from Bukedi in eastern Uganda, Minister of Foreign Affairs. Their view prevailed, and a decision was taken to give substantial aid. Subsequently, in January 1965, Gbenye and the three East African leaders, Obote, Nyerere, and Kenyatta, met at Mbale in eastern Uganda. Detailed arrangements regarding Uganda's program of support were worked out there, and the second in command of Uganda's army, Colonel Idi Amin, a northerner from Lango, was put in charge of the Uganda part of the operations.

Ibingira, it now seems reasonable to infer, remained opposed to the degree of commitment assumed by Uganda, but at that time little was known of this, or of the rift between him and Obote which the decision apparently occasioned, since Uganda's participation remained a state secret until an outline of its role was made public in 1966. What was public instead was the continuing dispute between Ibingira and Kakonge, which on at least two additional occasions after the 1964 UPC conference became a matter of general interest. On one of these, some supporters of Kakonge attacked Ibingira during a demonstration, and for this the latter brought a case before the UPC executive committee and obtained their suspension from the party. On the other occasion, Kakonge, this time supported by Obote, was nominated to fill a vacancy in the National Assembly, and Ibingira was among those who led the nearly successful fight to block his election. It was not to be long, however, before the Ibingira-Obote dispute would come into the open and overshadow all others.

In the middle of 1965, Obote went on a several week tour of China and Eastern Europe, and various debates over the merits of the trip occurred both while he was away and after his return. These exacerbated the division within UPC in two ways. In the course of the debates various UPC leaders were charged with being "agents" for one or another of the great powers, rumors of plots and counterplots spread, and the labels "pro-East" and "pro-West" came into regular use, in addition to "militant" and "moderate". Moreover, in the forefront of those attacking "communism in Uganda" and, in a more veiled fashion, Uganda's newly formed ties with the socialist countries, were several spokesmen for the Buganda establishment. Perhaps foremost among these was Daudi Ocheng, who, although a northerner from Acholi, was chosen by the lukiko in 1962 to be one of Buganda's representatives in the National Assembly and in time became Secretary General of KY. Differences on the Buganda question thus became inextricably bound up with differences on matters of foreign policy, on the one hand, and of internal security, on the other. This multiplication of the differences between what were becoming two camps deepened the rift between Obote and Ibingira at the same time that the language used had the effect of partially obscuring the basic issues involved.

Indeed, by late 1965, observers and participants alike were speaking
freely of two groups within UPC, an "Ibingira group" and an "Obote group",
and were describing the former as specifically opposed to Obote continuing
to be president of UPC and prime minister of the country. Included among
Ibingira's supporters in the cabinet were by this time Kirya, Lumu, Magezi,
and Matthias Ngobi, from Busoga (an easterner), then Minister of Agriculture.
Included among Obote's supporters were, as mentioned, Nekyon, Onama,
Ojera, and Odaka. Outside of the cabinet, in the functional divisions of
the national party organization and in the various district organizations,
each group had its adherents, so that to some there appeared to be not one
UPC but two. One stood for maintaining intact, for as long as possible,
the basic compromise arrangements which had so far provided the framework for Uganda's politics even if this required changes in the UPC leadership. The other stood for maintaining Obote's leadership in the party and
the country, even if this required ending the compromise arrangements
and developing a new set of rules for Uganda's politics.

As the regional composition of the two groups in the cabinet might
suggest, still another set of categories was sometimes used to describe
the division. Uganda a scarce fifty years ago was little more than a
British-Baganda imposed framework of overrule, a country in name only,
in which the colonial power, as a matter of policy, kept the contacts among
people from different areas to the minimum required by the colony's economy
and administrative system. When independence was won, the various tribal
communities were therefore necessarily still quite strong. Despite some
inroads on their strength, they also remained quite strong in the post-independence period, for the processes of modernization -- the formation of a national
state, the creation of a national economy, the rise of an urban-based class
structure -- are in general slow processes, and pre-existing, locally based,
ethnic and linguistic communities dissolve only gradually.

At the national level, though, loyalty to one or another particular
tribe was not especially apparent. Instead there occurred the loose three-way
grouping described earlier -- northerners (or, loosely, "Nilotics"), Baganda,
and non-Baganda Bantu. As was also mentioned before, when UPC was formed
it had virtually no Baganda among its leading members and, in regional
terms, was therefore essentially a coalition of northerners and non-Baganda
southerners. Just as the reasons for KY's existence began to be questioned
after independence, however, so too did the reasons for the existence of this
coalition, and UPC tended in time to dissolve into its two main regional
elements. In addition, the Baganda who joined UPC after independence
tended to associate themselves with the Bantu or southern grouping. The

division that was developing within the party thus came to have a regional cast, and the two wings acquired the labels "southerners" and "northerners", or "Bantus" and "Nilotics", in addition to the other terms used to refer to them.

That the UPC in general and the leadership in particular tended to divide along broadly north-south lines is fairly clear. Why this occurred is rather less clear. Some politicians, particularly some Baganda, tried consciously to bring such a division about, on the grounds that the UPC policy of reducing regional inequities by furthering the advance of northern districts generally and of individual northerners in particular, was being carried too far. But this explicitly regional appeal seems to have carried little weight among UPC leaders. Moreover, insofar as this argument gained any currency at all, it did so mainly after the split in UPC became generally known rather than before, so that the appeal seems to have been an effect or reflection of the division rather than a cause of it. More relevant to an explanation of the division, probably, is the gradual erosion that occurred in the post-independence period of the trust and confidence which the principal UPC leaders had developed in one another during the pre-independence period. Exactly how and why this erosion took place can probably not be known until the participants themselves describe what happened, but the following general considerations seem, prima facie, to be relevant.

A group such as the UPC leadership derives its cohesion not from an impersonally organized system of roles and authority relations, that is, not from the kind of system that holds a civil service or an army together, but from the personal knowledge the members have of one another and in particular from the trust and confidence they come to feel in each other's judgment and word. In such a group coalitions and alliances of course form -- for collective decisions must be reached, and unanimity is a rare condition -- but these tend to be unstable: new ones form as different issues come up and dissolve as the matters that occasion them are decided.

If the condition of trust within the group as a whole should become eroded, however, members will find themselves in ambiguous circumstances when making decisions. They will not know whose expressed views to take at face value and whose to discount, or who can be counted on to discharge a responsibility reliably and who can be expected to use the opportunity to further his own ends. Under such conditions they will tend to feel that, generally speaking, they are safer trusting those whose backgrounds are similar to their own and less safe trusting others. Coalitions and alliances will thus tend to form on the basis of similar backgrounds. Such alliances are usually stabler than those formed in connection with particular issues, though, since in the nature of the case the members' backgrounds do not change. They thus have a mechanical, repetitive quality to them, and in due course give rise to well-defined, continuing blocs.

In the kind of environment in which a group like the UPC leadership has to operate, there is one condition in particular that seems to have an especially corrosive effect on the degree of trust within the group. This condition develops when the members come to know that each is subject to considerable pressure and inducement from various outside groups to act in certain ways within the group, but have no way of knowing with any certainty whether or to what extent each has, in fact, been co-opted by or become a supporter of one or another outside interest. Known outside affiliations seem not to have strong negative effects, presumably just because they are known. They can be openly referred to in debate and taken into account when evaluating what a man says or when deciding whether or not he should be given a particular responsibility. But that is exactly what cannot be done when external affiliations are merely suspected and would be denied if openly broached. The thought that some among a man's colleagues are secretly in league with outsiders, particularly outsiders whose interests he does not share or may even actively oppose, and hence whose aim may well be to remove him from power -- it is this thought that when held by several members of the group, rapidly erodes whatever degree of trust they may have had in one another.

How far such general considerations go in explaining the division within the UPC leadership in 1964 and 1965 is, as was said, impossible to know at the present time. But there is some circumstantial information which makes them at least seem relevant. A number of countries -- the U. S., Russia, Britain, China, Ghana, and so forth -- were indeed actively involved in trying to influence Uganda policy. And UPC leaders, as well as others, did become concerned with the question of who was receiving what aid from whom for what purposes. But this question, once asked, can almost never be satisfactorily answered, and the possibility of a cumulative process of doubt and discord thereupon becomes very real. Conceivably the UPC leadership might have remained intact, despite the corrosive effects resulting from these influences, if the lines of conflict arising from the Buganda question had cut across the lines of conflict arising from the cold war pressures. But they paralleled them instead, and the strains from these two sources of tension increased at the same time and in the same degree. And when they were coupled with the regional blocs so engendered, the combined effect proved completely disruptive. Obote and his associates, on the one hand, and Ibingira and his associates, on the other, came increasingly to

doubt the others' intentions. In due course each group considered it had
enough information to assume its doubts were well-founded, and each prepared
to act against the other.

The split between the two wings was evident, as was said, in virtually
all of the functional and regional arms of the party. In late 1965 and early
1966 attention centered principally on control of the rapidly growing UPC
organization in Buganda, however, where an Obote-affiliated faction led
by Binaisa was opposed by an Ibingira-affiliated faction led by Lumu. The
increasing weakness of KY and its imminent demise, coupled with the
parallel growth of UPC, had induced a number of leading Baganda to decide
that the best protection for their interests lay in joining UPC, organizing
UPC chapters in Buganda, and, by using their delegate strength in support
of the "moderates", tempering national policy towards Buganda. The Buganda
Region UPC, which had limped along for several years with hardly more
than a token membership, thus suddenly found itself, in the middle of 1965,
acquiring new members at the rate of several thousand a week.

Most national politicians from Buganda, including all but one of the
Baganda ministers in the national government, and may other Baganda as
well, opposed what was sometimes referred to as "the Mengo clique". The
core of this group was formed by a number of Baganda notables who had
strong vested interests in the existing structure of political, economic, and
social power in Buganda and who in consequence pursued a policy aimed
at preserving intact for as long as possible, one, Buganda's relative autonomy
within Uganda, which protected the structure from the modernizing forces
in the national government, and two, the kabaka's powers, which formed the
apex of the structure of control and gave it its stability. However, only
the most "radical" or "militant" UPC politicians from Buganda had openly
and from the start attacked the Buganda establishment; the others had preferred
to work within the framework of compromise and to reform the system from
the top down. Hence it was that, at the time of its sudden growth, the
Buganda Region UPC was in the hands of the "militants". Faced with the
probable loss of their positions, because relatively few of the converts
from KY shared their "radical" views, the existing UPC leadership in
Buganda called a delegates' conference in August 1965, and held an election
that, essentially, confirmed them in their posts for another year. The action
was immediately challenged by the increasingly larger opposition faction,
and in December the UPC Central Executive Committee suspended two of
the Baganda "militants", Bidandi Ssali and Kinto Musoke, declared the August
elections invalid, and ordered new ones. The decision was subsequently
confirmed by the party's national executive, and in the new elections, in
February 1966, the Lumu-led "moderate" faction defeated the Binaisa-led
"radical" faction for control of the Buganda Region UPC.

The whole development deepened the split between the two UPC wings, beyond a point at which a compromise resolution of their differences in the interest of party unity could have been arranged, and it indicated that the "moderates" within UPC were clearly in a position to launch a potentially successful attack on Obote's leadership. It also made clear beyond a reasonable doubt that the Buganda question was at the heart of the differences and that the outcome of a showdown would inevitably determine in what manner, and on what terms, Buganda would be further incorporated into the evolving national society: either the compromise framework would be more or less preserved, and "moderate" Baganda, such as Lumu and Mayanja-Nkangi, the Buganda katikiro, would play a far more influential role than they had before, and thus in effect mediate between the conservative, vested interests in Buganda and the centralizing, modernizing forces in the national government; or the framework would be dispensed with, the more "radical", anti-establishment Baganda would come to have substantial influence in the national government, and a sustained attack would be launched on Buganda's autonomy, the kabaka's powers, and the whole "traditional" structure of interests and controls.

The Obote Revolution[3]

In April 1966, four years to the month after the UPC-KY coalition came into power, Uganda received a new constitution which both reflected the changes in the balance of power since independence and offered a new framework for its politics. The event was preceded by the preventive detention of Ibingira and four of his associates in February, and followed by Mutesa's exiling himself in London in June after the army had attacked and destroyed his palace.

At the time of the pre-independence constitutional negotiations, power in Uganda, insofar as it was held by Africans, was almost entirely locally-based power and thus was dispersed among the nearly dozen and a half territorial administrative divisions. Some of these local units had relatively large populations, some rather small; and within some, power was relatively centralized, while within others it was still further diffused among even smaller units. Buganda stood out in this situation because it was both very much larger and very much more centralized than any of the other units. In opposition to the centrifugal forces of these local centers stood only the protectorate government and the force of overrule. But both were about to depart, and those who would succeed to the central government positions, the leaders of the national parties, were, with few exceptions, men on the periphery of their area's local power structure. Thus, when Buganda protracted the constitutional negotiations in its successful fight for a decentralized or federal kind of state, in which local units would have a considerable measure of vested autonomy, it spoke to the actual distribution of power at that time. And the constitution which Uganda secured reflected, more or less accurately, not only Buganda's bargaining strength, but, more generally, that distribution of power as well.

As the preceding section suggests, however, a double- or triple-level redistribution of power began with independence. Power within the various district units, including the western kingdoms, was, at first slowly and later more rapidly, taken away from the specifically local notables by the national politicians, who used the resources of both the national party and the national government to mobilize and retain substantial local followings. In a few instances men highly placed or in control of a local power structure were able to use their position in the local structure to secure for themselves an important place in national politics. Mutesa and Nadiope are the prime examples. But for the most part local notables were only indirectly involved in the national arena, and they found their power and influence slipping into the hands of those more directly involved. Even in Buganda, it will be recalled, a national politician, Mayanja-Nkangi, replaced the highly respected but also specifically local political leader, Kintu, as katikiro. At the same time, many of the legal and constitutional powers of the various local units, which had seemed considerable at the time of independence, turned out not to be so vested as was thought and were increasingly circumscribed in principle by court decisions or in practice by the national government's financial controls. So, again, the locus of power was shifting away from the local level and to the national level. Finally, at the national level itself, centralization also occurred as a consequence of the defections from DP and KY and the corresponding growth of UPC: in time Uganda became virtually a one-party system, in the sense that the UPC executive and the cabinet came to be the sole effective centers of decision-making.

UPC itself, however, proved unable to withstand the strains from such a rapid and substantial concentration of power. It was not only that the leadership began to split. Also, and at first quite independently of this development, factional disputes, both within the UPC-organized local governments and the functional arms of the party (labor, youth, etc.), grew increasingly frequent and increasingly violent. Moreover, in several instances the party executive found its efforts to mediate between factions, or its attemps to enforce decisions from above, simply rebuffed, and it began to be apparent that it was incapable of resolving some intra-party disputes. This failure of the party's leaders to maintain control over the organization contributed to the growing tension among them. But of more importance, as the divisions evolved, the leadership virtually ceased making

efforts to settle intra-party factional fights. Instead its two wings began
taking opposite sides in the disputes, and as a result local-level tensions
increased the division within the leadership, while a division along lines
paralleling the division among the leaders developed in partically every
one of the party's branches and arms.

The gradual removal of power from local groups -- and in time from
the other political parties and other national organizations (such as trade
unions) as well -- and its concentration within UPC were thus paralleled
by the progressive disorganization and division of UPC. A simple inverse
function virtually describes the relation between these two developments,
the party's growing power in this period and its declining capacity to act.
It was almost as if the more power UPC acquired, relative to other collective
units, the less it was able to take collective actions and the more it became
simply an arena or context in which various contending groups carried on
their fights.

The sequence of events in the first six months of 1966 resulted
directly from this double, contradictory movement, and the actions taken
in this period were designed not only to anchor the degree of centralization
that had occurred by then, and to provide for further development in that
direction, but also to arrest and reverse the process of dissolution within
UPC. Whichever wing had won out in the struggle -- and at the end of 1965
and beginning of 1966 few observers were willing to place bets -- it would
have had to take actions along both these lines. This much seems clear.
Whether the particular actions in fact taken were equally necessary, or --
since this article is being written in the summer of 1966 -- will prove viable,
is difficult to say. In the event, Obote moved first and blocked the other
wing from acting, and it is therefore the actions he and his associates took
that actually matter.

The new constitution he introduced does essentially three things.
One, it vests all power in the national state: district or regional governments,
including Buganda, have no constitutionally defined powers and may exercise
only powers explicitly delegated to them by the National Assembly. Two,
it vests all executive power at the national level in a single office, that
of Executive President, and makes the abakama of Ankole, Buganda, Bunyoro,
and Toro ineligible for this office by making them ineligible for any public
office. And, three, the constitution specifically both divests Buganda of
its autonomy and alters its internal power structure. It may no longer
elect its members to the National Assembly indirectly, have an independent
civil service establishment, or maintain a parallel and largely independent
judicial system. Furthermore, its administrative chiefs no longer have

control over certain official lands (nor may they receive the rent from the
lands), and they no longer have the right to sit as voting members in the
Buganda lukiko (assembly). Finally, in a later action, the central government divided Buganda into four districts for administrative purposes and
put each under the direct supervision of a team of its own civil servants.

   The way for this radical reorganization of Uganda's political framework was prepared in February when, in rapid succession, Obote had the
leading members of the Ibingira-group arrested, declared he was assuming
emergency powers, suspended sections of the constitution -- notably those
defining the offices of President and Vice President -- removed the commander
of the army, Brigadier General Sabama O. Opoloto, an Itesot (easterner)
married to a daughter of a former katikiro of Buganda, replacing him with
Colonel Idi Amin, like himself a Langi, and charged the kabaka with having
secretly negotiated to bring foreign troops into Uganda. Then, on April
5th, the existence of a new constitution was announced to an abruptly convened
National Assembly, and after its contents were outlined, the assembled
members voted their approval, including their approval of Obote as the
first Executive President. Buganda refused to accept the new constitution,
tension built up, and in May its lukiko resolved that the central government
should remove itself within ten days from its offices in Entebbe and Kampala,
the country's main administrative cities, both of which lie geographically
within Buganda's boundaries. The central government, assuming that the
resolution probably prefigured a rebellion, moved quickly and arrested
three key administrative chiefs. The Baganda countryside, on hearing of
the arrests, then did in fact revolt, but in an apparently unco-ordinated
fashion: some police posts were attacked and overrun, some telephone wires
were cut, some roads to Kampala blocked off, and so forth. The government's response was swift and drastic. The army went directly to the
kabaka's palace in Mengo, adjacent to Kampala, and after what most
reports describe as a fierce day-long battle, in which, according to several
estimates, several hundreds from both sides were killed, it succeeded by
nightfall in reducing the buildings to rubble and scattering the remaining
defenders. Organized resistance was thus rapidly crushed, but the Buganda
countryside continued to be the scene of sporadic incidents, and mobile
army units had to patrol most parts of the kingdom for some time, while
the state of emergency, declared at the time the three chiefs were arrested,
stayed in effect for several months. Mutesa and his katikiro, Mayanja-
Nkangi, were at first believed killed in the siege, but each eventually
made his way to exile in London. Their absence, the state of emergency,
and the complete breakdown of the administration in the kingdom led the
government to attempt to restore order by dividing it into the four administrative areas mentioned earlier and assigning central government civil servants
supervise the work in these divisions. There matters stood, in the summer
of 1966.

Concluding Reflections

A politics so shaped by a single tension, however, must to some
extent be an incomplete politics, one mirroring only a part of the strains
to which the soceity is subject. And, indeed, other strains do exist in
modern Uganda, and its politics has been, in this sense, imcomplete.
Some of these, such as the civilian-military tensions or those between
northern and southern tribal groupings, have impinged directly on the
handling of the Buganda question and so have found expression in the political
alignments which that question has generated. And one tension, deriving
from the competitive relations between the Roman Catholic and Anglican
Churches, has had an independent effect on Uganda's politics. But several
others, notably the tensions deriving from class or economic differences
and from Uganda's relations with Kenya and Tanzania, have implied
alignments rather different from the alignments on the Buganda question
and have so far not played an important part in the country's politics, at
least not a part at all commensurate with their importance in the society
generally.

It seems unlikely that this condition will last much longer, however.
A politics in which basic strains are directly reflected in proportion to
their importance in a society, that is, a "complete politics", is a limiting
or theoretical condition which presumably rarely or never occurs empirically,
at least not in complex societies. But political systems do generally tend
towards completeness, to move or evolve in that direction. The reasons
for this tendency are several, but basically two ideas are involved. One,
a society's strains and tensions are held to breed discontent, and its basic
strains to breed widespread discontent; and two, such discontent is assumed
to find its way eventually into the society's political processes, by one means
or another. Often it happens because those who feel aggrieved succeed in
formulating their grievances, organizing themselves, and making their
complaints a public concern, thereby translating the underlying tensions
into politically consequential issues. Alternatively, the tensions may simply
continue to mount and the discontent to grow, in which case those affected
will eventually express themselves collectively in some form of overt,
often violent behavior and thereby automatically introduce the underlying
tensions into the political process. In one way or another, then, a society's
basic strains tend to become reflected in its politics, which is to say that
its politics tends to move towards completeness.

Something of this sort is likely to occur in Uganda, and it is therefore
well to bear in mind the limitations of the preceding analysis. For like its
subject matter, the analysis has also been incomplete, and for the same
reason: it has concerned itself almost wholly with the Buganda question and
has taken up other politically relevant strains in the society only insofar

as they have impinged on the handling of that question or have been reflected
in the alignments surrounding it. In particular, it has not examined the
economic sources of strain in present-day Uganda, since so far none of
the resulting tensions has in fact played an organizing part in Uganda's
politics. Some have not become sufficiently pronounced to give rise to
widespread discontent; some have been so overlaid with other tensions as
to obscure the economic basis of the discontent from those concerned;
some have been formulated and expressed by organized groups but owing
to the political leaders' concentration on the Buganda question and related
matters have not became salient political issues. For the reasons given
above, though, it seems likely that this situation will not continue and that
instead some of these will play a much more important part in Uganda's
politics in the future than they have in the past. Their identification at
this point will thus serve the double purpose of suggesting both some of the
limitations of the preceding analysis and some of the features of Uganda's
economy which, because they are sources of strain in the society, are likely
to give rise in the fairly short-run to politically important issues.

Uganda, like other East African countries, has a community of
Asians (Indians and Pakistanis) who form at most about one per cent of its
population and whose relations with Uganda's Africans have been a continual
source of strain. Although defined by some as a communal tension, it
seems to be basically a class tension, for its source is the Asians' heretofore
virtual monoply of the distributive sector of the economy (including produce
marketing and processing operations as well as retail trade). Their economic
power has been reduced somewhat in recent years, through government-
sponsored programs to develop producers' cooperatives and to Africanize
retail trade (and the tension has also lessened somewhat), but it remains
considerable nevertheless and is of obvious importance. For Uganda's
principal cash crops, cotton and coffee, are grown on thousands of small-
scale, family-run farms or shambas, not on plantations or estates. Those
engaged specifically in the marketing operations, through which these crops
are brought together and made ready for export, thus not only influence
Uganda's overseas earnings but, of more importance internally, they seem
visibly to control, and in fact do measurably affect, the cash earnings
received by the bulk of the population for their products. The tension has
been compounded, and to some extent obscured, by the Asian community's
aloofness and implicit claim to a social standing which most Africans are
unprepared to accord. But its basis is the Asians' visibly dominant economic
position, and as long as that remains, African discontent and resulting
anti-Asian boycotts and rioting -- instances of which have occurred in the
past, most recently in Buganda in 1959 -- will also remain potentially
important in Uganda's politics.

In an underdeveloped argicultural country, land is simultaneously
the most important means of production and the most important means of
subsistence, and its control is inevitably a locus of tension. So far large
land-holding has existed only in Buganda, where the administrative chiefs,
both in their private capacities and, until President Obote's 1966 reforms,
ex officio, have controlled extensive tracts. Any tension over control of
land has therefore been but one element in the more general tension in
Buganda between higher and lower, between the rulers and the ruled. The
economic tension is unlikely to remain so embedded, however, particularly
if large-scale, capitalistic farming should become more general than it
has been. But of probably greater potential importance is the role this
tension may come to play elsewhere in the country. For the government
is engaged in a program of surveying and registering the thousands of small
customary holdings throughout Uganda, preparatory to converting them
into privately-owned holdings in order to encourage the formation of a
market in land. Numerous local incidents have occurred in connection
with the surveying alone, but these would seem to be only the beginning.
For land markets in areas that combine subsistence farming with cash-
crop production commonly bring in their train speculative buying, tenant
farming, a particular form of debt bondage, and, politically the most
troublesome of all, a landless rural proletariat.

Although mainly an agricultural country, Uganda is not without
industrial development, and hence it is not without an urban labor force
and the associated tensions. These have not been reflected in its political
arena partly because the industrial labor force proper is still so small
but also partly because until recently Kenyans played a leading role in
Uganda's labor movement and as such had little influence on an independent
Uganda's politics. Both of these dampening effects are lessening now, at
the same time that school-leavers and graduates are migrating to the
industrial areas more rapidly than jobs are being created. Moreover, private
capital, now being drawn not only from expatriate sources but also and
increasingly from local mercantile sources, is becoming progressively
more important in Uganda's industrial development, and this capital is
by and large highly concentrated -- for example, one family-owned complex
of enterprises accounts for some ten per cent of the government's total
revenue from taxes. It thus seems likely that this classic tension will
also become increasingly pronounced.

Another class-like tension that has so far not played an important
part in post-independence politics revolves about the distribution of income
among urban-area Africans. On the surface this seems to derive from the
marked differences that exist in access to education and consequently in
educational attainments and associated styles of life. But the more fundamental
source of the tension is the highly skewed income structure that Uganda

inherited at independence and that initially came into being not in order to
elicit the kinds of effort and initiative needed in an independent economy
but in order to induce expatriates, and to some extent trained Asians and
Africans as well, to man the administrative posts of a dependent, colonial
polity and economy. The existence of such an income structure, and of
the highly visible differences in well-being it supports, is likely to become
increasingly difficult to justify, particularly as the economy moves into
a phase of import-substitution and consumer austerity, as it must if it is
to develop.[4]

Finally, brief mention should be made of the fact that politically
relevant strains within Uganda have arisen as a result of its association
with Kenya and Tanzania in the East African Common Services Organization
(EACSO). This has been mainly an economic association, concerned with
marketing and infrastructural matters, and only secondarily a political
association, but specifically political tensions have developed in the course
of the continuing negotiations which the three countries have carried on
regarding both the future of EACSO and, even more tension-inducing, the
possibility of political federation.

All of these sources of tension and strain exist in Uganda in varying
degrees, and some are already important loci of discontent. Nevertheless,
none has so far substantially influenced the organization or conduct of the
country's politics, and they have therefore not been taken into account in
the present analysis. At the same time, as the above mere listing indicates,
the preceding examination of Uganda's politics in terms of the role of the
Buganda question alone has by no means constituted an exhaustive treatment
of the subject, more broadly conceived.

Footnotes

1. The sources from which materials for the essay have been drawn are given at the end of the note on sources, pp. 289-290.

2. Although the Nilo-Hamites are ethnographically akin to the Nilotic and Sudanic peoples of the northern region of Uganda, at least more so than to the Bantu-speakers, their languages are not mutually intelligible with Nilotic languages. Moreover, probably because of colonial administrative practice, which put the Iteso together with the eastern Bantu tribes in the eastern region, the Iteso are today both socially and politically closer to the other tribes of the eastern region than to the tribes of the northern region. Hence the grouping of the Iteso for present purposes with the non-Baganda Bantu.

3. This is the title of by far the best account to date of events in the first half of 1966. See M. Crawford Young, "The Obote Revolution", Africa Report, June 1966, 8-14.

4. Space limitations preclude even a cursory presentation of the supporting argument. See Dudley Seers, "The Stages of Economic Development of a Primary Producer in the Middle of the Twentieth Century", The Economic Bulletin (Ghana), VII, 4:58-69 (1963); Celso Furtado, "The Dialectic of Development", Part I, Diagnosis of the Brazilian Crisis (Berkeley and Los Angeles, 1965); and Terence K. Hopkins, "On Economic Planning in Tropical Africa", Coexistence, I:77-88 (1964).

A Note on Sources

In 1961-1962 and again in 1963, when I was in Uganda doing field and archival research on the economic and political development of the Ankole District, the principal topic of conversation was, as it would naturally be at such a time in a country's history, its politics; to a large extent this essay is the fruit of those conversations. In addition I have made use of contemporary accounts of events, mainly those in The Uganda Argus, the major English language daily newspaper, and The East African Reporter, a fortnightly news magazine published in Nairobi, and The People, a weekly newspaper published in Uganda.

A study of Uganda's politics is, of course, of recent origin, and although several accounts of political developments exist, an authoritative work has yet to appear. Perhaps the most valuable background work published to date is the long paper by D. Anthony Low, Political Parties in Uganda, 1949-1962, Commonwealth Paper No. 8, Institute of Commonwealth Studies, University of London, 1962. The most authoritative account of recent events in the article by Young, referred to in Note 3. In addition, besides the Apter and Ingham books cited in full below, some other relevant works are:

Colin Legum, Must We Lose Africa? (London, 1954); George W. Shepherd, Jr., They Wait in Darkness (New York, 1955); Lloyd Fallers (ed.), The King's Men: Leadership and Status in Buganda on the Eve of Independence (New York, 1964); and Chapter 6 of A. J. Hughes, East Africa: The Search for Unity, Kenya, Tanganyika, Uganda and Zanzibar (Baltimore, 1963); R. Cranford Pratt, "Nationalism in Uganda, " Political Studies, IX:157-178 (1961); Lloyd Fallers, "Ideology and Culture in Uganda Nationalism, " American Anthropologist, LXIII:677-686 (1961). Robert O. Byrd, who studies the 1961 elections, has reported some of his materials in "Characteristics of Candidates for Election in a Country Approaching Independence: The Case of Uganda, " Midwest Journal of Political Science, VII:1-27 (1963). See also, Fred G. Burke, Local Government and Politics in Uganda (Syracuse, 1964), which gives detailed accounts for three districts, Bunyoro, Teso, and Bukedi. (There is to appear a monograph on constitutional and political development in Uganda by Grace Ibingira.)

Perhaps the main remark to make about most of these writings concerns their point of view. Because the field work on which they are based was carried out primarily in the 1950's, when the Baganda dominated the political scene both as nationalists and as traditionalists, most, as it were, look at the arena of Uganda politics from a window in Mengo, Buganda's capital. For observers in the 1960's, however, this has been by no means the best vantage point. In fact, there may no longer be one good vantage

point, which may well be the most important indicator of the changes that
have taken place in the 1960's.

As with Uganda's politics, so with its history, an authoritative study
remains to be written. A cursory account, presented largely from the point
of view of the protectorate administration, is Kenneth Ingham, The Making
of Modern Uganda (London, 1958). Numerous studies of the Baganda are in
print; among the best are: D. Anthony Low and R. Cranford Pratt, Buganda
and British Overrule, 1900-1955: Two Studies (New York, 1960); David
E. Apter, The Political Kingdom in Uganda: A Study in Bureaucratic Nationalism (Princeton, 1961); Peter Gutkind, The Royal Capital of Buganda (The
Hague, 1963); and D. A. Low, "The Advent of Populism in Buganda, "
Comparative Studies in Society and History, VI:424-444 (1963-1964).
Contemporary ethnographers and social anthropologist ordinarily include
some material on developments during overrule among the people they are
writing about. See, for example, F. K. Girling, The Acholi of Uganda,
Colonial Research Studies No. 30, Colonial Office (London, 1960) and Aidan
W. Southhall, Alur Society: A Study in Processes and Types of Domination
(Cambridge, n.d.). But of more value are ethnographic studies that focus
directly on the transformations which occurred under colonialism. See,
for example, Lloyd A. Fallers, Bantu Bureaucracy: A Study of Integration
and Conflict in the Political Institution of an East African People (Cambridge,
n.d.); and J. C. D. Lawrance, The Iteso: Fifty Years of Change in a Nilo-
Hamitic Tribe of Uganda (New York, 1957).

Among the more important studies of Uganda's economy, besides
the two five-year plans published by the government, are: The International
Bank for Reconstruction and Development, The Economic Development of
Uganda (Entebbe, 1961); The United Nations Economic and Social Council,
Social Commission, Report on the World Situation: Planning for Social and
Economic Development in Uganda, Bureau of Social Affairs, Department
of Economic and Social Affairs, United Nations Secretariat (New York,
1962) (E/CN.5/346/Add.9); Walter Elkan, The Economic Development of
Uganda (London, 1961); and C. C. Wrigley, Crops and Wealth in Uganda:
A Short Agrarian History, East African Studies No. 12, East African Institute of
Social Research (Kampala, 1959).

Two works specifically concerned with the Asian communities in
Uganda, Kenya, and Tanzania are: George Delf, Asians in East Africa
(London, 1963); and L. W. Hollingsworth, The Asians of East Africa
(London, 1960).

XI

Majimbo Schemes in Kenya and Uganda

Donald Rothchild
Department of Political Science, University of California, Davis

Uhuru involves much more than freedom from colonial rule. It suggests a large-scale transformation of the society brought about by demands for more schools, by the growth of cities, by greater activity of youth groups, by wider contact with the outside world, and many other forces of change. As a consequence, it is not only the expatriate community in a country that feels threatened by the impending change in the status quo that comes with the transfer of power, but many of the established indigenous elements of the pre-uhuru society as well.

No element in an African nation is more anxious about its status than the traditional leaders. These leaders sense the trend of the time, in particular the rising tide of hostility toward what is loosely described as "tribalism." They know they are frequently criticized for separatist, reactionary, and parochialist inclinations. They note that in Ghana the government has shorn traditional authorities of significant political responsibilities and that in Tanganyika authorities have restricted chiefs to "traditional functions," denying them a place of importance in the administration of the country. And they realize that in 1959 the All-African Peoples Conference in Accra denounced tribalism as a "evil practice" and called upon the independent governments of Africa "to suppress or modify /this/ institution."

Yet it by no means follows that because traditional authorities are on the defensive they are resigned to a fate of atrophy. This is far from the case. They understand only too clearly the warning implicit in the Accra resolutions; and, because they look with distrust upon any but the most binding of guarantees, they seek to entrench what they see as their peoples' interests firmly in the constitutional framework of their emergent countries.

What ensues from this demand for security is a struggle between two concepts of nationalism -- tribal and territorial. The pre-independence period in a number of cases was marked by a play of interests between regionalists and centralists. This power struggle led to such varying patterns as centralism in Guinea and Tanganyika, majimbo (or regionalism) in Kenya, and federalism in Nigeria. Traditional leaders naturally sought more decentralized constitutional arrangements such as federalism (or even sometimes autonomy), but they were compelled, in Kenya and in Uganda's western kingdoms and Busoga, to compromise on regionalism because of insufficient power at the bargaining table. The solution adopted has tended to reflect the particular power configuration within each country, smaller ethnic groups usually gaining much less recognition at the bargaining table than their more powerful neighbors.

Regionalism differs from federalism both in its allocation of powers and in its objectives. Whereas federalism seeks to build a nation by accommodating vigorous constituent parts, regionalism -- which is closer on the continuum to centralized (unitary) forms of government -- involves the devolution of limited powers upon a middle tier of government. Regionalism, therefore, represents a political and institutional compromise between federalism and a unitary system.

This paper seeks to make a comparative analysis of regionalism in Kenya and in Uganda's western kingdoms and Busoga. Buganda is not included because of its more genuine federal relationship with the Uganda government. In both Uganda and Kenya minority peoples forced majimbo upon the same departing colonial government and struggled to see it implemen-ted (before independence in the case of Kenya and after independence in the case of relevant Ugandan areas). Certain recurrent trends became evident in the process: the reasons for seeking a regionalist solution, the expedient nature of the compromise, the difficulties involved in implementing the scheme, and the restrictions placed upon the powers of the regions. Although the two cases are not identical, they are close enough to make valid comparison feasible.

In view of the minorities' determination to see a regional scheme implemented, this study also attempts to make a tentative appraisal of regionalism as a minority safeguard. Can group security be engineered by the adoption of majimbo-type machinery? Whatever the answer, the East African experience should be of great help in widening our understanding of the impact of constitutional arrangements on community relations.

I

Such factors as pride, administrative convenience, and the desire to build upon the foundation of traditional African institutions all helped to spur the call for regionalism. The western kingdoms and Busoga's demand for the same formal status as that granted Buganda grew in large part, for example, from feelings of ethnic vanity and a recognition of the fact that Buganda's special position had "paid off" throughout the period of British rule.[1]

Nevertheless, the primary impetus for regionalism sprang from fear. But for the intensity of minority anxieties, the drive to create regional bodies would have lacked energy and determination. For traditional and minority groups majimbo had appeal, although substantially less than that of a more decentralized arrangement such as federalism, as a means of firmly entrenching their position before the strains of independence appeared. Their fears and hopes became enmeshed as the day of uhuru approached. The western kingdoms and Busoga in Uganda and the Kalenjin, Masai, and Coastal peoples in Kenya welcomed an end to British rule. At the same time, however, they were uneasy over their future once the colonial scaffolding was torn away. Occasional, half-hearted statements appeared to the effect that a continuance of colonial rule was preferred to submergence in a unitary state, but these pronouncements often seemed more bargaining points than genuine policy positions.

Minority ethnic groups feared being swamped by other ethnic groups, by the central government, or by a combination of these forces. Ethnic fears could be detected in the western kingdoms' and Busoga's demand for federal status; their insistence was in part a product of fears stemming from Buganda's newly acquired federal relationship. A number of Embu leaders in Kenya expressed similar fears when presenting their case for being placed in a non-Kikuyu region. They feared "domination by some of our neighbours" as one Embu spokesman told the Kenya Boundaries Commission.[2] But nothing provoked greater anxiety than the possibility of an ethnic rival using the central government's power for expansionist purposes. References to "Kikuyu-Luo domination" evoked minority fears of land seizures and caused many a minority leader to urge the establishment of majimbo as a protection of his stake in society.

Fears of being overwhelmed by an unbridled central government were widespread. In Uganda Toro's katikkiro (prime minister), cabled the British Colonial Secretary making it "emphatically clear" that his people

would not support a unitary system.[3] Kenya African Democratic Union
(KADU) leaders reiterated this theme at countless public meetings. These
minority spokesmen resisted the attempt to transfer the "Westminster
model" in its pure form, recognizing the difficulty of limiting the energetic
executive under the British system. In part, then, their demand for federalism was a reaction to Britain's preference for a unitary system of government
in Kenya and Uganda. Unitary systems, KADU leaders argued, had failed
or had been perverted after independence because unitary forms of government tend to concentrate powers in the hands of one man or group. "Unfortunate
experiences in some ex-British Colonies have shown, " R. G. Ngala, Leader
of the Opposition, asserted, "just how easily the Westminster pattern of
Government can be perverted into a ruthless dictatorship. I assure you that
the adoption of an orthodox Westminster pattern for Kenya would inevitably
result in placing absolute power in the hands of a dictator."[4] The best
means of preventing central domination in Ngala's eyes was to spread power
among the regions.[5]

II

The agreement to set up regional institutions was less a concession
to minority fears than an effort to speed independence. Majority interests,
suspicious that the colonial power would use the minority issue to delay
uhuru or to create conditions which would perpetuate the colonial influence,
reluctantly agreed to devolve some powers and functions on to the constituent
parts. For the dominant African groups, inclusion of constitutional restraints
on central leadership (such as majimbo) contravened the principle of
"undiluted democracy" by allowing the minority to have checks on the will
of the majority.

Leaders in Uganda's western kingdoms and Busoga succeeded in
securing a "federal" relationship for their peoples just before the 1962
independence elections. Despite the kingdoms' limited size and financial
resources, these spokesmen insisted upon being accorded the same formal
status as that given Buganda in 1961. British officials were loath to reopen
the issue of full federal status only a few months after the 1961 constitutional
conference had completed its discussions. Nevertheless, they bowed -- in
principle but not in substance -- to the rising public clamor on the question.

Largely for political reasons, both parties united in supporting
the kingdoms' claims.[6] Not only did the Uganda People's Congress (UPC)
and the Democratic Party (DP) seek election support in these areas, but they

realized that the country's progress toward uhuru might be adversely affected
by any evidences of instability at that time. Many political leaders reasoned
that should the kingdoms carry out their threat to boycott the general elections unless they were first accorded federal status, the elections -- and
independence -- might well be delayed.[7] For party leaders the price was
small: to concede federal status in principle and to guarantee the positions
of the hereditary rulers. At once they came to substantial agreement
on the issue, and British officials had little choice but to accept the Ugandans'
lead. Consequently Colonial Secretary Reginald Maudling abandoned his
previous opposition to increased powers and to a federal relationship for
the kingdoms (and later Busoga). From this point Uganda moved forward
swiftly toward independence.

As early as 1961, many able observers of the Kenya scene held out
little hope for KADU's majimbo plans.[8] The Kenya African National Union
(KANU), the largest political group, was willing to give limited control
over tribal land, public health, and primary education to local authorities;
it looked disapprovingly, however, upon KADU's proposed federation of
six regions, each having a wide array of functions and powers. Why, then,
at the London conference in 1962 did KANU consent to a framework constitution which sought "maximum possible decentralization of the power of government to effective authorities capable of a life and significance of their own,
entrenched in a constitution and drawing their being and power from the
constitution and not from the Central Governments"?[9] Clearly KANU had
not undergone a change of heart; but its freedom of action was limited by
its lack of power at the bargaining table and its feeling of urgency about
independence.[10] KANU leaders knew that other delegations had been sent
home by the Colonial Office for failing to reach agreement, and they feared
a similar fate for themselves if the issue of regionalism caused a breakdown in negotiations. Consequently, a majority of Kenyans acted on this
issue much as the UPC did, and perhaps the other Uganda parties as well.
They accepted regionalism in order to take the next constitutional step
forward.

But because the most powerful party in each country felt that it had
conceded regionalism as a measure of expediency, it felt few qualms about
setting limits upon regional arrangements after the constitution had come
into effect. In 1963, Uganda's UPC headed off any illusions of their federal
status under the constitution the regions might have harbored by securing
passage of the Western Kingdoms and Busoga Act which established central
supremacy over these areas. And KANU, by winning a thumping majority
in the Kenya elections in 1963, received widespread backing even before

independence for its narrow interpretation of majimbo as "only a name for
dignified local authorities."[11] Certainly once Great Britain transferred
decisive powers to the popularly elected governments, regionalism proved
a brittle safeguard.

                                    III

During the debates on establishing regional bodies in Kenya and
Uganda, a great deal of confusion arose over terminology. Uganda's
constitution accorded the western kingdoms and Busoga "federal status";
all that actually seemed warranted by the powers these units possessed
was a frank recognition of the subordinate place of the constituent parts
in the governing of the country. The distinction in principle between federalism and regionalism seems clear enough, for whereas the former brings
together bodies co-ordinate in nature, the latter leaves the parts only a
limited autonomy. An examination of the basic laws in both countries, with
the exception of the Buganda-central government relationship, shows the
political systems to be far from genuinely federal.

For evidence that the regional assemblies were subordinate bodies
from the outset, it is necessary to examine the powers they wielded at their
zenith, that is, before the government clarified their post-independence
roles. In Uganda, the Munster Commission of 1961 proposed a semi-federal
relationship for the kingdoms of Bunyoro, Ankole, and Toro, which were to
have strong,legally-enforceable guarantees for traditional rulers and
institutions. "It is not necessary," the report observed, "to make special
provision for legislative powers in the kingdoms, since the councils will
have the ordinary powers of district councils."[12] Accordingly, the 1961
London conference made the kingdoms responsible for the same services
which devolved upon local administrations in the rest of the country.
Moreover, the central government would continue to "have ultimate responsibility for the administration of these services."[13] Although the 1962 constitutional conference raised Uganda's western kingdoms to full federal
status, the change had, in fact, little practical effect. Traditional rulers
and institutions received firm guarantees, but, beyond this point, the
conference was vague, leaving details on the substance of federal status
to future agreement. In view of the kingdoms' inability to shoulder heavy
administrative burdens and the central government's extensive delegated
and concurrent powers under the constitution, it is not surprising that
subsequent negotiations did little to challenge central hegemony. For
Minister of Regional Administration C. J. Obwangor, the center must be

firm so that the regions, the "concentric points, " could "run and ... prove themselves."[14] He and his colleagues had little difficulty establishing this conception of regionalism in Uganda.

Great efforts were made in Kenya to decentralize powers to regional authorities; at no time, however, was strong central leadership really in jeopardy. The Lancaster House conference of 1962, which agreed on a framework constitution, provided for six regions possessing "administrative powers and powers of making enactments having the force of law."[15] In applying this statement of principle, the constitution bestowed powers upon the regional assemblies in such fields as land transactions, local government, public health, education, and the maintenance of law and order. At most, these powers would seem to permit a very limited kind of autonomy;[16] this conclusion is enforced by examining the restrictions on exercising power in delegated fields. The report noted, for example, that the regions would have responsibility for the practical applications of local government, day-to-day security matters, certain parts of the public health program, and education through the intermediate level. But taken in conjunction with the extensive functions and powers of the national government (and in particular central police and emergency powers), it was apparent that majimbo represented less of a frontal assault on central dominance than many critics were willing to concede.

After the Lancaster House conference laid the basis for regionalism, legal experts of the Kenyan and British governments set about the task of filling in the framework of the constitution. Many crucial questions remained unsettled. On the one hand, the Kenya government's summary of the constitution strengthened central supremacy by vesting in it residual powers and supremacy over matters which were to be handled jointly with the regions. Even fields which are the exclusive responsibility of the regions can come under central government direction in the event of an emergency. Moreover, "in certain circumstances the Central Legislature will be able to assume the legislative or executive authority of a Regional Assembly if that Regional Assembly is impeding or prejudicing the exercise of the executive authority of the Central Government or failing to comply with a law made by the Central Legislature."[17] On the other hand, the regional structure was strengthened by a decision to abolish the right of a regional assembly to surrender its powers to the center. The government summary also provided for one central and seven regional civil services, each to have executive responsibility for appointments, promotions, and dismissals.[18]

In addition, it should also be noted that the Fiscal Commission had created a solid under-pinning for Kenyan regionalism by recommending that major sources of revenue be assigned to regional authorities. These included taxes on petrol and diesel fuels, to be distributed on a basis of derivation; a fixed percentage (35 per cent) of customs and excise taxes, to be distributed on a basis of population; and grants for regional police contingents.[19] Not only did the constitution include all of these fiscal recommendations, but it also empowered the regional assemblies to make laws with respect to taxes on entertainments, poll taxes, rates on land or buildings, and certain mineral royalties.[20]

For Duncan Sandys, the Colonial Secretary, this constitutional arrangement effectively reconciled a strong central government with an appreciable measure of regional autonomy.[21] KADU also spoke with confidence, seeing regionalism as an effective safeguard against majority domination of smaller ethnic groups. KANU leaders, however spoke with considerable restraint. Tom Mboya praised the constitutional agreement for saving Kenya from "senseless tribalism"; but he also warned that his party would "remove or amend any and all parts of the Constitution which are unworkable, expensive or hinder progress." Majimbo, Mboya declared, was "an experiment which must justify itself or perish."[22] Then, as the election approached, KANU speakers became more militant. They sought to whittle down the autonomous powers of the regional authorities, picturing these bodies as extensions of the local authorities rather than as a separate tier of government. As a consequence, the fate of regionalism in an independent Kenya became intimately intertwined with the election; and KANU won, opening the way to new efforts to tone down the strength of the regions. If the distribution of powers between a strong center and the subordinate parts did not prejudge this outcome in the first instance, the facts of Kenya politics did in the second.

IV

Although the decline of regionalism was precipitated in the end by political forces, it is important to note two factors which contributed to this outcome -- the cost of regionalism and the difficulty of drawing regional boundaries.

Cost is naturally a problem in developing countries. A regional solution, therefore, must be justified by its proponents in terms of the sizeable outlays involved. In determining priorities, various questions must be asked. Will regionalism, by offering safeguards to minorities, give these peoples the security and peace of mind to enable them to throw their full energies into the task of economic development? Moreover, although no one questions the need for local initiative, is regionalism the most effective means of securing local responsibility? If these questions can be answered affirmatively, then those who advocate majimbo may have good reason for contending that such a solution can be reconciled with the overall requirements of administrative efficiency.[23]

From the outset, it is useful to note, the weight of majority opinion opposed regionalism, as it would have federalism, on the grounds of cost and general efficiency. Majority sentiment favored central leadership and planning in economic affairs. It regarded regionalism with its multiplication of legislatures and civil services and with its intensification of ethnic consciousness, as working against rapid economic growth. Even KADU's R. G. Ngala, who in his enthusiasm for majimbo was "prepared to see a chaotic situation develop in Kenya before independence in order to get our rights,"[24] admitted that the establishment of regionalism would cause administrative complications.[25] Nevertheless, Ngala differed from his KANU opponents in feeling that the benefits of majimbo were well worth this price.

Because regionalism caused less disruption in Uganda, its cost was lower there than in Kenya. The various commissions and conferences which worked out the constitutional arrangements were careful not to create elaborate governmental machinery in the western kingdoms and Busoga and not to assign these regions more responsibilities than their limited human and fiscal resources could comfortably carry.[26] Since they were transferring services to authorities already in operation, costs were likely to be minimal.[27] Some duplication of administrative activities was involved to be sure, but its small scale accounts in part for the survival of elements of regionalism after Uganda's uhuru.

In Kenya, regionalism meant considerable financial outlays; hence the attack was fiercer. Jomo Kenyatta, testifying before the Boundaries Commission, bluntly stated that Kenya could not afford regionalism under existing financial conditions.[28] Critics of majimbo pointed to the costs of regional members' salaries, to the possible expense involved in building an administrative headquarters in the Western Region, and to the added complications for economic planning and development. Despite Ngala's assurances that the cost of putting a regional system into effect would not be heavy,[29] most observers had good reason to question whether Kenya could finance a third tier of government at the very time that the Economy Commission was recommending a drastic pruning of the staff and activities of the public (civil) service.

On the question of drawing regional boundaries, it is important to keep in mind that the overlap of ethnic groups in virtually endless variation throughout tropical Africa leaves the mapmaker with few "natural" boundaries between peoples. Since regionalism came into existence essentially to ease minority anxieties, it is not surprising that those peoples who were placed in a minority in each region (as some inevitably were) would fear and resent it. As a consequence, regionalism might well promote new minority frustrations and new claims to regional status. Perhaps federalism, at least in its Western experience, enjoys real advantages over regionalism in this respect; it permits frontiers to be artificial and therefore unrealistic in terms of ethnic factors. Regionalism, which must be factually realistic, is less able to bypass difficult political, ethnic, and/or economic problems.

Even though boundary questions are numerous in Uganda, it is difficult to find a definite connection between them and the elements regionalism adopted in that country. Certainly the parochialism inherent in a regional type of solution heightened a consciousness of tribal particularism and self-interest generally, but one would be mistaken to place the sole responsibility for Uganda's boundary conflicts at regionalism's door. For one thing, border disputes occurred between such districts as Bukedi and Bugisu which were in a unitary relationship with the center.[30] For another, boundary questions, as exemplified by the one between Buganda and Bunyoro over the so-called "lost counties," would have come to a head with the approach of independence whether or not Uganda had written regionalism into her basic law.

But, if it is impossible to precisely define the relationship between constitutional decentralization and the burgeoning of boundary questions in Uganda, it seems clear that some correlation does exist. Uganda's constitution, by accommodating the kingdoms' and Busoga's dignity, separateness, and desire for self-rule, fostered parochial ambitions throughout the country. As ethnic groups achieved a measure of self-determination and identity -- and sought to fulfill their aspirations -- they inevitably came into conflict with their neighbors. "The increased autonomy which Buganda will enjoy under the 1961 constitution," observed the Molson Report on the lost counties, "adds greatly to the apprehensions of the Banyoro."[31] Bunyoro's leaders interpreted Buganda's achievement of federal status as implying permanent detachment of the lost counties -- unless Bunyoro acted in a decisive manner to turn the tide prior to independence.

It is significant that Bunyoro's posture of determination and strength over the lost counties question paralleled its constitutional advance toward "federal" status. Bunyoro thus emerged as an important political factor on the modern Uganda scene, anxious to increase its size in keeping with its enhanced constitutional position. In the end, the spirit as well as the increased autonomy of a regional approach (and also irredentism, independence, and ethnic aspirations) became intertwined and made the Buganda-Bunyoro boundary problem one of the most acute in Uganda's history.

Unlike Uganda, it was Kenya's lack of well-entrenched regional units which gave rise to a series of boundary disputes. Provincial boundaries, as the Foster-Sutton commission on regional boundaries observed, had no sanctity. Rather than retain these provincial boundaries intact (as KANU wished) the commission recommended major boundary revisions. Complex boundary revision was part and parcel of the majimbo approach.

As the Kenya Boundaries Commission traveled from district to district holding hearings to ascertain popular desires on the question, it became aware of the full extent of group suspicions and hostilities. This open expression of fears and animosities could not have had any other effect than to raise tribal tensions to new heights. At the hearing, Abaluhya and Kipsigis delegations sought to be separated from the Luo, the Teso did not want to be included in a region with the Abaluhya, the Kamba did not wish to join the Masai or Kikuyu, and the Meru opposed association with the Kikuyu. The Somalis of the Northern Frontier District were bent upon complete secession from Kenya, and delegations from Mombasa and Kilifi did not want to integrate the Coastal Strip into the Coast region until the sultan of Zanzibar had given his final approval to such an action. The commission was hard put to square these wishes with the terms of reference which restricted it to providing for six regions and the Nairobi area.[32] That various peoples were left dissatisfied with its juggling efforts is hardly surprising.

Although both KANU and KADU leaders hailed the report of the Boundaries Commission as a party victory, they also found much in it to criticize. Secretary-General of KANU Tom Mboya expressed satisfaction with the room allocated for expansion to the predominantly-Kikuyu Central region and to the predominantly-Luo Nyanza region, but he regretted the large extent of European influence in the drawing of the Rift Valley Region lines as well as the fragmentation of the northern province. Nevertheless, Mboya considered the findings to be executive in nature and therefore final; they could only be altered, he maintained, if both KANU and KADU agreed to the changes, and if the British government consented. KADU's Ngala praised the report but called for "statesmanlike negotiation" over its discrepancies.[33]

Indeed, a number of boundary disputes followed the report's issuance; foremost of these was the rivalry over Kitale. The decision to place Kitale in the Rift Valley rather than in the Western Region left the latter without a capital and led quickly to a major political crisis in the country at large.

The Kitale question shows both how deep tribal emotions run on boundary issues as well as how difficult it is to put majimbo into practice. Abaluhya leaders were incensed over the Boundary Commission's decision to place Kitale, Trans Nzoia, and the western half of Uasin Gishu outside the Western Region. KADU Vice-president Masinde Muliro, declaring that his people must recover their bithright, asserted that the Abaluhya would employ "every force" to regain Kitale and the surrounding areas.[34] On several occasions he contended that the commission had failed to carry out the people's wishes because it acted on "evidence put forward for ulterior political motives."[35]

KADU's solution seemed clear enough -- to restore Kitale to the Abaluhya while holding party solidarity firm. The Kenya constitution seemed to facilitate KADU's task, for it provided that the regions could make boundary changes on a bilateral basis during the first six months of its coming into effect so long as the change involved less than five per cent of the inhabitants of the region affected. After that, the constitution required that both the regional assemblies must support the alteration by a two-thirds vote of all their respective members, with both houses of the National Assembly concurring.[36]

One hurdle for KADU leaders on the Kitale question was the maintenance of unity within their own ranks. They handled this problem with considerable finesse. That it could have been a serious situation is indicated by Kalenjin leader Moi's comment upon leaving a Nakuru conference where Kalenjin, Masai, and Abaluhya notables pledged their support to the Abaluhya's position on Kitale; Moi noted that the Kalenjin had put aside "strong feelings" on the transfer question in order to preserve the solidarity of KADU.[37] It was natural enough for the Kalenjin, Masai, and Abaluhya to have different and often conflicting views of their own self-interest; yet in this case they were able to surmount their differences and present a common front. KADU's major achievement in this regard came in September 1963, when the Rift Valley Regional Assembly approved, by twenty-one votes to five, the opening of negotiations on the transfer of Kitale to the Western Region. The one-sidedness of this vote should not, however, obscure the bitter emotions that accompanied this resolution. KADU had emerged from the crisis intact, but somewhat bruised. Further shocks were to follow.

Another hurdle was the KANU government at the center. KANU
Minister for Home Affairs Odinga, aroused opposition suspicions soon
after the Rift Valley resolution by indicating that he did not consider the
Kitale question settled. In response to a delegation of the Supreme Council
of Pokot, Saboat, Cherangoni, and Marakwet, he said that the Kenya government would not support the Rift Valley's resolution until all sides had had
a chance to present their claims.[38]

But could the central government legitimately intervene to block
the Kitale transfer? The constitution made the region's subordinate status
evident at almost every turn; yet on the question of boundary alteration
it was silent as to the center's rule, at least during the six-month period
after the constitution came into operation. In practice, however, the key
role played by the central government in the transfer question was soon
apparent. When the enactment, signed by the presidents of the Rift Valley
and Western regions, was forwarded to Oginga Odinga for ratification,
the minister for home affairs refused to sign the enactment until the people
affected by the transfer were first consulted. Thus, even though the transfer
of Kitale was officially noted in the Kenya Official Gazette, actual border
rectification was put off because of the disagreement between central and
regional authorities on the need for an expression of popular support on
the part of the population affected by the change.

V

Regionalism reached its high-water mark prior to the transfer of
power; its decline followed swiftly upon the heels of the transfer. The fact
that elements of regionalism survived in the post-independence period in
the East African countries does not negate the conclusion that regionalism
proved ineffective as a minority safeguard. But the clarification of the
subordinate status of regional authorities indicated the limitations of an
areal solution as a brake upon majoritarian power. In both countries minorities soon found regionalism insufficient protection.

In Uganda, any illusions the people of the western kingdoms and
Busoga might have harbored as to the meaning of "federal status" were
shattered by the events which followed independence. It will be remembered
that British officials only reluctantly conceded federal status prior to the
1962 general elections; however, they left to future agreements the interpretation of the powers to be allocated to the regions. Such an arrangement was
unsatisfactory, to be sure, but it was made necessary by the urgency

surrounding Uganda's <u>uhuru</u>. Then as <u>uhuru</u> celebrations quieted, the
central government got down to allocating functions and powers to the various
authorities. In October 1962, it published the administrations (Western
Kingdoms and Busoga) bill. There was an immediate outcry from spokesmen for the kingdoms, who raised objections over the drafters' unwillingness
to consult them about the bill's provisions; they who were dismayed at the
bill's failure to reflect the territories' federal status.

The minister of regional administrations secured a wide measure
of control over regional authorities. This control extended to regulating
all matters of finance, approving legislation, supervising administration,
and enforcing the performance of duties. Not only were the lists of functions
and sources of revenue permitted the regions strictly circumscribed, but
they were identical to those assigned to the districts.[39] It is, therefore,
little wonder that the kingdoms' leaders felt let down after examining the
fruits of their struggle to secure a federal relationship.

Because the bill was criticized widely, it was withdrawn from Parliament's agenda and Minister of Regional Administration Cuthbert J. Obwangor
began discussions in 1963 with the chief ministers of Bunyoro, Ankole,
Toro, and Busoga to find a basis of agreement. These talks were in vain.
Obwangor rejected all but minor modifications, and the kingdoms threatened
non-co-operation if the government "bulldozed" through Parliament a bill
similar to the original.

Just as a serious impasse seemed to be developing, Prime Minister
Obote entered the discussions and held a weekend of meetings with the chief
ministers. In a surprising turnabout, the impending deadlock disappeared,
for after several days of deliberations the two parties reached complete
agreement on the provisions of the bill. A crisis was thus averted. Moreover, the central government's retention of hegemony made Obote's coup
seem especially impressive; now the kingdoms and Busoga had accepted a
bill which was basically the same as its predecessor. Even if formal
concessions were made to the sensitivities of the rulers, in substance,
the minister of regional administrations retained extensive control over the
activities of the regions. Where the previous bill permitted him to issue
intructions in various circumstances, the new bill required him to consult
with the regional government on such matters as auditing fees, controlling
finance, or establishing tender boards. Instead of asserting that "the Minister
shall approve" of additional revenues, the new bill declared that the regions
may raise "such other revenues as may be agree between the government
and the Minister."[40] The regions were in fact little more free to initiate
and administer their policies than before; central approval was as vital a
factor as ever.

With the debate in the National Assembly on the kingdoms' bill, members of parliament recognized for the first time that federal status for these regions "meant nothing more than decentralization of powers."[41] The rulers' agreement with Obote assured overwhelming support for the revised bill. Prior to the final voting, Obwangor himself made the government's position clear. He disclaimed, on the one hand, any intention on the part of the center of "trying to undermine the federal status and powers that were obtained in the London Conference as well as in the Constitution."[42] On the other hand, he observed that "first and foremost we must know that when there is autonomy in these regions the point must be clear that the Central Government must retain the reins ... and, secondly, that we must be on the look-out and must precisely know to what extent, economically, politically, psychologically all this parochial fanaticism goes."[43] Because the center does hold the reins firmly under the Western Kingdoms and Busoga Act, regionalism is not an effective guarantee of minority rights for the peoples in those areas.

From the time the boundary report made its appearance in Kenya in December 1962, until the independence conference in September and October 1963, KANU voices rose higher and higher in denunciation of regionalism. Oginga Odinga's remark that "We will destroy these silly boundaries under the new Government headed by Jomo Kenyatta," was unique only for its candor and outspokenness.[44] Around the time the report was made public, there was a quiet hostility to it among KANU MPs. They seemed determined to modify the entire majimbo structure as soon as the first opportunity arose.

With the approach of the May elections, party positions on majimbo hardened. Both sides realized that the winner of the pre-independence election would determine the manner in which Kenya would be organized for many years. What was lacking was a consensus as to goals and values, creating a grim contest of parties and policies. As a consequence, majimbo's fate was to be determined not so much by practical considerations as by its identification with a winning or losing party.

KADU speakers stood firmly by the majimbo constitution. They charged KANU with seeking to sweep away the commitments agreed upon at London. They promised, on their part, to resist these threats by every legitimate means. A problem for KADU appeared early in the campaign with the emergence of the African People's Party (APP) under Kamba leader Paul Ngei. Could KADU form a coalition with this fiery ex-detainee who seemed to have little in common with KADU on the issue of regionalism? Again proving the old maxim that politics makes strange bedfellows, the two parties worked out an arrangement which only barely succeeded in papering over their

differences. APP's election manifesto avoided any endorsement of regionalism by recording the fact that the constitution had been agreed to by both
KANU and KADU and noting that "it would be unwise for any party to say
that it will destroy the Constitution while it is in power."

Throughout the campaign KANU stressed two somewhat conflicting
themes with regard to regionalism -- the constitutional framework was not
sufficiently flexible and the regions were merely glorified local authorities
with limited powers. On the first point, KANU objected to the rigid amending clause and the decision to decentralize certain police and civil service
responsibilities. "We have said, and we continue to say," wrote Minister
of Labor Tom Mboya, "that the Constitution ... is an experiment and it is
quite obvious that it contains a number of unworkable and unfair provisions."[45]
KANU's firm resolve was to amend the basic law, leaving the regions limited powers at best and scrapping regionalism entirely if, to note the words
of a party statement, "it is not able clearly to show its worth."[46]

KANU also belittled the functions and powers of the regions. Asserting
that KADU exaggerated regional powers and status, Mboya contended that
the regions "will not constitute Governments parallel to the Kenya Government.
They will be authorities exercising only the powers specifically given to
them. All the other powers belong to the Kenya Government."[47] There is
little question that the regions were subordinate units; and the powers of
the regions still remained vague and undefined. It was the outcome of the
election rather than the legal formula determined at Lancaster House in
1962 which was to be conclusive in shaping Kenya's constitutional patterns.

By the end of May the people of Kenya spoke. In the House of
Representatives, where the constituencies reflected population densities more
accurately than in the upper chamber, KANU won sixty-six seats; KADU,
thirty-one; APP, eight; the Northern Province United Association (NPUA),
three; and independents, four. In the Senate the results were as follows:
KANU, nineteen; KADU, sixteen; APP, two; and NPUA, one. Only in the
regions did KADU equal its rival; KANU gained control of Central, Eastern,
and Nyanza regions, and KADU secured majorities in the Coast, Western,
and Rift Valley regions. In terms of seats, however, KANU won 158 regional
assembly seats and KADU won fifty-one. KANU had won majority support
for its position on majimbo.

Now that it was evident that the internal power balance had swung
decisively in favor of KANU, the party gained self-assurance and attracted
new public support to itself. The most dramatic indication of the latter
came in September when APP leader Ngei led his colleagues across the floor
of the House to the government benches, specifically denouncing majimbo as

he went. Ngala, now clearly on the defensive, repeatedly reminded the
Kenyan and British governments of their joint commitment to the framework
constitution and warned of possible chaos or partition if the majimbo provisions
of the constitution were altered.

KADU leaders also maintained that the government was acting
unconstitutionally by failing to hand powers over to the regions. They
alleged that central authorities had intentionally blocked efforts by the
regions to assume these powers. Accordingly, on September 12, 1963,
Ngala tabled a motion in the House of Representatives deploring the government's failure to put the internal self-government constitution into effect.
"The Government, " he declared, "has dragged its feet on the implementation of this Constitution, because, since the new Constitution came into
being, only one power has been transferred and that is administration. "[48]
Such powers as local government, lands and probation had been retained
by the central government and, in view of the regions' readiness for the
handover, he could see no reason for further delays. Mboya, criticizing
this statement as misleading, noted that since internal self-government,
regional assemblies, law and order committees, commissioners of police,
civil secretaries, and government agents had all begun to act in their new
capacities. He conceded that "certain aspects of this Constitution $\underline{/}$ i.e.,
budgetary responsibility $\underline{/}$ have not as yet been fully implemented" but
deemed it "entirely unfair to suggest that in the light of the amount of
implementation which has already taken place, there is any hidden motive
in not having succeeded in implementing certain parts of the Constitution. "[49]

At heart, the issue was whether the government would implement
the form or the substance of majimbo. For Mboya, who threatened action
against any region which behaved as if its assembly were a government,
there was no doubt as to the supremacy of the Kenya government in all
aspects of the country's life.[50] He was joined in this by the Minister of
Home Affairs Odinga, who wrote a circular to all presidents of regional
assemblies and civil secretaries maintaining that the regions should refer
proposed legislation to his ministry before submitting it to the regional
assembly.[51] For KADU, the assemblies were much more than "regional
authorities, " and its spokesmen bristled over what they felt were efforts
of KANU ministers to belittle the significance of the regions. This conflict
of views could not be resolved, at least not until the next London conference
tackled the question.

With the approach of independence, KADU appeared more determined
than ever to preserve majimbo intact. In August 1963, KADU representatives
walked out of the preparatory constitutional talks, refusing to return until
basic constitutional changes were removed from the agenda. KADU National

Assembly members endorsed the walkout; they urged Ngala and his colleagues not to return unless the constitution were fully implemented. At this time, threats of secession became more commonplace. Typical was the warning of KADU executive officer, D. Lemomo: "If the Kenya Government insisted on major changes in the regional Constitution," he warned, "KADU would ask its delegation at the London talks to demand partition of the country between the two parties."[52] Others, such as M. J. Seroney (member for Nandi North), referred ominously to the Congo situation.[53] Seroney's decision to join KANU a few months later, however, points up just how much bluff was included in some of these threats. Finally, there were reports that KADU intended to boycott the London constitutional conference if the Kenya government failed to implement the constitution immediately; Ngala quashed these rumors in early September but not before they had circulated fairly widely.

As a consequence of the elections and the months of maneuvering that followed, it was a harassed KADU delegation and a rather confident KANU delegation which assembled in London for the final talks on the independence constitution. KADU sought to preserve the status quo, KANU to amend the constitution so as to increase central power. The British government was clearly on the spot. It wanted to move Kenya smoothly to independence and to reconcile national unity with the safeguarding of minority interests. Such a task was made particularly formidable by the lack of common ground between the two parties. Moreover, the Conservative government had little desire to antagonize its own right wing -- as well as European and KADU interests in Kenya -- by "betraying" promises made in 1962 at Lancaster House. The stage was set for a major crisis.

The conference opened on September 25, 1963, and lasted three and one-half weeks. During this period, three stages were discernible: the preliminary negotiations, the separate talks between the Colonial Secretary and the delegations, and the final showdown.

The initial statements were as anticipated. KANU leader Kenyatta demanded significant changes in the existing constitution, which he described as the consequence of "massive compromises, artificial feelings of mistrust and fear and arbitration by the Secretary of State." The constitution, he contended, lacked widespread support in Kenya. Therefore, in the interests of majority opinion and harambee (pull together) it should be amended.[54] Important changes sought included greater central control over police and planning, the establishment of a single public service commission, and the simplifying of the amending procedure. At no time did KANU insist upon abolishing the regional bodies as such. In fact, the Kenya government issued a statement early in the conference emphasizing its intention to transfer regional function before independence "as far as possible and practicable."[55] KANU sought to place central hegemony beyond dispute and to create a wider scope for central action. If they were thwarted in these aims, Kenyatta warned the conference, they would not feel themselves bound by the present basic law.

Ronald Ngala, speaking for the opposition, declared, in his turn, that the full implementation of the self-government constitution was absolutely vital. The need for conference agreement on certain "technical amendments" was apparent, but KADU would go no further. "On the basic changes which the Kenya Government is proposing, " he declared a few days later, "there is no alternative for us but to stand firm, come what may."[56] The extent of his determination can be seen by his hesitation over independence itself unless guarantees on majimbo were forthcoming.

The gulf between the two parties was so wide that Colonial Secretary Duncan Sandys soon substituted private discussions with the KANU and KADU delegations for further plenary sessions. During these discussions the two delegations hardly budged from their position. KANU continued to urge major constitutional modifications; KADU insisted that the British government prove its good faith by implementing the majimbo constitution. Just as something akin to a "phony war" seemed in the making, KADU members from both houses startled the conference by calling for the establishment of an independent "Republic State of Kenya." Kenyatta rejected this partition scheme and immediately broadcast an appeal for calm and order. KANU acted swiftly to regain the initiative. Kenyatta threatened to withdraw from the conference and to declare Kenya's independence unilaterally if Sandys went back on any previous agreements. His announcement received solid support from the KANU parliamentary group in Nairobi.

The center of the storm had arrived. Sandys had to act or a dangerous situation might engulf all Kenya -- majority and minority alike. In such circumstances, he had little choice but to mollify the KANU delegation. Kenyatta, by securing what amounted to a mandate from the nation on the majimbo question, had tilted the balance of power in his favor, and in the end Sandys was forced to reckon with this fait accompli. For regionalism, the portents were only too clear.

In the final, showdown stage of the conference, Sandys agreed to amend the constitutional framework of 1962; he did so on the grounds of enhancing the constitution's workability and durability. The amendments Sandys accepted included National Security Council control over the strength of all

police contingents, the right of the inspector general of police to transfer
police from contingent to contingent and to move police reinforcements
from one place to another, and the establishment of a single Public Service
Commission (instead of eight). And perhaps most important of all, he agreed
to a relaxation of the rigid amending clause (which required approval by
75 per cent of the House of Representatives and 90 per cent of the Senate)
with respect to various powers of the regional assemblies. Henceforth,
only 75 per cent of both houses or 75 per cent of one house and 2/3 of the
votes validly cast at a referendum would suffice. The latter change did not
apply to individual rights, tribal land rights, the districts, the Senate, the
composition of the regional assemblies, or the amendment clause itself.

What Sandys did was to move from the rigid guarantees of the
majimbo constitution to a more flexible basic law based on confidence in
present leaders. Prime Minister Kenyatta responded generously to this
tactic. In separate letters he advised the Colonial Secretary that no further
constitutional amendments were contemplated "except in so far as subsequent
experience shows these to be absolutely necessary," and that regional
powers would be transferred to the regions by the end of 1963.[57] A number of
these powers were transferred as promised; nevertheless, the Kenya government was careful to retain control of the financing of regional services
throughout the following year.

Thus regionalism survived the conference, but without firm roots.
In addition to the center's financial control, the functions and powers allocated to the regions were strictly circumscribed. Moreover, in the event
of an emergency, the executive authority of the central government extended
to all matters within the exclusive legislative competence of the regional
assemblies. And not only could the central government amend the powers
of the regional assemblies by a 75 per cent vote of support in both houses
(or a 2/3 majority in a referendum if one house did not endorse the change
by the requisite percentage), but it could take over and administer any
region which failed to carry out a function or service for which a central
direction was given. The range of central authority in this respect seemed
unusually extensive. The constitution provided that "the executive authority
of a Region shall be exercised so as (a) not to impede or prejudice the exercise
of the executive authority of the Government of Kenya; and (b) to ensure
compliance with any provision made by or under an Act of Parliament applying to that Region."[58] It left to central authorities the right to determine
whether the region had complied with its direction and to take necessary
action in the event of non-compliance. Regional assemblies had clearly
become subordinate bodies whose very survival depended upon KANU goodwill.

VI

Fearing possible domination by the central government, other ethnic groups, or both, minorities seek safeguards in the post-independence era. Regionalism appealed to certain minorities in Kenya and Uganda as the most reliable protection available to them in view of their relatively weak power position in the country at large. However, other and perhaps smaller ethnic groups felt that they would be better able to protect their interests under a strong central government than cut off and lost amid a larger ethnic group in a regional system.

Regionalism inspired minority confidence because it spread power on an areal basis. This decentralization of power seemed to leave indigenous local elites in control of the local situation, thereby disturbing the status quo only minimally. Nevertheless, such a view of majimbo was unrealistic, for it underestimated the dynamic implications of uhuru as a vehicle of political, social, and economic change. Federalism would have served the purposes of the minorities who desired protection more fully than regionalism, for the former reflected and perpetuated a balance of power in the society. But federalism was unobtainable, and regionalism could not assure security from oppression because it created an uneasy constitutional imbalance from the outset. By combining a strong center with a limited measure of regional autonomy, it established a political and institutional halfway house. A compromise situation of this sort does not seem likely, in a showdown, to prove an effective restraint against determined central action.

In part, majimbo suffered by its indentification with the departing colonial regime as the colonial power was the instrument through which the minorities obtained regionalism. Majority elements only reluctantly conceded regional arrangements and did so in Kenya and Uganda only to smooth and speed the way to independence. The majority elements viewed this concession as an expedient calculated to achieve a desired end. Consequently, they saw no reason to hesitate from interpreting regionalism narrowly in order to satisfy the needs of central leadership once independence came into effect or was assured.

The Western Kingdoms and Busoga Act of 1963, by defining and there-by limiting the jurisdiction of the regions, marked the demise of regionalism as a protection for the kingdoms against the Uganda government. Henceforth, only a policy of co-operation made sense. In Kenya, the shock came before uhuru, but the results were similar. Although Prime Minister Kenyatta did not announce his government's decision to place broad limitations on the powers and functions of the regional assemblies until August 14, 1964

(when he announced that Kenya would shortly become a republic and outlined
the country's proposed new constitution), it seems reasonable to contend,
as one observer has, that "majimbo ... died at the June election and this
/the Independence Conference/ is its Requiem."[59] In the end, the smaller
ethnic groups found they could not rely on any entrenched guarantees of a
colonially-bequeathed basic law, especially one which by definition lacked
balance or which failed to reflect the true power relations of the country.

Regionalism also paid the price of decentralizing tendencies the world
over. Centripetal forces have been building up in intensity in Kenya and
Uganda. The increasing prominence of the leading party and bureaucracy
in each country; growing central direction of the economy, education, and
the trade unions; and the declining importance of the legislature and parliamentary opposition all point to expanding central influence. Regional leaders
are no more able to stand against this trend than are other independent
centers of power. Central leaders by and large resent regional claims to
autonomy and look askance at such formal limitations on their powers as
regionalism, at least at present. Buganda's unity and power has enabled
it to counteract this trend to some extent, but Buganda, with its true federal
relationship, has erected defenses for its interests considerably more
durable than those offered by a majimbo arrangement.[60]

Regionalism, moreover, was condemned to a minor place by the
general air of suspicion that surrounded it. Without a consensus as to
majimbo's desirability and utility, it could hardly be expected to play a
vital role in these societies. Some consensus was achieved in Uganda on
the need to concede "federal status" to the Western kingdoms and Busoga
before the independence elections, but by the following year agreement was
reached which placed very real limitations on the kingdoms' freedom of
action. In contrast, in Kenya, there was little consensus between KANU
and KADU. They disagreed fundamentally on the desirability and meaning
of majimbo. Thus, the 1963 elections seemed more a "win all, lose all"
battle between adversaries than a truly political situation in which there is
a spirit of give and take and the loss of an election does not necessarily
mean irrevocable defeat for a policy.

The failure of regionalism in the post-colonial era, then, is not
necessarily a final commentary upon regional structures as an administrative device -- one giving expression to group self-determination or encouraging
local initiative -- but rather a commentary upon regionalism as a constitutional
mechanism designed to act as a safeguard for certain minority interests
under East African conditions. Kenya's and Uganda's experience indicates
that some traditional minorities initially placed more faith in the majimbo

mechanism than logically seemed warranted. It should have been evident from the outset that political, constitutional, and sociological factors virtually precluded regionalism from acting as an effective brake on central power. Inability to appraise regionalism's potential in a realistic manner caused imprudent hopes to be aroused and unnecessary frustrations to result. Yet the ability of local leaders to grasp quickly the essential meaning of the new constitutional arrangement for themselves and to work out an accommodation with central authorities over their place in the post-independence political framework accounts in large part for the survival of certain features of regionalism in the political life of East Africa.

Footnotes

1. For a fuller discussion of this point, see Donald Rothchild and Michael Rogin, "Uganda," in Gwendolen Carter (ed.), National Unity and Regionalism in Eight African States (Ithaca, 1965).

2. East African Standard (Nairobi), Aug. 25, 1963, 5.

3. Uganda Argus (Kampala), Aug. 22, 1960, 3.

4. East Africa and Rhodesia, Feb. 15, 1962, 585.

5. Ibid., Feb. 22, 1962, 609-610; Kenya Weekly News, Jan. 18, 1963, 9.

6. Uganda Argus, March 2, 1962, 1; March 3, 1962, 1.

7. Indeed, Prime Minister Benedicto Kiwanuka did announce his government's opposition to holding elections in the kingdoms until they were granted federal status. Both the Uganda People's Congress and Kabaka Yekka, suspicious of the motives behind any call for postponement, immediately rejected this suggestion.

8. See Clyde Sanger, "Kenya African Split Deepens," Manchester Guardian Weekly, 14:7 (Oct. 5, 1961).

9. Report of the Kenya Constitutional Conference, 1962, Cmnd. 1700 (London, 1962), 17.

10. "KANU or Chaos? ...," Spearhead, 1:5 (Jan. 1963).

11. Statement by Mboya, East African Standard, Jan. 21, 1963, 5.

12. Report of the Uganda Relationships Commission, 1961 (Entebbe, 1961), 57.

13. Report of the Uganda Constitutional Conference, Cmnd. 1523 (London, 1961), 18.

14. National Assembly Debates (Uganda), 2nd series, IX:74, 75 (March 20, 1963).

15. Report of the Kenya Constitutional Conference, 17.

16. Whereas KADU interpreted the constitution as being federal in nature, "KANU ... said Kenya would still be a unitary state and these regional powers would be no more than an English county council possessed." Clyde Sanger, "East African Notes: Divided Kenya," Spearhead, 10:3 (Nov. 1962).

17. Kenya Constitution, Summary of the Proposed Constitution for Internal Self-Government, Cmnd. 1970 (London, 1963), 4.

18. A seventh region was created for the predominantly Somali Northern Frontier District.

19. Report of the Fiscal Commission (Nairobi, 1963), 19-20. For a discussion of the impact of the commission's recommendations, see Clyde Sanger and John Nottingham, "The Kenya General Election of 1963," Journal of Modern African Studies, II:14, 15, 16, 39-40 (March 1964).

20. "Constitution of Kenya," Kenya Gazette Supplement, No. 30 (April 18, 1963), Ch. VII, Sect. 133.

21. East African Standard, March 9, 1963, 1.

22. Ibid., March 11, 1963, 3.

23. For opposing views on the relationship of regionalism to economic development see An Outline Programme for Economic and Social Development in Kenya, A Study Prepared at the Request of the Kenya African National Union (London, 1962), and Statement by Mr. R. G. Ngala to Introduce KADU's Plan "Land Tenure and Pastoral Development for Independent Kenya" (Mimeograph) (Nairobi, 1962).

24. East African Standard, Feb. 20, 1963, 1.

25. Legislative Council Debates (Kenya), XC, 2nd Sess. (Oct. 16, 1962), col. 43.

26. Report of the Uganda Relationships Commission, 1961, 49.

27. For an estimate of the fiscal effects of transferring the services, see the Report of the Uganda Fiscal Commission (Entebbe, 1962), 9.

28. Kenya, Report of the Regional Boundaries Commission, Cmnd. 1899 (London, 1962), 45.

29. East Africa and Rhodesia, Feb. 22, 1962, 610.

30. See Uganda Protectorate, Report of the Commission Appointed to Review the Boundary between the Districts of Bugisu and Bukedi (Entebbe, 1962).

31. Uganda, Report of a Commission of Privy Counsellors on a Dispute between Buganda and Bunyoro, Cmnd. 1717 (London, 1962), 16.

32. To meet this requirement, the commission somewhat reluctantly included the Northern Frontier District in the Coast Region. This situation was remedied shortly afterward when a seventh region was created for the NFD. See Cmnd. 1899, 16. It is interesting that the government subsequently used regionalism to demonstrate to the people of the NFD that they had significant rights and liberties under the constitution. East African Standard, Sept. 12, 1963, 5.

33. Ibid., Dec. 21, 1962, 1.

34. East African Standard, Jan. 7, 1963, 5. He also warned Britain of another Congo occurring if Kitale were not transferred to the Western Region. Ibid., Jan. 14, 1963, 5.

35. Ibid., Jan. 16, 1963, 5, Jan. 3, 1963, 5, and Daily Nation (Nairobi), Dec. 28, 1962, 2.

36. Constitution of Kenya (April 18, 1963), Ch. XIII, Sect. 226.

37. East African Standard, March 18, 1963, 1.

38. Ibid., Sept. 19, 1963, 1, and Reporter (Nairobi), Sept. 21, 1963, 11-12.

39. See Special Supplement to the Uganda Gazette, LV, No. 27 (Oct. 26, 1962), and Uganda Protectorate, Local Administrations Ordinance, 1962 (Entebbe, 1962). "Surprisingly enough," notes Fred G. Burke, "the central government has greater control over the legislative process in the federal states than in the district administrations. The Kingdoms and Busoga Act requires that before a bill is introduced into the Assembly it must first be forwarded to and approved by the Minister of Regional

Administrations. The legislative process in the district administrations does not require prior approval of draft bills by the minister although his approval is required before local legislation becomes law." Local Government and Politics in Uganda (Syracuse, 1964), 5.

40. Cf. Special Supplement to the Uganda Gazette Extraordinary, LVI (March 12, 1963).

41. National Assembly Debates (Uganda), IX:44 (March 20, 1963), A. Kisekka (a member of the National Assembly of Uganda, representing Mengo South).

42. Ibid., 70.

43. Ibid., 74.

44. Daily Nation, Dec. 22, 1962, 2, 6.

45. Tom Mboya, "Constitution Must Not Be Too Rigid," East African Standard, May 15, 1963, 4.

46. Ibid., May 24, 1963, 15.

47. Ibid., May 9, 1963, 5.

48. House of Representatives Debates (Kenya), I, 1st Sess. (Sept. 12, 1963), col. 1866.

49. Ibid., col. 1888.

50. East African Standard, June 13, 1963, 1.

51. Reporter, Aug. 10, 1963, 10.

52. East African Standard, Sept. 26, 1963, 1.

53. Reporter, Aug. 31, 1963, 12.

54. Ian Matheson, "Jomo Gets Tough on Majimbo," Daily Nation, Sept. 26, 1963, 1, and East African Standard, Sept. 26, 1963, 1, 3.

55. Daily Nation, Sept. 30, 1963, 1.

56. East African Standard, Sept. 30, 1953, 1.

57. Kenya, Independence Conference, 1963, Cmnd. 2156 (London, 1963), 10.

58. "Constitution of Kenya, " Kenya Gazette Supplement, No. 105 (Dec. 10, 1963), Ch. VI, Sect. 106.

59. John Nottingham, "Kenyatta's Freedom, " Venture, 11:8 (Dec. 1963). In his statement on the future role of the regional assemblies, Prime Minister Kenyatta assured the House of Representatives that his government intended to retain regional authorities. However, he intended to control them by denying these bodies exclusive executive authority or legislative competence in any matter which should be planned and directed on a national scale (education, agriculture, health, economic and social development, and the utilization of land); by centralizing the public service and the police authorities; and by permitting the central government to determine what taxes the local government authorities would levy and what services they should provide. East African Standard, Aug. 15, 1964, 5.

60. At the same time it is important to note that Buganda's defenses are by no means impregnable. In August 1964, the alliance between the UPC and Kabaka Yekka crumbled, and thirteen KY members of parliament crossed to the opposition benches. Moreover, two important Uganda High Court decisions since independence have enhanced the power of the central government at the expense of Buganda. In April 1964, the court maintained that nothing in the Uganda constitution required the government of Uganda to transfer police stations in Buganda to the kabaka's police force, and in the following month, the court upheld the central government's interpretation of its method of computing grants to the kabaka's government.

XII

Party and State Relations in Guinea

Lucy Behrman
Department of Political Science, University of Pennsylvania

In self-governing African states, party and government relationships have been constantly changing since independence. It has been necessary for all the ruling African parties to readjust and redefine their ideas
of the role of the party in relation to the government. Enough material
has been accumulated for students of African politics to study in detail the
reactions and changes in governing African parties since independence.
Such studies will not, of course, indicate what the final stage (if there is
such a thing) will be in African party-state relationships, but they will be
extremely valuable for the understanding of African government processes.

In the hope of providing at least the beginnings of a case study on
Guinea, this paper will present material on the Guinean administration
and on the Parti Démocratique de Guinée (PDG).[1] We will briefly discuss
the administration before independence, the changes which have been made
in the government structure since independence, the organization of the party
and, finally, the relations between the PDG and the administration. In
order to provide a framework in which to evaluate the developments in
Guinea, we will begin by discussing the impact of independence on dominant
parties in African states as it has been dealt with by Joseph Nye, James
Coleman, and Carl Rosberg. It should be noted here, however, that this
writer disagrees with the conclusions which the latter two writers draw
about Guinea. Coleman and Rosberg, in concord with Victor Du Bois,
see the PDG and the the administration as working together as one unit.[2]
The thesis of this paper, in contrast, based on observations made in
Guinea in 1963 and in the writings of Sekou Touré, is that there has been
a continuing conflict between party and administration in Guinea which has
not been resolved to the present day.

I

The most recent major work dealing with single-party states and
the factors which have affected the ruling African parties is Political Parties
and National Integration in Tropical Africa, edited by James Coleman and
Carl Rosberg. Some of the points the editors make, especially in their
concluding discussion, are quite relevant to this paper. The editors,
however, distinguish between two types of one-party states, the "revolutionary-

centralizing" type and the "pragmatic-pluralist" type. According to their criterion, Guinea, Mali, Ghana, and Tanzania fit into the former category as they have regimes which "seek to absorb and control all forms of associational life in /their countries./"[3] The revolutionary-centralizing classification is therefore relevant to this paper; discussion of developments in pluralist regimes will be omitted.

Coleman and Rosberg list a number of factors which have forced African parties to reassess their position since independence.[4] In the first place, the editors suggest that the governing party may lose its major reason for existence once it has succeeded in expelling the colonizers from the country. After independence, ruling parties are forced to take on jobs formerly held by Europeans. The parties must accept responsibility for their country's development and order, and often have to act in a coercive manner. As a result, they lose the psychological advantage they had when challenging the alien rulers.

Another possible influence on the development of the ruling party is the rise to power of individual Africans. These leaders may become so independent that the party will find itself, with the state organization, merely an adjunct of their personal power.

Modernization in itself may create factors which threaten the position of the ruling party. Modernization causes new demands, and it also tends to give rise to new groups (for example, students without jobs) which may form pockets of resistance to the policies of the party. Similarly, modernization usually includes the creation of an army which itself may become an important force in African politics. As Coleman and Rosberg point out, the Tanganyika African National Union (TANU) was helpless in 1964 in the face of a strike for higher pay by a few hundred soldiers.[5]

A problem more relevant to Guinea, however, is the tendency which Coleman and Rosberg note for party personnel to be diverted to administrative tasks. Few Africans are trained to handle technical and managerial problems, and, with the removal of the Europeans from the administration, these few are attracted to the governing and development of the country. As a result, the party organization faces a serious weakening through loss of personnel.

The attraction of party personnel into the government may be a manifestation of the overall growing dominance of the formal government structure over the party organization. Positions in the government

bureaucracy can become considerably more important than offices in the
national party as the process of modernization calls for increasing numbers
of managerial and technical workers. Coleman and Rosberg, supported
by William Foltz and Joseph Nye, believe that there is a discernible trend
in this direction in independent African states.[6] That there is evidence of
such a trend in many African states is not questioned here. However, it
seems an overstatement to say that in all African states the power of the
bureaucracy will eventually supersede that of the party. In Guinea, at
least, the party has not declined in importance and the state has not gained
power over the party.

Coleman and Rosberg are quite aware that African ruling parties
can react in a great many ways to the factors discussed above, particularly
the potential growth in power of the bureaucracy. They discuss two tendencies
which they believe are evident in the development of African one-party
states: the "no-party" state and the "party-state."[7] In the first alternative,
the African ruling party loses most of its power to the government apparatus.
In the most extreme case, the party which may have been very powerful
before independence, will become merely a unifying symbol for the country,
providing ideology which legitimatizes the role of the government. In his
article, "The Impact of Independence on Two African Nationalist Parties,"
Nye shows that TANU is no longer as important in Tanzania as the administrative organization. TANU personnel give their attention to their government
jobs, resulting in debilitation of the party. TANU is, of course, still important
as "a focus for identity and as a boundary of consensus"; it is the administration,
however, which makes and carries out day-to-day decisions.[8]

Nye did not discuss the concept of the party-state which Coleman and
Rosberg present as another possible reaction to the factors mentioned
above. In this second alternative, the dominant party does not lose its
power. Structurally, however, the party hierarchy fuses with the government on all levels. Thus, the party does not decline, but neither does the
administration; rather the two form together a party-state structure staffed
by the same personnel who hold office in both organizations. As an example
of this second alternative Coleman and Rosberg point to Guinea where, they
believe, the PDG has quite closely approximated the party-state. Ghana,
in contrast, provides for them an example of a country in which incomplete
fusion has taken place resulting in a state in which the party is still in
isolated dominance.[9]

As Coleman and Rosberg explain them, the concepts of the no-party
state and the party-state are clearly distinguishable from each other.
However, the no-party and the party-state concepts may be more confusing

than helpful in understanding the developing relations between African parties
and administrations. For it is quite misleading to call Tanzania a no-party
state, although it fulfills the criterion as a state in which there has been
a "progressive decline of the party as the center of power and decision-
making."[10] The implication of the words no-party is that the party will
become nothing more than a tool of the administration. In Tanzania, on
the contrary, the party is still very important although it no longer makes
day-to-day policy decisions. Furthermore, TANU personnel have not given
up their positions in the party; rather the party and administrative structures
have fused by having considerable overlapping membership.[11] The latter
characteristic is cited by Coleman and Rosberg as evidence of a tendency
towards a party-state. And yet, one could not include Tanzania in the
party-state classification because TANU definitely has declined in power
relative to the administration. Possibly, the no-party and the party-state
concepts should be replaced by other concepts which take into account more
factors than have been considered so far. In any case, as Nye suggests,
it is necessary to consider African parties on a spectrum.[12] Students of
African politics must clarify the precise differences between the parties
by filling the spectrum. Once this has been done, it will be possible to make
some meaningful generalizations about tendencies in African party development.

II

It is necessary, at this point, to leave this general discussion of
factors affecting African parties and trends in party development to examine
the specific case of Guinea. Today, the PDG is confronted with a number
of problems: the complaints of students, especially those studying outside
of Guinea; the predictable resentment of Guinean citizens when government
plans go astray (as for example, when the state distribution of food goods
had to be ended in 1963); and the strains which arise when societies are forced
to change old ways and adapt to government-sponsored modernization schemes.
Many families cannot understand why chiefdom was abolished; they do not
want to join voluntary work groups; and they resent internal migration
regulations which prevent them from freely going to Conakry to live off
their relatives working there. Most families resent taxes which they do
not understand. The need to implement economic plans, serious in any
developing society, is doubly serious in Guinea where the dominant role of
the state and the loss of some foreign aid after independence, has created
a demand for technically and managerially skilled workers. This scarcity
offers at least a potential threat to the strength of the party organization.

Before 1946, the Guinean administrative system was essentially a
hierarchical one headed by a governor who was responsible to the governor

general in Dakar.[13] The governor was advised by a small council which was
largely appointed by him. Guinea was divided into eighteen regions or
cercles which were administered by commandants de cercles who filled the
same role as Napoleon's prefects in France, being responsible for all that
went on in their regions. As early as 1919 an appointed conseil de notables
indigènes was set up in each cercle to advise the commandant.

Many of the cercles were cut up into subdivisions headed by assistant
administrators who were responsible to the commandants. Beginning in 1920 three
urban centers -- Conakry, Kindia, and Kankan -- had special administrative
status as communes, which meant that these towns were ruled by French
mayors responsible directly to the commandant of the region. The mayors
were assisted by appointed councils of which half the members were African.
The lowest divisions in the cercle were the cantons and the villages, headed
by designated African chiefs, whose job it was to supply labor for public
works projects, recruit men for the army, and collect taxes. Except on
the lowest commune level and sometimes on the subdivision level, the civil
servants who staffed the administrative system were Frenchmen educated
at the Ecole Nationale d'Administration in France. Locally-trained men
and educated Africans could rise only as high as assistant administrators.

Following World War II, a few changes were made in the administrative system, such as the addition of the Territorial Assembly in Conakry,
growing out of the old appointed governor's council. The assembly in 1952
had fifty members, eighteen elected by the French citizens and thirty-one
by the African subjects (the governor was the fiftieth member). By 1954,
Guinea was sending three deputies to the French National Assembly, two
senators to the Council of the Republic, five councillors to the Grand Council
of the French Union and four to the Union Assembly. In that same year
three towns -- Mamou, Labe and Siguiri -- were permitted to gain administrative status as communes while the original three communes advance their
status to municipalities and were granted elective councils, although their
mayors were still appointed by the governor.

Under the Loi Cadre in 1956, which opened the way for responsible
government in Guinea, a council of government was chosen from the leading
party in the now enlarged Territorial Assembly. Because the PDG held
fifty-eight of the sixty assembly seats, the council's twelve members
were PDG men, and Sekou Touré held the highest post as vice-president
of the council. Touré dominated the council, although the governor of Guinea
was himself president and held veto and reserved powers.

The elimination of the chiefs from the administrative system was
carried out in 1957 under the aegis of the new council. In most West African
countries chiefs have been a source of opposition to modernization. Guinea
was no exception to this rule, and Sekou Touré was opposed by a formidable
group of chiefs with a strong base of power in the Foulah region. His ability
to remove the chiefs from the administration was, therefore, a clear
indication of Touré's control of the country as well as of his political
acumen. In place of chiefs, elective councils headed by presidents were set
up in the villages and cantons.[14] In this same year the Conseil de Notables
Indigènes which advised the commandant became elective, and the customary
courts were abolished.

III

Guinea became independent on October 2, 1958. The new constitution,
passed on November 12, replaced the governor with a president elected for
a seven-year term. The territorial assembly became a unicameral legislature
which could not be dissolved by the president as it could formerly by the
governor.[15] It was restrained, however, by the president's power to initiate
referenda on laws and constitutional amendments. The new cabinet, which
had been chosen from the old council, was no longer responsible to the
assembly; but like the pre-1946 council, it was responsible to the president --
an interesting reversion to an earlier, colonial, form.[16]

On the national level, the ministries were reorganized to enable the
government to control and organize the economy of Guinea. Like the leaders
in many other African states, Guinea's leaders envisioned the development
of the economy as possible only through rigorous state planning, government
ownership in some industries, and tight government controls on private
industry. Guinea's economy was in particularly dire straits immediately
after independence because the French cut off all forms of aid and withdrew
their personnel. In order to revitalize the economy, PDG leaders named
several ministers of economic affairs.[17] They also created an agency for
exterior commerce and an agency for interior commerce (comptoirs)
which were divided into various enterprises, each responsible for the purchase
(wholesale) and sale (retail) of different products.[18]

It was hoped that the various enterprises, especially those dealing
with the buying and selling of food, would be able to sell their products
throughout the country at fixed prices. Traditionally, prices in the interior
had been much higher than on the coast; had it worked as planned, the
comptoir reform would have equalized the situation. Unfortunately, however,

the comptoir reform did not work very well.[19] The Guinean government had neither the personnel nor the experience necessary to move from a mostly private economy to a completely publically-controlled one, and the distribution of imports in Guinea broke down rapidly. Finally on November 1, 1963, the government enterprises which had distributed retail goods were closed.

The Guinean government retained those enterprises, created at the same time as the comptoir system, dealing with what the PDG calls basic economic activities -- including railways, roads, air transport, electricity, mining and banking.[20] These operations have been relatively more successful than the comptoir system, perhaps because they controlled sectors of the economy formerly administered and organized by the colonial government or simply handled relations with large foreign monopolies exploiting Guinean resources.

A second major reason for the reorganization of ministries was to decentralize responsibility. Under French rule, all important decisions were made by the governor in Conakry, while local decisions were handled by the commandants, who, however, were bound to ask for the approval of the governor. President Touré has attempted to allow greater powers to the commandants (now called governors) and other regional officials, but, on the whole, this attempt has not succeeded. Lower officials, including governors, are afraid to act without higher approval. As Touré himself points out: "What paralyzes action is often the fear of assuring responsibility for it, the fear of involving oneself in error."[21]

The result of this fear to take responsibility is often inactivity and inefficiency. An example of this fear occurred in 1963 when a group of Americans was sent to Mamou to work on a partially completed project. They were warmly received and then left to sit in their lodging or stand idly at the worksite as essential materials were not available. Lower government and party officials were even afraid to allow them to walk about the town freely, and officials at the cercle level would not act without permission from officials in Conakry, who were either at an economic conference, or out of the country.

In general, efforts to decentralize have not changed the role of the regional administrative structure. There have, however, been two additions to the personnel in charge of regional administration. First, national inspectors are now sent to each region by many national government enterprises and ministries. There are inspectors for labor, health, and social affairs, commerce, education, and planning and development. Most important is

inspector of youth, who has the right to sit ex-officio on the Bureau Politique
Fédéral (BPF) of the PDG in his region. All the inspectors oversee actions
which are taken in their various fields. They are generally not from the
region to which they are sent, and their interests are far more national
than regional because their possibilities of promotion and advancement rest
in Conakry.

The second addition to regional administration in Guinea was the
appointment in 1964 of four national ministers, each one responsible for one
geographical area of the country. Guinea is divided into four districts each
containing several cercles. The districts are: Lower Guinea (whose minister
is M. Kaba Mamady), Middle Guinea (whose minister is General Diane
Lansana), Upper Guinea (whose minister is Dr. Diallo Abdourahman),
and the Forest Area (whose minister is Keita N'Famara). These four
ministers may be intended to take over the responsibilities of the former
secretary of the interior, Sinkoun Kaba, whose name was not mentioned in
the list of government members announced in November 1964.[22]

Despite the presence of national inspectors in each region and the
creation of area ministers, the position of the governor is little changed.
Each region, of course, has a governor (the former commandant) who was
appointed, until the changes in 1964, by the secretary of the interior with
the approval of the president. Governors will probably be appointed in the
future by the minister of the appropriate area. The governor is responsible
for his region and directs all government activities including such special
projects as factories or government enterprises. He is advised by the
inspectors and by a general council of between ten and forty members, which
is elected for five years and sits for two sessions a year. Like the old
council, its functions are merely advisory, although it has one new claim
to importance in its control over the regional budget.

Under the old system the governor and his advisers drew up the
budget, but now the chief of finance, a member of the general
council, draws up the budget which is based on locally collected taxes. In
essence there is little difference between the old and new systems since the
governor's approval is still necessary, and the secretary of the interior
(now the minister of the area) must approve the budget before it goes into
effect. The second in command to the governor is the secretary-general,
who advises the governor and takes over in his absence. This post, incident-
ally, also existed under the colonial administration.

In 1959 the municipalities were abolished because it was believed
that the municipal governments merely duplicated the work of the
arrondissement and regional governments. Some towns in Guinea, however,
still have special status as regions in themselves. Thus Conakry is divided

into two federations and administered as a separate region while Kerouane
and Fria, which have economic importance, were given the same status.
Most recently Yomou, another economically important town, has been
added to the list.

By the beginning of 1964, twenty-nine regions replaced the eighteen
cercles of colonial times. (The capital region is divided into two federations
so the number of regions is sometimes calculated as thirty.) Once change
projected in 1963 would subdivide some of the larger regions, so in all
probability the number of regions will increase. The regions are divided
into 168 arrondissements (no longer called subdivisions as under the French),
each headed by a commandant d'arrondissement (no longer called assistant
administrator), who is responsible to the governor.[23]

One other important change in the administration was decided by
the PDG in 1962. This change led to the elimination of village councils which
had occupied the base position in the pyramidal administrative structure. In
his essay on Guinea in African One-Party States, L. Gray Cowan pointed
out that while there had been considerable discussion of the need to resolve
the dual authority of the party and the administration at least on the village
level, the PDG leadership had decided against elimination of the latter,
believing that "the dividing line between the authority of the administrators
and the local party officials /is/ that separating technical authority from the
political realm of policy making."[24] In late 1962, however, this decision
was reversed. Apparently Sekou Touré concluded that the village party
leaders could manage village affairs without destroying the principle of
separation of party and state. As a result, below the level of the commandant
d'arrondissement there is no governmental officer, elected or otherwise.
The position of mayor of the village is occupied by the president of the village
PDG committee which now carries out the functions of the former village
councils.[25]

While such a brief resume of the administrative structure and its
changes since the PDG took office does not do justice to the complexities
of the system, it does make some fundamentals clear. It shows that the
original hierarchical administration of ten or twenty years ago remains
with few basic changes. The most important of these changes are the
disappearance of the chiefs[26] from the system and, subsequently, the elimination of the base of the pyramid -- the village councils and presidents. Other
changes have been superficial refinements and additions to the old system.
Some government reforms, as the creation of interprises and reorganization
of ministries, have had very important purposes. However, the administration itself remains organized in the same way that it was before independence
and has nearly the same outlook and responsibilities as it had before. In

Government and PDG Structure

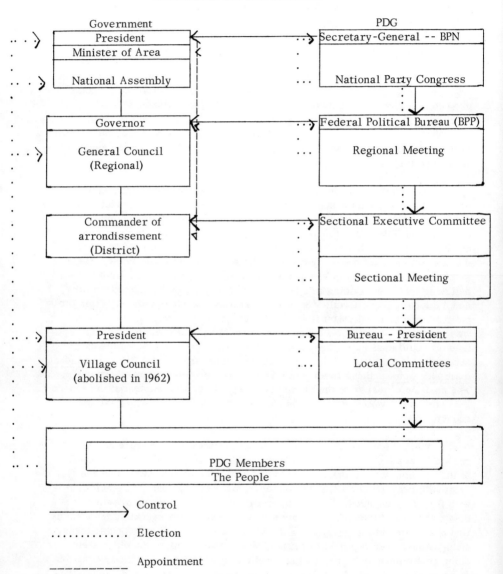

	Control
....	Election
----------	Appointment

one way, of course, the administration is not at all the same as it was under the French. Where there was no hierarchy there are now two, the second being the party which actually shares in the government of the country.[27]

IV

The actual structure of the party can be quickly summarized since it has grown up over the last few years but not really changed.[28] It parallels the government structure on every level (see diagram). At the base in each town, quartier, or village is one local committee which in theory includes all the inhabitants. At the head of each committee is an executive bureau of ten members, three of whom are the leaders of the local women's committee, while two others are appointed by the local branch of the youth organization, Jeunesse de la Révolution Démocratique Africaine (JRDA).[29] The remaining members are elected annually by the local general meeting.

At the present time the number of local committees is very much in flux. In 1963 the party estimated that there were 7,164 such committees.[30] In the fall of 1964, however, Sekou Touré announced a series of reforms which changed this number. He stated that local committees would be created in government enterprises and in factories, and that the number of committees in quartiers would be reduced, especially in Conakry. This reform was necessary because "certain committees represented only one or three families and the votes taken in the heart of the committees were influenced by family discipline."[31]

The members of the executive bureaus of all the local committees in an arrondissement attended the general meeting of the section (the party term for the arrondissement area). From the sectional general meeting the seventeen-member sectional executive committee, is elected biannually. Of the seventeen, two must be women from the sectional women's committee and two must represent the sectional JRDA (one male and one female). Above the section is the regional (or federal) general meeting composed of all members of the sectional executive committees in the region. From this meeting, a seven-member federal political bureau (BPF) is elected biannually; the BPF head is the secretary-general of the party in the region. On the regional level a regional conference also exists, which includes the BPF, five representatives from each sectional executive committee, and the members of the conseil général. The regional conference meets every three months and is responsible for implementing in the region the policies decided on by higher PDG officials.[32]

At the top of the party hierarchy all the federal political bureaus (thirty in number) and the members of the sectional executive committees come together to form the National Party Congress (Congrès Nationale)

which meets every three years. From the congress the seventeen-
member Bureau Politique National (BPN) is elected, the highest member of
which is the secretary-general of the whole party. On the national level
there also is a general meeting or congress of the JRDA and one of the
women's organizations, each of which is headed by a national bureau and has
committees and bureaus corresponding to every party level.

Along side the National Party Congress and not part of the formal
party apparatus, exists the Conseil Nationale de la Révolution (CNR). The
latter includes specifically the members of the BPN and the members of all
the BPF's. In actual fact, a large number of other people have the right to
attend CNR sessions as they do to go to the National Party Congress. Members
of the government, presidents of local committees, members of the National
Council of the JRDA, the heads of the Confédération Nationale des Travailleurs
Guinéens (CNGT), and many others are invited to attend CNR meetings.[33]
The CNR held its first meetings in 1964, in April and in September, and also
held a number of regional information sessions throughout Guinea. The
purpose of the council is not to supercede the BPN and the National Congress
in their direction of the PDG and of government policy. Instead, it discusses
important policy issues -- specifically economic problems -- and produces
resolutions approving party and government policy or suggesting changes.
In time the CNR could take over the role of the National Congress but at
present it is a super-party council which stands above and outside the regular
party organization.

The entire party organization is held together by a belief in "democratic
centralism, " meaning that decisions once made at the top must be carried
out without question by lower echelons of the party. The decisions themselves
are supposedly arrived at after considering the opinions of the Guinean people,
which are transmitted through the party by the popularly elected PDG officers.[34]

V

In theory the party and the state have specific functions. Although
the state is responsible for carrying out the laws, the party is the guiding
force in the country, mobilizing the people and creating policy. Even the
legislators are merely technicians since the laws they formulate are taken
from the policy decisions of the BPN. The authority of the party cannot be
denied, for as President Touré said (my translation):

> In reality, the Party should always be in advance of the
> Administration because as soon as, in a village or in a
> region, it lets itself be outdistanced by the Administration,
> in such cases, it loses its preeminent role and this situation
> abounds in continual conflicts of authority between the Party
> and the Administration.[35]

The administration, however, is not dispensable, nor can the two systems
merge with each other. The president warns:

> We sometimes witness conflicts of competence which establish
> themselves between technicians and administrative officials, be-
> tween administrative officials and political cadres. These conflicts
> of competence are a manifestation of an evident lack of good will
> and an illustration of a lack of conscience for popular interest.
>
> Now, in our political action, the only preeminence which we
> recognize is that of the interest of the people. The defense of
> this interest, the ways chosen to satisfy the legitimate aspira-
> tions of the populations, the orientation given to the activities
> of the Nation, come back to the people for whom the Parti
> Démocratique de Guinée is the means of action and of expression.
> In this is the preeminence of the Party and in no case will this
> preeminence be subjected to technical or administrative consider-
> ations which put in question the decisions of the Party.
>
> This is recognized and admitted. It is equally recognized and
> admitted that it is not the Party which can resolve technical
> problems or substitute itself for the administrative organiza-
> tion.[36]

In an attempt to reinforce the separation between party and state
structure, the PDG has forbidden certain administrators to run for office
in the party -- including governors of regions, secretary generals, commandant
d'arrondissement, police officials, magistrates, judges, and others.[37] This
ruling is meant to prevent the same men from dominating both the party and
the administration, at least on the regional level, for the most important
positions on that level are included in this list.

Despite all attempts to prevent them, conflicts persist. What is
particularly interesting about these conflicts, as far as this paper is concerned,
is that in most cases the party has seemed to succeed in asserting its superiority.

This is true in spite of the recent halt in state distribution of goods which some observers thought must signal a de-emphasis on planning and the party. In fact, evidence of the party's preeminence can still be found at every level of party and state structures.

On the national level, what first strikes the observer of Guinean politics is that the outstanding personalities in the party are the same men who head the state. Thus Sekou Touré is the secretary general of the PDG and is also the president of the Republic; Saifoulaye Diallo, who seconds President Touré in the PDG, is presently the minister of state in charge of finances and planning. Most of the other ministers, including L. L. Beavogui, Ismael Touré, and N'Famara Keita are also important members of the BPN as is the head of the National Assembly, Leon Maka.

In the light of their dual positions, which of their offices -- party or state -- do these national leaders consider the most important? This question, however logical it may appear, is not actually a fair one. These national leaders are each in charge of some very important aspect of Guinean life. None of them can help but devote the major part of his time to the administration of the country, that is, to the state structure. Yet the PDG is not slighted. Sekou Touré, Saifoulaye Diallo, and the others act according to instructions, which they themselves help formulate in the BPN. It is through the party that new policies are formed and then announced. Even comments on significant international events are made first by leaders acting in their party capacities. For example, when Diallo Telli was not nominated to the post of secretary-general of the OAU in 1963 because Guinea had angered the UAM states, [38] Sekou Touré made his first comments on the matter at a branch meeting of the PDG in Conakry. More dramatically, the arrest of students and teachers and the expulsion of Russian Ambassador Daniel Solod, after the teachers strike, was ordered by the BPN, while the official Guinean position on the incident was first made clear at a PDG meeting held on December 26, 1961, in Labé.[39] In other words, as ministers the national leaders act as technicians for the major innovations which are decided on by the party; crisis decisions are also made by the party.

On the regional level the phenomenon of the same people dominating both structures is not encountered; the division between the two is clear. Important regional officers cannot hold party offices, although the governor sits ex officio on the BPF. At this level, because there are two structures staffed by two different groups, it is much easier to see how the party and state interact. The region of Mamou serves as an example, illustrating several instances of party and state relations.

Mamou has approximately 120, 000 people and is one of the most important regions in Guinea.[40] Located in the Fouta Djalon, it is the center of the cattle raising area and has some of the most fertile soil in the country, as well as a very favorable climate. The region also has several commercial enterprises, including a Russian-built canning factory, an experimental chicken farm, and an agricultural testing center. Mamou is a crossroads for all of the interior of Guinea, because the major town (also named Mamou) is located on the railroad where it branches, on line going to Labé, the other to Kankan.

The governor of Mamou, Condé Sory, is an older man and seems to be widely respected.[41] Nonetheless, it is interesting to note that on most important ceremonial occasions during the summer of 1963, it was Doukouré Aboubacar, the secretary general of the party in the region, who gave the major address although the governor made an appearance. On national holidays the secretary-general gave the keynote speeches at the local celebrations. When Associate Justice Douglas of the United States Supreme Court visited Mamou and stayed in the governor's guest house, it was Doukouré Aboubacar who gave the official welcome at a ceremony in his honor.

On a more day-to-day basis, the governor works in the regional offices with his aides, seeming active and important; yet once again the regional head of the party seems to have greater influence. For example, in handling the complex relations with the Russians while the canning factory was being built, party men (and mostly national party men) made the decisions.[42] The governor can permit visitors to the factory, yet this does not indicate that he controls the functioning of that factory. Even the investissement humain; the voluntary work program is handled in Mamou by the party and not by the government, a situation noticeably different from Tanganyika's where, as Nye says, "The party administration was less efficient ... than the colonial Community Development Department, and gradually the organization of self-help projects became primarily a government responsibility."[43] In Mamou the governor (or a lower state official), may choose the site of a work project and must supply necessary materials; but party men handle voluntary work projects. They call up the "volunteers" from each quartier on a weekly basis and punish those who do not appear or who refuse to work.

Another way of evaluating the position of the regional administrative personnel relative to the party officials would be to see which structure provides the quickest way to advancement. It seems, not surprisingly, that this would be the party.[44] In Mamou in 1963 two of the most outstanding men were in the party hierarchy. One, Sane Mamadou Lamine, who was in 1960 only the JRDA representative to the section of the Mamou-ville, was in 1963 the regional

inspector of youth, both a party and regional office; and by 1964 he was promoted
to a national position. The second, Kaba Mory, presently the JRDA representative to the section of Mamou-ville and the chief of finance, was promoted to
Mamou from Kankan shortly before 1963, and seems to be moving rapidly
upwards in the party.

It is not easy, however, to prove that regional party positions are
more promising as the administration   as well as the party is staffed by men
who are not from the Mamou region. Since independence, President Touré
has stressed the need to break tribal and regional ties in order to promote
national allegiances. Even in the Foulah regions, where opposition to the
government has always been the strongest, he has been markedly successful
in integrating the party and administration. Mamou, which is a Foulah region,
has a Malinké from Kankan as governor, a Soussou from Nalou as secretary-
general and as commandants of its six arrondissements it has a Malinké from
Kouroussa, a Foulah from Géoual, a Foulah from Labé, a Soussou from
Conakry, a Malinké from Youkounkoun, and a Malinké from Kankan. On the
party side, the same wide distribution of backgrounds can be seen. On the
BPF, which has seven members, including the governor and the youth inspector
who is a Malinké from Kankan, there is a Foulah from Timbo, a Foulah from
Labé, two Soussou from Kindia, and a Malinké from Kankan.[45]

Obviously the administration, as well as the party, functions on
a national basis. A regional commandant d'arrondissement can be promoted
or demoted by being shifted to a different region, or he can become the governor
of a region or a member of the national government. In order to draw any
valid conclusion on which man -- the party man or the state employee --
has the best opportunities for advancement, a careful study on all the promotions
and demotions in a region would be necessary. Such a survey is, of course,
not yet available for Mamou; without it, this line of questioning must be deferred.

On a level much below that of the governor and the secretary-
general of the party there are several examples in Mamou of PDG usurpation
of government functions. The most flagrant of these involves the actions of
the party militia, whose job in theory is to keep order at party gatherings
and maintain checks on PDG members, insuring the payment of dues and
attendance at meetings. But in Mamou the militia does far more than that.
The regular police in khaki uniforms are commonly to be seen in the police
station or around the governor's mansion, while the red, yellow, and green
belts of the militia can be spotted all over the town of Mamou, even directing
traffic. Local Lebanese merchants and African citizens are sometimes
threatened by the militia and some have been arrested and jailed for displeasing
the party. There is no evidence that the regular police restrict the militia

in any way.

On the lowest rung of all in Mamou, in the quartiers of the towns
and in the villages, the PDG has unquestioned superiority. In the first place
there is no longer a government structure at this level, and party men head
the villages. Party men interpret national laws to the people and mobilize
citizens (which fact alone gives the PDG an important advantage over the
administration).

Particularly indicative of the party technique on the quartier level
is the JRDA-sponsored effort to educate people by having them participate
in competitive sports, plays, songs, and dances. Sports do not need additional
comment; they simply arouse interest and enthusiasm. But the other activities
are more unusual. Each play, song, or dance is on a theme of concern to
the party. Thus one begins "He Faranci barawa la guinée Kafoko Faranci
bejewa" (the French have left, Guinea told the French to leave); and so it
continues until the benefits of independence and the wickedness of colonialism
have been explained. Even though they are being indoctrinated, the young
people, especially the uneducated, seem most eager about these competitions,
for they are being indoctrinated in the easiest of all possible ways -- by
amusing themselves. Loyalties are being built to the state represented by
the PDG and Sekou Touré.[46]

Even allowing for differences between party and state structures
in Mamou and in other regions, the evidence presented up to this point seems
incontrovertible: in Guinea, the PDG has grown more, rather than less,
powerful since independence. At the same time the position of the administration has been very unclear. It has not fused with the party, as Coleman and Rosberg
contend, but remains distinct from it. In fact, the two organizations are
continually conflicting with each other, the conflicts being particularly noticeable on the regional level. Throughout the struggles between the party and
administrative personnel it has been the party view which has tended to
predominate. One cannot, of course, be completely confident that the situation
will always remain the same. Thus it is interesting to note Sekou Touré's
comment in November 1963, explaining the fact that the PDG is not mentioned
in the constitution. Touré said: "Since the party has the people completely
within its bosom, it is normal that one can proclaim that the national sovereignty
is expressed through the party. If we place in the Constitution that the Party
is the supreme organ of the Nation, we would be in conformity with reality.
But we do not know the realities of tomorrow."[47] at present, then, the
PDG is the most important organization in Guinea; it may not be in the future.

VI

Before this discussion can be closed, one major question remains to be answered. Is there any evidence to indicate why the PDG has reacted as it has to independence? Why is the Guinean party clearly the most important force in the state when in Tanzania the once highly organized and powerful government party has been subordinated to the administration? The answer is certainly not that Guinea has more trained men than Tanzania with which to staff the administration and the party. One observer has suggested that the preeminence of the PDG stems from the habit of power and authority which the party acquired before independence.[48] But this explanation does not show why TANU, which also had acquired considerable authority, lost some of its power after independence. A partial answer might be that the traditions of the French and British in the two administrative systems were so dissimilar that the Guinean administration just naturally submitted to the party. This explanation, however, does not seem to be valid as the administrative system in Guinea was the sole vehicle of authority until the PDG took power.

The difference between the PDG and TANU is probably caused, at least partially, by the differing ideologies of the party leaders. It is tempting, indeed, to make an analogy between the Guinean situation and that of the Soviet Union. It is difficult to make comparisons between African countries and the Soviet state; nevertheless, it is true that the industrialization of the USSR and the resultant creation of a large powerful managerial class has not caused the decline of the Russian Communist Party. One important reason the Communist Party has retained its position is that the Soviet system is based on an ideology whose primary principle (since Lenin) has been the leadership role of the party. In Guinea too, Sekou Touré's voluminous writings place the PDG in a clearly Marxist-Leninist position of leadership. The PDG directs the affairs of Guinea as an expression of the will of the people. As the material presented here has shown, the party is organized like a Communist party, and is based on the same theory of democratic centralism. There are considerable differences between Sekou Toure's idea of socialism and Soviet Communism, but it is nonetheless true that his concept of the role of the party, its relation to the people and to the administration are very similar to that of Russian leaders. In contrast to Sekou Touré, Julius Nyerere and other TANU leaders do not use Marxist concepts in their writings. The role of the party apparently concerns them much less than the practical day-to-day problems of Tanzania.[49] It is not the purpose of this discussion to treat the philosophy of the Tanganyikan leaders, but it is at least suggested that the de-emphasis on the party in Tanzania, as contrasted to the Guinean situation, may be related to the attention given the position of the party by Guinean Marxist-oriented party leaders.

It is perhaps dangerous to cite ideology as even a partial explanation
for the differences between Guinea and Tanzania as this raises the whole
question of the real importance of ideology in politics. It is by no means clear
what the role of ideology is in the Soviet Union. In Guinea party leaders
openly state that their political beliefs can and will be changed according
to the problems they face. President Touré has pointed out that the role of
the party may someday change; in another place he has written that the PDG
was concerned with the welfare of the people and not with doctrines. He said:

> The PDG, for its part, thinks that socialism is a
> means and that the end ... is the moral and material
> well-being of the People. It is in terms of this end
> that our social structure and our economic and cultural
> practices are chosen and determined.
>
> The PDG refuses ... to condition the People in terms
> of such and such doctrine; in contrast it means to define
> the concrete application of the content of such and such
> doctrine according to the present and future interests of
> the people.[50]

Nonetheless through training and experience, Sekou Touré has learned
to accept a certain role for the PDG which will change only very gradually
(if it does indeed change). Touré's cast of mind, a strongly Marxist-Leninist
one, is also that of the most important PDG leaders, and it cannot help but
affect the position of the party in Guinea. Nevertheless, there is not at
present any complete answer to the question of why the party in Guinea
continues to dominate the state. There are undoubtedly a large number of
important factors which have not been considered. Guinea's international
position at independence and its economic crisis after the French withdrawal
certainly influenced the development of Guinean party-state relations. Even
the differences in structure between PDG and TANU may have been important
in shaping the positions which the two occupy in their respective countries.
Much more research will have to be done before the developments in Guinea
can be understood.

Footnotes

1. A major part of this paper is based on interviews with party and state officials obtained during a two-month visit to Guinea in the summer of 1963.

2. There are also some minor disagreements between the material presented by Victor Du Bois and what is presented in this paper, mostly relating to the organization of the PDG. James S. Coleman and Carl G. Rosberg (eds.), Political Parties and National Integration in Tropical Africa (Berkeley, 1964), 200-206, 678.

3. Ibid., 671

4. Ibid., 655-691.

5. Ibid., 677.

6. Ibid., 675. See Joseph Nye, "The Impact of Independence on Two African Nationalist Parties, " this volume.

7. Colemen and Rosberg, Political Parties, 676-679.

8. In his paper Nye presents a counter-example of a party which has strengthened its position since independence. This is the Uganda Peoples Congress (UPC) which has used the government bureaucracy to build up its own organization. The UPC is not discussed in this paper because the circumstances in Uganda are so unlike those in Tanzania, on the one hand, and Guinea on the other. Uganda is not a highly centralized state, and the UPC was not a tightly organized, powerful party before independence. See Nye, this volume.

9. Coleman and Rosberg, Political Parties, 678-679.

10. Ibid., 676.

11. See Nye.

12. Ibid.

13. For further material on the pre-independence administrative system see Virginia Thompson and Richard Adloff, French West Africa (Stanford, 1957), 132-139, 179-203. See also U. S. Department of the Army

(Special Warfare), Area Handbook: Guinea, prepared by the Special Operations Research Office, American University, Washington, D. C., 1960.

14. For an account of the way Touré handled the elimination of chiefs, consult the minutes of the Conférence de Commandants de Cercle de la Guinée, held at Conakry, July 25-27, 1957, in Sekou Touré, Guinée, Prélude à l'Independence (Paris, 1958).

15. As of November 22, 1964, the assembly is known as l'Assemblée Nationale Populaire. "Guinée, " Afrique Nouvelle (Nov. 27 - Dec. 3, 1964), 4.

16. The provisions of the new constitution also bear a close resemblance to the constitution of the Fifth Republic in France. See Sekou Touré, L'Expérience Guinéenne et Unité Africaine (Paris, 1960), 263-275

17. In the new government, announced in November 1964, there were seven ministers and secretaries of state dealing with the economic development of Guinea: the minister and secretary in charge of the plan and of finances, Diallo El Hadj Saifoulaye and Balde Ousmane, respectively; the minister and secretary in charge of economic development, Toure Ismael and Fofana Karim, respectively; the minister for rural economy, Barry Sory; the minister for interior commerce, Camara Oumar Dine; and the minister for exterior commerce, Diakhite Moussa. There were altogether twenty-four ministers in the government. "Guinée: d'importantes réformes sont intervenues, " Afrique Nouvelle (Nov. 20-26, 1964), 4.

18. For a complete list of the planning agencies and their functions see Sekou Touré, La Révolution Guinéenne et le Progrès Social, VI (Conakry, 1962), 157-173.

19. Although the comptoir system did not work well, in some areas it was a very popular reform. For example, in Mamou, a town of about 10,000 people in Middle Guinea, the comptoir was still the focal point of the town in the summer of 1963. Imported food, including flour, rice, and staples of all types, was considerably cheaper in the government store than it was in Lebanese shops. People lined up for hours when a shipment came to the comptoir, and they depended on it for everything but local products.

20. "Guinée: Définition des enterprises de l'Etat, des entreprises mixtes et privées, " Afrique Nouvelle (June 5-11, 1964), 4.

21. La Révolution Guinéenne, 76.

22. "Guinée: d'importantes réformes, " 4.

23. The change from subdivision to arrondissement and from assistant administrator to commandant was made in early 1963. The switch in name indicated an attempt to give greater authority to the lower government official. The change came as part of the government's effort to decentralize responsibility. "Guinée: Réformes administratives, " Afrique Nouvelle (Feb. 7, 1963), 4; and Sekou Touré, La Révolution Guinéenne et le Progrès Social, VI, Edition Speciale (Conakry, 1962), 620-621.

24. L. Gray Cowan, "Guinea, " in Gwendolen Carter (ed.), African One-Party States (Ithaca, 1962), 210.

25. There has been no mention of this reform in most of the sources available in the United States. Afrique Nouvelle, which usually reports major Guinean administrative reforms, has not mentioned the elimination of village councils. In the Mamou region in the summer of 1963 I was told repeatedly by party officials that this reform had taken place. In Mamou it was evident that party men ran the quartiers and villages which seemed to have no administrative offices. The first written reference to this reform appears to be in Sekou Touré, La Révolution Guinéenne, Edition Speciale, 621, 626. Hopefully later volumes of Touré's writings will provide more information on this measure.

26. The fact that chiefs have been technically eliminated from the administration does not mean that on the lower levels and on the regional level their power has been completely destroyed. It appears to be quite common for the village PDG leaders to be chiefs in their own right. More generally, especially in the Fouta Djalon, former almamys and other Moslem leaders still command a great deal of respect.

27. The PDG also existed under the French. However, there were not two organizations responsible for the government in colonial times.

28. For information on the growth of the PDG and its rise to power see Ruth Schachter Morgenthau, Political Parties in French-speaking West Africa (Oxford, 1964), 219-254.

29. Until 1963 JRDA stood for Jeunesse du Rassemblement Démocratique Africain. Since independence the PDG has no longer been a member of the Rassemblement Démocratique Africain, so it was thought wise to change the meaning of the initials of the youth group.

30. Sekou Touré, "Au nom de la révolution," IX, Conférences Hebdomadaires, (Conakry, 1962), 117; and La Révolution Guinéenne, Edition Speciale, 626.

31. "Guinée: d'importantes reformes," 4.

32. For further information on the organization of the party see Touré, Conférences, 117-124; and La Révolution Guinéenne, Edition Speciale, 621-625.

33. For information on who may attend the CNR see "Communiqué du BPN à propos des assises du CNR," Horoya (Sept. 13-14, 1964), 4. Also, Sekou Touré, La Révolution Guinéenne, Edition Speciale, 625.

34. See Sekou Touré, "Les Principes du centralisme démocratique," L'Expérience Guinéenne, 541-542.

35. Conférences Hebdomadaires, 41.

36. La Révolution Guinéenne, 77.

37. See Touré, Conférences, 119.

38. "OAU Foreign Ministers Meet in Dakar," Africa Report, VIII:19 (Oct. 1963).

39. "Both East and West Blamed for Guinea Unrest," Africa Report, VII:10 (Jan. 1962).

40. This figure is Kaba Mory's, the chief of finance; the population figure suggested by the Area Handbook is 81,000. The actual number is probably somewhere between the two.

41. Recently Condé Sory was replaced by Diallo Tellivel.

42. Interviews with regional leaders in Mamou, August 1963.

43. Nye, "Impact of Independence," this volume.

44. People in Mamou stated that men without education or technical training must enter the party organization if they wish to rise rapidly to an important position. For men with training and education the situation is more open; the party still provides a means of rapidly advancing to better jobs,

but such men also find good jobs in the administrative system. The whole
situation is complicated by the general bias of the PDG against higher education.
In the past Touré has openly stated that he felt men with too much training or
education tended to be corrupted and to lose their contacts with the people.
As a result highly educated men are at a disadvantage at the top levels of
both the party and the administration in Guinea.

45. The author has lists of other party officials and administrative
personnel in Mamou which show that a wide distribution of backgrounds extends
downwards to a very low level.

46. The administration does not seek to build loyalties among the
Guinean people since this is by definition the major task of the PDG.

47. Afrique Nouvelle, Nov. 21-27, 1963, 4.

48. W. J. Le Melle, "A Concept of the Modern African State: A
Critique of the Political Philosophy of Sekou Touré" (unpubl. diss., University
of Denver, 1963), 132.

49. For a discussion of Julius Nyerere's political philosophy see
Harvey Glickman, "Dilemmas of Political Theory in an African Context:
The Ideology of Julius Nyerere," this volume.

50. La Révolution Guinéenne, Edition Speciale, 598.